Power Shortcuts...
EXCEL 4.0

by

Phyllis Romanski
and
Susan Rothenberg

MIS:
PRESS

A Subsidiary of
Henry Holt and Co., Inc.

First Edition—1993

ISBN 1-0555828-237-8

Printed in the United States of America.

10 9 8 7 6 5 4 3 2 1

MIS:Press books are available at special discounts for bulk purchases for sales promotions, premiums, fund-raising, or educational use. Special editions or book excerpts can also be created to specification.

For details contact: Special Sales Director
MIS:Press
a subsidiary of Henry Holt and Company, Inc.
115 West 18th Street
New York, New York 10011

Dedication

This book is dedicated to Uncle Joe,
who still doesn't use these "newfangled" inventions.

Acknowledgments

We would like to thank all of the people who have helped to make this book happen:

Lois Karp, for her love and support.

Paul Landsman and Joe Gruner, of Landsman and Gruner, who are always there when you need them.

Matt Wagner, of Waterside Productions, who keeps us in mind when interesting projects come along.

Steve Berkowitz, our publisher, for his patience and understanding with interminable delays.

Elizabeth Gehrman, our editor, for her patience and flexibility.

And, last but not least, our clients, who put up with being put off while this book was being written.

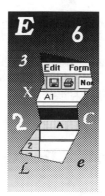

INTRODUCTION

Excel is one of the most popular spreadsheet programs on the market today for a reason—its power and flexibility. Most people who use Excel set up classic spreadsheets, and rarely take advantage of the programs' full capablity. This book will introduce you to one of Excel's most powerful features—the macro. Macros allow you to perform simple repetitive mouse or keystroke combinations quickly, and with macro programming language, you can write an entire program within Excel.

This book explains the concepts of the function and command macro feature, and leads you, step-by-step, through the creation of simple and complex macros. As you progress to more complex macros, all of the concepts involved, such as branching and looping within a program module, are explained and illustrated. This book will allow you to harness the programming power of Excel by teaching you the programming concepts you need to know to accomplish your goal. You will also learn how to create your own data forms and dialog boxes, and incorporate them into custom macros.

What You Need to Know

Power Shortcuts…Excel 4.0 assumes that you are already at least an intermediate-level user of Excel. You do not need to know any programming or programming concepts. Complete explanations and illustrations of all the basic concepts used in programming will be explained. This book will explain the database and chart features, but will not explain the basic spreadsheet layout or mouse or keystroke movements for spreadsheets.

Preparing to Use This Book

All of macros you will learn to create are included in the disk included with this book. The disk also contains a sample chart of linked accounts and spreadsheets. Before you copy these documents onto your hard drive, create a separate directory for them. This way you can locate the files quickly and, if you decide to expand the program, all of the files will be in the same directory.

Additional Information

Key combinations are indicated by a plus sign. For example, Shift+F1 means that you should hold down the Shift key while pressing the F1 function key. The commands in this book assume that you are using a mouse, although in some instances, alternative keyboard combinations are given for those who do not use a mouse. It is strongly suggested that you use a mouse in Excel.

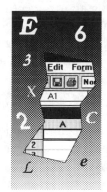

CONTENTS

Chapter 1

USING FUNCTIONS

What Is a Function?

Excel has two kinds of functions: **worksheet functions** and **macro functions**. Worksheet functions are formulas that perform calculations and produce a result based on the values in the calculation. Macro functions allow you to build "mini programs" using the macro function commands. You can use macro functions to record commands and keystrokes and play them back at a later time. Macros produced using the macro functions provided in Excel can be simple (like automating the print feature) or highly complex. In this book, we will start with simple worksheet and macro functions and progress to sophisticated functions used to produce a basic accounting system.

A worksheet function consists of a built-in **formula** (the function name) and an **argument** (the information used by the function to produce a new value). The function performs on the argument(s) the calculation specified by the function name and produces a result.

For example, in the following function:

```
=SUM(6,5,3)
```

SUM is the built-in formula or function name, and the information enclosed in parentheses (6,5,3) are the arguments. The result of the function is 14 (the sum of 6+5+3). In this function, SUM is replacing the plus operator (+) and 6, 5, and 3 are the arguments used to produce the new value.

Macro functions are **worksheet functions**, **command-equivalent functions**, and **action-equivalent functions**. Using a command-equivalent function is the same as choosing a command from the menu bar. For example, using the command-equivalent function COLUMN.WIDTH is the same as clicking on Format in the menu bar and then clicking on Column Width. You can use an action-equivalent function to perform an action that does not require a command. For example, the action-equivalent function SELECT is the same as selecting a cell, a worksheet object, or a chart object.

The Syntax of Functions

All functions employ the same basic syntax. Chapter 3 lists all of the macro functions available in Excel and the correct syntax for each. If your function's syntax is incorrect, Excel displays a message informing you that there is an error in the formula. The basic syntax of a function is:

```
=FUNCTION NAME(argument or arguments)
```

A function must always begin with an equal sign (=). This is followed by the function name, such as SUM. The function name is followed by argument(s) enclosed in parentheses.

In this book, the following syntax will be used for functions: function names will be in boldface uppercase letters, required arguments will be in boldface lowercase letters, and optional arguments will be in lightface lowercase letters. For example, in the following function:

```
=SUM(number1,number2,...)
```

the function name, SUM, and the required argument, number1, are in boldface; the argument number2 is not in boldface and is therefore optional. If the function name is followed by an empty set of parentheses, the function does not accept an argument. You must, however, include the parentheses in the function.

As a rule, you should not use spaces in functions. You may use upper- or lowercase letters when typing a function. The maximum number of arguments that can be included in a function is 30, and the total number of characters cannot exceed 1,024. The most characters that can be used in any one argument in a function is 255.

When the arguments in a function are followed by an ellipsis (...), you can have more than the number of arguments listed for that function. For example, in the function

`=`**`SUM(number1`**`,number2,...)`

the arguments number1 and number2 are separated by commas and followed by an ellipsis. This indicates not only that all of the arguments must be separated by commas, but also that you can enter more than two arguments in the function, so long as the arguments are of the same data type. Furthermore, the argument (number1,number2,...) consists of two number arguments followed by an ellipsis. Therefore, any values used in arguments in the SUM function must be number values.

There are several ways to express values in an argument. Nonsequential values are separated by commas. For example, in the functions

`=SUM(5,6,3)` and `=SUM(C6,C9,C15)`

the three values in each argument are nonsequential and are separated by commas.

Values consisting of sequential groups of cells (known as ranges) are separated by a colon (:). (Periods [.] are used in Lotus 1-2-3 and can also be used in Excel 4.0.) For example, in the function

`=SUM(C5:C12)`

the values are separated by a colon (:), indicating that they represent a range.

You can also use values consist of both nonsequential and sequential groups of cells. For example, in the function

`=SUM(C5:C12,D8:D14,E4:E10)`

the ranges are separated by colons, and the nonsequential values are separated by commas.

Using Functions

If you know the name and syntax of the function you want to use, you can type the function directly into a cell in the worksheet or macro sheet.

NOTE

If you are entering a function and cannot remember the argument(s), you can paste the argument(s) into the function by typing the equal sign (=), the function name, and the opening parenthesis, and then pressing Ctrl+A.

If you do not know the exact name of the function you want to use, you can find and then select it using the Paste Function command in the Formula menu. The function, including its argument(s), will appear in the formula bar. To use the Paste Function command:

1. Open the worksheet or macro sheet.
2. Select the cell in which you want to use the function.
3. Click on Formula in the menu bar to open the Formula menu.
4. Click on Paste Function to display the Paste Function dialog box, as shown in Figure 1.1.

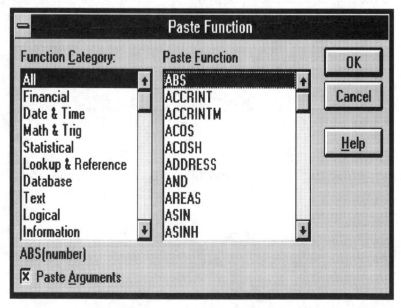

Figure 1.1 *The Paste Function dialog box.*

5. The Paste Category list box lists the types of functions available in Excel. You can select any of these function types. See Chapter 3 for a detailed discussion of the function types used in worksheets and macros.

6. The Paste Function list box lists the functions available in the function category you selected. The default function category is All, and all of the worksheet functions available in Excel are listed in the Paste Function list box when that category is selected.

7. Select the function you want in the Paste Function list box.

8. Click on OK.

9. The correct syntax for the function appears in the formula bar, and looks like this:

```
=FUNCTION(argument1,argument2)
```

The formula begins with an equal sign (=), and is followed by the built-in formula (or function), which is followed by a parenthetical expression that contains the syntax for the values or arguments you are going to use in the formula. You must replace the arguments with the values or cell addresses that contain the values you want to use in the formula. These values can be numbers, individual cells, or ranges. If you clear the Paste Arguments check box, your formula will not include the syntax for the arguments, and will look like this:

```
=FUNCTION()
```

10. Edit the arguments in the function in the formula bar to reflect the number, cell, or range of cells you want to include in the function.

11. Copy this function to any cell or range of cells where you want the same function to occur. Note that the cell or range references in the function change to reflect the new cell address of the function.

 When you copy a function, its formatting is also copied.

NOTE

Arguments in Functions

The arguments in a worksheet function determine the result of the function calculation, the arguments in a command or action-equivalent macro function determine the action the function will perform. If a function name is followed by an empty set of parentheses, the function will not accept arguments. For example, the function =FALSE() does not accept arguments and will always return the logical value FALSE. If the function name is followed by optional arguments only, you may choose whether or not you wish to include any arguments in the function. For example, in the function =DIRECTORY(path_text), the argument is optional. If you choose to omit the argument, you must enter the function as =DIRECTORY(). If you include the argument, the function is entered as =DIRECTORY("c:\excel\library").

Types of Arguments

There are six argument types that can be used in a function, each requires a specific data type to be used in the argument.

▼ **Numbers.** Numbers used as arguments in functions can be positive or negative. You can use whole numbers or decimals.

▼ **Text.** Text used as an argument must be enclosed in quotation marks (" "). If you want quotation marks to *appear* in the function, you must add an extra set.

For example, in the function =LEN("this is a ""test"""), the words *this is a* are enclosed in quotation marks. The word *test* was originally enclosed in quotation marks, and when used in the function must be enclosed in two sets of quotation marks. Thus, the following appears in the function: *This is a "test"*.

Text arguments in functions can be used in many ways: to search for text, name documents and workbooks, compare text strings, find and/or open documents, find the length of text strings, and return the number of characters in the string as a result.

Named ranges used in arguments must be enclosed in quotation marks. In the function =LEN("this is a ""test"""), the function counts all of the characters (including spaces and punctuation) in the string enclosed in quotation marks, and returns a value of 16. The first quotation mark after the open parenthesis and the last quotation mark before the close parenthesis are not counted, and only one set of the double quotation marks surrounding the word *test* are counted as part of the string. The inside quotation marks are identified as text. Remember, text arguments can have a maximum of 255 characters, including spaces and punctuation.

▼ **Logical values.** There are only two logical values you can use as arguments in a function: TRUE and FALSE. Logical values can be used to enable or disable actions, or they can be the result of an action or comparison. For example, the function =MESSAGE(logical,text) displays text in the message area of the formula bar when the logical value is TRUE, and removes all messages from the message area of the formula bar when the logical value is FALSE. Logical values are also used with **conditionals**, such as IF and WHILE, that allow you to perform actions conditionally. If the result is TRUE, an action will be performed; if the result is FALSE, a different action will be performed.

▼ **Error values.** Error values are the result of a function in which either the syntax or the arguments are incorrect. Error values are preceded by a number sign (#), and will appear in the cell in which you entered the function. Some of the error values you might see are #NAME?, #NULL, #DIV/0!, #N/A, #VALUE|, #REF!, and #NUM!.

▼ **References.** References are the addresses of cells, ranges, or nonadjacent ranges. When you use a reference as an argument in a function, the contents of the cells being referenced are used as the argument. For example, the function =SUM(A1,B1) will add the value of the contents of cells A1 and B1. The function =SUM(A1:A10) will add the value of the contents of all cells in the range A1:A10. Excel interprets a range as one argument in a function. For example, the function =SUM(A1:A10,B1:B10) will add the values of the contents of all of the cells in the range A1:A10 and B1:B10. The ranges are separated by commas, indicating that each range is a separate argument.

▼ **Arrays.** Arrays can be used as the arguments of formulas in a function. A complete explanation of arrays can be found later in this chapter. You can enter more than one value as an argument in an array.

Most of the functions tell you which data type is to be used by naming the argument (the **argument name**). For example, in the function

```
=SUM(number1,number2,...)
```

the arguments are named number1 and number2. Since the argument name is *number*, the data type you use in the argument must be a number. In the function

```
=DIRECTORY(path_text)
```

the argument name includes the word *text*, so the data type used in the argument must be text. The argument names reference, logical, and array indicate that you must use the corresponding data types for your arguments.

Converting Data Types

If you enter an argument that contains an incorrect data type into a function, Excel will try to convert the data in the argument. For example, the function =LEN(text) requires that a text data type be used in the argument. If you enter the function =LEN("data"), all of the characters between the opening and closing quotation marks will be counted and the function will return a value of 4. If you enter a number type argument instead of a data type argument in the function, Excel will convert the number to text. For example, the function =LEN(12345) contains a number type argument (12345) instead of a data type argument. Excel will convert the number to a text value of 12345, and will count all of the characters between the opening and closing quotation marks. The value of the function =LEN(12345) will be returned as 5. Excel will try to convert numbers, text, and logical values to the correct data type. Following is a list of data types and how they are converted.

▼ **Arguments that should be numbers but are entered as text.** If you enter text (data enclosed in quotation marks) in an argument that requires a number, Excel will try to convert the text to a number. If the data is in any standard number, time, date, or currency format, Excel will ignore the quotation marks and treat the data as numbers. For example, the function =SUM("1","2") is incorrect since the arguments *1* and *2* are data type arguments. Since *1* and *2* can be recognized by Excel as standard numbers, Excel will convert the text to the number type 1 and 2, and the function will produce a result of 3.

▼ **Arguments that should be numbers but are entered as logical values.** If you enter a logical value in an argument that requires a number, Excel will convert the logical value TRUE to a 1 and a logical value FALSE to a 0.

▼ **Arguments that should be text but are entered as numbers.** If you enter a number or numbers in an argument that requires text, Excel will enclose the number or numbers in quotation marks and use them as text. For example, the function =LEN(12345) contains the number type argument (12345) instead of a data type argument. Excel will convert the number to a text value of *12345* and will count all of the characters between the opening and closing quotation marks. The value of the function =LEN(12345) will be returned as 5.

▼ **Arguments that should be text but are entered as logical values.** If you enter a logical value in an argument that requires text, Excel will enclose the logical value in quotation marks and use it as text. For example, the function =LEN(TRUE) contains the logical value TRUE instead of text in its argument. Excel will convert the logical value to TRUE and the function will return a value of 4.

▼ **Arguments that should be logical values but are entered as numbers.** If you enter a number in an argument that requires a logical value, Excel will convert a 0 to FALSE and all other numbers to TRUE. For example, the function =MESSAGE(logical,text) requires a logical value for its first argument. If you entered the function as =MESSAGE(0), Excel would convert the number to the logical value FALSE and would remove any messages in the message area of the status bar. If you entered a number other than 0, Excel would convert the number to the logical value TRUE.

▼ **Arguments that should be logical values but are entered as text.** If you enter text in an argument that requires a logical value, the text *TRUE* and *FALSE* will be converted to the logical values TRUE and FALSE. All other text will be ignored.

Using Commas in Arguments

Arguments in functions are separated by commas. The commas indicate to Excel which value corresponds to which argument in a function. For example, the function

```
=FUNCTION(number,logical,text)
```

contains three data types as arguments: the first argument is *numbers*, the second is *text*, and the third is *logical*. If you omit the second argument and enter the function as

```
FUNCTION(10,Text)
```

Excel will assume that the first argument is a number, which is correct. It will assume the second argument is an incorrect logical value (Text), and will ignore it. Since only two arguments are included in the function, Excel will assume that the third argument was omitted. If you want Excel to know that the second argument is the one that was omitted, you must enter the function as follows:

```
=FUNCTION(10,,Text)
```

In this function, the first argument is a number; the second argument is replaced by a **placeholder**, the commas, which indicates that the argument has no value; and the third argument is text. When you use a placeholder instead of a value in an argument, Excel substitutes a value for the argument. The value substituted for an omitted argument depends upon what data type has been omitted. If the data type is numbers, the value is 0. If the data type is logical, the value is FALSE. If the data type is text, the value is "" (empty text). If the data type is reference, the value is usually the active cell or selection.

In some instances you do not want to use a placeholder. For example, if you enter the function =MIN(1,5,7) you will receive a result of 1 (the smallest number used by the arguments). If you enter =MIN(,1,5,7) you will receive a result of 0. This function uses four arguments. The first argument is indicated by a placeholder. Since the value of the argument is omitted, Excel substitutes the value of 0, giving the function a result of 0.

Be careful when using placeholders, since they can cause inaccurate results. If you are using the function to determine the smallest number in a row on a worksheet, for instance, and include extra commas, your result will not be accurate. Since placeholders affect the number of arguments that Excel includes in a function, using extra commas can also affect the way some functions are calculated. For example, the function =AVERAGE(4,3,14) will produce a result of 7. The function =AVERAGE(4,,3,14) will produce a result of 5.25. In the first example, Excel adds the numbers and averages the total by 3 (three arguments); in the second example, Excel adds the numbers and averages the total by 4 (three arguments plus the placeholder).

Using Parenthetical Expressions in Formulas and Functions

So far, we have used simple functions (formulas) to perform calculations and produce a result. For example, the function =SUM(1,2) was used to produce a result of 3. The result of the formula was calculated by performing the instructions of each operator in the order in which it was encountered. For example, the formula =50-10+30 produces a result of 70. This result is obtained taking the number 50, subtracting 10, and then adding 30. If you use more than one type of operator in a formula, Excel performs the calculations based on the order shown below.

Operator	Description
:	Range
Space	Intersection
.	Union
–	Negation (single operand)
%	Percent
^	Exponentiation
* and /	Multiplication and division
+ and –	Addition and subtraction
&	Text joining
= < > <= >= <>	Comparison

Parentheses also change the order in which calculations are performed. For example, if we used the formula =10+5*2, the result would be 20. The formula would first multiply 5 * 2, then add the result to 10. If we wanted the result to reflect 2 multiplied by the result of 10 + 5, this formula would not work. We would have to use a parenthetical expression to indicate to Excel the order in which the calculations were to be performed. A parenthetical expression tells Excel to perform the calculation on the result of the values enclosed in it. For example, the formula =(10+5)*2 tells Excel to add 10 and 5 and multiply the result by 2 to give you 30.

Parenthetical expressions can be used anywhere in a formula or function, and you can use as many parenthetical expressions as you wish in a formula or function. More than one parenthetical expression must be used if you want more than one operation in your formula calculated in a specific order.

To illustrate, let's look at three formulas, each using the same values:

=10+10*2-5-3 will produce the result 22
=10+(10*2)-5-3 will produce the result 32
=10+(10*2)-(5-3) will produce the result 28

It is the placement of the parentheses that determines the result. If your formula does not produce the value you expected, check to see whether you need to use a parenthetical expression, or make sure any that are used are placed correctly.

Parenthetical expressions are included in the syntax of all functions; for example, =SUM(number1,number2,...). You can, however, build more complex formulas that combine functions and other parenthetical expressions. For example: If the value of each cell in the range A1:A5 is 10, the value of cell B1 is 10, and the value of cell B2 is 5, then =SUM(A1:A5)–B1–B2*2 will produce the result 30. This result is obtained by adding the values of cells A1:A5 for a total of 50, subtracting the value of cell B1 (10) for a total of 40, multiplying cell B2 (5) by 2 (multiplication precedes subtraction in the order in which Excel performs calculations), for a total of 10, which is then subtracted from 40. Combining a function and a parenthetical expression as follows: =SUM(A1:A5)-(B1-B2)*2 produces a result of 40. This formula takes the sum of the values of cells A1:A5 (50), subtracts B2 from B1 for a total of 5, multiplies 5 by 2 for a total of 10, then subtracts 10 from 50.

Using Arrays in Formulas and Functions

Arrays can simplify formula entry in your worksheet. A single array can produce the same result as several formulas. For example, suppose you wanted to compute the square root of all of the values in cells A1:A7 and see the results in cells B1:B7. You could enter a formula into cells B1, B2, B3, B4, B5, B6, and B7, or you could enter the formula into cell B1 and then copy it to cells B2:B7. An even quicker way to calculate the square root of the values in cells A1:A7 would be to use an array. When you use an array, you can replace all seven formulas in cells B1:B7 with one formula and achieve the same results.

Entering an Array Formula into a Range of Cells

Let's enter an array formula into the worksheet shown in Figure 1.2 that will produce the same result as entering a formula into each of the cells in the Totals column, G3:G14.

1. Create the worksheet shown in Figure 1.2.

	A	B	C	D	E	F	G	H
1	Sales		Jan.	Feb.	Mar.	Apr.	Totals	
2								
3	Dresses		$2,500.00	$1,375.00	$1,260.98	$400.00	$5,535.98	
4	Skirts		920.00	1,400.67	1,200.00	998.00	4,518.67	
5	Blouses		700.00	1,020.00	950.00	825.00	3,495.00	
6	Slacks		700.00	921.00	840.00	250.00	2,711.00	
7	Jackets		2,047.98	975.00	770.00	1,400.00	5,192.98	
8	Suits		670.00	1,500.00	625.87	650.50	3,446.37	
9	Coats		3,800.00	2,000.45		3,500.00	9,300.45	
10	Handbags		300.00	110.00	600.00		1,010.00	
11	Earrings				825.00	300.00	1,125.00	
12	Bracelets					175.00	175.00	
13	Belts				250.00		250.00	
14	Hair Bows					98.00	98.00	
15								
16	Totals		$11,637.98	$9,302.12	$7,321.85	$8,596.50	$36,858.45	
17								
18								

FIG102.XLS

Figure 1.2   *The Sales worksheet.*

2. Click on cell H3.

3. Select the range of cells in which you want the results of your formula to appear. We want to total the accounts for each item in the worksheet, so we will select cells H3:H14. Rows 3 through 14 contain all of the items for which income from sales was received in January, February, March, and April.

4. Enter the following formula:

```
=C3:C14+D3:D14+E3:E14+F3:F14
```

This formula contains four ranges, each separated by the plus operator (+). When the array is created, Excel will use the values of the first cell address in each range and will perform the action indicated by the operator (+). Cell H3 will contain the sum of the values of C3, D3, E3, and F3. Excel will then go on to the next cell address in the range and produce the sum of the values of C4, D4, E4, and F4. Next Excel will add the values of cells C5, D5, E5, and F5. Excel will continue to add the values of the corresponding cell addresses until it reaches the end of the range, C14, D14, E14, and F14. This single formula will produce twelve values, one for each row in the range. If you click on cells H3:H14, you will see that each cell contains the formula you originally entered in cell H3.

5. To create the array press Ctrl+Shift+Enter. Excel will automatically surround your formula with brackets ({ }) and copy it to each cell in the range. The totals for all accounts in each item will appear in your selected cells (H3:H14), as shown in Figure 1.3. If you compare these values with the values in the Totals column (column G) you will see that they are the same.

	A	B	C	D	E	F	G	H
1	Sales		Jan.	Feb.	Mar.	Apr.	Totals	
2								
3	Dresses		$2,500.00	$1,375.00	$1,260.98	$400.00	$5,535.98	5535.98
4	Skirts		920.00	1,400.67	1,200.00	998.00	4,518.67	4518.67
5	Blouses		700.00	1,020.00	950.00	825.00	3,495.00	3495
6	Slacks		700.00	921.00	840.00	250.00	2,711.00	2711
7	Jackets		2,047.98	975.00	770.00	1,400.00	5,192.98	5192.98
8	Suits		670.00	1,500.00	625.87	650.50	3,446.37	3446.37
9	Coats		3,800.00	2,000.45		3,500.00	9,300.45	9300.45
10	Handbags		300.00	110.00	600.00		1,010.00	1010
11	Earrings				825.00	300.00	1,125.00	1125
12	Bracelets					175.00	175.00	175
13	Belts				250.00		250.00	250
14	Hair Bows					98.00	98.00	98
15								
16	Totals		$11,637.98	$9,302.12	$7,321.85	$8,596.50	$36,858.45	
17								
18								

Figure 1.3 *The Sales worksheet with array totals.*

Excel views an array range as a single entity and does not allow you to edit sections of it. You cannot clear or delete individual cells or ranges that are contained in the array range. You cannot insert cells into an array range. Any of these actions will result in an error message. To return to the worksheet, click on OK in the error message, and press Esc. If you want to perform any editing in an array range, you must first convert the formulas to constant values.

 You can format cells in an array range independently. You can also copy a cell or range of cells in an array to another part of the worksheet. When you copy a cell or range of cells from an array range to another part of a **N O T E** worksheet, Excel will change the cell addresses in the formula to reflect the new address, just as it does with any formula based on relative references.

Deleting an Array Range

You cannot delete individual cells or ranges of cells within an array range. You can, however, delete the entire range:

1. Select the array range.
2. Click on Edit in the menu bar to open the Edit menu.
3. Click on Delete.
4. Choose OK.

Clearing an Array Range

You cannot clear an individual cell or ranges of cells within an array range. You can, however, clear the entire array range:

1. Select the array range.
2. Click on Edit in the menu bar to open the Edit menu.
3. Click on Clear.
4. Choose OK.

Converting the Formulas in an Array Range to Constant Values

When you convert the formulas in an array range to constant values, the formula in each cell takes on the value reflected in that cell. For example, if cell A1 shows a value of 10 and cell A2 shows a value of 15, when you convert the formulas in these cells to a constant value, the formula in cell A1 will be replaced by the value 10, and the formula in cell A2 will be replaced by the value 15. Once you have converted the array range into a range that contains constant values, the array is no longer in effect and each cell can be edited individually; you can delete and/or clear individual cells or ranges of cells, and you can insert cells into the rows or columns that contained the array. To convert the formulas in an array range to constant values:

1. Select the array range.
2. Click on Edit in the menu bar to open the Edit menu.
3. Click on Copy.
4. Click on Edit in the menu bar again.
5. Click on Paste Special to display the Paste Special dialog box.
6. Under Paste, select the Values option.
7. Click on OK.

Using Array Constants

You have just created an array using cell references. Excel used the values in those referenced cells to produce the results of the array formula. You can also enter an array formula using values instead of cell addresses, or using a combination of both. When you enter values instead of cell references into an array formula, these values are referred to as **array constants**. When you enter an array constant in an array formula, you must surround its values with brackets ({ }) and separate each value with a comma (,). For example, suppose you wanted to calculate the state and city tax you paid on the total of each item sold in the month of January, February, March, and April. The state tax is 5 percent and the city tax is 3 percent. You could enter a single formula that would calculate each tax (state and city) for each total. The formula would look like this:

```
=G3:G14*{.05,.03}
```

Each cell in the range G3:G14 contains a value that reflects the total for each item sold. This is followed by an operator informing Excel that the value contained in each cell in the range is going to be multiplied. The brackets that enclose the values .05 and .03 indicate that these are array constants (constant values instead of cell references). To see the results of this array formula using the worksheet shown in Figure 1.3:

1. Select the range I3:J14.
2. Enter the formula =G3:G14*{.05,.03} into cell I3.
3. Press Ctrl+Shift+Enter.

You have created an array range in which Columns I and J contain the results of the formula and show you the state and city tax for the total amount in sales of each item.

Using an Array Constant in a Function to Project a Trend

You can also include array constants and array formulas in functions. Arrays are frequently used in functions to project trends. For example, you would like calculate the total sales for the next three months. You already know the total sales for January, February, March, and April. We will use an array constant in a function to calculate the total sales for the next three months based on the total sales for the previous four months. To predict the sales for the months of May, June, and July:

1. Open a blank worksheet.
2. Enter the titles and amount of total sales for the months of January, February, March, and April, as shown in Figure 1.4.

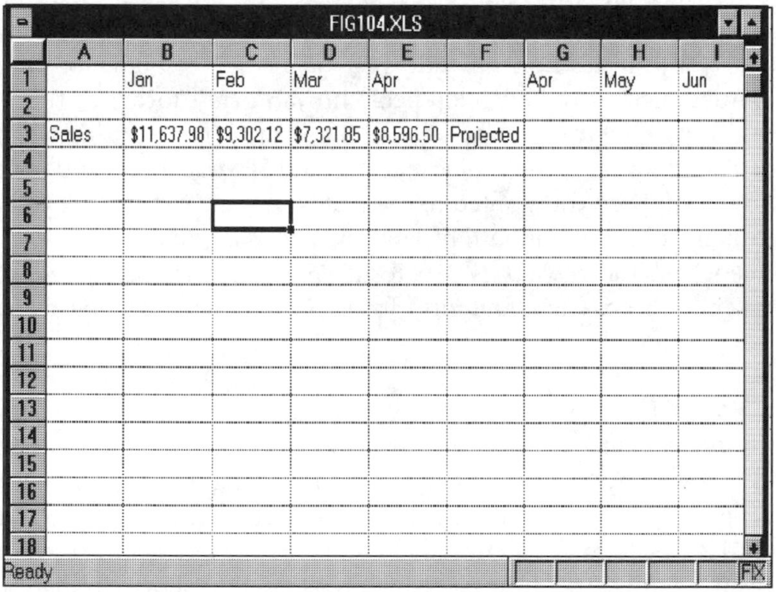

Figure 1.4   Sales for January, February, March, and April.

3. Select cells G3:I3.
4. Click on Formula in the menu bar to open the Formula menu.
5. Click on Paste Function to display the Paste Function dialog box.
6. Select TREND in the Paste Function list box.

7. Click on OK.

8. The TREND function is displayed in the formula bar. You will notice that the syntax for the argument (enclosed in parentheses) contains three possible types of arguments, separated by commas. We are going to add a fourth argument, an array constant, but we are not going to use the second and third arguments. Since Excel identifies each new argument by the comma that separates it from the others, we need to tell Excel that the second and third arguments are blank, and that the array constant is the fourth argument. If we do not, Excel will try to calculate the formula using the array constant as the second argument type, and an error will result. To tell Excel to calculate the values of the first and fourth argument types, edit the formula to read:

   `=TREND(B3:E3,,{5,6,7}`

   This formula tells Excel that it is going to calculate a trend using the values in the first argument (the values contained in the cells in B3:E3), skip the second and third arguments, and calculate the fifth, sixth, and seventh values (the values 4,5,6 contained in the array constant) for the trend.

9. Press Ctrl+Shift+Enter to create the formula. The values in cells B3, C3, D3, and E3 (sales for January, February, March, and April) have been used to project the values in cells G3, H3, and I3 (projected sales for the months of May, June, and July), as shown in Figure 1.5.

	A	B	C	D	E	F	G	H	I
1		Jan	Feb	Mar	Apr		Apr	May	Jun
2									
3	Sales	$11,637.98	$9,302.12	$7,321.85	$8,596.50	Projected	6438.435	5327.964	4217.493

Figure 1.5 *Projected sales for April, May, and June.*

Customizing Functions

You can create your own **custom functions** on macro sheets. Custom functions are used the same way as worksheet functions. Any formula or group of formulas that can be entered on a worksheet can be combined with built-in functions to create your custom functions.

For example, suppose you want to calculate your net income for the month. You need to subtract expenses from income. Your income is made up exclusively of sales, and your worksheet has only one figure for each sale: the amount of the sale plus New York City's 8.25 percent sales tax. Since you do not keep the sales tax, it has to be subtracted from total sales in order for your net income to be accurate. You could write a formula to determine the dollar value of 8.25 percent of the total sales for the month. You could then write another formula to deduct the dollar amount of the sale tax and expenses to determine your net income. Assume your sales for the month totalled $10,000 and your expenses were $6,000. Your formulas would look like this:

```
=10000*.0825 = 825 (the amount of sales tax)
=10000-825-6000=3175 (net income for the month)
```

You could streamline the process even more by entering one formula to subtract the 8.25 percent sales tax and expenses from total sales:

```
=10000-(10000*.0825)-6000=3175
```

Since you will want to know the amount of your net income every month, you could enter this formula into your worksheet for each month, or you could create a custom function, as shown in Figure 1.6. If you create a custom function, you simply have to enter into the function the totals of your sales and expenses and the tax rate for each month; the function will automatically calculate the result. You can create functions that allow you to enter either values or cell or range references as arguments.

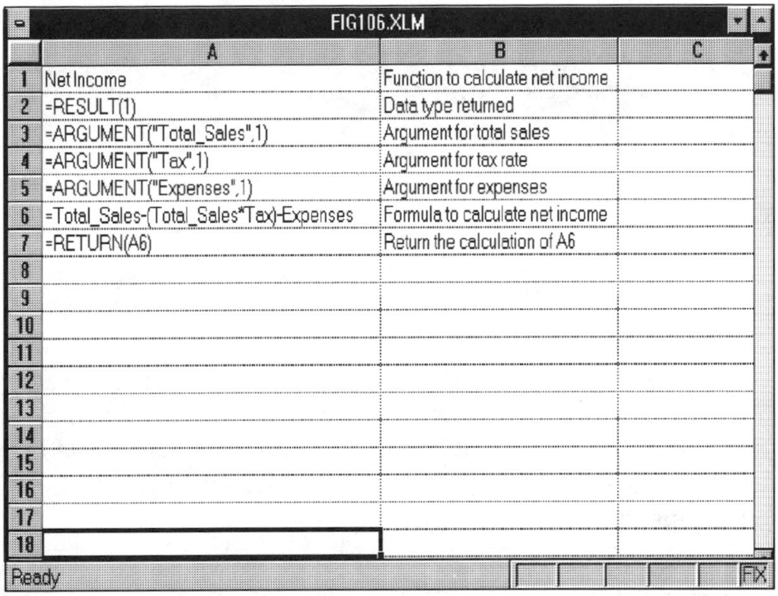

	A	B	C
1	Net Income	Function to calculate net income	
2	=RESULT(1)	Data type returned	
3	=ARGUMENT("Total_Sales",1)	Argument for total sales	
4	=ARGUMENT("Tax",1)	Argument for tax rate	
5	=ARGUMENT("Expenses",1)	Argument for expenses	
6	=Total_Sales-(Total_Sales*Tax)-Expenses	Formula to calculate net income	
7	=RETURN(A6)	Return the calculation of A6	

FIG106.XLM

Ready

Figure 1.6 *Function with arguments Total_Sales, Tax, and Expenses.*

Designing a Custom Function

A custom function consists of three parts: the arguments, the formulas, and the result. When you use a built-in function, you supply values for the existing arguments in the function. When you create a function, you determine how many arguments will be used, and what type of data each argument will accept. After you define the arguments in your custom function, you must create the formula to use the arguments. Finally, you must specify the data type of the result.

Designing the Arguments in a Custom Function

The first step in creating a custom function is designing the arguments used to perform the calculation. Arguments are defined using the ARGUMENT function. The first argument you define using the ARGUMENT function will be the first argument used in the function, the second argument you define will be the second argument used in the function, and so on. The ARGUMENT function uses the following syntax:

```
=ARGUMENT(name_text,data_type_num,reference)
```

The first argument is name_text. If you do not specify a reference argument, this argument is required. The name_text argument defines a name for the value of the argument. When you paste the function, this name appears as the argument name in the function. For example, Figure 1.6 defines three argument names: Total_Sales, Tax, and Expenses. If you name the function Net_Income and then use the Paste Function command on the Formula menu in your worksheet, the following function will appear in the formula bar:

```
=MACRO.XLM!Net_Income(Total_Sales,Tax,Expenses)
```

The name_text argument

The first name after the equal sign is the name of the macro sheet on which the function is located. The second name is the function name, which is followed by arguments enclosed in parentheses. The name for each argument in the function was defined by the name_text argument in the ARGUMENT function when you created your function. Names that have been defined using the name_text argument can be used in other formulas and functions throughout the macro sheet.

 Do not use names for arguments that have been defined elsewhere on the macro sheet. For example, if you already had a cell or range named Total_Sales, you should not use Total_Sales for your name_text argument. **WARNING** If you try to do this, a conflict will arise and your results will be inaccurate.

The data_type_num argument

The second argument in the ARGUMENT function is the data_type_num argument. Use this argument to require a specific data type for your arguments. If you omit the data_type_num argument, Excel will assign a default data_type_num of 7 to the argument, which will allow the user to enter numbers, text, or logical values into the argument using the custom function. If you want to restrict the user to entering a text data type for the argument, you must specify a data_type_num argument of 2. For example, if you want to allow only text entries for the argument name Total_Sales, you would enter the following into the ARGUMENT function:

```
=ARGUMENT("Total_Sales",2)
```

The first argument (name_text) defines the name for the value of the argument, and the second (data_type_num) specifies that only text entries will be accepted for the value of Total_Sales. Each data type you can specify in an argument is shown in the following table, along with its value.

Data type	Value
Number	1
Text	2
Logical	4
Reference	8
Error	16
Array	64

An argument can be a formula, a reference to a single cell, or a constant value, as long as it produces a result that is allowed by the data type. For example, if you specify a data type of 1 in the first argument of the NET_INCOME function, the user can enter any of the following arguments (where cell A1 contains a number):

```
=NET_INCOME(50+50)
```

```
=NET_INCOME(A1)
```

```
=NET_INCOME(100)
```

Each of the arguments used above will produce a number, and will satisfy the requirements of the data type you specified. If you specify a data type of 64 in the first argument of the NET_INCOME function, the user can enter a formula, a cell reference, a range, or a constant value.

If you want to specify more than one data type for an argument, you can add the values of the different data types together. For example, if you want to allow either text or a logical value in your argument, you would add the value of the text data type (2) to the value of the logical data type (4), and enter type data type for the argument as 6. Your argument would look like this:

```
=ARGUMENT("Total_Sales",6)
```

When the function is used, the argument Total_Sales will allow only text or logical value data types to be used.

If you enter a data type into an argument that does not match the data type you specified in the ARGUMENT function, Excel will attempt to convert the argument to the correct data type. If the data in the argument cannot be converted, you will receive an error message.

The reference argument

When you use the reference argument in the ARGUMENT function, Excel places the value you enter into the custom function in the referenced cell or range. If you want to enter a single value, the reference must refer to a single cell. If you want to enter an array, the reference must refer to a range of cells large enough to include the entire array. Once you have entered the argument value in a reference, you can refer to the referenced cell or cell in other formulas or functions in the macro sheet. If you have used the reference argument in the ARGUMENT function, the name_text argument is optional. If you have a data_type_num value that specifies a reference data type, you cannot use the reference argument.

You can save space on your worksheet by using the name_text argument and the appropriate data type value instead of the reference argument. Using the name_text argument also insures that the argument always refers to the correct cell or cells. For example, you can use the ARGUMENT function with name_text and data_type_num to create an argument that will accept a referenced cell. The argument would look like this: =ARGUMENT("Total_Sales",1). It will allow you to enter a number, a cell reference, or a formula as a value in the argument. The argument =ARGUMENT("Total_Sales",8) will allow you to enter a cell reference as a value in the argument.

Using Arrays in Custom Functions

If you want to enter a range or an array into a custom formula, you must use the value for data_num_type that specifies an array (64). This value allows you to enter a range, a cell reference, a constant value, or a formula into the argument. If you try to enter an array constant into an argument that is not specified as an array type, Excel will use the first value in the range or array constant and ignore the rest. If you try to enter an array range into an argument that is not specified as an array type, Excel will return an error value of #VALUE.

Designing the Formulas in a Function

Formulas used in custom functions can include the name defined in the name_text argument, the cells referenced in the reference argument, references to cells in the macro sheet that contain values, and other functions.

Designing formulas that use defined names

You can create formulas in a function that use the name defined in the ARGUMENT function. In Figure 1.6, for example, the formula for the Net_Income function looks like this:

```
=Total_Sales-(Total_Sales*Tax)-Expenses
```

Total_Sales is the name defined for the first argument, Tax is the name defined for the second argument, and Expenses is the name defined for the third argument. The value of the data_type_num for all of the arguments is 1. When you use the Paste Function command in the Formula menu, the Net_Income function appears in the formula bar and looks like this:

```
=MACRO.XLM!Net_Income(Total_Sales,Tax,Expenses)
```

The values you enter for the arguments (a value can be a formula, cell reference, or number and satisfy the requirements of the data type specified) are passed to the names defined for each argument. If you use the value 100 for Total_Sales, the value .05 for Tax, and the value 10 for Expenses, your function will look like this:

```
=MACRO.XLM!Net_Income(100,.05,10)
```

The values you entered into each of the arguments are passed to the defined names; and Total_Sales now has a value of 100, Tax now has a value of .05, and Expenses now has a value of 10. The values you entered for each argument name are used in the following formula to produce a result of 85:

```
=Total_Sales-(Total_Sales*Tax)-Expenses
```

The value of "Total_Sales" is 100, minus the value of "Total_Sales" multiplied by .05 (100*.05=5) to produce a value of 95, minus the value of "Expenses" (10) to produce a value of 85.

If cell A1 contains the value 100, cell A2 contains the value .05, and cell A3 contains the value 10, you could enter the cell references in the Net_Income function and produce the same result. For example, the function

```
Net_Income(Total_Sales,Tax,Expenses)
```

would use the value A1 for the first argument, A2 for the second argument, and A3 for the third argument. Your function would look like this:

```
=MACRO.XLM!Net_Income(A1,A2,A3)
```

Using the formula =Total_Sales–(Total_Sales*Tax)–Expenses, this function would produce a result of 85. Cell A1 contains the value of Total_Sales (100). That is subtracted from the result of Total_Sales times the value of Tax, which is contained in cell A2 and equals .05. This produces a value of 95 (100–(100*.05)), minus the value of Expenses, which is contained in cell A3.

Defining formulas that use constant values or a cell reference

Formulas used in a function do not have to reflect the value of an argument. You can use a constant value or a cell reference to produce a value in the formula, as shown in Figure 1.7.

	A	B	C
1	Net Income	Function to calculate net income	0.0825
2	=RESULT(1)	Data type returned	
3	=ARGUMENT("Total_Sales",1)	Argument for total sales	
4	=ARGUMENT("Expenses",1)	Argument for expenses	
5	=Total_Sales-(Total_Sales*$C$1)-Expenses	Formula to calculate net income	
6	=RETURN(A5)	Return the calculation of A6	

Figure 1.7 *Function with cell reference used as an argument.*

The custom function in Figure 1.7 includes two arguments: the argument for the defined name Total_Sales, and the argument for the defined name Expenses. There is no argument for the value of tax. When the formula for the function is entered it looks like this:

```
=Total_Sales-(Total_Sales*.0825)-Expenses
```

or this:

```
=Total_Sales-(Total_Sales*$C$1)-Expenses
```

In the first example, the values for the arguments are entered by the user as values for the named arguments, and the value for tax is the constant value (.0825). When Excel calculates this formula it takes this value of Total_Sales minus the value of Total_Sales times the constant value, minus the value of Expenses. In the second example, the value for tax is the referenced cell C1, which contains the value .0825. When

Excel calculates the formula, it subtracts the value of Total_Sales from the value of Total_Sales times the value of the contents in cell C1, minus the value of Expenses.

Defining formulas that use functions

You can create formulas in a custom function that use Excel's built-in functions, as shown in Figure 1.8.

	A	B
1	Net Income	Function to calculate net income
2	=RESULT(1)	Data type returned
3	=ARGUMENT("Total_Sales",64)	Argument for total sales
4	=ARGUMENT("Tax",1)	Argument for tax rate
5	=ARGUMENT("Expenses",1)	Argument for expenses
6	=SUM(Total_Sales)-SUM(Total_Sales)*Tax-Expenses	Formula to calculate net income
7	=RETURN(A6)	Return the calculation of A6

Figure 1.8 *Function with a range entered as an argument.*

The custom function in Figure 1.8 includes three arguments: an argument for Tax that specifies a number data type, an argument for Expenses that specifies a number data type, and an argument for Total_Sales that specifies an array data type. This argument allows you to enter a range as the value of the argument. When the formula for this function is entered, it looks like this:

```
=SUM(Total_Sales)-SUM(Total_Sales)*Tax-Expenses
```

This formula uses the SUM function to add the values of the contents of the cells in the range A1:A5 (the value of each cell in the range A1:A5 is 2,000) to calculate the value of Total_Sales (10,000). The value of Total_Sales is then multiplied by the value of Tax (10000*.0825=825), and subtracted from the value of Total_Sales (10000–825=9175). The value of Expenses (6000) is then subtracted (9175–6000), for a result of 3,175.

Designing the Result of a Function

You must use the RESULT function if you want to specify the data type for the result of a custom function, or if you want the result of your function to return an array or a reference. If you do not use the RESULT function, Excel will use a default result that will allow number, text, and logical values as the data types for the results of your custom function. The syntax for the RESULT function is:

```
=RESULT(type_num)
```

The type_num argument specifies the data type of the value that is returned by the function. The numbers used for the type_num argument correspond exactly to the numbers used for the data_type_num arguments listed earlier in this chapter. The RESULT function must be entered before any other formulas in the function, including the ARGUMENT and RETURN functions.

Writing a Custom Function

Writing a custom function is a two-step process.

1. Create the custom function on a macro sheet.
2. Name the custom function.

Excel calculates the arguments and formulas in a custom function starting in the first cell of the custom function, and continuing down each cell in the column until the RETURN function is encountered. You must always enter the arguments and formulas for your custom formats in a column.

Entering a Custom Function into a Macro Sheet

To enter a custom function into a macro sheet:

1. Open the macro sheet.
2. If you want to specify a data type for the result of the function, enter the RESULT function.

3. Enter the ARGUMENT function for each argument you want to use in the function.

4. Enter the formula to calculate the result.

5. Use the RETURN function to end the function. The syntax of the RETURN function is =RETURN(value). The value argument in the RETURN function tells Excel to return the value of the formula in the cell used for the argument. For example, if the formula for a custom function is located in cell A7, the RETURN function would look like this:

   ```
   =RETURN(A7)
   ```

   The RETURN function will return the result of the formula located in cell A7 in the custom function.

6. Save the macro sheet.

Naming a Custom Function

To name a custom function:

1. Select the first cell of the custom function.
2. Click on Formula in the menu bar to open the Formula menu.
3. Click on Define Name to display the Define Name dialog box.
4. Type the name you want to give the custom function into the Name text box.
5. Select the Function option button if you want the name of the custom function to appear in the Paste Function dialog box.
6. Select a category in the Category drop-down box, if you do not wish to accept the default category *User Defined*.
7. Click on OK.

Using a Custom Function

Before you can use a custom function, you must open the macro sheet on which it was saved. There are two way you can use a custom function: if you know the name of the function and the syntax of its arguments, you can type the function into the worksheet; otherwise you must paste it.

To type a custom function into a worksheet:

1. Type the name of the macro sheet that contains the function followed by an exclamation point (!).

2. Type the function name directly after the exclamation point.

3. Type the opening parentheses, the function arguments separated by commas, and the closing parentheses directly after the function name. Your custom function should look like this:

```
=MACRO.XLM!Net_Income(10000,.0825, 6000)
```

To paste a custom function:

1. Select the cell in which you want to paste the function.

2. Click on Formula in the menu bar to open the Formula menu.

3. Click on Paste Function to open the Paste Function dialog box. The Function Category All is selected, and the Paste Function list box displays a list of all of the worksheet functions available in Excel. Custom functions are at the end of the list.

4. Select the custom function you want to use.

5. Click on OK.

6. Edit the arguments in the function in the formula bar to reflect the values you want to use in the function.

7. Press Enter when you have finished editing.

Error Messages

If the custom function you create contains a formula that Excel cannot calculate, you will receive an error value in the cell that contains the formula. If the formula contains a reference to a cell that contains an error value, the formula will also produce an error value. The error values in Excel are:

▼ **#DIV/0!.** This error value means that a formula is trying to divide by 0.

▼ **#N/A.** This error value used in a custom function means that you have omitted a required argument in the function.

▼ **#NAME?.** This error value means that you have used a name that Excel doesn't recognize in an argument or formula.

▼ **#NULL.** This error value means that you have specified an intersection of two areas that do not intersect.

▼ **#NUM.** This error value means you have used a number that is unacceptable in the function. For example, the function SQRT requires a positive number. If you enter a negative number for the value of the argument, the result will be #NUM.

▼ **#REF!.** This error value means that you have used a cell reference that is not valid. You might have deleted cells to which other formulas refer, or copied or moved cells over the cells to which other formulas refer.

▼ **#VALUE.** This error value means that you have entered an argument that does not use the specified data type, and Excel cannot convert the argument to the correct data type.

SIMPLE MACROS

What Is a Macro?

Macros are mini programs. The simplest macro is a **keystroke macro**. Instead of repeating the same sequence of keystrokes (or mouse movements) every time you want to perform an action, you can record a macro to accomplish the action. For example, suppose you use different fonts in your worksheets. Instead of having to click on Format, Font, and then make the selections in the Font dialog box, you could create a macro to automatically select each font for you. This type of key-stroke macro is known as a **command macro**. When you record a command macro, Excel records the instructions (or mouse movements) for each action you perform. These instructions are known as **macro functions**, and are stored on a macro sheet. You can either store the macro on the Excel global macro sheet or on a macro sheet you have created. If you store the macro on the global macro sheet, it is automatically available when you execute Excel. If you store it on a macro sheet that you created, you must open the macro sheet before you can use the macro. When you **run** (execute) the macro, all of the macro functions are performed in the order in which they were recorded.

Command macros can be assigned to tools, buttons, or other graphic objects, and Excel allows you to design your own command macros. You can design custom dialog boxes and menus, execute commands on the basis of user input, and create an entire custom program using the macro command language. These macros are generally used to simplify user input, and to insure that the output is in a similar format. As we progress through this book, we will create all of these kinds of macros.

Creating a Simple Macro

You can create simple macros by using mouse movements and/or keystrokes in the document window. You can use these macros to automate any series of commands you use frequently. For example, if you commonly use certain formats in your worksheets, you could create a macro that duplicates the actions necessary to create each format. Then, when you want to use a certain format for a section of your worksheet, you just have to click your mouse. If you need to change your format on the current worksheet, you can format the worksheet and create a macro for that format at the same time. Once you have created the macro, you can invoke it any number of times.

To create a simple macro:

1. If you have an open document on the screen (including a blank worksheet), click on Macro in the menu bar and then click on Record. If no document is open, click on File in the menu bar and then on Record Macro. This displays the Record Macro dialog box, as shown in Figure 2.1.

2. In the Name text box, type a name for the macro. Excel will suggest the default name Record, followed by a number that corresponds to the next available number in the macro sheet. For example, the first macro you create on the macro sheet will have the suggested name Record1; if you accept this name, the second macro you create will have the suggested name Record2. You should give your macros names that will make it easy for you to identify the task the macrowwill accomplish. For example, if you create a macro to change the default font from 10 point to 12 point, you might want to name your macro *Font12*. All macros in Excel are automatically given an .XLM extension.

3. In the Key text box, type the shortcut keystroke you want to use to execute the macro. Excel will suggest a letter that you can use just as you use any other shortcut key in Excel. You do not have to accept the suggested shortcut key. You should be careful, however, not to use any of the built-in Excel shortcut keys (such as Ctrl+B) or a shortcut key that already exists on an open macro sheet. If a macro sheet has two macros with the same shortcut key, Excel will execute only one macro when the shortcut key is used, and you will not be able

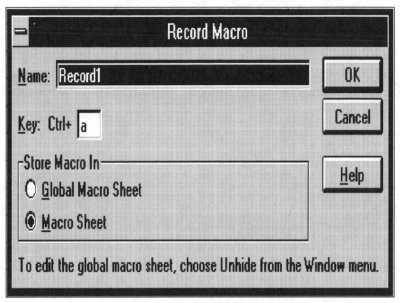

Figure 2.1   *The Record Macro dialog box.*

to use the shortcut key for the other macro. If you have more than one macro sheet open and they each contain a macro with the same shortcut key, Excel will run whichever macro comes first alphabetically. The other macro will be ignored. Excel will not suggest a shortcut key that is a built-in shortcut key-stroke or that already exists on an open macro sheet. If you are not certain that the shortcut key you want to use is unique, accept the suggested letter. You must use a single letter for your shortcut keystroke combinations. Shortcut keys are case-sensitive; Excel recognizes upper- and lowercase letters as unique. If you use a lowercase letter, you execute the macro using Ctrl+letter; if you use an uppercase letter, you execute the macro using Ctrl+Shift+letter.

4. Select the option button you want in Store Macro In.

You can choose to store the macro in the global macro sheet, a new macro sheet, or a macro sheet you have already created. If you store it in the global macro sheet, the macro is automatically available to you when you start Excel. Therefore, it is a good idea to record macros you will want to use on many worksheets in the global macro sheet. If you are creating macros for a specific worksheet, you will probably want to record them to a specially created macro sheet.

To create a macro sheet, choose the Macro Sheet option button. The next time you record a macro during the current Excel session, the name of the macro sheet you created will appear in the Macro Sheet option, and the next macro you record will be added to the newly created macro sheet. If you have an existing macro sheet for the worksheet and want to add macros to the existing macro sheet:

1. Open the macro sheet (if the macro sheet is open but is not visible on the screen, click on Window in the menu bar and click on the macro name to bring it to the top of the document window).

2. Select an empty cell in the macro sheet.

3. Click on Macro in the menu bar.

4. Click on Set Recorder. When you record your macro, it will be added to the existing macro sheet in the location you selected.

5. Click on OK. The Macro Record dialog box is no longer on the screen and you are ready to start recording your macro.

6. Perform the actions you want to record (you can record mouse movements and/or keystrokes).

7. Click on Macro in the menu bar.

8. Click on Stop Recorder.

Once you begin recording your macro, Excel will record every mouse movement and keystroke you make. As you perform each mouse movement and keystroke, it will appear in the document as Excel records each action and creates the macro. Let's assume you are creating a group of worksheets that will all have the same title. Let's create a macro that will place the title on each new worksheet.

1. If you do not have a blank worksheet in your document window, open one.

2. Click on Macro in the menu bar.

3. Click on Record to display the Record Macro dialog box.

4. In the Name text box, type the name *JuneTitl* (this macro will create the titles for worksheets for the month of June).

5. In the Key text box, type the letter t, the first letter in the word *title*. (This shortcut key can be executed by pressing Ctrl+t.)

6. Since this macro will be used only for the worksheets created for the month of June, select the Macro Sheet option button.

7. Click on OK.

8. Type *ABC Company — June 1992* in cell A1 and press Enter.

9. Click on Macro in the menu bar.

10. Click on Stop Recorder.

You now have a title for the month of June in cell A1 on your worksheet, and you have created a macro that will place the same title in cell A1 of any worksheet when you invoke the macro during this session of Excel. If you wish to run the macro during subsequent sessions of Excel, you must save the macro.

Saving a Macro

Macros are not automatically saved when you create them. The macro sheet remains open until you exit Excel. When you exit Excel, you will receive a message asking whether you want to save the changes to the macro sheet. To save the macro, choose Yes. If you created the macro on the global macro sheet or on an existing macro sheet, the sheet will be saved with the macro. If you have created a new macro sheet, the File/Save As dialog box will be displayed. Type in the name you want for the new macro sheet, and click on OK; when you save the macro sheet the macro is saved with it. Let's save our newly created macro sheet:

1. Exit Excel.
2. A dialog box appears asking whether you want to save the changes in your macro sheet. Select Yes.
3. The File/Save As dialog box is displayed on your screen.
4. Type the name you want for your macro sheet in the File Name text box. Since this macro sheet is going to be used for worksheets for the month of June, name it JUNE.XLM.
5. Click on OK.

The macro sheet is now saved, along with any macros you created.

Macros created during a session in Excel are temporary, and can be used only during the current session. If you want to use the macro during subsequent sessions, you **must** save your macro when you exit Excel.

N O T E

Running a Macro

When you create a macro, the actions you select are performed in the document while they are being recorded in the macro. To perform these actions automatically elsewhere in the document or in a new document, run the macro. To do this:

1. If the macro was created and saved on a macro sheet other than the global macro sheet, you must open the macro sheet.
2. Click on Macro in the menu bar.
3. Click on Run to display the Run dialog box, as shown in Figure 2.2.

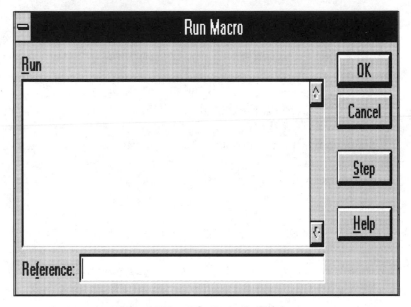

Figure 2.2   *The Run dialog box.*

4. Select the name of the macro you want to run.
5. Click on OK.

Or, use the shortcut key to run the macro.

Let's run the Junetitl macro.

1. Open the JUNE.XLM macro sheet.
2. Either click on Macro/Run, select the macro name and click on OK. **Or** press Ctrl+t.

Excel types *ABC Company — June, 1992* in cell A1 of the new worksheet.

When you execute a macro that inserts text into your document, the macro will overwrite any existing text in that location.

WARNING

Stopping a Macro While It Is Running

To stop a macro while it is running:

1. Press Esc.
2. A dialog box appears asking if you want to halt the macro, step through the macro, continue running the macro, or go to the cell where the macro was stopped.
3. Click on Halt.

The execution of the macro was aborted when you pressed Esc. All of the actions performed by the macro up until that point will appear on the worksheet or macro sheet.

Replacing a Macro

Suppose you want to change the name of ABC Company in your Junetitl macro. You could edit the macro (see Chapter 4), or simply recreate the macro using the same macro name. If the macro is short, it is usually easier to recreate it than to edit it. To recreate a macro using an existing macro name:

1. Open the macro sheet. If the macro sheet is open but not visible, click on Windows in the menu bar and click on the name of the macro sheet to bring it to the top of the document window.
2. Select the first cell of the macro you want to recreate.
3. Click on Macro in the menu bar.
4. Click on Set Recorder.
5. Bring your document to the top of the document window.
6. Click on Macro in the menu bar.
7. Click on Record to display the Record Macro dialog box.
8. In the Name text box, type the name of the existing macro.
9. In the Key text box, type the shortcut key letter of the existing macro.
10. Under Store Macro In, the Macro Sheet option button should be selected.
11. Click on OK.
12. Confirm that you want to overwrite the existing macro.
13. Perform the actions you want to record (mouse movements and/or keystrokes).
14. Click on Macro in the menu bar.
15. Click on Stop Recorder.

Let's replace the Junetitl macro with one that types *ABC Company, Inc. — June, 1992.*

1. If you do not have a blank worksheet in your document window, create one.

2. Either open the JUNE.XLM macro sheet or, if it is already open, bring it to the top of the document window.

3. Select the first cell of the macro you wish to change. Notice that all of the commands in a macro are listed in a column under the cell that contains the macro name and the shortcut key in parentheses.

4. Click on Macro in the menu bar.

5. Click on Set Recorder.

6. Change your document window so that the blank worksheet is visible.

7. Click on Macro in the menu bar.

8. Click on Record to display the Record Macro dialog box.

9. Type *Junetitl* in the Name text box.

10. Type *t* in the Key text box.

11. Under Store Macro In, the Macro Sheet option button should be selected. Notice that the name of the macro sheet in which you set the recorder appears.

12. Click on OK.

13. Confirm that you want to overwrite the Junetitl macro.

14. Type *ABC Company, Inc. — June, 1992* in cell A1.

15. Click on Macro in the menu bar.

16. Click on Stop Recorder.

The new macro has been created, replacing the old version.

If you do not save the changes to the macro sheet when you exit Excel, the new macro will not be saved and the old macro will not be replaced.

WARNING

Creating a Multicommand Macro

Simple macros can perform more than one menu command. For example, you could create a macro that would type a two-line title for your worksheets and change the font size for one line and the bottom cell border for the other line. Let's create a new macro for our June worksheets that contains the title used in Junetitl and another line for Week1, Week2, Week3, and Week4. Let's change the font for the text in the first line to 12 point, and change the bottom cell border for the second line.

1. Open the JUNE.XLM macro sheet (if it is already open, bring the macro sheet to the top of the document window).

2. Click on the first cell in the first empty column (Excel will record the macro in this column).

3. Click on Set Recorder.

4. Bring a blank worksheet to the top of the document window or, if a blank worksheet does not exist, create one.

5. Click on Macro in the menu bar.

6. Click on Record to display the Record Macro dialog box.

7. In the Name text box, type the name *Tottitle* to indicate that the title used is the complete title for all June worksheets.

8. In the Key text box, the logical letter to type would be *t*, but since it has already been used, you cannot use it again. However, since macro shortcut keys are case-sensitive, you can use an uppercase T. Therefore, in the Key text box, type *T*.

9. Under Store Macro In, the Macro Sheet option button is selected.

10. Click on OK.

11. In cell A1 type *ABC Company, Inc. — June, 1992*.

12. In cell C3 type *Week1*, in cell D3 type *Week2*, in cell E3, type *Week3* and in cell F3 type *Week4*.

13. Select cell A1 and click on Format in the menu bar. Click on Font to display the Font dialog box and change the font size to 12 point. Click on OK.

14. Select the cells whose borders you want to change (C3, D3, E3 and F3). Click on Format in the menu bar, then click on Border to display the Border dialog box. Change the bottom border to a heavier line. Click on OK.

15. Click on Macro in the menu bar.

16. Click on Stop Recorder.

You have just created a macro that will type two lines of text in your worksheet, change the font size in one line, and change the border style in the other line. The macro can be invoked at any time during the current Excel session. If you want to use the macro during subsequent sessions in Excel, you must save the changes to the macro sheet when you exit Excel.

Running the Macro

To see how your new macro looks:

1. Create a blank worksheet in the document window.
2. If you have exited Excel (saving the changes to the macro sheet), open the macro sheet.
3. Click on Macro in the menu bar, click on Run, select the Tottitl macro and click on OK. Or press Ctrl+Shift+t.

The text you recorded is typed in the appropriate location in your worksheet, and is formatted according to the formatting commands you performed during the macro recording session.

Pausing the Recorder while Recording a Macro

You can pause the recorder at any time while recording a macro. While the recorder is paused, all mouse movements and keystrokes are ignored and will not be recorded in the macro. The recorder will remain paused until you start it again.

To pause the recorder:

1. Click on Macro in the menu bar.
2. Click on Stop Recorder.

To start recording to the macro again:

1. Click on Macro in the menu bar.
2. Click on Start Recorder.

Creating Macros in More than One Macro Sheet

If you want to create macros in more than one macro sheet in the same Excel session, you must open each macro sheet for which you want to create a macro.

Creating Macros in Several Macro Sheets During the Same Excel Session

For the first macro you want to create:

1. Open the macro sheet in which you want the macro to be created.
2. Select the first empty cell in the first empty column.
3. Click on Menu in the menu bar.
4. Click on Set Recorder.
5. Select the worksheet in which you wish to create the macro.
6. Click on Macro in the menu bar.
7. Click on Record to open the Record Macro dialog box.
8. In the Name text box, type the name you wish to give the macro.
9. In the Key text box, type the shortcut key letter to wish to use for the macro.
10. Under Store Macro In, select the Macro Sheet option button. The name of the macro sheet in which you selected Set Recorder is displayed in the Macro Sheet option.
11. Perform the actions you want to record.
12. Click on Macro in the menu bar.
13. Click on Stop Recorder.

The macro sheet in which you selected Set Recorder will remain the default macro sheet. If you want to record a macro in a different macro sheet, repeat steps 1 through 13.

> If you want to record a macro to the global macro sheet, you do not have to open the macro sheet or select Set Recorder. You simply have to select the Global Macro Sheet option button in the Record Macro dialog box.
>
> **N O T E**

Creating More than One Macro Sheet During an Excel Session

If you want to create more than one macro sheet during an Excel session, you cannot use the Macro menu. Once you have created a macro sheet, it becomes the Macro/Record/Macro Sheet option button default and all new macros are created on the sheet. If you have opened other existing macro sheets, you can use the Set Recorder command to change the Macro Sheet option button default. However, you can use the Set Recorder command only for an open, existing macro sheet. To create a new macro:

1. Click on File in the menu bar.
2. Click on New to display the New dialog box.
3. Click on Macro Sheet.
4. Click on OK.

Your new macro sheet has been created and opened, and appears in your document window. To record a macro to the new macro sheet, follow steps 2 through 13 in "Creating Macros in Several Macro Sheets During the Same Excel Session."

Assigning a Macro to a Button or Tool

You can assign a macro to a button that you place on a worksheet or macro sheet, or you can create a button and record a macro for it. You can create a custom tool for a macro or change an existing tool and assign a macro to it. Assigning a macro to a button or tool makes it easier to run—you do not have to remember the shortcut keys to invoke the macros, or go through many other steps to execute the macro. Instead, you simply click on the button or tool to run the macro.

When you create a button, it is embedded in the worksheet or macro sheet on which it is created. If you want to use the button in another document, you must either copy the button to the document, or create a new button on the document. When you create a tool, the tool is available whenever the toolbar is displayed, regardless of what document is in the document window.

Creating a Button and Recording a Macro for It

If you want to create a button and record a macro to one of several existing macro sheets you are using, remember to use the Set Recorder command in the Macro menu to set the Macro Sheet default to the sheet in which you want to create the macro. To create a button and record a macro for it:

1. Click on Options in the menu bar.
2. Click on Toolbars to display the Toolbars dialog box.
3. Select Utility, then click on Show.
4. Click on the Button tool in the Utility toolbar, as shown in Figure 2.3.

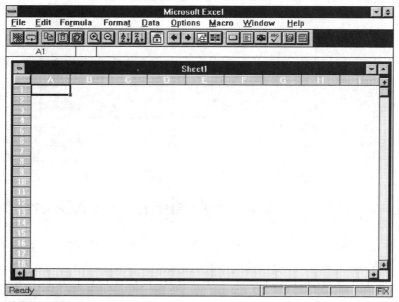

Figure 2.3   *The Button tool is sixth from the right on the toolbar.*

5. Place your insertion point where you want the button to be located. Drag until the button is the size you want. If you want your button to be square, hold down the Shift key while dragging.

6. When you release the mouse button, your button box appears on the screen with the text *Button* and a number in it. The Assign To Object dialog box appears on the screen, as shown in Figure 2.4.

7. Click on Record in the dialog box.
8. Perform the actions you want to record.
9. Click on Macro in the menu bar.
10. Click on Stop Recorder.

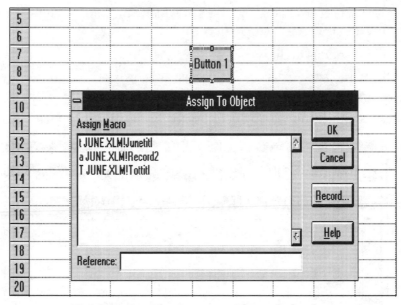

Figure 2.4   *The Assign to Object dialog box.*

Creating a Button and Assigning a Macro to It

To create a button and assign an existing macro to it:

1. Click on Options in the menu bar.
2. Click on Toolbars to display the Toolbars dialog box.
3. Select Utility, then click on Show.
4. Click on the Button tool in the Utility toolbar.
5. Place your insertion point where you want the button to be located. Drag until the button is the size you want. If you want your button to be square, hold down the Shift key while dragging.
6. When you release the mouse button, your button box appears on the screen with the text "Button" and a number in it. The Assign To Object dialog box appears on the screen.
7. Select the macro you want to assign to the button.
8. Click on OK.

Changing the Macro Assigned to a Button

To change the macro assigned to a button or to assign a different macro to the button, or to clear a macro from a button:

1. Press Ctrl and click on the button.
2. Click on Macro in the menu bar.
3. Click on Assign to Object to display the Assign To Object dialog box.
4. Select the macro you want to assign to the button. If you want to clear a macro assigned to the button, delete the macro name in the Reference box.
5. Click on OK.

Changing the Text in the Button

When you create a button it contains the text *Button* and a number. Even when you record or assign a macro to it, the text in the button does not change to reflect the name of the macro. You cannot tell by looking at the button what macro will be run when you click on it. To change the text in the button to make it easy to identify the macro it will invoke:

1. If a macro is assigned to the button, press Ctrl and click on the button; otherwise just select the button.
2. Place your insertion point in the button where you want to change the text. Insert, delete, and edit the text just as you would edit text in the formula bar in a worksheet.
3. Click on any cell outside the button.

Text in a button bar does not appear in the formula bar, but is edited in exactly the same way as text in a worksheet.

N O T E

Formatting the Button Text

You can change the text alignment and orientation and the font in a button.

1. If a macro is assigned to the button, press Ctrl and click on the button; otherwise just select the button.

2. If you want to change the font of some of the characters in the button; select the characters you want to change. If you want to change the font of all of the characters in the button, or if you want to change the text alignment and/or orientation, do not select any of the text.

3. Click on Format in the menu bar.

4. Click on Font to display the Font dialog box. Or, click on Text to display the Text dialog box.

5. Select the options you want in the dialog box you have chosen.

6. Click on OK.

Deleting a Button

To delete a button from a worksheet or macro sheet:

1. If a macro is assigned to the button, press Ctrl and click on the button; otherwise just select the button.

2. Click on Edit in the menu bar.

3. Click on Clear.

The button is no longer visible on the worksheet or macro sheet. When you save the document, the button will be permanently deleted.

Creating a Custom Tool and Recording a Macro for It

You can create a custom tool, assign it to any toolbar, and record a macro for it. If you want to create a tool and record a macro to one of several existing macro sheets you are using, remember to use the Set Recorder command in the Macro menu to set the Macro Sheet default to the macro sheet in which you want to create the macro. To create the custom tool:

1. Click on Options in the menu bar.

2. Click on Toolbars to display the Toolbars dialog box.

3. Click on the Customize button to display the Customize dialog box.

4. Select Custom in the Categories list box. The tools you have available to you appear in the Tools box, as shown in Figure 2.5.

5. Drag the tool you want to use for your macro to the location on the toolbar where to want to add to tool.

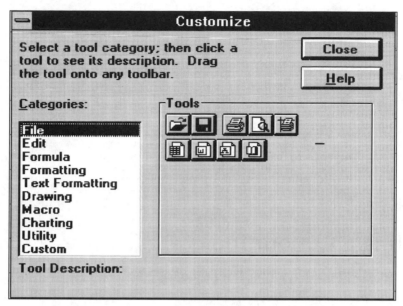

Figure 2.5   *The Cusomize dialog box.*

6. The Assign To Tool dialog box is displayed.

7. Click on Record to display the Record Macro dialog box.

8. In the Name text box, type the name you want to give the macro.

9. In the Key text box, type the shortcut key letter you want to assign to the macro.

10. The Macro Sheet option button under Store Macro In should be selected and should display the name of the macro sheet you selected with the Set Recorder command. If you want to add the macro the global macro sheet, select the Global Macro Sheet option button.

11. Click on OK.

12. Perform the actions you want to record.

13. Click on Macro in the menu bar.

14. Click on Stop Recorder.

Creating a Tool and Assigning a Macro to It

To create a custom tool and assign an existing macro to it:

1. Click on Options in the menu bar.

2. Click on Toolbars to display the Toolbars dialog box.

3. Click on the Customize button to display the Customize dialog box.

4. Select Custom in the Categories list box. The tools you have available to you appear in the Tools box.

5. Drag the tool you want to use for your macro to the location on the toolbar where to want to add to tool.

6. The Assign To Tool dialog box is displayed.

7. In the Assign Macro list box, select the macro you want to assign to the tool.

8. Click on OK to return to the Customize dialog box.

9. Click on Close.

Deleting a Custom Tool

If you want to delete a custom tool from a toolbar:

1. Click on Options in the menu bar.

2. Click on Customize to display the Customize dialog box.

3. Drag the custom tool from the toolbar to any other location where there is no toolbar.

4. Click on Close.

 When you delete a customized tool from a toolbar, the tool is permanently deleted. If you want to add the tool again, you must recreate the custom tool.

Keeping a Record of Your Macros

If you have added several macros to the global macro sheet and/or created several macro sheets, you may find it difficult to remember what macros you have recreated. You might find it useful to keep a log of all of the macros and macros sheets you create.

Chapter 3

MACRO FUNCTIONS AND ARGUMENTS

The Syntax of Functions

All functions employ the same basic syntax. If the syntax of your function is incorrect, Excel will display a message informing you that there is an error. The basic syntax of a function is:

```
=FUNCTION NAME(argument or arguments)
```

A function must begin with an equal sign (=). This is followed by the function name, such as SUM. The function name is followed by the argument(s) enclosed in parentheses.

The following syntax will be used for all functions: function names will be in bold-face, uppercase letters; required arguments will be in boldface; and optional arguments will be in lightface type. For example, in the following function:

```
=SUM(number1,number2,...)
```

the function name, SUM, and the required argument, number1, are bold; the argument number2 is not bold and is therefore optional. If the function name is followed by an empty set of parentheses, the function does not accept an argument. You must, however, include the parentheses in the function.

When a function name is followed by a question mark (?), the dialog box that corresponds to the function name is displayed. If the arguments are omitted, the choices in the dialog box appear as the Excel default; if the arguments in the function are included, the arguments appear in the corresponding text boxes or check boxes in the dialog box.

As a rule, you should not use spaces in functions. You may use upper- or lowercase letters when typing a function. The maximum number of arguments that can be included in a function is 30 and the total number of characters cannot exceed 1,024. The most characters that can be used in any one argument in a function is 255.

The Chart Menu Functions

The following functions are the equivalent of executing Chart menu commands or tools.

ADD.ARROW

The ADD.ARROW function adds an arrow to the active chart. Inserting this function in a macro sheet is the equivalent of choosing the Add Arrow command from the Chart menu or clicking the Chart Arrow tool. To use the ADD.ARROW function, a chart must be the active document.

Use with macro sheets only.

Syntax

```
=ADD.ARROW()
```

LEGEND

The LEGEND function adds or deletes a legend in a chart. Inserting this function in a macro sheet is the same as choosing the Add Legend or Delete Legend command from the Chart menu.

Use with macro sheets only.

Syntax

```
=LEGEND(logical)
```

Logical is a value specifying which command LEGEND is equivalent to. If logical is TRUE, LEGEND is equivalent to the Add Legend command. If logical is FALSE, LEGEND is equivalent to the Delete Legend command. The default (if logical is omitted) is TRUE.

ADD.OVERLAY

The ADD.OVERLAY function adds an overlay to a 2-D chart. Inserting this function in a macro sheet is the equivalent of choosing the Add Overlay command from the full Chart menu.

Use with macro sheets only.

Syntax

```
=ADD.OVERLAY()
```

AXES

The AXES function controls the appearance of the axes on a chart. Inserting this function in a macro sheet is the equivalent of choosing the Axes command from the Chart menu. There are two forms of syntax for this function, depending upon whether you are using a 2-D chart or a 3-D chart.

Use with macro sheets only

Syntax for 2-D Charts

```
=AXES(x_main,y_main,x_over,y_over)
=AXES(x_main,y_main,x_over,y_over)
```

Syntax for 3-D Charts

```
=AXES(x_main,y_main,z_main)
=AXES?(x_main,y_main,z_main)
```

X_main corresponds to the (x) axis on the main chart; y_main corresponds to the (y) axis on the main chart; z_main corresponds to the (z) axis on the 3-D main chart;

x_over corresponds to the (x) axis on the overlay chart; and y_over corresponds to the (y) axis on the overlay chart.

Arguments are logical values. If the argument is TRUE, the corresponding axis displayed. If the argument is FALSE, the corresponding axis is hidden. If the argument is omitted, the corresponding axis is displayed (the default).

CALCULATE.NOW

The CALCULATE.NOW function calculates all open documents when calculation is set to manual. Inserting this function in a macro sheet is equivalent to choosing the Calculation command from the Options menu and then choosing the Calc Now button.

Use with macro sheets only.

Syntax

```
=CALCULATE.NOW()
```

DELETE.ARROW

The DELETE.ARROW function deletes the selected arrow in a chart. Inserting this function in a macro sheet is equivalent to choosing the Delete Arrow command from the Chart menu. To select an arrow before deleting it, use the SELECT function (see the "Command Functions" section later in this chapter). You can also use the CLEAR function (see the "Edit Functions" section later in this chapter) to delete an arrow.

Use with macro sheets only.

Syntax

```
=DELETE.ARROW()
```

DELETE.OVERLAY

The DELETE.OVERLAY function deletes an overlay from a chart. Inserting this function in a macro sheet is equivalent to choosing the Delete Overlay command from the Chart menu.

Use with macro sheets only.

Syntax

```
=DELETE.OVERLAY()
```

EDIT.SERIES

The EDIT.SERIES function creates or changes a chart series by inserting a new series formula or modifying an existing series formula in a chart. EDIT.SERIES is usually used to change the data that is plotted in a chart. Inserting this function in a macro sheet is equivalent to choosing the Edit Series command from the Chart menu. To delete a series, first select the series using the SELECT function, then delete it using the FOR-MULA function. You can also use the CLEAR function to delete a series. The SELECT, FORMULA, and CLEAR functions are explained later in this chapter.

Use with macro sheets only.

Syntax

```
=EDIT.SERIES(series_num,name_ref,x_ref,y_ref,z_ref,plot_order)
=EDIT.SERIES?(series_num,name_ref,x_ref,y_ref,z_ref,plot_order)
```

Series_num is the number of the series you want to change. If this value is 0 or omitted, a new data series is created.

Name_ref is the name of the data series. It can be an external reference to a single cell, a name defined as a single cell, or a name defined as a sequence of characters. It can also be text (for example, January, 1993).

X_ref is an external reference to the name of the worksheet and the cells that contain the data for the X axis in the chart.

Y_ref is an external reference to the name of the worksheet and the cells that contain the data for the Y axis in the chart.

Z_ref is an external reference to the name of the worksheet and the cells that contain the data for the Z axis in a 3-D chart.

Plot_order is a number indicating whether the data series is plotted first, second, third, and so forth, in the chart. Some rules apply:

1. No two series can have the same plot order.
2. When you assign a plot order to a series, all other plot orders in the series are increased by one.
3. If you omit plot_order, Excel will plot that series last.
4. The maximum value for plot_order is 255.

GRIDLINES

The GRIDLINES function allows you display or hide the gridlines in a chart. Inserting this function is equivalent to choosing the Gridlines command from the Chart menu.

Use with macro sheets only.

Syntax

    =GRIDLINES(x_major,x_minor,y_major,y_minor,z_major,z_minor)
    =GRIDLINES?(x_major,x_minor,y_major,y_minor,z_major,z_minor)

X_major corresponds to the major coordinates on the X axis; x_minor corresponds to the minor coordinates on the X axis; y_major corresponds to the major values on the Y axis; y_minor corresponds to the minor values on the Y axis; z_major corresponds to the major values on the Z axis; and z_minor corresponds to the minor values on the Z axis.

Arguments are logical values. If the argument is TRUE, the gridlines are displayed. If the argument is FALSE, the gridlines are hidden. The default argument is FALSE.

SELECT.CHART

The SELECT.CHART function is used to select an entire chart. To select sections of a chart, use the SELECT function (Chart Items) explained later in this chapter. Inserting this function is equivalent to choosing the Select Chart command from the Chart menu.

Use with macro sheets only.

Syntax

    =SELECT.CHART()

The Control Menu Functions

The following functions are the equivalent of executing Control menu commands.

CLOSE

The CLOSE function closes the active window. Inserting this function in a macro sheet is equivalent to choosing the Close command from the application Control menu. You can specify whether the document should be saved before the window is closed.

Use with macro sheets only.

Syntax

`=CLOSE`(save_logical)

Save_logical is a value that specifies whether to save the file before closing the window. If you specify TRUE for the save_logical value, the file is saved. If you specify FALSE for the save_logical value, the file is not saved. If you omit a save_logical value from the function and you have made changes to the file, a dialog box is displayed asking whether you want to save the file.

APP.MAXIMIZE

The APP.MAXIMIZE function maximizes the Excel window. Inserting this function in the macro sheet is equivalent to choosing the Maximize command from the Control menu for the application window.

Use with macro sheets only.

Syntax

`=APP.MAXIMIZE()`

WINDOW.MAXIMIZE

The WINDOW.MAXIMIZE function changes the active window from its normal size to full size. Inserting this command in a macro sheet is the equivalent of pressing Ctrl+F10 or double-clicking the title bar.

Use with macro sheets only.

Syntax

`=WINDOW.MAXIMIZE`(window_text)

Window_text specifies which window to switch to and maximize. Window_text is text enclosed in quotation marks or a reference to a cell containing text. If window_text is omitted, the active window stays the same.

APP.MOVE

The APP.MOVE function moves the Excel window to a designated location on the screen. Inserting this function in a macro sheet is equivalent to choosing the Move command from the Control menu for the application window. If the window has been maximized you will get an error value if you use this function.

Use with macro sheets only.

Syntax

=APP.MOVE(x_num,y_num)
=APP.MOVE?(x_num,y_num)

X_num specifies the horizontal position of the Excel window measured in points from the left edge of the screen to the left edge of the window; and y_num specifies the vertical position of the Excel window measured in points from the top edge of the screen to the top edge of the window.

If you use the function=APP.MOVE?(), no dialog box is displayed. Instead, you can move the window using the keyboard or mouse. If you include x_num or y_num values in the function, the window is moved to the specified coordinates and you are left in move mode.

WINDOW.MOVE

The WINDOW.MOVE function moves the active window to a specified location in the workspace. Inserting this function in a macro sheet is equivalent to choosing the Move command from the Control menu in Microsoft Excel for Windows or moving a window by dragging its title bar or icon.

Use with macro sheets only.

Syntax

=WINDOW.MOVE(x_pos,y_pos,window_text)
=WINDOW.MOVE?(x_pos,y_pos,window_text)

X_pos specifies the horizontal position, measured in points, to which you want to move the window. A point is 1/72 of an inch. The position is measured from the left edge of the workspace to the left edge of the window.

Y_pos specifies the vertical position, measured in points, to which you want to move the window. The position is measured from the top edge of your workspace to the top edge of the window.

Window_text specifies which window to move. Window_text is text enclosed in quotation marks or a reference to a cell containing text. If window_text is omitted, the active window is moved.

APP.RESTORE

The APP.RESTORE function restores the Excel window to its previous size and location. Inserting this function in a macro sheet is equivalent to choosing the Restore command from the Control menu for the application window.

Use with macro sheets only.

Syntax

```
=APP.RESTORE()
```

WINDOW.RESTORE

The WINDOW.RESTORE function changes the active window back to its previous size. Inserting this function into a macro sheet is equivalent to pressing Ctrl+F5 or double-clicking the title bar or the icon (if the window has been minimized).

Use with macro sheets only.

Syntax

```
=WINDOW.RESTORE(window_text)
```

Window_text specifies which window to switch to and restore. Window_text is text enclosed in quotation marks or a reference to a cell containing text. If window_text is omitted, the active window is restored.

APP.SIZE

The APP.SIZE function changes the size of the Excel window. Inserting this function in a macro sheet is the equivalent of choosing the Size command from the Control menu for the application window.

Use with macro sheets only.

Syntax

```
=APP.SIZE(x_num,y_num)
=APP.SIZE?(x_num,y_num)
```

X_num specifies the width, in points, of the Microsoft Excel window; and y_num specifies the height, in points, of the Microsoft Excel window.

If you use the function=APP.SIZE?(), no dialog box is displayed. Instead, you can manually drag the border of the window using the keyboard or mouse. If you include x_num or y_num values in the function, the window is sized according to the specified coordinates and you are left in size mode.

WINDOW.SIZE

The WINDOW.SIZE function changes the size of the active window by moving the lower-right corner of the window a specified number of points. The upper-left corner of the window will not be affected. Inserting this function in a macro sheet is equivalent to choosing the Size command in the Control menu or using a mouse to adjust the sizing borders of a window. You cannot use this function to size a window that has been minimized to an icon or maximized to full size. You must first restore the window to its original size.

Use with macro sheets only.

Syntax

```
=WINDOW.SIZE(width,height,window_text)
=WINDOW.SIZE?(width,height,window_text)
```

Width specifies the width of the window in points, height specifies the height of the window in points, and window_text specifies which window to size. Window_text is text enclosed in quotation marks or a reference to a cell containing text. If window_text is omitted, the active window is sized.

A point is 1/72 of an inch.

The Data Menu Functions

The following functions are equivalent to executing Data menu commands or tools.

CONSOLIDATE

This function allows you to summarize data from multiple ranges on multiple worksheets into a separate worksheet. The CONSOLIDATE function is equivalent to choosing the Consolidate command on the Data menu.

Use with macro sheets only.

Syntax

=**CONSOLIDATE**(source_refs,function_num,top_row,left_col,create_links)

=**CONSOLIDATE?**(source_refs,function_num,top_row,left_col,create_links)

Source_refs refers to the names of the worksheet and the ranges that you want to consolidate. Source_refs must be set up as external references, and must be in text form. Source_refs must always be given as an array. For example:

=CONSOLIDATE("INCOME.XLS!January","EXPENSES.XLS!Jan")

will combine the range named *January* on the Income worksheet and the range named *Jan* on the Expenses worksheet into a single range on one worksheet. If you need to add or delete a source_ref from a consolidation on a worksheet, you must redo the CONSOLIDATE function.

Function_num specifies one of the eleven functions that you can use to consolidate data. If you omit function_num, the default function SUM will be used. The following table lists the functions that are available to you:

Function_num	Function	Use
1	AVERAGE	Returns the average of all the arguments.
2	COUNT	Counts all of the cells containing numbers in the arguments.
3	COUNTA	Counts all of the cells that are not blank in the arguments.
4	MAX	Returns the largest number in the arguments.
5	MIN	Returns the smallest number in the arguments.
6	PRODUCT	Multiplies the values in the arguments.
7	STDEV	Estimates the standard deviation of a population based on a sample given as arguments.
8	STDEVP	Estimates the standard deviation of an entire population with the entire population given as arguments.
9	SUM	Adds the numbers in the arguments.
10	VAR	Estimates the variance of a population given as arguments.
11	VARP	Estimates the variance of an entire population using the entire population as arguments.

Top_row and left_col are logical values that refer to the categories in the top row and/or left columns. If the value is TRUE, Excel will use the categories in the top row and/or left column of the arrays in source_refs to consolidate the data. For example, you want to consolidate by Totals, and the data you are consolidating is in one location in the first source document and in another location on the second source document. Since Excel uses the labels on the source worksheets to determine the category names and ranges, choosing TRUE would consolidate all of the ranges labeled Totals in the consolidated worksheet no matter where they are located in the source worksheets. If the value is FALSE or omitted, Excel will consolidate by position. FALSE should be used if you are consolidating data from a series of identical worksheets.

Create_links allows you to create links from the source data to the consolidated data so that the consolidated data is updated automatically when the source data is changed. If you omit create_links, you must reconsolidate the data every time you want to update the consolidated data. To reconsolidate the data, use the CONSOLI-DATE function with no arguments. Excel will reconsolidate the data using the arguments on the existing consolidation.

CROSSTAB.CREATE

The CROSSTAB.CREATE function creates a cross-tabulation table from specified data in a database. It is equivalent to choosing the Crosstab command from the Data menu, which activates the Crosstab Wizard. It is strongly recommended that you use the macro recorder rather than the CROSSTAB.CREATE function to create a cross-tabulation table.

Use with macro sheets only.

Syntax

```
=CROSSTAB.CREATE(rows_array,columns_array,values_array,create_out-
line, Create_names,multiple_values,auto_drilldown,new_sheet)
=CROSSTAB.CREATE?()
```

Rows_array is a two-dimensional array that specifies a set of fields that appear in each row of the cross-tabulation table. Rows_array consists of the following elements:

▼ Field_name specifies a field name as either as text or as a reference to a cell you wish to include in the cross-tabulation table.

▼ Grouping_index specifies how to group numeric and date values in the cross-tabulation table. For numeric fields, the grouping_index is the size of the group. For text fields, or to specify no grouping at all, use 0. The grouping_index for date values is as follows:

Index	Description of group
0	No grouping or text field
1	Group by days
2	Group by weeks
3	Group by months
4	Group by thirty-day periods
5	Group by quarters
6	Group by years

▼ From specifies the value for the starting field. If the field is numeric, From is a number; if the field is a character field, From is a text string; if the field is a data field, From is a serial number or date enclosed in quotation marks (" "). Enter FALSE for the From value to specify that you wish to start at the minimum possible value for the field.

▼ To specifies the value for the ending field. If the field is numeric To is a number; if the field is a character field To is a text string; if the field is a data field, To is a serial number or date enclosed in quotation marks (" "). If you enter FALSE for the To value, you specify that you wish to end at the maximum possible value for the field.

▼ Subtotals represents a string of seven characters. Each character in the string corresponds to a type of subtotal. If you want a type of subtotal, set the character in the string to Y. If you want to skip a type of subtotal, set the character in the string to N. Following is a list of the type of subtotals and their corresponding position within the character string.

Position	Type of subtotal
1	Sum
2	Count
3	Average
4	Minimum
5	Maximum
6	Standard deviation
7	Variance

Columns_array is a two-dimensional array that specifies a set of fields that appear in each column of the cross-tabulation table. Columns_array consists of the same elements as Rows_array.

Values_array is a two-dimensional array the identifies each field that appears as a value field in the cross-tabulation table. Following is a list of the elements that comprise the Values_array.

▼ Field_label specifies a label for the summary field.

▼ Summary_expression is a text string that identifies the expression (including an aggregation operator) to compute.

▼ Display_items is a five-character text string that specifies whether to display certain values. To specify a display value, type Y for the corresponding character. To omit a display value, type N for the corresponding character. The Display_items values and their correspond positions in the character string are as follows:

Position	Type of display
1	Values
2	Row percent
3	Column percent
4	Total percent
5	Index

▼ Use_all_values is a logical value that indicates what values to use when calculating subtotals and percentages. If the logical value is TRUE, the CROSSTAB.CREATE function uses any table values that it needs, even values that appear outside the From and To range. These values will not, however, appear in the cross-tabulation table. if the logical value is FALSE, the CROSSTAB.CREATE function will use only values that appear in the cross-tabulation table.

Create_outline is a logical value. If the logical value is TRUE, the argument creates an outline for the cross-tabulation table; if the logical value is FALSE, the argument does not create an outline.

Create_names is a logical value. If the logical value is TRUE, the argument creates names for the values from the cross-tabulation table; if the logical value is FALSE, the argument does not create names for the values. Names can be used instead of cell addresses for rows and columns.

Multiple_values is a numerical value that indicates how to handle multiple summaries. Following is a list of multiple_values and their descriptions:

Value	Description
1	Inner columns
2	Outer columns
3	Inner rows
4	Outer rows

Auto_drilldown is a logical value. If TRUE, the argument places drilldown formulas in the result cells, if FALSE, the argument does not place drilldown formula in the result cells.

New_sheet is a logical value. If TRUE, the argument creates the cross-tabulation table on a new sheet; if FALSE, the argument creates the cross-tabulation table on the existing sheet.

The CROSSTAB.CREATE() function will access the Crosstab Wizard.

CROSSTAB.DRILLDOWN

The CROSSTAB.DRILLDOWN function performs a database query that retrieves records that are summarized in the cell. This function is equivalent to double-clicking on a cell that contains a summary value in a cross-tabulation table.

Use with macro sheets only.

Syntax

```
=CROSSTAB.DRILLDOWN()
```

CROSSTAB.RECALC

The CROSSTAB.RECALC function recalculates a cross-tabulation table. This function is equivalent to the Recalculate Existing Crosstab command in the Data menu.

Use with macro sheets only.

Syntax

```
=CROSSTAB.RECALC(rebuild)
```

If the logical value rebuild is TRUE, the CROSSTAB.RECALC function recreates the cross-tabulation table from row, column, and value definition. If the logical value is FALSE or omitted, the CROSSTAB.RECALC function recalculates the cross-tabulation with its current layout and elements.

DATA.DELETE

The DATA.DELETE function deletes data that matches the specified criteria in the defined database. This function is equivalent to using the Delete command on the Data menu.

Use with macro sheets only.

Syntax

```
=DATA.DELETE()
=DATA.DELETE?()
```

The first example will delete all of the records that match the specified criteria in the defined database without any warning message. The second example will display a message warning you that matching records will be deleted and will give you a choice of approving or canceling the action. If you approve, all of the records that match the specified criteria will be deleted. If you cancel, the action will be canceled, and the records will not be deleted.

EXTRACT

The EXTRACT function extracts records that match specified criteria in the criteria range and copies them into a separate extract range. This function is equivalent to using the Extract command on the Data menu.

Use with macro sheets only.

Syntax

```
=EXTRACT(unique)
=EXTRACT?(unique)
```

Unique is a logical value. If the value is TRUE, Excel excludes duplicate records from the extract list. If the value is FALSE or omitted, Excel includes all records that match the criteria in the extract list. If EXTRACT is followed by a question mark (?), the Extract dialog box will be displayed on the screen.

DATA.FIND

The DATA.FIND function selects records that match the specified criteria in the defined database. This function is equivalent to using the Find and Exit Find command on the Data menu.

Use with macro sheets only.

Syntax

```
=DATA.FIND(logical)
```

If the DATA.FIND function returns a logical value of TRUE, this function will find and select all of the records that match the selected criteria. If the DATA.FIND function returns a logical value of FALSE, this function will execute the Exit Find command.

DATA.FIND.NEXT

The DATA.FIND.NEXT function finds the next record that matches the specified criteria in the defined database. This function is equivalent to using the Down Arrow key after selecting the Find command from the Data menu. If the DATA.FIND.NEXT function cannot find any more matching records, it will return a value of FALSE. You will hear a beep and your insertion point will remain in the last matching record.

Use with macro sheets only.

Syntax

```
=DATA.FIND.NEXT()
```

DATA.FIND.PREV

The DATA.FIND.PREV function finds the previous record that matches the specified criteria in the defined database. This function is equivalent to using the Up Arrow key after selecting the Find command from the Data menu. If the DATA.FIND.PREV function cannot find any more matching records, it will return a value of FALSE. You will hear a beep and your insertion point will remain in the last matching record.

Use with macro sheets only.

Syntax

```
=DATA.FIND.PREV()
```

DATA.FORM

The DATA.FORM function displays the data form for the defined database. If you have created a custom data form for the database it will be displayed; otherwise, the default data form will be displayed. This function is equivalent to using the Form command in the Data menu. If no database has been defined, the DATA.FORM function will return an error value of #VALUE.

Use with macro sheets only.

Syntax

```
=DATA.FORM()
```

PARSE

The PARSE function is usually used when you have imported data from another application. If the imported data is lumped together in one column, PARSE allows you to separate the data into several adjacent columns. This command is equivalent to choosing the Parse command on the Data menu.

Use with macro sheets only.

Syntax

```
=PARSE(parse_text,destination_ref)
=PARSE?(parse_text,destination_ref)
```

Parse_text indicates how many columns you want to split the data into and how many characters you want in each column. If parse_text is omitted, Excel will make the decision.

Destination_ref refers to the upper-left corner of the range where you want the parsed text to be located. If destination_ref is omitted, the parsed text will be placed in the current selection and will replace the original data in that selection.

DATA.SERIES

The DATA.SERIES function enters an interpolated or incrementally increasing or decreasing series of numbers or dates based upon the current selection. This function is equivalent to using the Series command in the Data menu.

Use with macro sheets only.

Syntax

=**DATA.SERIES**(rowcol,type_num,date_num,step_value,stop_value,trend)

=**DATA.SERIES?**(rowcol,type_num,date_num,step_value,stop_value,trend)

Rowcol can have a value of either 1 or 2 and indicates where the series should be placed. If you enter 1 for rowcol, the series will be extended in rows; if you enter 2, the series will be extended in columns. If you omit rowcol, the series will be entered based upon the size and shape of the current selection.

Type_num can have a value of 1, 2, 3, or 4 and specifies the type of series. If the value is 1 or is omitted, the series type is linear. If the value is 2, the series type is growth. If the value is 3, the series type is date, and if the value is 4, the series type is autofill and Excel will perform an autofill operation.

Date_num is a number from 1 to 4 that specifies whether to increment by day, weekday, month, or year. If the value is 1, the series will increment by day. If the value is 2, the series will increment by weekday. If the value is 3, the series will increment by month, and if the value is 4, the series will increment by year. You can use the date_num argument only if you have selected 3 (date) for the type_num argument.

Step_value is a number that tells Excel the step value for the series. If step_value is omitted, the value defaults to 1.

Stop_value is a number. When the series has reached the number specified by stop_value, the series will stop. If stop_value is omitted, the function will continue to fill the series until it reaches the end of the selected range.

Trend is a logical value. If trend is TRUE, Excel will generate an exponential or linear trend. If trend is FALSE or is omitted, Excel will generate a standard data series.

SET.CRITERIA

The SET.CRITERIA function defines the name Criteria for the selected criteria range on the database. This function is equivalent to using the Set Criteria command in the Data menu.

Use with macro sheets only.

Syntax

```
=SET.CRITERIA()
```

SET.DATABASE

The SET.DATABASE function defines the name Database for the selected database range on the database. This function is equivalent to using the Set Database command in the Data menu.

Use with macro sheets only.

Syntax

```
=SET.DATABASE()
```

SET.EXTRACT

The SET.EXTRACT function defines the name Extract for the selected extract range on the database. This function is equivalent to using the Set Extract command in the Data menu.

Use with macro sheets only.

Syntax

```
=SET.EXTRACT()
```

SORT

The SORT function sorts selected data by rows or columns in ascending or descending value. You can sort using up to three sort keys. This function is equivalent to using the Sort command in the Data menu.

Use with macro sheets only.

Syntax

```
=SORT(sort_by,key1,order1,key2,order2,key3,order3)
```

Sort_by must have a value of either 1 or 2. If the value is 1, the data will be sorted by rows; if the value is 2, the data will be sorted by columns.

Key1 is an external reference to the cell or range you want to use as the first sort key. If the cell or range you want to use as the sort key is in the active worksheet, precede the address or named range with an exclamation point (!). For example, SORT(1,!A3) will sort the selected rows using column A for the first sort key.

Order1 specifies whether to sort the row or column contained in key1 in ascending or descending order. A 1 will sort in ascending value, and a 2 will sort in descending value.

Key2,order2,key3, and order3 work in exactly the same way as key1 and order1, except that key2 and order2 refer to the second sort key, and key3 and order3 refer to the third sort key.

TABLE

The TABLE function creates a table based on the input formulas and values on a worksheet. Data tables are used to perform "what-if" analysis by changing certain values on a worksheet and noting how values in other cells are affected. This function is equivalent to choosing the Table command in the Data menu.

Use with macro sheets only.

Syntax

```
=TABLE(row_ref,column_ref)
=TABLE?(row_ref,column_ref)
```

Row_ref specifies the cell to use as the row input for the table, and column_ref specifies the cell to use as the column input for the table. Row_ref and column_ref are entered either as external references to the cell address on the active worksheet — for example, TABLE(!$A$4,!$B$4) — or as an R1C1 type of reference — for example, TABLE("R1C4","R2C4"). If you use the R1C1 type of reference, the cell address is assumed to be relative to the active cell in the selection.

The Edit Menu Functions

The following functions are the equivalent of executing Edit menu commands or tools.

CLEAR

The CLEAR function clears formulas, formats, or notes from the active worksheet or formulas, formats, or charts from the active chart. Inserting this command into a macro sheet is the equivalent of choosing the Clear command from the Edit menu.

Use with macro sheets only.

Syntax

```
=CLEAR(type_num)
=CLEAR?(type_num)
```

Type_num is a number from 1 to 4.

In a worksheet or macro sheet, type_num 1 clears all (formulas, formats, and notes); type_num 2 clears formats; type_num 3 clears formulas; and type_num 4 clears notes, including sound notes. If you omit the type_num part of the formula, Excel will default to the value of 3 for both worksheets and macro sheets.

In a chart, type_num 1 clears all; type_num 2 clears the chart format or pictures; and type_num 3 clears all data series. If you omit the type_num part of the formula, Excel will automatically default to a value of 1.

In a chart with a single point or an entire data series selected, type_num 1 clears the selected series; and type_num 2 clears the format in the selected point or series. If you omit the Type-num part of the formula, Excel will automatically default to delete the selected item.

COPY

The COPY function copies data or objects from a cell or range and pastes them in a specified location. This function is equivalent to choosing the Copy and Paste commands in the Edit menu.

Use with macro sheets only.

Syntax

```
=COPY(from_reference,to_reference)
```

From_reference is an external reference to the cell or range you want to copy. If from_reference is omitted, Excel assumes that you want to copy the current selection.

To_reference is an external reference to the cell or range where you want to paste the copied data or objects. If the to_reference is to a single cell and you are copying a range of cells, the single cell in the to_reference will become the upper-left corner of the range when it is pasted.

COPY.PICTURE

The COPY.PICTURE function copies a chart or range of cells to the Clipboard as a graphic. Use this function when you want to create an image of a chart or range of cells to use in another application. This function is equivalent to choosing the Copy Picture command from the Edit menu (to access this command in the Edit menu, depress Shift when you click on Edit).

Use with macro sheets only.

Syntax

```
=COPY.PICTURE(appearance_num,size_num,type_num)
=COPY.PICTURE?(appearance_num,size_num,type_mu,)
```

The number value for the first argument (appearance_num) specifies how to copy the picture. If appearance_num is 1 or omitted, the picture is copied as closely as possible to the picture on the screen. If appearance_num is 2 the picture is copied the way it would look if you printed it.

Size_num is available only if you are copying a chart. It specifies whether to copy the chart in the size shown on the screen (using a value of 1) or in the size in which it would be printed (using a value of 2). If the argument is omitted and you are copying a chart, Excel will default to a value of 1.

Type_num specifies the format in which the picture will be copied. A value of 1 will use a picture format and a value of 2 will use a bitmap format.

COPY.TOOL

The COPY.TOOL function copies a tool face to the Clipboard. This function is equivalent to using the Copy Tool Face command in the Edit menu to copy a selected tool.

Use with macro sheets only.

Syntax

```
=COPY.TOOL(bar_id,position)
```

Bar_id specifies the name or number of the toolbar that contains the tool face you want to copy and position specifies the position of the tool in the toolbar. Position starts with 1 at the left of the toolbar (horizontal) or at the top of the toolbar (vertical).

CUT

The CUT function cuts or moves data or objects from a cell or range and pastes them in a specified location. This function is equivalent to choosing the Cut and Paste commands in the Edit menu.

Use with macro sheets only.

Syntax

```
=CUT(from_reference,to_reference)
```

From_reference is an external reference to the cell or range you want to cut or move. If from_reference is omitted, Excel assumes that you want to cut or move the current selection.

To_reference is an external reference to the cell or range where you want to paste the data or objects. If the to_reference is to a single cell and you are moving a range of cells, the single cell in the to_reference will become the upper-left corner of the range when it is pasted.

EDIT.DELETE

The EDIT.DELETE function deletes selected cells and shifts the remaining cells to close up the empty space. This function is equivalent to choosing the Delete command from the Edit menu.

Use with macro sheets only.

Syntax

```
=EDIT.DELETE(shift_num)
=EDIT.DELETE?(shift_num)
```

Shift_num specifies whether to move the remaining cells up or to the left or to delete the entire row or column. The following table shows the values that can be used in shift_num and the result of each value.

Shift_num	Result
1	Shifts cells left
2	Shifts cells up
3	Deletes entire row
4	Deletes entire column

If you omit shift_num and either a single cell or a horizontal range is selected, the remaining cells will shift up. If you omit shift_num and a vertical range is selected, the remaining cells will shift left.

FILL.DOWN

The FILL.DOWN function copies the formats and contents of the cells in the top row of a selection to the cells in the rest of the rows in the selection.

Use with macro sheets only.

Syntax

```
=FILL.DOWN()
```

FILL.LEFT

The FILL.LEFT function copies the formats and contents of the cells in the right column of a selection to the cells in the rest of the columns in the selection.

Use with macro sheets only.

Syntax

```
=FILL.LEFT()
```

FILL.RIGHT

The FILL.RIGHT function copies the formats and contents of the cells in the left column of a selection to the cells in the rest of the columns in the selection.

Use with macro sheets only.

Syntax

```
=FILL.RIGHT()
```

FILL.UP

The FILL.UP function copies the formats and contents of the cells in the bottom row of a selection to the cells in the rest of the rows in the selection.

Use with macro sheets only.

Syntax

```
=FILL.UP()
```

INSERT

The INSERT function inserts blank cells or ranges or pastes cells or ranges into a work-sheet and shifts the selected cells to accommodate the new ones. This function is equivalent to choosing the Insert command from the Edit menu.

Use with macro sheets only.

Syntax

```
=INSERT(shift_num)
=INSERT?(shift_num)
```

where shift_num specifies the result of the argument according to the number value entered. The following table lists the number values you can use and the result.

Shift_num	Result
1	Shift cells up
2	Shift cells down
3	Shift entire row
4	Shift entire column

If you have selected an entire row or column, shift_num is ignored.

INSERT.OBJECT

The INSERT.OBJECT function creates an embedded object whose source data is supplied by another application. This function is equivalent to choosing the Insert Object command in the Edit menu.

Use with macro sheets only.

Syntax

```
=INSERT.OBJECT(object_class)
=INSERT.OBJECT?(object_class)
```

where object_class is the classname text string that identifies the application and object you are embedding.

PASTE

The PASTE function pastes all of the components (formats, formulas, values, and notes) of the data or objects that were cut or copied using the Cut or Copy command. This function is equivalent to choosing the Paste command in the Edit menu.

Use with macro sheets only.

Syntax

=PASTE(to_reference)

To_reference specifies the cell or range where you want to paste. If to_reference is omitted, the data or object is pasted to the current selection.

PASTE.LINK

The PASTE.LINK function is used when you want to paste data or objects that were copied and create a link with the source of the data or objects. When you use PASTE.LINK, the pasted data or objects will automatically be updated when changes are made in the source. This function is equivalent to choosing the Paste Link command in the Edit menu.

Use with macro sheets only.

Syntax

=PASTE.LINK()

PASTE.PICTURE

The PASTE.PICTURE function pastes a picture of the contents of the Clipboard into the worksheet without linking the source to the pasted picture. This function is equivalent to choosing the Paste Picture command from the Edit menu.

Use with macro sheets only.

Syntax

```
=PASTE.PICTURE()
```

PASTE.PICTURE.LINK

The PASTE.PICTURE.LINK function pastes a picture of the contents of the Clipboard into the worksheet and links the source to the picture so that changes to the source will be updated automatically in the picture. This function is equivalent to choosing the Paste Picture Link from the Edit menu.

Use with macro sheets only.

Syntax

```
=PASTE.PICTURE.LINK()
```

PASTE.SPECIAL

The PASTE.SPECIAL function pastes the specified components from the copied data into the current worksheet selection. The PASTE.SPECIAL function has four syntax forms. Syntax 1 pastes from a worksheet into a worksheet or macro sheet, syntax 2 pastes from a worksheet into a chart, syntax 3 pastes from a chart into a chart, and syntax 4 pastes from another application.

Use with macro sheets only.

Syntax 1

Use to paste from a worksheet to a worksheet or macro sheet.

```
=PASTE.SPECIAL(paste_num,operation_num,skip_blanks,transpose)
=PASTE.SPECIAL?(paste_num,operation_num,skip_blanks,transpose)
```

Paste_num specifies what to paste as follows:

Paste_num	Pastes
1	All
2	Formulas
3	Values
4	Formats
5	Notes

Operation_num specifies what operation to perform when pasting. The following table list the available operations.

Operation_num	Actions
1	None
2	Add
3	Subtract
4	Multiply
5	Divide

Skip_blanks is a logical value that, when TRUE, instructs Excel to skip blanks in the copy area when pasting. If skip_blanks is FALSE, Excel pastes normally.

Transpose is a logical value that, when TRUE, transposes rows and cloumns when pasting. If transpose is FALSE, Excel pastes normally.

Syntax 2

Use to paste from a worksheet to a chart.

```
=PASTE.SPECIAL(rowcol,series,categories,replace)
=PASTE.SPECIAL?(rowcol,series,categories,replace)
```

Rowcol must use either the number 1 or 2 and specifies whether the values that correspond to a data series are in rows or columns. The number 1 is used for rows and the number 2 is used for columns.

Series is a logical value. If the value is TRUE, Excel uses the contents of the cell in the first column of each row (or the first cell in each column, depending upon the value of rowcol) as the name of the data series in that row or column. If the value is FALSE, Excel uses the contents of the cell in the first column of each row (or the first row of each column) as the first data point of the data series.

Categories is a logical value that, if TRUE, uses the contents of the first row (or column) as the categories for the chart. If FALSE, Excel uses the contents of the first row (or column) as the first data series in the chart.

Replace is a logical value that, if TRUE, applies categories and replaces existing categories with information from the copied range. If the value is FALSE, Excel applies new categories without replacing any old ones.

Syntax 3

Use to paste from a chart to a chart.

```
=PASTE.SPECIAL(paste_num)
=PASTE.SPECIAL?(paste_num)
```

Paste_num specifies what to paste. A value of 1 pastes all formats and data series, a value of 2 paste formats only, and a value of 3 pastes formulas (data series) only.

Syntax 4

Use to paste from another application

```
=PASTE.SPECIAL(format_text,pastelink_logical)
=PASTE.SPECIAL?(format_text,pastelink_logical)
```

Format_text is a text string that specifies the type of data you want to paste from the Clipboard. Among the types of data you can paste are Text and Picture.

Pastelink_logical is a logical value that, if TRUE, links the pasted information to the source document, as long as the source application supports linking. If the value is FALSE, the information is pasted without a link.

EDIT.REPEAT

The EDIT.REPEAT function repeats the same actions and commands that can be repeated by using the Repeat command in the Edit menu.

Use with macro sheets only.

Syntax

```
=EDIT.REPEAT()
```

UNDO

The UNDO function will undo the same actions and commands that can be undone by using the Undo command in the Edit menu.

Use with macro sheets only.

Syntax

```
=UNDO()
```

The File Menu Functions

The following functions are the equivalent of executing File menu commands or tools.

FILE.CLOSE

The FILE.CLOSE function closes the active document. If you are in a workbook, FILE.CLOSE closes all of the documents in the workbook. If you want to close just a window in a document, use the CLOSE function instead of FILE.CLOSE. This function is the equivalent of choosing the Close command from the File menu.

Use with macro sheets only.

Syntax

=FILE.CLOSE(save_logical)

Save_logical is a logical value that specifies whether to save the file before closing it.

If you are using a single active file:

▼ If the value is TRUE, Excel saves the file.

▼ If the value is FALSE, Excel does not save the file.

▼ If you omit the argument and you have made changes to the file, Excel will display a dialog box asking whether you want to save the file.

If you are in a workbook:

▼ If the value is TRUE, Excel save changes to all of the documents in the workbook.

▼ If the value is FALSE, Excel does not save changes to any of the documents in the workbook.

▼ If you omit the argument Excel will display a dialog box for the workbook and for each unbound document in the workbook that has been changed, asking whether you want to save the changes to that document.

When you use the FILE.CLOSE function, Excel will not run any auto_close macros before it closes the document.

CLOSE.ALL

The CLOSE.ALL function closes all protected, unprotected, and hidden windows. If you have made changes in any document in any of the windows, Excel will display a dialog box asking whether you want to save the document.

Use with macro sheets only.

Syntax

```
=CLOSE.ALL()
```

FILE.DELETE

The FILE.DELETE function is used to delete files from a disk. In macros this function is generally used to delete temporary files created by the macros. This function is the equivalent to choosing the Delete command from the File menu.

Use with macro sheets only.

Syntax

```
=FILE.DELETE(file_text)
=FILE.DELETE?(file_text)
```

File_text is the name (enclosed in parenthesis just like any text string) of the file you wish to delete.

CHANGE.LINK

The CHANGE.LINK function changes a link from one supporting document to another. This function is equivalent to choosing the Change button from the File menu's Links dialog box.

Use with macro sheets only.

Syntax

```
=CHANGE.LINK(old_text,new_text,type_of_link)
=CHANGE.LINK?(old_text,new_text,type_of_link)
```

Old_text is a text string of the path from the active dependent document you want to change.

New_text is a text string listing the path of the link you want to change to.

Type_of_link is a number value that specifies what type of link you want to change. A 1 specifies an Excel link and a 2 specifies a DDE link.

LINKS

The LINKS function generates an array of the names of all linked documents in the specified document. This function is equivalent to choosing the Links command in the File menu.

Use with macro sheets only.

Syntax

`=LINKS(document_text,type_num)`

Document_text is the name of the document whose external references you want to list. If document_text is omitted, Excel will return the external references in the active document. If the document specified by the argument is not open, or if the document contains no external references, Excel will return an error value of #N/A.

Type_num is a number that specifies the type of linked documents to return. The following table lists which numbers will return the specified type of linked documents.

Type_num	Returns
1	Microsoft Excel Link
2	DDE Link
3	Reserved
4	Not applicable
5	Publisher
6	Subscriber

OPEN.LINKS

The OPEN.LINKS function is used with LINKS to open document links to a specific document. This function is equivalent to choosing the Links command from the File menu.

Use with macro sheets only.

Syntax

`=OPEN.LINKS(document_text1,document_text2,...,read_only,type_of_link)`
`=OPEN.LINKS?(document_text1,document_text2,...,read_only,type_of_link)`

Document_text1,document_text2, and so forth, are the names of the supporting documents. The arguments can be in the form of text, arrays, or references that contain text. You can use as many as twelve document_text arguments in the OPEN.LINKS function.

Read_only is a logical value. If the value is TRUE, changes to the document cannot be saved. If the value is FALSE, changes to the document can be saved.

Type_of_link is a number that specifies what type of linked documents to return.

Type_num	Returns
1	Microsoft Excel Link
2	DDE Link
3	Reserved
4	Not applicable
5	Publisher
6	Subscriber

If you want to open all of the links in an open document, you can use the LINK.OPEN with the LINKS function. For example, the following formula will open all of the links in the document when the document is opened: OPEN.LINKS(LINKS()).

UPDATE.LINK

The UPDATE.LINK function updates a link to another document. This function is equivalent to choosing the Update button for the selected link from the File menu's Links dialog box.

Use with macro sheets only.

Syntax

`=UPDATE.LINK`(link_text,type_of_link)

Link_text is a text string that includes the entire path of the linkl. If link_text is omitted, you can only update links from the active document to other Excel documents.

Type_of_link specifies the type of link to update. If type_of_link has a value of 1, the argument updates Excel links. If type_of_link has a value of 2, the argument updates DDE links.

NEW

The NEW function creates a new document or opens a template. This function is equivalent to choosing the New command from the File menu.

Use with macro sheets only.

Syntax

=NEW(type_num,xy_series,add_logical)

=NEW?(type_num,xy_series,add_logical)

Type_num informs Excel of the type of document you wish to open. If type_num is omitted, the new document will be the same type as the document in the active window. The following table lists the documents you can create.

Type_num	Document
1	Worksheet
2	Chart
3	Macro sheet
4	International macro sheet
5	Workbook
Text string	Template

Xy_series is a value that specifies how data is arranged in a chart when you create a new chart. The following table shows the values you can use and the result of those values.

Xy_series	Result
0	Displays a dialog box if the selection is not clear
1 or omitted	The first row/column is the first data series
2	The first row/column contains the category (x) axis labels
3	The first row/column contains the x-values. The new chart is an xy (scatter) chart.

Add_logical is a logical value that specifies whether to add the created document to the open workbook. If the value is TRUE, the document is added; if the value is FALSE, the document is not added. If you created a workbook, the add_logical value is ignored.

PAGE.SETUP

The PAGE.SETUP function allows you to determine the printed appearance of your documents. This function is equivalent to choosing the Page Setup command from the File menu. There are two types of syntax for PAGE.SETUP. Syntax 1 is used if the active document is a worksheet or a macro, syntax 2 is used if the active document is a chart. The arguments in the PAGE.SETUP function correspond to the text and check boxes in the Page Setup dialog box.

Syntax 1

Use with worksheets and macro sheets.

```
=PAGE.SETUP(head,foot,left,right,top,bot,hdng,grid,h_cntr,v_cntr)
=PAGE.SETUP?(head,foot,left,right,top,bot,hdng,grid,h_cntr,v_cntr)
```

Syntax 2

Use with charts.

```
=PAGE.SETUP(head,foot,left,right,top,bot,bot,size,h_cntr,v+cntr,
orient,paper_size,scale,pg_num)
=PAGE.SETUP?(head,foot,left,right,top,bot,bot,size,h_cntr,v+cntr,
orient,paper_size,scale,pg_num)
```

Head specifies the text and formatting codes, as listed in the following table, for the document header.

Foot specifies the text and formatting codes, as listed in the following table, for the document footer.

Formatting Code	Result
&L	Left-aligns the characters that follow the code.
&C	Centers the characters that follow the code.
&R	Right-aligns the characters that follow the code.
&B	A toggle that turns bold printing on or off. If bold is on, this code will turn it off; if bold is off, this code will turn it on.
&I	A toggle that turns italic printing on or off.
&U	A toggle that turns underline printing on or off.

Formatting Code	Result
&S	A toggle that turns strikeout printing on or off.
&D	Prints the current date.
&T	Prints the current time.
&F	Prints the name of the document.
&P	Prints the page number.
&P+number	Prints the page number plus number.
&P-number	Prints the page number minus number.
&&	Prints a single ampersand (&).
&"fontname"	Prints the characters that follow the code in the font specified by "fontname." You must include the quotation marks.
&nn	Prints the characters that follow the code in the font size specified by nn. The size is a number which corresponds to the point size you want to use.
&N	Prints the total number of pages in the document.

Left is a number that specifies the left margin; right is a number that specifies the right margin; top is a number that specifies the top margin; bot is a number that specifies the bottom margin.

Hdng is a logical value. If the value is TRUE, the row and column headings will be printed; if the value is FALSE, the row and column headings will not be printed. Hdng can only be used in the worksheet and macro sheet form of the function.

Grid is a logical value. If the value is TRUE, the gridlines in the worksheet or macro sheet will be printed; if the value is FALSE, the gridlines will not be printed. This argument can only be used in the worksheet and macro sheet form of the function.

H-cntr is a logical value that, if TRUE, centers the text horizontally on the page when it prints.

V_cntr is a logical value that, if TRUE, centers the text vertically on the page when it prints.

Orient is a number value that determines the direction in which your document will print. If you use a number value of 1, the document will print in portrait; if you use a number value of 2, the document will print in landscape.

Paper_size is a number value that specifies the size of the paper, as shown in the following table.

Paper_size	Paper type
1	Letter
2	Letter (small)
3	Tabloid
4	Ledger
5	Legal
6	Statement
7	Executive
8	A3
9	A4
10	A4 (small)
11	A5
12	B4
13	B5
14	Folio
15	Quarto
16	10x14
17	11x17
18	Note
19	ENV9
20	ENV10
21	ENV11
22	ENV12
23	ENV14
24	C Sheet
25	D Sheet
26	E Sheet

Scale is a number value that represents the percentage to increase or decrease the document size when it prints. Scale is ignored if the printer you are using does not support scaling.

To reduce or enlarge a document when it prints, set scale to the percentage by which you want to reduce or enlarge.

For worksheets and macro sheets, you can specify the number of pages that the printout of the document should be scaled to fit. Set scale to a two-item horizontal array; the first item should be equal to the width and the second to the height. If you want to change the scaling on only one item, set the corresponding value of the other item to #N/A.

If you want to fit the print area on one page, set the value of scale to TRUE.

Pg_num specifies the number of the first page. Pg_num must be equal to or greater than 1.

A pg_order of 1 specifies pagination as top to bottom and then right. A pg_order of 2 specifies pagination as left to right and then down.

Bw_cells is a logical value that specifies whether to print cells and text boxes in color. This argument is ignored if your printer does not support color printing. If the value is TRUE, Excel prints cell text and borders in black, and cell backgrounds in white. If the value is FALSE, Excel prints cell text, borders, and background patterns in color.

Size is a number value that specifies how you want a chart printed on the page. This argument can be used only for charts. The following table lists the options available in the size argument.

Size	Size to print the chart
1	Screen size
2	Fit to page
3	Full page

PRINT

The PRINT function prints the active document. This function is equivalent to choosing the Print command from the File menu. The argument in the PRINT function correspond to the check boxes, options, and edit boxes in the Print dialog box.

Use with macro sheets only.

Syntax

```
=PRINT(range_num,from,to,copies,draft,preview,print_what,quality,
v_quality)
=PRINT?(range_num,from,to,copies,draft,preview,print_what,quality,
v_quality)
```

Pg_num is a number value that specifies which pages to print. If the number value is 1, all of the pages will be printed. If the number value is 2, a specified range of pages will be printed. If you select the number value 2, you must include the from and to arguments.

From specifies the first page to be printed. If you did not select a number value of 2 for the pg_num argument, this argument will be ignored.

To specifies the last page to be printed. This argument will be ignored unless you specified a value of 2 for pg_num.

Copies specifies the number of copies to print. If this argument is omitted, the default number of 1 will be used.

Draft is a logical value. If the value is TRUE, the Fast, but no graphics checkbox is enabled. If the value is FALSE or omitted, the Fast, but no graphics checkbox is disabled.

Preview is a logical value. If the value is TRUE, the active document will be previewed on the screen before it is printed; if the value is FALSE or omitted, the document will not be previewed.

Print_what is a number value that specifies what parts of a worksheet or macro sheet will print. If the active document is a chart, the print_what argument is ignored. If the argument is omitted, the current setting remains in effect. The following table shows the numbers values and their results.

Print_what	Result
1	Prints sheet only
2	Prints notes only
3	Prints sheet and then notes

Quality specifies the DPI output quality you want. This argument corresponds to the Print Quality box in the Print dialog box and allows you a choice of high, medium, low, and draft. If the argument is omitted, the current setting remains in effect.

V_quality values correspond to the choices allowed in the Print Quality box in the Print dialog box if you have specified a printer where the vertical and horizontal resolution is not equal (such as a dot-matrix). If the argument is omitted, the current setting remains in effect.

PRINT.PREVIEW

The PRINT.PREVIEW function previews the active document on the screen. This function is equivalent to choosing the Print Preview command in the File menu.

Use with macro sheets only.

Syntax

```
=PRINT.PREVIEW()
```

QUIT

The QUIT function closes all open documents and exits Excel. If you have not saved changes to any open documents, Excel displays a message asking whether you want to save them. This function is equivalent to choosing the Exit command in the File menu. The QUIT function can be used in an auto_close macro to exit Excel whenever a particular worksheet or macro sheet is closed.

Use with macro sheets only.

Syntax

```
=QUIT()
```

If you have cleared error-checking by using an ERROR(FALSE) function, QUIT will exit Excel without asking whether you want to save any changes to the open documents.

SAVE

The SAVE function saves the active document. Inserting this function in a macro sheet is the equivalent of choosing the Save command from the File menu. Save will save the file to the same name and path. If you want to specify a password, create a backup file, or save the file to a different name, type, or path, use the SAVE AS function.

Use with macro sheets only.

Syntax

```
=SAVE()
```

SAVE.AS

The SAVE.AS function saves the active file, while allowing you to change the filename, type, and path. It also allows you to designate a password, backup file option, or save the file as a template or add-in document. Inserting this function into a macro sheet is the equivalent of choosing the Save As command from the File menu.

Use with macro sheets only.

Syntax

`=SAVE.AS(document_text,type_num,prot_pwd,backup,write_res_pwd, read_only_rec)`

`=SAVE.AS?(document_text,type_num,prot_pwd,backup,write_res_pwd, read_only_rec)`

In the SAVE.AS function, Document_text specifies the name of a document to save. If saving to a different directory, specify the full path.

Type_num represents a number that specifies the file format in which you want to save the document. The following table lists the file formats and their corresponding number.

Type_num	File format
1 or none	Normal
2	SYLK
3	Text
4	WKS
5	WK1
6	CSV
7	DBF2
8	DBF3
9	DIF
10	Reserved
11	DBF4
12	Reserved
13	Reserved
14	Reserved

Type_num	File format
15	WK3
16	Microsofe Excel 2.x
17	Template
18	Add-in macro
19	Text (Macintosh)
20	Text (Windows)
21	Text (MS-DOS)
22	CSV (Macintosh)
23	CSV (Windows)
24	CSV (MS-DOS)
25	International macro
26	International add-in macro
27	Reserved
28	Reserved
29	Microsoft Excel 3.0

The following list shows which type_num values can be used with each document type.

Document type	Type-num
Worksheet	All except 10, 12-14, 18, 25-28
Chart	1, 16, 17, 29
Macro Sheet	1-3, 6, 9, 16-29
Workbook	1, 15

Prot_pwd is a password given as text or as a reference to a cell containing text. You may not exceed fifteen characters.

Backup allows you to create a backup of the file. If backup is TRUE, a backup file will be created. If backup is FALSE, no backup will be created. If backup is omitted, the status remains unchanged.

Write_res_pwd corresponds to the Write Reservation Password box in the Save Options dialog box. This will allow anyone to open a file that has been saved with a password, but only users with the password can write to the file.

Read_only_rec is a logical value corresponding to the Read-Only Recommended check box in the Save Options dialog box. If read_only_rec is TRUE, the file is saved as a read-only recommended document. If read_only_rec is FALSE, the file is saved as a normal document. If read_only_rec is omitted, the status remains unchanged.

 To close a document without saving changes, set type_num to 0 and omit all other changes (=SAVE.AS(0)). This allows you to close a file without overwriting it and without a prompt asking if you want to save **N O T E** changes.

SAVE.WORKBOOK

The SAVE.WORKBOOK function saves the workbook to which the active document belongs. Inserting this function into a macro sheet is the equivalent of choosing the Save Workbook command from the File menu.

Use with macro sheets only.

Syntax

```
=SAVE.WORKBOOK(document_text,type_num,prot_pwd,backup,write_res_pwd,
read_only_rec)
=SAVE.WORKBOOK?(document_text,type_num,prot_pwd,backup,write_res_pwd
,
read_only_rec)
```

See SAVE.AS for an explanation of the arguments.

The Format Menu Functions

The following functions are the equivalent of executing Format menu commands or tools.

VIEW.3D

The VIEW.3D function adjusts the view of the active 3-D chart by allowing you to view the chart from different angles. Inserting this function into a macro sheet is the equivalent of choosing the 3-D View command from the Format menu.

Use with macro sheets only.

Syntax

=VIEW.3D(elevation.perspective,rotation,axes,height%,autoscale)
=VIEW.3D?(elevation.perspective,rotation,axes,height%,autoscale)

Elevation is a number from –90 to 90, measured in degrees, that specifies the viewing elevation of the chart. Elevation is limited to 0 to 44 for 3-D bar charts and 0 to 80 for 3-D pie charts. The elevation argument corresponds to the Elevation box in the 3-D View dialog box.

▼ If elevation is 0, the chart is viewed straight on.
▼ If elevation is 90, the chart is viewed from above.
▼ If elevation is –90, the chart is viewed from below.
▼ If elevation is omitted, it is assumed to be 25.

Perspective is a number from zero to 100 percent that specifies the perspective (apparent distance) of a chart. Perspective is ignored on 3-D and pie charts. The perspective argument corresponds to the Perspective box in the 3-D View dialog box.

▼ A higher perspective simulates a closer view.
▼ If perspective is omitted, it is assumed to be 30.

Rotation is a number from 0 to 360, measured in degrees, that specifies the rotation of the chart around the (Z) axis. Rotation is limited to 0 to 44 for 3-D bar charts. If rotation is omitted, it is assumed to be 30. The rotation argument corresponds to the Rotation box in the 3-D View dialog box.

Axes is a logical value that specifies whether axes are fixed in the plane of the screen or can rotate with the chart. Axes is TRUE for 3-D bar charts and ignored for 3-D pie charts. The axes argument corresponds to the Rotation box in the 3-D View dialog box.

▼ If axes is TRUE, the axes are locked to the plane of the screen.
▼ If axes is FALSE, the axes can rotate.
▼ If the axes argument is omitted and the chart view is 3-D, axes is FALSE.
▼ If the axes argument is omitted and the chart view is not 3-D, axes is TRUE.

Height% is a number from 5 to 500 that specifies the height of the chart as a percentage of the length of the base. If the height% argument is omitted, it is assumed to be 100. The height% argument corresponds to the Height box in the 3-D View dialog box.

Autoscale is a logical value that scales the chart. The autoscale argument corresponds to the Auto Scaling box in the 3-D View dialog box. If autoscale is set to TRUE, automatic scaling is used. If autoscale is set to FALSE, automatic scaling is not used. If the autoscale argument is omitted, the settings are not changed.

ALIGNMENT

The ALIGNMENT function aligns the contents of selected cells. Inserting this function into a macro sheet is the equivalent to choosing the Alignment command from the Format menu.

Use with macro sheets only.

Syntax

```
=ALIGNMENT(horiz_align,wrap,vert_align,orientation)
=ALIGNMENT?(horiz_align,wrap,vert_align,orientation)
```

Horiz-align is a number from 1 to 7 that specifies the type of horizontal alignment in the selected cell or cells. If the horiz-align argument is omitted, the horizontal alignment is not changed. The following table lists the types of horizontal alignment and their corresponding numbers.

Horiz-align	Horizontal alignment
1	General
2	Left
3	Center
4	Right
5	Fill
6	Justify
7	Center across selection

Wrap is a logical value that determines whether or not to wrap text in a cell. If wrap is set to TRUE, the text is wrapped in the cell. If wrap is set to FALSE, the text is not wrapped in the cell. If the wrap argument is omitted, wrapping does not change. The wrap argument corresponds to the Wrap Text check box in the Alignment dialog box.

Vert-align is a number from 1 to 3 that specifies the vertical alignment of text in the selected cell or cells. If the vert_align argument is omitted, vertical alignment does not change. The following table lists the types of vertical alignment and their corresponding numbers.

Vert-align	Vertical alignment
1	Top
2	Center
3	Bottom

Orientation is a number from 0 to 3 that specifies the orientation of text in the selected cell or cells. If the orientation argument is omitted, orientation does not change. The following table lists the types of orientation and their corresponding numbers.

Type	Orientaton
0	Horizontal
1	Vertical
2	Upward
3	Downward

FORMAT.AUTO

The FORMAT.AUTO function formats the selected cell or cells using the built-in (table) formats. Inserting this function in a macro sheet is the equivalent of choosing the AutoFormat command from the Format menu.

Use with macro sheets only.

Syntax

=FORMAT.AUTO(format_num,number,font,alignment,border,pattern,width)
=FORMAT.AUTO?(format_num,number,font,alignment,border,pattern,width)

Format_num is a number corresponding to the formats in the Table Format list box in the AutoFormat dialog box. If this argument is omitted, the number is assumed to be 1.

The following arguments are logical values corresponding to the Formats To Apply boxes in the AutoFormat dialog box. If the value is TRUE, the box is selected. If the value is FALSE, the box is cleared. If the argument is omitted, the value is TRUE.

Argument	Corresponding check box
Number	Number check box
Font	Font check box

Argument	Corresponding check box
Alignment	Alignment check box
Border	Border check box
Pattern	Pattern check box
Width	Column Width/Row Height check box

BORDER

The BORDER function adds a border to the selected cell, range, or object, using the border styles available in the Border dialog box. Inserting this function into a macro sheet is the equivalent of choosing the Border command from the Format menu.

Use with macro sheets only.

Syntax

`=(BORDER(outline,left,right,top,bottom,shade,outline_color,left_color, right_color,top_color,bottom_color)`

`=(BORDER?(outline,left,right,top,bottom,shade,outline_color,left_color, right_color,top_color,bottom_color)`

Outline,left,right,top, and bottom are numbers from 0 to 7 corresponding to border styles in the Border dialog box. The following table lists the argument and its corresponding border style.

Argument	Border style
0	No border
1	Thin line
2	Medium line
3	Dashed line
4	Dotted line
5	Thick line
6	Double line
7	Hairline

Shade applies shading to the selected cell, range, or object.

Outline_color,left_color,right_color,top_color, and bottom_color are numbers from 1 to 16 that correspond to the Color box in the Border dialog box. Zero corresponds to automatic color.

BRING.TO.FRONT

The BRING.TO.FRONT function brings the selected object or objects to the forefront, placing them on top of all other objects. Inserting this function into a macro sheet is the equivalent of choosing the Bring To Front command from the Format menu.

Use with macro sheets only.

Syntax

```
=BRING.TO.FRONT()
```

CELL.PROTECTION

The CELL.PROTECTION function allows you to lock or hide the contents of a cell. In order to use this function, the document must be protected. Inserting this function into a macro sheet is the equivalent of choosing the Cell Protection command from the Format menu.

Use with macro sheets only.

Syntax

```
=CELL.PROTECTION(locked,hidden)
=CELL.PROTECTION?(locked,hidden)
```

In this function, the arguments are logical values corresponding to check boxes in the Cell Protection dialog box. If an argument is TRUE, the box is selected. If an argument is FALSE, the box is cleared. If an argument is omitted, the setting remains unchanged.

Locked corresponds to the Locked check box. The default is TRUE.

Hidden corresponds to the Hidden check box. The default is FALSE.

COLUMN.WIDTH

The COLUMN.WIDTH function changes the width of the columns in the specified reference. Inserting this function into a macro sheet is the equivalent of choosing the Column Width command from the Format menu.

Use with macro sheets only.

Syntax

```
=COLUMN.WIDTH(width_num,reference,standard,type_num,standard_num)
=COLUMN.WIDTH?(width_num,reference,standard,type_num,standard_num)
```

Width_num specifies, in units of one character, how wide you want the columns to be. If standard is set to TRUE or if type_num is included, width_num is ignored.

Reference specifies the columns for which you want to change the width, and must be either an external reference to the active worksheet (for example, !$B:$C, or !Database), or an R1C1 style reference in the form of text (for example, B1:D5, or Database).

If Reference is a relative R1C1 reference in the form of text, it is assumed to be relative to the active cell. If Reference is omitted, it is assumed to be the current selection.

Standard is a logical value corresponding to the Use Standard Width check box in the Column Width dialog box.

If Standard is TRUE, the column width is set to the default width and width_num is ignored. If Standard is FALSE or omitted, the width is set to the width_num or type_num.

Type_num is a number from 1 to 3 corresponding to the Hide, Unhide, or Best Fit option, respectively, in the Column Width dialog box. The following chart lists the type_num and the action taken.

Type_num	Action taken
1	Hides the column selection and sets the column width to 0.
2	Unhides the column selection by setting the column width to the value set before the selection was hidden.
3	Sets the column selection to a best-fit width.

If any arguments in the function conflict with the type_num setting, the other arguments will be ignored and the type_num setting will be used.

Standard_num specifies, in points, the standard width. If standard_num is omitted, the setting is unchanged. Changing the value of standard_num changes the width of all columns except those that have been set to a custom value.

FORMAT.FONT

The FORMAT.FONT function allows you to set the font for cells, text boxes, buttons, and chart items. Inserting this function in a macro sheet is equivalent to choosing the Font command from the Format menu.

Use with macro sheets only.

Syntax 1

Syntax 1 sets the font for cells.

```
=FORMAT.FONT(name_text,size_num,bold,italic,underline,strike,color,
outline,shadow)
=FORMAT.FONT?(name_text,size_num,bold,italic,underline,strike,color,
outline,shadow)
```

Syntax 2

Syntax 2 sets the font for text boxes and buttons on worksheets and macro sheets.

```
=FORMAT.FONT(name_text,size_num,bold,italic,underline,strike,color,
outline,shadow,object_id_text,start_num,char_num)
=FORMAT.FONT?(name_text,size_num,bold,italic,underline,strike,color,
outline,shadow,object_id_text,start_num,char_num)
```

Arguments correspond to the check boxes or options in the Font dialog box. Arguments that correspond to check boxes are logical arguments. If the argument is TRUE, the box is selected. If the argument is FALSE, the box is cleared. If an argument is omitted, the setting remains the same.

Name_text is the name of the font (for example, Courier); size_num is the font size, in points; bold puts the selection in boldface type; italic puts the selection in italic type; underline underlines the selection; and strike corresponds to the Strikeout check box.

Color is a number from 0 to 16 corresponding to the colors in the Font dialog box. Zero is automatic.

Outline and shadow are supported by Microsoft Excel for the Macintosh. These arguments are ignored by Microsoft Excel for Windows.

Object_id_text identifies the text box you want to format (for example, Text 1). If this argument is omitted, the text is the selected text box is formatted.

Start_num specifies the first character to be formatted. If this argument is omitted, the first character is assumed to be 1 (the first character in the text box).

Char_num specifies the number of characters to format. If this argument is omitted, all of the characters in the text box, beginning with start_num, are formatted.

Backgd is a number from 1 to 3 specifying which type of background to apply to the text in a chart. The following table lists the types of background and their corresponding numbers.

Backgd	Type of background applied
1	Automatic
2	Transparent
3	Opaque

Apply is used with data labels only. This argument corresponds to the Apply To All check box.

GROUP

The GROUP function is used to combine objects so they can be moved or sized together. When you use this function, Excel combines the objects into a single object and labels or identifies them (for example, Group 1). If a group is already selected, the function returns the #Value! error value and interrupts the macro. Inserting this function in a macro sheet is the equivalent of choosing the Group command from the Format menu.

Use with macro sheets only.

Syntax

```
=GROUP()
```

FORMAT.LEGEND

The FORMAT.LEGEND function sets the position and orientation of the legend on a chart and returns TRUE. If the legend is not selected, Excel returns an error message. Inserting this function in a macro sheet is the equivalent of choosing the Legend command from the Format menu.

Use with macro sheets only.

Syntax

```
=FORMAT.LEGEND(position_num)
=FORMAT.LEGEND?(position_num)
```

Position_num is a number from 1 to 5 specifying the position of the legend. The following chart lists the position_num and corresponding positions.

Position_num	Position of legend
1	Bottom
2	Corner
3	Top
4	Right
5	Left

FORMAT.MAIN

The FORMAT.MAIN function formats a chart. Selecting this function is the equivalent of choosing the Main Chart command from the Format menu.

Use with macro sheets only

Syntax

=FORMAT.MAIN(type_num,view,overlap,gap_width,vary,drop,hilo,angle,
gap_depth,chart_depth,up_down,series_line,labels)

=FORMAT.MAIN?(type_num,view,overlap,gap_width,vary,drop,hilo,angle,
gap_depth,chart_depth,up_down,series_line,labels)

Type_num is a number from 1 to 13 specifying the type of chart. The following table lists type_num and corresponding charts.

Type_num	Chart type
1	Area
2	Bar
3	Column
4	Line
5	Pie
6	XY (scatter)
7	3-D area
8	3-D column
9	3-D line
10	3-D pie
11	Radar
12	3-D bar
13	3-D surface

View is a number specifying one of the views in the Data View box in the Main Chart dialog box. The view varies according to the type of chart.

Overlap is a number from −100 to 100 specifying the position of bars or columns. Overlap corresponds to the Overlap box in the Main Chart dialog box. Overlap is ignored if type_num is not 2 or 3.

▼ If overlap is a positive number, it specifies the percentage of overlap for bars or columns. For example, if overlap is 50, one half of a bar or column would be covered by an adjacent bar or column. A value of 0 prevents bars or columns from overlapping.

▼ If overlap is a negative number, bars or columns are separated by the specified percentage of the maximum available distance between any two bars or columns.

▼ If overlap is omitted, it is assumed to be 0.

Gap_width is a number from 0 to 500 specifying the space between bar or column clusters as a percentage of the width of a bar of column. Gap_width corresponds to the Gap Width box in the Main Chart dialog box. Gap_width is ignored unless type_num is 2, 3, 8, or 12. If gap_width is omitted, it is assumed to be 50, or if a value was previously set, it is unchanged.

The following arguments are logical values corresponding to boxes in the Main Chart dialog box. If an argument is TRUE, the box is selected. If an argument is FALSE, the box is cleared. If an argument is omitted, the setting is unchanged.

Vary corresponds to the Vary By Categories box. This argument applies only to charts with one data series, and cannot be used with area charts.

Drop corresponds to the Drop Lines box. This argument applies only to area and line charts.

Hilo corresponds to the Hi-Lo Lines box. This argument applies only to line charts.

Angle is a number from 0 to 360 specifying, in degrees, the angle of the first pie slice in a pie chart. If the argument is omitted, it is assumed to be 0 or, if previously set, unchanged.

Gap_depth is for 3-D charts only. Gap_depth is a number from 0 to 500 specifying the depth of the gap in front of and behind a bar, column, area, or line as a percentage of the depth of the bar, column, area, or line. This argument corresponds to the Gap Depth box in the Main Chart dialog box. If gap_depth is omitted and the chart is a 3-D chart, it is assumed to be 50 or, if previously set, unchanged. If gap_depth is omitted and the view is side-by-side, stacked, or stacked 100%, gap_depth is assumed to be 0 or, if previously set, unchanged.

Chart_depth is for 3-D charts only. Chart_depth is a number from 20 to 2,000 specifying the visual depth of the chart as a percentage of the width of the chart. This argument corresponds to the Chart Depth box in the Main Chart dialog box. If chart_depth is omitted, it is assumed to be 100 or, if previously set, unchanged.

The following arguments are logical values corresponding to check boxes in the Main Chart dialog box. If the argument is TRUE, the box is selected. If the argument is FALSE, the box is cleared. If the argument is omitted, the setting is unchanged.

Up_down corresponds to the Up/Down Bars check box. This argument can be used only with line charts.

Series_line corresponds to the Series Lines check box. This argument can be used only with stacked bar and column charts.

Labels corresponds to the Radar Axis Labels check box. This argument can be used only with radar charts.

DELETE.FORMAT

The DELETE.FORMAT function deletes the specified custom number format. When you delete a custom number format, all numbers formatted with that number are formatted with the General format. Inserting this function into a macro sheet is equivalent to using the Number command from the Format menu to delete a format.

Use with macro sheets only

Syntax

```
=DELETE.FORMAT(format_text)
```

Format_text is the custom format given as a text string. If you specify a built-in format, Excel returns the #Value! error value.

FORMAT.NUMBER

The FORMAT.NUMBER function formats numbers, dates, and times in selected cells. Inserting this function into a macro sheet is equivalent to choosing the Number command from the Format menu.

Use with macro sheets only.

Syntax

```
=FORMAT.NUMBER(format_text)
=FORMAT.NUMBER(format_text)
```

Format_text is a format string specifying which format to apply to the selection.

OBJECT.PROPERTIES

The OBJECT.PROPERTIES function determines how the selected object or objects are attached to the cells beneath them and whether or not they are printed. Inserting this function into a macro sheet is equivalent to choosing the Object Properties command from the Format menu.

Use with macro sheets only.

Syntax

```
=OBJECT PROPERTIES(placement_type,print_object)
=OBJECT PROPERTIES?(placement_type,print_object)
```

Placement_type is a number from 1 to 3 specifying how to attach the selected object or objects. If the argument is omitted, the settings are unchanged. If an object is not selected, the function interrupts the macro and returns a #Value! error value. Following is a chart that lists placement_type and corresponding methods of attachment (the way an object is attached determines how the object is moved or sized with the cells).

If placement_type is	The selected object is
1	Moved and sized with cells
2	Moved but not sized with cells
3	Not affected by moving and sizing cells

Print_object is a logical value specifying whether to print the selected object(s). If the argument is TRUE or omitted, the objects are printed. If the argument is FALSE, the objects are not printed.

OBJECT.PROTECTION

The OBJECT.PROTECTION function allows you to lock or unlock a selected object or lock the text if the object is a text box or button. You cannot use this function to unlock an object if document protection is selected for objects in the Protect Document dialog box. Inserting this function into a macro sheet is the equivalent of choosing the Object Protection command from the format menu.

Use with macro sheets only.

Syntax

```
=OBJECT.PROTECTION(locked,lock_text)
=OBJECT.PROTECTION?(locked,lock_text)
```

Locked is a logical value that determines whether the selected object is locked or unlocked. If locked is TRUE, the object is locked. If locked is FALSE, the object is unlocked.

Lock_text is a logical value that determines whether text in a text box or button can be changed. This argument applies only if the object is a text box or button. If the argument is TRUE or omitted, text cannot be changed. If the argument is FALSE, text can be changed.

FORMAT.OVERLAY

The FORMAT.OVERLAY function formats an overlay chart. Inserting this function into a macro sheet is equivalent to choosing the Overlay command from the Format menu.

Use with macro sheets only.

Syntax

```
=FORMAT.OVERLAY(type_num,view,overlap,gap_width,vary,drop,hilo,angle,
series_dist,series_num,up_down,series_line,labels)
=FORMAT.OVERLAY?(type_num,view,overlap,gap_width,vary,drop,hilo,angle,
series_dist,series_num,up_down,series_line,labels)
```

Type_num is a number from 1 to 63 specifying the type of chart. The following chart lists type_num and corresponding charts.

Type_num	Chart type
1	Area
2	Bar
3	Column
4	Line
5	Pie
6	XY (scatter)
11	Radar

View is a number specifying one of the views in the Data View box in the Overlay dialog box. The view varies according to the type of chart.

Overlap is a number from −100 to 100 specifying the position of bars or columns. Overlap corresponds to the Overlap box in the Overlay dialog box. Overlap is ignored unless type_num is 2 or 3.

▼ If overlap is a positive number, it specifies the percentage of overlap for bars or columns. For example, if overlap is 50, one half of a bar or column is covered by an adjacent bar or column. A value of 0 prevents bars or columns from over-lapping.

▼ If overlap is a negative number, bars or columns are separated by the specified percentage of the maximum available distance between any two bars or columns.

▼ If overlap is omitted, it is assumed to be 0.

Gap_width is a number from 0 to 500 specifying the space between bar or column clusters as a percentage of the width of a bar of column. Gap_width corresponds to the Gap Width box in the Overlay dialog box. Gap_width is ignored unless type_num is 2 or 3. If gap_width is omitted, it is assumed to be 50, or if a value was previously set, it is unchanged.

Several of the following arguments are logical values corresponding to boxes in the Overlay dialog box. If an argument is TRUE, the box is selected. If an argument is FALSE, the box is cleared. If an argument is omitted, the setting is unchanged.

Vary corresponds to the Vary By Categories box. This argument cannot be used with area charts.

Drop corresponds to the Drop Lines box. This argument applies only to area and line charts.

Hilo corresponds to the Hi-Lo Lines box. This argument applies only to line charts.

Angle is a number from 0 to 360 specifying, in degrees, the angle of the first slice in a pie chart. If the argument is omitted, it is assumed to be 0 or, if previously set, unchanged.

Series_dist is number 1 or 2 and specifies automatic or manual series distribution. If series_dist is 1 or omitted, automatic series distribution is used. If series_dist is 2, manual series distribution is used and you must use the series_num argument to specify which series is first.

Series_num is the number of the first series in the overlay chart. This argument corresponds to the First Overlay Series box in the Overlay dialog box. If series_dist is 1, this argument is ignored.

Up_down corresponds to the Up/Down Bars check box. This argument can be used only with line charts.

Series_line corresponds to the Series Lines check box. This argument can be used only with stacked bar and column charts.

Labels corresponds to the Radar Axis Labels check box. This argument can be used only with radar charts.

PATTERNS

The PATTERNS function changes the appearance of the selected cells or objects or one selected chart item at a time. Inserting this function into a macro sheet is equivalent to choosing the Patterns command from the Format menu. The PATTERNS function has eight syntax forms.

Use with macro sheets only.

Syntax 1

Syntax 1 is used with cells.

```
=PATTERNS(apattern,afore,aback)
=PATTERNS?(apattern,afore,aback)
```

Syntax 2

Syntax 2 is used with lines (arrows) on worksheets or charts.

```
=PATTERNS(lauto,lstyle,lcolor,lwt,hwidth,hlength,htype)
=PATTERNS?(lauto,lstyle,lcolor,lwt,hwidth,hlength,htype)
```

Syntax 3

Syntax 3 is used with text boxes, rectangles, ovals, arcs, and pictures on worksheets or macro sheets.

```
=PATTERNS(bauto,bstyle,bcolor,bwt,shadow,aauto,apattern,afore,aback,
rounded)
=PATTERNS?(bauto,bstyle,bcolor,bwt,shadow,aauto,apattern,afore,aback,
rounded)
```

Syntax 4

Syntax 4 is used with chart plot areas, bars, columns, pie slices, and text labels.

```
=PATTERNS(bauto,bstyle,bcolor,bwt,shadow,aauto,apattern,afore,aback,
invert,apply)
=PATTERNS?(bauto,bstyle,bcolor,bwt,shadow,aauto,apattern,afore,aback,
invert,apply)
```

Syntax 5

Syntax 5 is used with chart axes.

```
=PATTERNS(lauto,lstyle,lcolor,lwt,tmajor,tminor,tlabel)
=PATTERNS?(lauto,lstyle,lcolor,lwt,tmajor,tminor,tlabel)
```

Syntax 6

Syntax 6 is used with chart gridlines, hi-lo lines, drop lines, lines on a picture line chart, and picture charts of bar, column, and 3-D column charts.

```
=PATTERNS(lauto,lstyle,lcolor,lwt,apply)
=PATTERNS?(lauto,lstyle,lcolor,lwt,apply)
```

Syntax 7

Syntax 7 is used with chart data lines.

```
=PATTERNS(lauto,lstyle,lcolor,lwt,mauto,mstyle,mfore,mback,apply)
=PATTERNS?(lauto,lstyle,lcolor,lwt,mauto,mstyle,mfore,mback,apply)
```

Syntax 8

Syntax 8 is used with picture chart markers.

```
=PATTERNS(type,picture_units,apply)
=PATTERNS?(type,picture_units,apply)
```

The following arguments correspond to check boxes, list boxes, and options in the Patterns dialog box. The default is the current setting in the dialog box.

Aauto is a number from 0 to 2 specifying settings regarding the object's surface area. The following table lists the numbers and their corresponding area settings.

If aauto is	Area settings are
0	Custom set by the user
1	Automatic
2	None

Aback is a number from 1 to 16 corresponding to the area background colors in the Patterns dialog box.

Afore is a number from 1 to 16 corresponding to the area foreground colors in the Patterns dialog box.

Apattern is a number corresponding to the area patterns in the Patterns dialog box. If an object is selected, apattern can be a number from 1 to 19. If a cell is selected, apattern can be a number from 0 to 18. If a cell is selected and apattern is 0, no pattern is applied.

Apply is a logical value corresponding to the Apply To All check box. This argument is used only with a chart data point or a data series. If the argument is TRUE, formatting changes are applied to all items that are similar to the selected item on the chart. If the argument is FALSE, formatting changes are applied only to the selected item on the chart.

Bauto is a number from 0 to 2 specifying border settings. The following table lists the numbers and corresponding border settings.

If bauto is	Border settings are
0	Custom set by the user
1	Automatic
2	None

Bcolor is a number from 1 to 16 corresponding to the sixteen border colors in the Patterns dialog box.

Bstyle is a number from 1 to 8 corresponding to the eight border styles in the Patterns dialog box.

Bwt is a number from 1 to 4 corresponding to the four border weights in the Patterns dialog box. The following table lists the numbers and their corresponding border weights.

If bwt is	Border weight is
1	Hairline
2	Thin
3	Medium
4	Thick

Hlength is a number from 1 to 3 specifying the length of the arrowhead. The following table lists the numbers and their corresponding lengths.

If hlength is	Arrowhead length is
1	Short
2	Medium
3	Long

Htype is a number from 1 to 3 specifying the style of the arrowhead. The following table lists the numbers and their corresponding styles.

If htype is	Arrowhead style is
1	No head
2	Open head
3	Closed head

Hwidth is a number from 1 to 3 specifying the width of the arrowhead. The following table lists the numbers and their corresponding widths.

If hwidth is	Arrowhead width is
1	Narrow
2	Medium
3	Wide

Invert is a logical value corresponding to the Invert If Negative check box in the Patterns dialog box. This argument is used only with data markers. If invert is TRUE, the pattern in the selected item is inverted if it corresponds to a negative number. If invert is FALSE, the inverted pattern is removed from the selected item corresponding to a negative number.

Lauto is a number from 0 to 2 specifying line settings. The following table lists the numbers and their corresponding settings.

If lauto is	Line settings are
1	Custom set by the user
2	Automatic
3	None

Lcolor is a number from 1 to 16 corresponding to the sixteen line colors in the Patterns dialog box.

Lstyle is a number from 1 to 8 corresponding to the eight line styles in the Patterns dialog box.

Lwt is a number from 1 to 4 corresponding to the four line weights in the Patterns dialog box. The following table lists the numbers and their corresponding line weights.

If lwt is	Line weight is
1	Hairline
2	Thin
3	Medium
4	Thick

Mauto is a number from 0 to 2 specifying marker settings. The following table lists the numbers and their corresponding marker settings.

If mauto is	Marker settings are
0	Custom set by the user
1	Automatic
2	None

Mback is a number from 1 to 16 corresponding to the sixteen marker background colors in the Patterns dialog box.

Mfore is a number from 1 to 16 corresponding to the sixteen marker foreground colors in the Patterns dialog box.

Mstyle is a number from 1 to 9 corrresponding to the nine marker styles in the Patterns dialog box.

Picture_units is the number of units you want each picture to represent in a scaled, stacked picture chart. This argument can be used only with type 3 picture charts.

Rounded is a logical value corresponding to the Round Corners check box. If rounded is TRUE, the corners of text boxes and rectangles are rounded. If rounded is

FALSE, the corners of text boxes and rectangles are square. Rounded is ignored if the selection is an arc or an oval.

Shadow is a logical value corresponding to the Shadow check box. Shadow is not used with area charts or bars in bar charts. If shadow is TRUE, a shadow is added to the selected item. If shadow is FALSE, the shadow is removed. Shadow is ignored if the selection item is an arc.

Tlabel is a number from 1 to 4 specifying the position of tick labels. The following table lists the numbers and their corresponding label positions.

If tlabel is	Tick label position is
1	None
2	Low
3	High
4	Next to axis

Tmajor is a number from 1 to 4 specifying the type of major tick marks. The following table lists the numbers and their corresponding type of major tick marks.

If tmajor is	Type of major tick mark is
1	None
2	Inside
3	Outside
4	Cross

Tminor is a number from 1 to 4 specifying the type of minor tick marks. The following table lists the numbers and their corresponding types of minor tick marks.

If tminor is	Type of minor tick mark is
1	None
2	Inside
3	Outside
4	Cross

Type is a number from 1 to 3 specifying the type of pictures to use in a picture chart. The following table lists the numbers and their corresponding picture types.

If type is	Pictures are
1	Stretched to reach a particular value
2	Stacked on top of one another to reach a particular value
3	Stacked on top of one another, but you specify the number of units each picture represents

ROW.HEIGHT

The ROW.HEIGHT function is used to change the height of the rows in a reference. Inserting this function into a macro sheet is equivalent to choosing the Row Height command from the Format menu.

Use with macro sheets only.

Syntax

=ROW.HEIGHT(height_num,reference,standard_height,type_num)

=ROW.HEIGHT?(height_num,reference,standard_height,type_num)

Height_num specifies, in points, how high you want the rows to be. If standard_height is set to TRUE, height_num is ignored.

Reference specifies the rows whose height you want to change, and must be either an external reference to the active worksheet (for example, !$B:$C, or !Database), or an R1C1 style reference in the form of text (for example, B1:D5, or Database).

If reference is a relative R1C1 reference in the form of text, it is assumed to be relative to the active cell.

If reference is omitted, it is assumed to be the current selection.

Standard_height is a logical value that sets the row height determined by the font.

If standard_height is TRUE, the row height is set to a standard height, depending upon the font of each row. Height_num is ignored. If Standard is FALSE or omitted, the row height is set to the height_num.

Type_num is a number from 1 to 3 corresponding to the Hide, Unhide, or Best Fit option, respectively, in the Row Height dialog box. The following table lists the type_num and the action taken.

Type_num	Action taken
1	Hides the row selection and sets the row height to 0.
2	Unhides the row selection by setting the row height to the value set before the selection was hidden.
3	Sets the row selection to a best-fit height.

If any arguments in the function conflict with the type_num setting, the other arguments will be ignored and the type_num setting will be used.

SCALE

The SCALE function changes the position, formatting, and scaling of the selected axis of the active chart. This command is equivalent to choosing the Scale command from the Format command in the Chart menu. To use the SCALE function, a chart must be the active document. There are five syntax forms that can be used with the SCALE function. Syntax 1 is used if the selected axis is a category (x) axis on a 2-D chart and the chart is not a scatter (xy) chart. Syntax 2 is used if the selected axis is a value (y) axis on a 2-D chart and the chart is not a scatter (xy) chart. Syntax 3 is used to change the position, formatting, and scaling of the selected category (x) axis on a 3-D chart. Syntax 4 is used if the selected axis is a value (y) axis on a 3-D chart. Syntax 5 is used to change the position, formatting, and scaling of the selected value (y) axis on a 3-D chart.

Use with macro sheets only.

Syntax 1

```
=SCALE(cross,cat_labels,cat_marks,between,max,reverse)
=SCALE?(cross,cat_labels,cat_marks,between,max,reverse)
```

The selected axis is a category (x) axis on a 2-D chart. The arguments used in this function correspond to the text and check boxes in the Scale dialog box.

Cross is a number that corresponds to the Value (Y) Axis Crosses At Category box. This number determines where the x and y axes will intersect in the chart. The default is 1. If the argument max is TRUE, any value entered for cross will be ignored.

Cat_labels determines the number of categories between tick labels on the category axis. The default is 1.

Cat_marks determines the number of categories between tick marks on the category axis. The default is 1.

Between tells Excel where the value (y) axis will cross between categories. If the cat_labels argument is omitted or is 1, this argument does not apply.

Max is a logical value that, if TRUE, tells Excel to position the intersection of the x and y axis at the maximum category value. If max is TRUE, any argument for cross is ignored.

Reverse is a logical value that, if TRUE, reverses the order of the categories in the x axis. The default is FALSE.

Syntax 2

=SCALE(min_num,max_num,major,minor,cross,logarithmic,reverse,max)

=SCALE?(min_num,max_num,major,minor,cross,logarithmic,reverse,max)

The selected axis is a value (y) axis on a 2-D chart. The first five arguments used in this function correspond to the range variables in the Scale dialog box. Each of these arguments can be either a number or the logical value TRUE. The last three arguments are logical values only.

Min_num determines the minimum value for the value (y) axis. If the argument is a number, that number is used for the value. If the logical value TRUE is used, Excel determines the minimum value.

Max_num determines the maximum value for the value (y) axis. If the argument is a number, that number is used for the value. If the logical value TRUE is used, Excel will determine the maximum value for the y axis.

Major determines the major unit of measure on the y axis. If the argument is a number, that number is used to determine the major unit of measure, if the logical value TRUE is used, Excel will determine the major unit of measure.

Minor determines the minor unit of measure on the y axis. If the argument is a number, that number is used to determine the minor unit of measure; if the logical value TRUE is used, Excel will determine the minor unit of measure.

Cross determines where the value (y) axis and the category (x) axis intersect. If the logical value TRUE is used, Excel will use the default position.

Logarithmic is a logical value that corresponds to the Logarithmic Scale check box in the Scale dialog box. Entering a value of TRUE is the equivalent of selecting the check box. Entering a value of FALSE is equivalent to clearing the check box.

Reverse is a logical value that, if TRUE, reverses the order of the categories in the y axis. The default is FALSE.

Max is a logical value that, if TRUE, tells Excel to position the intersection of the x and y axis at the maximum category value.

Syntax 3

```
=SCALE(cat_labels,cat_marks,reverse,between)
=SCALE?(cat_labels,cat_marks,reverse,between)
```

The selected axis is a category (x) axis on a 3-D chart. The arguments in this function correspond to the text and check boxes in the Format Scale dialog box.

Cat_labels determines the number of categories between tick labels on the category axis. The default is 1.

Cat_marks determines the number of categories between tick marks on the category axis. The default is 1.

Reverse is a logical value that, if TRUE, reverses the order of the categories in the x axis. The default is FALSE.

Between tells Excel where the value (y) axis will cross between categories. If the cat_labels argument is omitted or is 1, this argument does not apply.

Syntax 4

```
=SCALE(series_labels,series_marks,reverse)
=SCALE?(series_labels,series_marks,reverse)
```

The selected axis is a series (y) axis on a 3-D chart.

Series_labels determines the number of series between tick labels on the series axis. The default is 1.

Series_marks determines the number of series between tick marks on the series axis. The default is 1.

Reverse is a logical value that, if TRUE, reverses the order of the series in the y axis. The default is FALSE.

Syntax 5

```
=SCALE(min_num,max_num,major,minor,cross,logarithmic,reverse,min)
=SCALE?(min_num,max_num,major,minor,cross,logarithmic,reverse,min)
```

The selected axis is a value (z) axis on a 3-D chart. The first five arguments used in this function correspond to the range variables in the Scale dialog box. Each of these arguments can be either a number or the logical value TRUE. The last three arguments are logical values only.

Min_num determines the minimum value for the value (z) axis. If the argument is a number, that number is used for the value. If the logical value TRUE is used, Excel determines the minimum value.

Max_num determines the maximum value for the value (z) axis. If the argument is a number, that number is used for the value. If the logical value TRUE is used, Excel will determine the maximum value for the z axis.

Major determines the major unit of measure on the z axis. If the argument is a number, that number is used to determine the major unit of measure; if the logical value TRUE is used, Excel will determine the major unit of measure.

Minor determines the minor unit of measure on the z axis. If the argument is a number, that number is used to determine the minor unit of measure; if the logical value TRUE is used, Excel will determine the minor unit of measure.

Cross determines where the xy plane crosses. If the logical value TRUE is used, Excel will use the default position.

Logarithmic is a logical value that corresponds to the Logarithmic Scale check box in the Scale dialog box. Entering a value of TRUE is the equivalent of selecting the check box. Entering a value of FALSE is equivalent to clearing the check box.

Reverse is a logical value that, if TRUE, reverses the order of the categories in the y axis. The default is FALSE.

Min is a logical value that, if TRUE, tells Excel to position the intersection of the xy plane at the minimum category value.

SEND.TO.BACK

The SEND.TO.BACK function sends selected objects to the back or hides them behind other objects. If the selection is not an object or a group of objects, this functions interrupts the macro and returns a #Value! error value. Inserting this macro in a macro sheet is equivalent to choosing the Send To Back command from the Format menu.

Use with macro sheets only.

Syntax

```
=SEND.TO.BACK()
```

APPLY.STYLE

The APPLY.STYLE function applies a previously defined style to the current selection. Inserting this function in a macro sheet is equivalent to choosing theStyle command from the Format menu and selecting a style.

Use with macro sheets only.

Syntax

=**APPLY.STYLE**(style_text)
=**APPLY.STYLE?**(style_text)

Style_text is the name, in a text string, of a previously defined style. If style_text is not defined, the function interrupts the macro and returns a #Value! error. If style_text is omitted, the Normal style is applied to the selection.

FORMAT.TEXT

The FORMAT.TEXT function is used to format a selected worksheet text box or button or any text item on a chart. Inserting this function in a macro sheet is equivalent to choosing the Text command from the Format menu.

Use with macro sheets only.

Syntax

=**FORMAT.TEXT**(x_align,y_align,orient_num,auto_text,auto_size,show_key, show_value)
=**FORMAT.TEXT?**(x_align,y_align,orient_num,auto_text,auto_size,show_key, show_value)

X_align is a number from 1 to 4 specifying the horizontal alignment of the text. The following table lists the numbers and their corresponding horizontal alignment.

X_align	Horizontal alignment
1	Left
2	Center
3	Right
4	Justify

Y_align is a number from 1 to 4 specifying the vertical alignment of the text. The following table lists the numbers and their corresponding vertical alignment.

Y_align	Vertical alignment
1	Top
2	Center
3	Bottom
4	Justify

Orient_num is a number from 0 to 3 specifying the orientation of the text. The following table lists the numbers and their corresponding orientation.

Orient_num	Text orientation
1	Horizontal
2	Vertical
3	Upward
4	Downward

The following arguments correspond to check boxes and are logical values. If the argument is TRUE, the check box is selected. If the argument is FALSE, the check box is cleared. If the argument is omitted, the current settings are used.

Auto_text corresponds to the Automatic Text check box. If the selected text was created with the Attach Text command from the Chart menu and edited, auto_text restores the original text. This argument is ignored for text boxes on worksheets and macro sheets.

Auto_size corresponds to the Automatic Size check box. If you have changed the size of the border around the selected text, this argument restores the border to automatic size.

Show_key corresponds to the Show Key check box. This argument can be used only with an attached data label on a chart.

Show_value corresponds to the Show Value check box. This argument can be used only with an attached data label on a chart.

The following table lists each text item and the arguments that can be used with it.

Text item	Arguments that apply
Worksheet text box or button	X-align,y_align,orient_num,auto_size
Attached data label	All arguments
Unattached text label	X-align,y_align,orient_num,auto_size
Tickmark label	Orient_num

UNGROUP

The UNGROUP function separates a grouped object from the group, turning it into an individual object. This allows you to work with the object outside of the group.

Inserting this function in a macro sheet is the equivalent of choosing the Ungroup command from the Format menu.

Use with macro sheets only.

Syntax

```
=UNGROUP()
```

The Gallery Menu Functions

The following functions are the equivalent of executing Gallery menu or toolbar commands while in the Chart menu.

GALLERY.3D.AREA

The GALLERY.3D.AREA function changes the format of the active chart to a 3-D area chart. This command is equivalent to choosing the 3-D Area command from the Gallery command in the Chart menu or clicking the Gallery Area tool. To use the GALLERY.3D.AREA function, a chart must be the active document.

Use with macro sheets only.

Syntax

```
=GALLERY.ED.AREA(type_num)
=GALLERY.3D.AREA?(type_num)
```

Type_num corresponds to the number of the 3-D area chart in the 3-D Area dialog box that you wish to select.

GALLERY.3D.BAR

The GALLERY.3D.BAR function changes the format of the active chart to a 3-D bar chart. This command is equivalent to choosing the 3-D Bar command from the Gallery command in the Chart menu, or clicking the Gallery Bar tool. To use the GALLERY.3D.BAR function, a chart must be the active document.

Use with macro sheets only.

Syntax

```
=GALLERY.ED.BAR(type_num)
=GALLERY.3D.BAR?(type_num)
```

Type_num corresponds to the number of the 3-D bar chart in the 3-D Bar dialog box that you wish to select.

GALLERY.3D.COLUMN

The GALLERY.3D.COLUMN function changes the format of the active chart to a 3-D column chart. This command is equivalent to choosing the 3-D Column command from the Gallery command in the Chart menu, or clicking the Gallery Column tool. To use the GALLERY.3D.COLUMN function, a chart must be the active document.

Use with macro sheets only.

Syntax

```
=GALLERY.ED.COLUMN(type_num)
=GALLERY.3D.COLUMN?(type_num)
```

Type_num corresponds to the number of the 3-D column chart in the 3-D Column dialog box that you wish to select.

GALLERY.3D.LINE

The GALLERY.3D.LINE function changes the format of the active chart to a 3-D line chart. This command is equivalent to choosing the 3-D Line command from the Gallery command in the Chart menu, or clicking the Gallery Line tool. To use the GALLERY.3D.LINE function, a chart must be the active document.

Use with macro sheets only.

Syntax

```
=GALLERY.ED.LINE(type_num)
=GALLERY.3D.LINE?(type_num)
```

Type_num corresponds to the number of the 3-D line chart in the 3-D Line dialog box that you wish to select.

GALLERY.3D.PIE

The GALLERY.3D.PIE function changes the format of the active chart to a 3-D pie chart. This command is equivalent to choosing the 3-D Pie command from the Gallery command in the Chart menu, or clicking the Gallery Pie tool. To use the GALLERY.3D.PIE function, a chart must be the active document.

Use with macro sheets only.

Syntax

```
=GALLERY.ED.PIE(type_num)
=GALLERY.3D.PIE?(type_num)
```

Type_num corresponds to the number of the 3-D pie chart in the 3-D Pie dialog box that you wish to select.

GALLERY.3D.SURFACE

The GALLERY.3D.SURFACE function changes the format of the active chart to a 3-D surface chart. This command is equivalent to choosing the 3-D Surface command from the Gallery command in the Chart menu, or clicking the Gallery Surface tool. To use the GALLERY.3D.SURFACE function, a chart must be the active document.

Use with macro sheets only.

Syntax

```
=GALLERY.3D.SURFACE(type_num)
=GALLERY.3D.SURFACE?(type_num)
```

Type_num corresponds to the number of the 3-D surface chart in the 3-D Surface dialog box that you wish to select.

GALLERY.AREA

The GALLERY.AREA function changes the format of the active chart to an area chart. This command is equivalent to choosing the Area command from the Gallery command in the Chart menu, or clicking the Gallery Area tool. To use the GALLERY.AREA function, a chart must be the active document.

Use with macro sheets only.

Syntax

```
=GALLERY.AREA(type_num,delete_overlay)
=GALLERY.AREA?(type_num,delete_overlay)
```

Type_num corresponds to the number of the area chart in the Area dialog box that you wish to select and delete_overlay is a logical value that specifies whether to delete an overlay chart. The delete_overlay argument corresponds to the Add Overlay and Delete Overlay commands in the Chart menu. If delete_overlay is TRUE, Excel will delete the existing overlay chart and apply the new format to the main chart. If delete_overlay is FALSE, Excel will apply the new format to either the main chart or the overlay chart, depending on the location of the selected series. The default for delete_overlay is FALSE.

GALLERY.BAR

The GALLERY.BAR function changes the format of the active chart to a bar chart. This command is equivalent to choosing the Bar command from the Gallery command in the Chart menu, or clicking the Gallery Bar tool. To use the GALLERY.BAR function, a chart must be the active document.

Use with macro sheets only.

Syntax

```
=GALLERY.BAR(type_num,delete_overlay)
=GALLERY.BAR?(type_num,delete_overlay)
```

Type_num corresponds to the number of the bar chart in the Bar dialog box that you wish to select, and delete_overlay is a logical value that specifies whether to delete an overlay chart. The delete_overlay argument corresponds to the Add Overlay and Delete Overlay commands in the Chart menu. If delete_overlay is TRUE, Excel will delete the existing overlay chart and apply the new format to the main chart. If delete_overlay is FALSE, Excel will apply the new format to either the main chart or the overlay chart, depending on the location of the selected series. The default for delete_overlay is FALSE.

GALLERY.COLUMN

The GALLERY.COLUMN function changes the format of the active chart to a column chart. This command is equivalent to choosing the Column command from the Gallery command in the Chart menu, or clicking the Gallery Chart tool. To use the GALLERY.COLUMN function, a chart must be the active document.

Use with macro sheets only.

Syntax

```
=GALLERY.COLUMN(type_num,delete_overlay)
=GALLERY.COLUMN?(type_num,delete_overlay)
```

Type_num corresponds to the number of the column chart in the Column dialog box that you wish to select, and delete_overlay is a logical value that specifies whether to delete an overlay chart. The delete_overlay argument corresponds to the Add Overlay and Delete Overlay commands in the Chart menu. If delete_overlay is TRUE, Excel will delete the existing overlay chart and apply the new format to the main chart. If delete_overlay is FALSE, Excel will apply the new format to either the main chart or the overlay chart, depending on the location of the selected series. The default for delete_overlay is FALSE.

COMBINATION

The COMBINATION function changes the format of the active chart to a combination chart. This command is equivalent to choosing the Combination command from the Gallery command in the Chart menu, or clicking the Gallery Combination tool. To use the COMBINATION function, a chart must be the active document.

Use with macro sheets only.

Syntax

```
=COMBINATION(type_num)
=COMBINATION?(type_num)
```

Type_num corresponds to the number of the combination chart in the Combination. When you use the COMBINATION function, both the main chart and the overlay chart will be formatted with the style of chart you selected for type_num.

GALLERY.LINE

The GALLERY.LINE function changes the format of the active chart to a line chart. This command is equivalent to choosing the Line command from the Gallery command in the Chart menu, or clicking the Gallery Line tool. To use the GALLERY.LINE function, a chart must be the active document.

Use with macro sheets only.

Syntax

```
=GALLERY.LINE(type_num,delete_overlay)
=GALLERY.LINE?(type_num,delete_overlay)
```

Type_num corresponds to the number of the line chart in the Line dialog box that you wish to select and delete_overlay is a logical value that specifies whether to delete an overlay chart. The delete_overlay argument corresponds to the Add Overlay and Delete Overlay commands in the Chart menu. If delete_overlay is TRUE, Excel will delete the existing overlay chart and apply the new format to the main chart. If delete_overlay is FALSE, Excel will apply the new format to either the main chart or the overlay chart, depending on the location of the selected series. The default for delete_overlay is FALSE.

GALLERY.PIE

The GALLERY.PIE function changes the format of the active chart to a pie chart. This command is equivalent to choosing the Pie command from the Gallery command in the Chart menu, or clicking the Gallery Pie tool. To use the GALLERY.PIE function, a chart must be the active document.

Use with macro sheets only.

Syntax

```
=GALLERY.PIE(type_num,delete_overlay)
=GALLERY.PIE?(type_num,delete_overlay)
```

Type_num corresponds to the number of the pie chart in the Pie dialog box that you wish to select and delete_overlay is a logical value that specifies whether to delete an overlay chart. The delete_overlay argument corresponds to the Add Overlay and Delete Overlay commands in the Chart menu. If delete_overlay is TRUE, Excel will delete the existing overlay chart and apply the new format to the main chart. If delete_overlay is FALSE, Excel will apply the new format to either the main chart or the overlay chart, depending on the location of the selected series. The default for delete_overlay is FALSE.

GALLERY.RADAR

The GALLERY.RADAR function changes the format of the active chart to a radar chart. This command is equivalent to choosing the Radar command from the Gallery command in the Chart menu, or clicking the Gallery Radar tool. To use the GALLERY.RADAR function, a chart must be the active document.

Use with macro sheets only.

Syntax

```
=GALLERY.RADAR(type_num, delete_overlay)
=GALLERY.RADAR?(type_num, delete_overlay)
```

Type_num corresponds to the number of the radar chart in the Radar dialog box that you wish to select, and delete_overlay is a logical value that specifies whether to delete an overlay chart. The delete_overlay argument corresponds to the Add Overlay and Delete Overlay commands in the Chart menu. If delete_overlay is TRUE, Excel will delete the existing overlay chart and apply the new format to the main chart. If delete_overlay is FALSE, Excel will apply the new format to either the main chart or the overlay chart, depending on the location of the selected series. The default for delete_overlay is FALSE.

GALLERY.SCATTER

The GALLERY.SCATTER function changes the format of the active chart to an XY (Scatter) chart. This command is equivalent to choosing the XY (Scatter) command from the Gallery command in the Chart menu or clicking the Gallery tool. To use the GALLERY.SCATTER function, a chart must be the active document.

Use with macro sheets only.

Syntax

```
=GALLERY.SCATTER(type_num, delete_overlay)
=GALLERY.SCATTER?(type_num, delete_overlay)
```

Type_num corresponds to the number of the XY (scatter) chart in the XY (Scatter) dialog box that you wish to select and delete_overlay is a logical value that specifies whether to delete an overlay chart. The delete_overlay argument corresponds to the Add Overlay and Delete Overlay commands in the Chart menu. If delete_overlay is TRUE, Excel will delete the existing overlay chart and apply the new format to the main chart. If delete_overlay is FALSE, Excel will apply the new format to either the main chart or the overlay chart, depending on the location of the selected series. The default for delete_overlay is FALSE.

SET.PREFERRED

The SET.PREFERRED function makes the format of the active chart the preferred format. When used in conjunction with the PREFERRED function, this function will change the format of the active chart to the format selected by SET.PREFERRED. When used in conjunction with the PREFERRED function, the SET.PREFERRED function also changes the default format that Excel uses for new charts. This command is equivalent to choosing the Preferred command from the Gallery command in the Chart menu. To use the SET.PREFERRED function, a chart must be the active document.

Use with macro sheets only.

Syntax

```
=SET.PREFERRED()
```

PREFERRED

The PREFERRED function changes the format of the active chart to the format selected by SET.PREFERRED. This command is equivalent to choosing the Preferred command from the Gallery command in the Chart menu, or clicking the Gallery Area tool. To use the PREFERRED function, a chart must be the active document.

Use with macro sheets only.

Syntax

```
=PREFERRED()
```

The Formula Menu

The following functions are the equivalent of executing Formula menu commands or tools.

APPLY.NAMES

The APPLY.NAMES function replaces references or values in selected cells with the names defined for them. If no names are defined, the #Value! error is returned. Inserting this function in a macro sheet is equivalent to choosing the Apply Names command from the Formula menu.

Use with macro sheets only.

Syntax

=**APPLY.NAMES**(`name_array`,`ignore,use_rowcol,omit_col,omit_row,order_num,`
`append_last`)
=**APPLY.NAMES?**(`name_array,ignore,use_rowcol,omit_col,omit_row,order_num,`
`append_last`)

Name_array is the name or names to apply as text in an array. If the names in the argument have already replaced the references or values, the #Value! error is returned.

Several of the following arguments correspond to check boxes and options in the Apply Names dialog box. Arguments that apply to check boxes are logical values. If an argument is TRUE, the check box is selected. If an argument is FALSE, the check box is cleared. If the argument is omitted, the settings are unchanged.

Ignore corresponds to the Ignore Relative/Absolute check box.

Use_rowcol corresponds to the Use Row and Column Names check box.

Omit_col corresponds to the Omit Column Name If Same Column check box. If Use_rowcol is FALSE, this argument is ignored.

Omit_row corresponds to the Omit Row Name If Same Row check box. If Use_rowcol is FALSE, this argument is ignored.

Order_num determines which named range appears first when a reference is replaced by both a named row and a named column. The following table lists the order number and corresponding order or range names.

Order_num	Order of range names
1	Row Column
2	Column Row

Append_last is a logical value that determines whether the names most recently defined are replaced. If this argument is TRUE, the definitions of the names in name_array and the last names defined are replaced. If this argument is FALSE, only the definitions of the names in name_array are replaced.

CREATE.NAMES

The CREATE.NAMES function assigns each column and row in the selected range the same name as the name in the first column and row. Inserting this function in a macro sheet is the equivalent of choosing the Create Names command from the Formula menu.

Use with macro sheets only.

Syntax

```
=CREATE.NAMES(top,left,bottom,right)
=CREATE.NAMES?(top,left,bottom,right)
```

Arguments are logical values corresponding to check boxes in the Create Names dialog box. If an argument is TRUE, the box is selected. If an argument is FALSE or omitted, the box is cleared.

Top corresponds to the Top Row check box; left corresponds to the Left Column check box; bottom corresponds to the Bottom Row check box; right corresponds to the Right Column check box.

DEFINE.NAME

The DEFINE.NAME function defines a name in the active worksheet or macro sheet. Inserting this function into a macro sheet is equivalent to choosing the Define Name command from the Formula menu.

Use with macro sheets only.

Syntax

```
=DEFINE.NAME(name_text,refers_to,macro_type,shortcut_text,hidden
category)
=DEFINE.NAME?(name_text,refers_to,macro_type,shortcut_text,hidden
category)
```

Name_text is the text name. Names must start with a letter, cannot include spaces or symbols, and cannot look like cell references.

Refers_to describes the values to which name_text should refer. The following table lists the reference values and their corresponding name_text definitions.

If refers_to is	Then name_text is
A number, text, or logical value	Defined to refer to that value
An external reference	Defined to refer to those cells
A formula in the form of text	Defined to refer to the formula
Omitted	Defined to refer to the current selection

Macro_type is a number from 1 to 3 that indicates the type of macro. This argument is used only if the macro sheet is the active document. The following chart lists macro_type numbers and their corresponding types.

Macro_type	Type of macro
1	Custom function (function macro)
2	Command macro
3 or omitted	None

Shortcut_text is a text value that specifies the macro shortcut key. This must be a single letter. This argument is used only if the macro sheet is the active document.

Hidden is a logical value that determines whether the defined name is hidden. If the argument is TRUE, the name is defined as a hidden name. If the argument is FALSE or omitted, the name is defined as a normal name.

Category corresponds to categories in the Function Category list box. Categories can be text or numbered, starting with the first category in the list (1). If the category is text and is not listed in the categories list, a new category is created and your custom function is assigned to it.

FORMULA.FIND

The FORMULA.FIND function searches the cells of a worksheet for specified text strings. If the text string is found, FORMULA.FIND returns a value of TRUE; if the text string is not found, FORMULA.FIND returns a value of FALSE. Using this function in a macro is equivalent to choosing the Find command in the Formula menu.

Use with macro sheets only.

Syntax

```
=FORMULA.FIND(text,in_num,at_num,by_num,dir_num,match_case)
=FORMULA.FIND?(text,in_num,at_num,by_num,dir_num,match_case)
```

Text is the text string you want to find. In_num is a number value from 1 to 3 which specifies the type of cell data where you want to search.

In_num	Searches
1	Formulas
2	Values
3	Notes

At_num is a number that specifies whether to search for cells that contain text only or to broaden the search to include cells that contain text as well as other characters.

At_num	Searches for text as
1	The entire string (the only value in the cell)
2	Either an entire string or part of a longer string

By_num is a number that specifies whether to search by rows or columns. If you enter the number 1 as your argument, Excel will search by rows; if you enter the number 2, Excel will search by columns.

Dir_num is a number that specifies whether to search for the next occurrence of the text string or the previous occurrence. The default number is 1, which searches for the next occurrence of the string. If you enter 2 as your argument, Excel will search for the previous occurrence of the text string.

Match_case is a logical value. If the value is TRUE, Excel will search for exact—that is, case-sensitive—matches of the text string. If the value is FALSE or omitted, Excel will search for all occurrences of the text string regardless of case.

GOAL.SEEK

The GOAL.SEEK function calculates the values you need to return a specific value (which is called a **goal**). For example, if you want a formula to return a specific value, GOAL.SEEK calculates the values needed in the formula to return the value. This function is equivalent to choosing the Goal Seek command in the Formula menu.

Use with macro sheets only.

Syntax

```
=GOAL.SEEK(target_cell,target_value,variable_cell)
=GOAL.SEEK?(target_cell,target_value,variable_cell)
```

Target_cell refers to either the cell address or to the named reference to the cell that contains the formula. If the target_cell does not contain a formula, Excel will display an error message.

Target_value is the value you want the formula in target_cell to return.

Variable_cell is the single named cell that you want Excel to change so that the formula in target_cell returns the value supplied in target_value. The formula in target_cell must contain the named reference to variable_cell, or Excel will not be able to provide a solution. For example, suppose you wanted to calculate the amount of sales you need monthly to provide an annual income from sales of $24,000. In a cell named *Sales,* you have a formula that looks like this:

```
=Month x 12
```

where month is the named reference to a single cell. You could then calculate how much you need to sell each month by entering the following function:

```
=GOAL.SEEK("Sales",24,000,"Month")
```

This would produce a value of $2,000, which is stored in the named cell *Month.*

FORMULA.GOTO

The FORMULA.GOTO function searches through all open documents and finds and selects a named area or a range of cells by cell address. This function is equivalent to choosing the Goto command in the Formula menu.

Use with macro sheets only.

Syntax

=FORMULA.GOTO(reference,corner)
=FORMULA.GOTO?(reference,corner)

Reference is either an external reference to a document, an R1C1 type of reference (remember that when you use the R1C1 reference it must be enclosed in quotation marks: "R1C1"), or the named area or cell address you want to select. If reference is omitted, Excel assumes you want to select a named area or cell address that was selected by a previous FORMULA.GOTO function. If you omit reference and have not used another FORMULA.GOTO function, you will receive an error message.

Corner is a logical value. When corner is TRUE, Excel scrolls through the document and places the upper-left cell selected in reference in the upper-left corner of the active window. If corner is FALSE or omitted, Excel scrolls normally.

NOTE

The NOTE function is used to create a cell note or to replace specified characters in a cell note with other text. This function is equivalent to choosing the Note command in the Formula menu.

Use with macro sheets only.

Syntax

=NOTE(add_text,cell_ref,start_char,num_chars)
=NOTE?()

Add_text is a text string that can contain up to 255 characters that you want to include in a note. Add_text must always be enclosed in quotation marks. If add_text is omitted, Excel will delete the entire note, including sound, unless you specify empty text. To specify empty text, use quotation marks (" ") with no text between them.

Cell_ref is the address or named reference of the cell to which you wish to add a note. If cell_ref is omitted, the note will be added to the active cell.

Start_char is the number of the character (starting from the first character of the existing note and counting characters and spaces) where you want to add text to the note. If start_char is omitted, Excel assumes the character to be 1. If you specify a start_num that is larger than the number of characters contained in a note, Excel will add the text to the end of the note. If you are creating a note, Excel ignores any arguments specified in start_char and adds text starting from character 1.

Num_chars specifies the number of characters you want to replace with new text. If num_chars is omitted, Excel assumes that you want to replace the entire note.

OUTLINE

The OUTLINE function creates an outline and defines the settings to automatically create outlines. This function is equivalent to choosing the Outline command in the Formula menu.

Use with macro sheets only.

Syntax

```
=OUTLINE(auto_style,row_dir,col_dir,create_apply)
=OUTLINE?(auto_style,row_dir,col_dir,create_apply)
```

Auto_style is a logical value that, when TRUE, automatically turns on outlining styles.

Row_dir is a logical value that, when TRUE, specifies that the summary rows are below the detail.

Col_dir is a logical value that, when TRUE, specifies that the summary columns are to the right of the detail.

Create_apply is a numerical value that uses a 1 to create an outline using the current settings, or a 2 to apply outlining styles to the selection based on outline levels. If create_apply is omitted, an outline is created using the auto_styles, row_dir, and col_dir settings.

FORMULA

The FORMULA function enters a formula or a value in the active cell or referenced area in a worksheet or chart. The FORMULA function has two syntax types: type 1 is used for worksheets, type 2 is used for charts.

Syntax 1

```
=FORMULA(formula_text,reference)
```

Syntax 1 is used in worksheets, where formula_text is a number, a reference, text, a formula, or a reference to a cell that contains any of the above. If formula_text is a formula, it must be entered using the R1C1 style, and it must be enclosed in parenthesis.

For example, if you want to add a formula to cell D2 that subtracts the contents of cell B2 from cell A1, you would type the following:

```
=FORMULA("=RC[-2]-R1C1")
```

If formula_text is text, a number, or a logical value, the value is entered as a constant.

Reference is the cell in the active worksheet or an external reference where the formula_text is to be added.

Syntax 2

```
=FORMULA(formula_text)
```

Syntax 2 is used in charts where formula_text is the text label or Series formula that you want to enter into a chart. If the current selection is a text label and the formula_text can be treated as a text label, the current selection is replaced with formula_text. If the formula_text can be treated as a text label and there is no current selection, or the current selection is not a text label, a new text label is created. If the current selection is a Series formula, and the formula_text can be treated as a Series formula, the current selection is replaced with formula_text. If formula_text can be treated as a Series formula and the current selection is not a Series formula, a new Series formula is created.

LIST.NAMES

The LIST.NAMES function lists all of the names (except hidden names) defined on your worksheet, as well as the cells to which the names refer, whether a macro is a command macro or a custom function. It also lists the shortcut key for all command macros, and the category to which each custom function is assigned. This function is equivalent to choosing the Paste Name command in the Formula menu and clicking on Paste List.

Use with macro sheets only.

Syntax

```
=LIST.NAMES()
```

If you want to list all of the five types of information that Excel returns with the LIST.NAMES function, you must either have a single cell currently selected, or your selection must be five or more columns wide. LIST.NAMES pastes each type of information for a name in a separate column in one row. Column 1 contains the cell names, column 2 contains the cells to which the names refer,and column 3 contains the number 1 if the name refers to a custom function, 2 if the name refers to a command macro, and 0 if the name refers to anything else. Column 4 contains the shortcut keys for command macros, and column 5 contains the category name or number for custom functions. If your selection contains more than a single cell and fewer than five columns, LIST.NAMES will include the information for only as many columns as you have selected, and will omit the rest.

 When you use LIST.NAMES, any information that was originally contained in the selected cells will be replaced by the information returned by the LIST.NAMES function.

WARNING

FORMULA.REPLACE

The FORMULA.REPLACE function searches for and replaces characters in the cells in your worksheet. This function is equivalent to choosing the Replace command in the Formula menu.

Use with macro sheets only.

Syntax

    =FORMULA.REPLACE(find_text,replace_text,look_at,look_by,active_cell,
    match_case)
    =FORMULA.REPLACE?(find_text,replace_text,look_at,look_by,active_cell,
    match_case)

Find_text is the text for which you are searching. You can use the DOS wildcards to search for text. An asterisk (*) matches any sequence of characters, and a question mark (?) matches any single character.

Replace_text is the text you want to use to replace find_text.

Look_at is a number. If 1, look_at specifies that you want find_text to match the entire contents of the cell. If look_at is 2 or omitted, find_text will search for any string of matching characters in a cell.

Look_by is a number that specifies whether to search horizontally or vertically through the worksheet. If look_by is 1, Excel searches by rows; if look_by is 2, Excel searches by columns.

Active_cell is a logical value. If active_cell is TRUE, find_text is replaced in the active cell only. If active_cell is FALSE or omitted, find_text will be replaced in all of the cells in the current selection or, if a single cell is selected, find_text will be replaced in the entire document.

Match_case is a logical value that, if TRUE, instructs Excel to search for exact matches including upper and lower case; if match_case is FALSE, the search is not case-sensitive.

SCENARIO.ADD

The SCENARIO.ADD function allows you to define specified values as a scenario. A scenario is a set of values that you use as input for a model on your worksheet. This function is equivalent to choosing the Scenario Manager command in the Formula menu and then clicking on Add.

Use with macro sheets only.

Syntax

```
=SCENARIO.ADD(scen_name,value_array)
```

Scen_name is the name of the scenario you wish to add and value_array is the array of values you want to use as input for the model on your worksheet. The values must be in same order as the input cells listed in Changing Cells in the Scenario Manager dialog box. If value_array is omitted, Excel assumes that it contains the current values of the input cells.

SCENARIO.CELLS

The SCENARIO.CELLS function defines the changing cells in a scenario. The changing cells are the cells you will use as input cells for the values you will enter when you display a scenario. This function is equivalent to choosing the Scenario Manager command in the Formula menu and editing the Changing Cells text box.

Use with macro sheets only.

Syntax

```
=SCENARIO.CELLS(changing_ref)
=SCENARIO.CELLS?()
```

Changing_ref are the references to the cells you want to use as input cells for the model. You can use named references or cell addresses.

SELECT.LAST.CELL

The SELECT.LAST.CELL function will select the last cell in the worksheet that contains a value, format, or formula, or that is referred to in a formula or name. This function is equivalent to choosing the Select Special command in the Formula menu and clicking the Last Cell option.

Use with macro sheets only.

Syntax

```
=SELECT.LAST.CELL()
```

SELECT.SPECIAL

The SELECT.SPECIAL function selects a group of cells whose contents match a specified category. For example, you could select all of the cells that contain notes. This function is equivalent to choosing the Select Special command in the Formula menu.

Use with macro sheets only.

Syntax

```
=SELECT.SPECIAL(type_num,value_type,levels)
=SELECT.SPECIAL?(type_num,value_type,levels)
```

Type_num is a number that specifies the category of cells you want to select:

Type_num	Category
1	Notes
2	Constants
3	Formulas
4	Blanks
5	Current region
6	Current array
7	Row differences
8	Column differences
9	Precedents
10	Dependents

Type_num	Category
11	Last cell
12	Visible cells only (applies to outlines)
13	All objects

Value_type is a number that specifies the type of formula or constant you want to select. Value_type can be used only when num_type is 2 (constants) or 3 (formulas). The following table shows which number is used to select each value_type.

Value_type	Selects
1	Numbers
2	Text
3	Logical values
4	Error values

If you want to select more that one type, you can add values. For example, to select both numbers and text, you would add 1 (the value_type for numbers) and 2 (the value_type for text), and enter a value_type of 3 for your argument. The default value_type is 23, which selects all value_types.

Levels is a number that specifies how precedents and dependents are selected. This argument can be used only when type_num is 9 or 10. A number 1 for levels selects direct only, a number 2 for levels selects all levels.

SHOW.ACTIVE.CELL

The SHOW.ACTIVE.CELL function scrolls through the active window until the active cell is displayed. If the active cell is an object, Excel will return a #VALUE! error and halt the macro. This function is equivalent to choosing the Show Active Cell command in the Formula menu.

Use with macro sheets only.

Syntax

```
=SHOW.ACTIVE.CELL()
```

The Macro Menu Functions

The following functions are the equivalent of executing Macro menu commands.

ASSIGN.TO.OBJECT

The ASSIGN.TO.OBJECT function assigns a macro to be run when a specified object is clicked with the mouse. This function is equivalent to choosing the Assign To Object command from the Macro menu.

Use with macro sheets only.

Syntax

```
=ASSIGN.TO.OBJECT(macro_ref)
=ASSIGN.TO.OBJECT?(macro_ref)
```

Macro_ref is the external reference to, or name of, the macro you want to run when the object is clicked with the mouse. If macro-ref is omitted, ASSIGN.TO.OBJECT is turned off, and the macro no longer runs when the object is clicked.

ASSIGN.TO.TOOL

The ASSIGN.TO.TOOL function assigns a macro to be run when a specified tool is clicked with the mouse. This function is equivalent to choosing the Assign To Tool command from the Macro menu.

Use with macro sheets only.

Syntax

```
=ASSIGN.TO.TOOL(bar_id,position,macro_ref)
```

Bar_id specifies the name or number of the toolbar that contains the tool to which you want to assign the macro, and position specifies the position of the tool within the toolbar. Position starts with 1 at the left (horizontal) or top (vertical) of the toolbar. Macro_ref is the external reference to, or name of, the macro you want to run when the tool is clicked with the mouse. If macro-ref is omitted, ASSIGN.TO.TOOL is turned off, and the macro no longer runs when the tool is clicked. When ASSIGN.TO.TOOL is turned off and the tool is a built-in tool, Excel will perform the default action for the tool when it is clicked. If the tool is a custom tool, Excel will display the Assign To Tool dialog box when the tool is clicked.

RESUME

The RESUME function resumes a paused macro. If a macro is not paused, the RESUME function returns a #Value! error. Inserting this function into a macro sheet is the equivalent of choosing the Resume command from the Macro menu.

Use with macro sheets only.

Syntax

=**RESUME**(type_num)

Type_num is a number from 1 to 4 specifying how to resume.

Type_num	How the macro resumes
1 or omitted	If paused by a Pause function, continues running the macro. If paused from the Single Step dialog box, returns to the dialog box.
2	Halts the paused macro. Use this option if one macro runs a second macro that pauses, and you want to halt only the paused macro. The HALT function halts all macros.
3	Continues running the macro.
4	Opens the Single Step dialog box.

RUN

The RUN function plays a macro. Inserting this command into a macro sheet is equivalent to choosing the Run command from the Macro menu.

Use with macro sheets only.

Syntax

=**RUN**(reference,step)
=**RUN?**(reference,step)

Reference is a reference to the macro you want to run or a number from 1 to 4 specifying an Auto macro to run. If reference is a range, the Run function begins with the macro function in the upper-left cell of reference. Reference can be an external reference to a macro not in the active document. If reference is omitted, the macro function in the active cell is carried out.

If reference is	The macro specified is
1	All Auto_Open macros
2	All Auto_Close macros
3	All Auto_Activate macros
4	All Auto_Deactivate macros

Step is a logical value specifying whether the macro is to be run in single-step mode. If step is TRUE, the macro is run in single-step mode. If step is FALSE or omitted, the macro is run normally.

The Options Menu Functions

The following functions are the equivalent of executing Options menu commands or tools.

CALCULATE.DOCUMENT

The CALCULATE.DOCUMENT function calculates the active document. Inserting this macro into a macro sheet is equivalent to choosing the Calculation command from the Options menu and then choosing the Calc Document button. If the active document is a chart, the function returns the #Value! error.

Use with macro sheets only.

Syntax

```
=(CALCULATE.DOCUMENT())
```

CALCULATE.NOW

The CALCULATE.NOW function calculates all open documents. Inserting this function into a macro sheet is equivalent to choosing the Calculation command from the Options menu and then choosing the Calc Now button.

Use with macro sheets only.

Syntax

```
=CALCULATE.NOW()
```

CALCULATION

The CALCULATION function determines when and how open documents are calculated. Inserting this function into a macro sheet is equivalent to choosing the Calculation command from the Options menu. The arguments correspond to check boxes and options in the Calculation dialog box. Arguments that correspond to check boxes are logical values. If an argument is TRUE, the box is selected. If an argument is FALSE, the box is cleared.

Use with macro sheets only.

Syntax

=CALCULATION(**type_num,**iter,max_num,max_change,update,precision,
date_1904,calc_save,save_values,alt_exp,alt_form)

=CALCULATION?(type_num,iter,max_num,max_change,update,precision,
date_1904,calc_save,save_values,alt_exp,alt_form)

Type_num is a number from 1 to 3 indicating the type of calculation.

Type_num	Type of calculation
1	Automatic
2	Automatic except tables
3	Manual

Iter corresponds to the Iteration check box; default is FALSE.

Max_num is the maximum number of iterations; default is 100.

Max_change is the maximum change of each iteration; default is 0.001.

Update corresponds to the Update Remote Reference check box; default is TRUE.

Precision corresponds to the Precision As Displayed check box; default is FALSE.

Date_1904 corresponds to the 1904 Date System check box; default is FALSE.

Calc_save corresponds to the Recalculate Before Save check box; default is TRUE.

Save_values corresponds to the Save External Link Values check box; default is TRUE.

Alt_exp corresponds to the Alternate Expression Evaluation check box.

Alt_form corresponds to the Alternate Formula Entry check box.

COLOR.PALETTE

The COLOR.PALETTE function copies a color palette from an open document to the active document. Inserting this function into a macro sheet is equivalent to choosing the Color Palette command from the Options menu and then choosing a file from the Copy Colors From box in the Color Palette dialog box.

Use with macro sheets only.

Syntax

```
=COLOR.PALETTE(file_text)
=COLOR.PALETTE?(file_text)
```

File_text is the name of a document, in a text string, from which you want to copy a color palette. If the document is not open, a #Value! error is returned and the macro is interrupted.

PRECISION

The PRECISION function controls how values are stored in cells. Inserting this macro into a macro sheet is equivalent to choosing the Calculation command from the Options menu and selecting or clearing the Precision As Displayed check box in the Calculation dialog box.

Use with macro sheets only.

Syntax

```
=PRECISON(logical)
```

Logical is a logical value corresponding to the Precision as Displayed check box. If logical is TRUE, the box is selected and future entries are stored at full precision (15 digits). If logical is FALSE or omitted, the values are stored as they are displayed.

EDIT.COLOR

The EDIT.COLOR function defines the color for one of the sixteen color palette boxes. Inserting this function into a macro sheet is equivalent to choosing the Color Palette command from the Options menu, and then selecting the Edit button in the dialog box. Your monitor and video card must be capable of supporting the color you select.

Use with macro sheets only.

Syntax

```
=EDIT.COLOR(color_num,red_value,green_value,blue_value)
=EDIT.COLOR?(color_num)
```

Color_num is a number from 1 to 16 specifying one of the sixteen color palette boxes for which you want to set the color.

Red_value, green_value, and blue_value are numbers from 0 to 255, specifying how much red, green, and blue are in each color. If all color values are set to 255, the resulting color is white. If all color values are set to 0, the resulting color is black.

DISPLAY

There are two syntax forms for the DISPLAY function. Syntax 1 determines whether formulas, gridlines, row and column headings, and other screen attributes are displayed. Inserting this function into a macro sheet is equivalent to selecting options and check boxes in the Display dialog box in the Options menu.

Syntax 2 determines which commands on the Info window are in effect. Inserting this function into a macro sheet is equivalent to choosing commands from the Info menu.

Use with macro sheets only.

Syntax 1

```
=DISPLAY(formulas,gridlines,headings,zeros,color_num,outline,
page_breaks,object_mum)
=DISPLAY?(formulas,gridlines,headings,zeros,color_num,outline,
page_breaks,object_mum)
```

Formulas corresponds to the Formulas check box.

Gridlines corresponds to the Gridlines check box.

Headings corresponds to the Row & Column Headings check box.

Zeros corresponds to the Zero Values check box.

Color_num is a number from 0 to 16 that corresponds to the gridline and heading colors in the Display dialog box.

Outline corresponds to the Outline Symbols check box.

Page_breaks corresponds to the Automatic Page Breaks check box.

Object_num is a number from 1 to 3 that corresponds to the display options in the Object box. The following table shows the object_num and its corresponding value.

Object_num	Corresponds to
1 or omitted	Show all
2	Show placeholders
3	Hide

Syntax 2

```
=DISPLAY(cell,formula,value,format,protection,names,precedents,
dependents,note)
```

The arguments correspond to commands on the Info menu with the same names. All of the arguments except precedents and dependents are logical values.

Precedents is a number from 0 to 2 that specifies which precedents to list and dependents is a number from 0 to 2 that specifies which dependents to list. The following table shows the precedent or dependent number and what is listed.

Precedents or dependents	List
0	None
1	Direct only
2	All levels

WORKGROUP

The WORKGROUP function creates a group. Inserting this function into a macro sheet is equivalent to choosing the Group Edit command from the Options menu.

Use with macro sheets only.

Syntax

```
=WORKGROUP(name_array)
=WORKGROUP?(name_array)
```

Name-array is a list of open, unhidden worksheets and macro sheets, as text, that you want to include in a group. Charts cannot be part of a group.

PROTECT.DOCUMENT

The PROTECT.DOCUMENT adds or removes protection from an active worksheet, macro sheet, workbook, or chart. Inserting this command into a macro sheet is equivalent to choosing Protect Document and Unprotect Document from the Options or Chart menu.

Use with macro sheets only.

Syntax

```
=(PROTECT.DOCUMENT(contents,windows,password,objects)
=(PROTECT.DOCUMENT?(contents,windows,password,objects)
```

Contents is a logical value corresponding to the Cells check box (worksheets or macro sheets), the Chart check box (charts), or the Contents check box (workbooks). If the argument is TRUE, the box is selected. If the argument is FALSE, the box is cleared.

Windows is a logical value that corresponds to the Windows check box in the Protect Document dialog box. If the argument is TRUE, the box is selected. If the argument is FALSE, the box is cleared.

Password is specified as text.

Objects is a logical value applying only to worksheets and macro sheets. This argument corresponds to the Objects check box in the Protect Document dialog box. If the argument is TRUE, the box is selected. If the argument is FALSE, the box is cleared.

REMOVE.PAGE.BREAK

The REMOVE.PAGE.BREAK removes manual page breaks. Inserting this function into a macro sheet is equivalent to choosing the Remove Page Break command from the Options menu.

Use with macro sheets only.

Syntax

```
=REMOVE.PAGE.BREAK()
```

SET.PAGE.BREAK

The SET.PAGE.BREAK function sets manual page breaks in a worksheet. Inserting this function into a macro sheet is equivalent to choosing the Set Page Break command from the Options menu.

Use with macro sheets only.

Syntax

```
=SET.PAGE.BREAK()
```

SET.PRINT.AREA

The SET.PRINT.AREA function determines the area that is printed when you print the document. Inserting this function into a macro sheet is equivalent to choosing the Set Print Areas command from the Options menu.

Use with macro sheets only.

Syntax

```
=SET.PRINT.AREA()
```

SET.PRINT.TITLES

The SET.PRINT.TITLES function determines whether titles for rows or columns are printed. Inserting this function into a macro sheet is equivalent to choosing the Set Print Titles command from the Options menu.

Use with macro sheets only.

Syntax

```
=SET.PRINT.TITLES(titles_for_columns_ref,titles_for_rows_ref)
=SET.PRINT.TITLES?(titles_for_columns_ref,titles_for_rows_ref)
```

Titles_for_columns_ref is a reference to the row to be used as a title for columns.

Titles_for_rows_ref is a reference to the column to be used as a title for rows.

SPELLING

The SPELLING function checks the spelling of words. Inserting this command into a macro sheet is equivalent to choosing the Spelling command from the Options menu.

Use with macro sheets only.

Syntax

`=SPELLING(custom_dic,ignore_uppercase,always_suggest)`

Custom_dic is the filename of the custom dictionary to be used (if necessary).

Ignore_uppercase is a logical value that corresponds to the Ignore Words In Uppercase check box. If the argument is TRUE, the box is selected. If the argument is FALSE, the box is cleared.

Always_suggest is a logical value that corresponds to the Always Suggest check box. If the argument is TRUE, the box is selected. If the argument is FALSE, the box is cleared.

SHOW.TOOLBAR

The SHOW.TOOLBAR function hides or displays a toolbar. Inserting this function into a macro sheet is equivalent to choosing the Show Toolbars button or Hide Toolbars button in the Toolbars dialog box.

Use with macro sheets only.

Syntax

`=SHOW.TOOLBAR(bar_id,visible,dock,x_pos,y_pos,width)`

Bar_id is the number or name of the toolbar(s) you want to display.

Visible is a logical value that specifies whether the toolbar is visible or hidden. If the argument is TRUE, the toolbar is visible. If the argument is FALSE, the toolbar is hidden.

Dock is a number from 1 to 5 that specifies the docking location of the toolbar. The following table shows the dock numbers and their corresponding positions.

Dock	Position of toolbar
1	Top of workspace
2	Left edge of workspace
3	Right edge of workspace
4	Bottom of workspace
5	Floating (not docked)

X_pos specifies the horizontal position, measured in points, of the toolbar. A point equals 1/72 of an inch. In a docked toolbar, x_pos is measured horizontally from the left edge of the toolbar to the left edge of the docking area. In a floating toolbar, x_pos is measured horizontally from the left edge of the toolbar to the right edge of the right-most toolbar in the left docking area.

Y_pos specifies the vertical position, measured in points, of the toolbar. In a docked toolbar, y_pos is measured vertically from the top edge of the toolbar to the top edge of the toolbar's docking area. In a floating toolbar, y_pos is measured vertically from the top edge of the toolbar to the top edge of the workspace.

SHOW.INFO

The SHOW.INFO function determines the display of the Info window. Inserting this function in a macro sheet is equivalent to choosing the Workspace command from the Options menu and then selecting the Info Window check box.

Use with macro sheets only.

Syntax

```
=SHOW.INFO(logical)
```

Logical is a logical value that controls the display of the Info window. If the argument is TRUE, Excel switches to the Info window. If the argument is FALSE, and the current window is the Info window, Excel switches to the document linked to the Info window.

WORKSPACE

The WORKSPACE function changes the workspace settings in a document. Inserting this function into a macro sheet is equivalent to choosing the Workspace command from the Options menu.

Use with macro sheets only.

Syntax

=**WORKSPACE**(fixed,decimals,r1c1,scroll,status,formula,menu_key,remote,
entermove,tools,notes,nav_keys,menu_key_action,drag_drop,show_info)
=**WORKSPACE?**(fixed,decimals,r1c1,scroll,status,formula,menu_key,remote,
entermove,tools,notes,nav_keys,menu_key_action,drag_drop,show_info)

Arguments correspond to check boxes and text boxes in the Workspace dialog box. Where arguments correspond to check boxes, they are logical values. If the argument is TRUE, the box is selected. If the argument is FALSE, the box is cleared.

Fixed is a logical value that corresponds to the Fixed Decimal check box.

Decimals specifies the number of decimal places. This argument is ignored if Fixed is FALSE or omitted.

R1C1 is a logical value that corresponds to the R1C1 check box.

Scroll is a logical value that corresponds to the Scroll Bars check box.

Status is a logical value that corresponds to the Status Bar check box.

Formula is a logical value that corresponds to the Formula Bar check box.

Menu_key is a text value that indicates an alternate menu key. This argument corresponds to the Alternate Menu Or Help Key box.

Remote is a logical value that corresponds to the Ignore Remote Requests check box.

Entermove is a logical value that corresponds to the Move Selection After Enter/Return check box.

Tools is a logical value. If the argument is TRUE, the Standard toolbar is displayed. If the argument is FALSE, all toolbars are hidden.

Notes is a logical value that corresponds to the Note Indicator check box.

Nav_keys is a logical value that corresponds to the Alternate Navigation Keys check box.

Menu_key_action is the number 1 or 2 that specifies options for the alternate menu or Help key. If menu_key_action is 1, the Excel menus are activated. If menu_key_action is 2, the Lotus 1-2-3 Help menu is activated.

The Window Menu Functions

The following functions are the equivalent of executing Window menu commands or tools.

ARRANGE.ALL

The ARRANGE.ALL function rearranges and resizes all of the open windows and rearranges icons. Inserting this function into a macro sheet is equivalent to choosing the Arrange command from the Windows menu. This function also synchronizes the scrolling of windows in the active document.

Use with macro sheets only.

Syntax

```
=ARRANGE.ALL(arrange_num,active_doc,sync_horiz,sync_vert)
=ARRANGE.ALL(arrange_num,active_doc,sync_horiz,sync_vert)
```

Arrange_num is a number from 1 to 6 specifying how you want the windows to be arranged as shown in the following table.

Arrange_num	Result
1 or omitted	Tiled (also used to arrange icons)
2	Horizontal
3	Vertical
4	None
5	Horizontally arranges and sizes the windows based on the position of the active cell
6	Vertically arranges and sizes the windows based on the position of the active cell

Active_doc is a logical value. If active_doc is TRUE, Excel arranges windows only on the active document. If active_doc is FALSE, Excel arranges all of the open windows.

Sync_horiz is a logical value, and can only be used if active_doc has a logical value of TRUE. If sync_horiz is TRUE, Excel synchronizes horizontal scrolling. If sync_horiz is FALSE, the windows will not be synchronized when you scroll horizontally.

Sync_vert is a logical value and can be used only if active_doc has a logical value of TRUE. If sync_vert is TRUE, Excel synchronizes vertical scrolling. If sync_vert is FALSE, the windows will not be synchronized when you scroll vertically.

HIDE

The HIDE function hides the active window. This function is equivalent to choosing the Hide command from the Windows menu.

Use with macro sheets only.

Syntax

    =HIDE()

FREEZE.PANES

The FREEZE.PANES function is used to split the active window into panes and create frozen panes, or to freeze or unfreeze existing panes. This is equivalent to choosing the Freeze Panes command from the Window menu.

Use with macro sheets only.

Syntax

    =FREEZE.PANES()
    =FREEZE.PANES(logical,col_split,row_split)

When the function is used without any arguments, the active window will be split into panes above and to the left of the active cell, then the panes will be frozen.

When the function is used with arguments, logical is a logical value that, if TRUE, freezes panes if they exist. If no panes exist, the argument will create panes, split them at the specified position, and freeze them. If the panes are already frozen, the function is ignored.

If logical is FALSE, the panes are unfrozen. If no panes exist, the function is ignored.

If logical is omitted, the function creates and then freezes panes. If no panes exist, the function freezes any existing panes if they are not currently frozen, or unfreezes existing if they are currently frozen.

Col_split indicates the location at which to split the window vertically and is measured in columns from the left of the window.

Row_split indicates the location at which to split the window horizontally, and is measured in rows from the top of the window. Col_split and row_split are ignored unless the value of logical is TRUE and split panes do not already exist.

NEW.WINDOW

The NEW.WINDOW function creates a new window for an active worksheet or macro sheet. This function is equivalent to choosing the New Window command on the Window menu.

Use with macro sheets only.

Syntax

```
=NEW.WINDOW()
```

SHOW.CLIPBOARD

The SHOW.CLIPBOARD function displays the contents of the clipboard in a new window if the clipboard is already available on the desktop. If the clipboard is not already available, you must use the SHOW.CLIPBOARD function twice—the first time to make the clipboard available, and the second time to display the contents of the clipboard.

Syntax

```
=SHOW.CLIPBOARD()
```

SPLIT

The SPLIT function splits the active window into panes, allowing you to view different sections of the active document simultaneously. This function is equivalent to choosing the Split command from the Window menu.

Use with macro sheets only.

Syntax

```
=SPLIT(col_split,row_split)
```

Col_split indicates the location to split the window vertically, and is measured in columns from the left of the window. To remove a vertical split, use a value of 0 for the col_split argument.

Row_split indicates the location at which to split the window horizontally, and is measured in rows from the top of the window. To remove a horizontal split, use a value of 0 for the row_split argument.

UNHIDE

The UNHIDE function displays hidden windows. This function is equivalent to choosing the Unhide command from the Window menu.

Use with macro sheets only.

Syntax

```
=UNHIDE(window_text)
```

Window_text is the name of the window to unhide. If the window_text argument is used and the window you want to unhide is not open, you will receive an error message and the macro will be halted.

VIEW.SHOW

The VIEW.SHOW function shows a view. It is equivalent to selecting a view and choosing Show in the Views dialog box from the View command in the Window menu.

Use with macro sheets only.

Syntax

```
=VIEW.SHOW(view_name)
=VIEW.SHOW?(view_name)
```

View_name spacifies the name of a view in the active document. The argument must be text enclosed in quotation marks.

ZOOM

The ZOOM function enlarges or reduces a document in the active window. This function is equivalent to choosing the Zoom command from the Window menu.

Use with macro sheets only.

Syntax

`=ZOOM`(magnification)

Magnification is either a logical value or a number that specifies the size of the document. If magnification is TRUE or omitted, the current selection is enlarged or reduced to completely fill the active window. If magnification is FALSE, the document is restored to normal size. If you use a number value for magnification, you can specify the percentage of enlargement or reduction by any number from 10 to 400.

The Command Functions

These functions are used in macros to execute commands that are not necessarily available in a menu.

A1.R1C1

The A1.R1C1 function specifies whether the row and column headings will be displayed in the A1 style reference or in the R1C1 style reference.

Use with macro sheets only.

Syntax

`=A1.R1C1`(logical)

Logical is a logical value. If it is TRUE, all worksheets and macros sheets use the A1 style of reference; if it is FALSE, all worksheets and macros sheets use the R1C1 style of reference.

ACTIVATE

The ACTIVE function switches to a different window if more than one window is open, or to a different pane if the window is split.

Use with macro sheets only.

Syntax

`=ACTIVATE`(window_text,pane_num)

Window_text is text enclosed in parentheses that specifies the name of the window to which you want to switch. If a document is displayed in more than one window and window_text does not specify which window to switch to, Excel will switch to the first window that contains the document. If a document is not displayed in more than one window, and window_text is omitted, the active window will not be changed.

Pane_num is a number indicating which pane to switch to. If pane_num is omitted and the document has more than one pane, the active pane will not be changed. The following table lists the numbers available in pane_num and the pane that each number activates.

Pane_num	Activate
1	Activates the upper-left pane. If the window is not split, this is the only existing pane. If the window is split horizontally, this is the upper pane. If the window is split vertically, this is the left pane.
2	Activates the upper-right pane. If the window is split only vertically, this is the right pane. If the window is split only horizontally, an error occurs.
3	Activates the lower-left pane. If the window is split only horizontally, this is the lower pane. If the window is split only vertically, an error occurs.
4	Activates the lower-right pane. If the window is split in only two panes, either horizontally or vertically, an error occurs.

ACTIVATE.NEXT

The ACTIVATE.NEXT function switches to the next window, or to the next document in a workbook.

Use with macro sheets only.

Syntax

```
=ACTIVATE.NEXT()
=ACTIVATE.NEXT(workbook_text)
```

When the first example is used, Excel switches to the next window (this is equivalent to pressing Ctrl+F6).

When the workbook_text argument is used, Excel switches to the next document in the workbook specified by the workbook_text argument. The workbook_text argument is the name of the workbook for which you want to activate a window.

ACTIVATE.PREVIOUS

The ACTIVATE.PREVIOUS function switches to the previous window, or switches to the previous document in a workbook.

Use with macro sheets only.

Syntax

```
=ACTIVATE.PREVIOUS()
=ACTIVATE.PREVIOUS(workbook_text)
```

When the first example is used, Excel switches to the previous window (this is equivalent to pressing Ctrl+Shift+F6).

When the workbook_text argument is used, Excel switches to the previous document in the workbook specified by the workbook_text argument. The workbook_text argument is the name of the workbook for which you want to activate a window.

CANCEL.COPY

The CANCEL.COPY function is equivalent to pressing Esc after you cut or copy a selection.

Use with macro sheets only.

Syntax

```
=CANCEL.COPY(render_logical)
```

Render_logical is a logical value that, if TRUE, places the contents of the Excel Clipboard on the clipboard. If the logical value is FALSE, the contents are not placed on the clipboard.

CHART.WIZARD

The CHART.WIZARD function formats a chart. This is equivalent to choosing the ChartWizard tool on either the standard or Chart toolbar.

Use with macro sheets only.

Syntax

=**CHART.WIZARD**(long,**ref**,gallery_num,type_num,plot_by,categories,
ser_titles,legend,title,x_title,y_title,z_title)
=**CHART.WIZARD?**(long,**ref**,gallery_num,type_num,plot_by,categories,
ser_titles,legend,title,x_title,y_title,z_title)

Long is a logical value that determines the type of ChartWizard tool to which the CHART.WIZARD function is equivalent. If long is TRUE or omitted, CHART.WIZARD is equivalent to using the five-step ChartWizard tool. If long is FALSE, CHART.WIZARD is equivalent to using the two-step ChartWizard tool, and gallery_num, type_num, legend, title, x_title, y_title, and z_title are ignored.

Ref is a reference to the cells on the active worksheet containing the source data for the chart, or, if the chart has already been created, the object identities of the chart.

Gallery_num is a number from 1 to 14 that specifies the type of chart you want to create, as shown in the following table:

Gallery_num	Chart
1	Area
2	Bar
3	Column
4	Line
5	Pie
6	Radar
7	XY (Scatter)
8	Combination
9	3-D area
10	3-D bar
11	3-D column
12	3-D line
13	3-D pie
14	3-D surface

Type_num specifies the formatting option you want to use, and corresponds to the options shown in the dialog box of the Gallery command. The options begin with the number 1.

Plot_by is either 1 or 2, and determines whether the data of each data series is in rows or columns. If the argument is 1, the data series is in rows; if the number is 2, it is in columns. If plot_by is omitted, Excel will use an appropriate value for the chart that is being created.

Categories is either 1 or 2, and determines whether the first row or column contains a list of x_axis labels, or data for the first data series. The value 1 specifies x_axis labels, and 2 specifies the first data series. If categories is omitted, Excel uses the appropriate value for the chart that is being created.

Ser_titles is either 1 or 2, and determines whether the first row or column contains series titles or data for the first data point in each series. The value 1 specifies series titles, and 2 specifies the first data point. If ser_titles is omitted, Excel uses the appropriate value for the chart that is being created.

Legend is either 1 or 2, and specifies whether to include a legend in the chart. If the value is 1, a legend is included; if it is 2 or omitted, there will be no legend.

Title specifies the text that you want to use as a chart title. If this argument is omitted, no title is specified.

X_title specifies the text that you want to use as an x_axis title. If this argument is omitted, no title is specified.

Y_title specifies the text that you want to use as a y_axis title. If this argument is omitted, no title is specified.

Z_title specifies the text that you want to use as a z_axis title. If this argument is omitted, no title is specified.

CREATE.DIRECTORY

The CREATE.DIRECTORY function creates a directory or folder. You must load FILEFNS.XLA from the Library directory for this function to be available.

Use with macro sheets only.

Syntax

```
=CREATE.DIRECTORY(path_text)
```

Path_text is the name of the directory or folder you want to create inside the current directory or folder, or the complete path location and name for a new directory or folder.

CREATE.OBJECT

The CREATE.OBECT function draws an object on a worksheet or macro sheet, and returns a value identifying the object created.

Use with macro sheets only.

Syntax 1

For lines, rectangles, ovals, arcs, pictures, text boxes, and buttons.

```
=CREATE.OBJECT(obj_type,ref1,x_offset1,y_offset1,ref2,x_offset2,
y_offset2,text,fill)
```

Syntax 2

For polygons.

```
=CREATE.OBJECT(obj_type,ref1,x_offset1,y_offset1,ref2,x_offset2,
y_offset2,array,fill)
```

Syntax 3

For embedded charts.

```
=CREATE.OBJECT(obj_type,ref1,x_offset1,y_offset1,ref2,x_offset2,
y_offset2,xy_series,fill,gallery_num,type_num)
```

Obj_type is a number from 1 to 10 that specifies the type of object you want to create, as shown in the following table.

Obj_type	Object
1	Line
2	Rectangle
3	Oval
4	Arc
5	Embedded chart
6	Text box
7	Button
8	Picture (created with the camera tool)
9	Closed polygon
10	Open polygon

If you want to create a chart or a picture, you must use the COPY function before the CREATE.OBJECT function.

Ref1 is a reference to the column from which the upper-left corner of the object is drawn, or from which the upper-left corner of the object's bounding rectangle is defined.

X-offset1 is the horizontal distance from the upper-left corner of the object or the upper-left corner of the object's bounding rectangle, to the mouse pointer. X_offset1 is measured in points. Each point is 1/72 of an inch. If x_offset1 is omitted, it is assumed to be 0.

Y_offset1 is the vertical distance from the upper-left corner of ref1 to the upper-left corner of the object or the object's bounding rectangle, to the mouse pointer. It is also measured in points. If y_offset1 is omitted, it is assumed to be 0.

Ref2 is a reference to the cell from which the lower-right corner of the object is drawn, or from which the lower-right corner of the object's bounding rectangle is defined. If offsets are not defined, the object will be drawn from the upper-left corner of ref2 to the upper-left corner of ref2.

X-offset2 is the horizontal distance from the upper-left corner of the object, or the upper-left corner of the object's bounding rectangle, to the mouse pointer. X_offset2 is measured in points. Each point is 1/72 of an inch. If x_offset2 is omitted, it is assumed to be 0.

Y_offset2 is the vertical distance from the upper-left corner of ref2 to the upper-left corner of the object or the object's bounding rectangle, to the mouse pointer. It is also measured in points. If y_offset2 is omitted, it is assumed to be 0.

Text specifies the text that will appear in a text box or button. If object_type is 7 and text is omitted, the button will be named *Button n*, where *n* is a number. If object_type is not 6 or 7, text is ignored.

Fill is a logical value. If fill is TRUE, the object is filled. If fill is FALSE, the object is transparent. If fill is omitted, the object is filled with an applicable pattern for the object that is being created.

Array is a reference to a range of cells that contain values or an *n*-by-2 array of values, that indicate the position of each vertex (a point that is defined by a pair of coordinates in one row of the argument array) in a polygon relative to the upper-left corner of the polygon's bounding rectangle. If the number of characters in the formula is greater than 1,024, you must use the EXTEND.POLYGON function listed later in this chapter.

Xy_series is a number from 0 to 3 that specifies how data is arranged in a chart and corresponds to the options in the First Row/Column Contains dialog box. If the number is 0, a dialog box is displayed if the selection is ambiguous; if the number is 1 or omitted, the first row/column is the data series; if the number is 2, the first row/column contains the category (x) axis labels; and if the number is 3, the first row/column contains the x-values and the created chart is an xy (scatter) chart. This argument is ignored unless the object_type is 5.

Gallery_num is a number from 1 to 14 that specifies the type of embedded chart you want to create.

Gallery_num	Chart
1	Area
2	Bar
3	Column
4	Line
5	Pie
6	Radar
7	XY (Scatter)
8	Combination
9	3-D area
10	3-D bar
11	3-D column
12	3-D line
13	3-D pie
14	3-D surface

Type_num is a number that specifies the formatting option for a chart and corresponds to the formatting options in the dialog box of the Gallery command. The first formatting option is 1.

CUSTOMIZE.TOOLBAR?

The CUSTOMIZE.TOOLBAR? function displays the Customize Toolbar dialog box. This function is equivalent to choosing the Toolbars command from the Options menu and then choosing Customize.

Use with macro sheets only.

Syntax

`=CUSTOMIZE.TOOLBAR?`(category)

Category is a number from 1 to 10 that specifies which category of tools you want to display in the dialog box. If this argument is omitted, the previous setting is used.

Category	Category of tools
1	File
2	Edit
3	Formula
4	Formatting (non-text)
5	Text formatting
6	Drawing
7	Macro
8	Charting
9	Utility
10	Custom

DELETE.DIRECTORY

The DELETE.DIRECTORY function deletes an empty directory or folder. If the directory or folder you wish to delete is not empty, the function returns a value of FALSE. You must load FILEFNS.ZLA from the Library directory in order to use this function.

Use with macro sheets only.

Syntax

```
=DELETE.DIRECTORY(path_text)
```

Path_text is the name of the directory or folder in the current directory or folder you want to delete, or the full path of the directory or folder you want to delete.

DELETE.FORMAT

The DELETE.FORMAT function deletes a specified custom number format. This function is equivalent to deleting the format using the Number command from the Format menu.

Use with macro sheets only.

Syntax

```
=DELETE.FORMAT(format_text)
```

Format_text is the custom format given as a text string enclosed in quotation marks.

DEMOTE

The DEMOTE function demotes the selected rows or columns in an outline. This function is equivalent to clicking the Demote button while in an outline.

Use with macro sheets only.

Syntax

```
=DEMOTE(row_col)
=DEMOTE?(row_col)
```

Row_col is a 1 or a 2. If the value is 1 or omitted, rows are demoted. If the value is 2, columns are demoted. If the selection consists of an entire row or rows, then rows are demoted even if the value of row_col is 2. If the selection consists of an entire column or columns, then columns are demoted even if the value of row_col is 1.

DUPLICATE

The DUPLICATE function duplicates a selected object. If an object is not selected, the function returns an error value and the macro is interrupted.

Use with macro sheets only.

Syntax

```
=DUPLICATE()
```

EXTEND.POLYGON

The EXTEND.POLYGON function adds vertices to a polygon. A vertex is a point on a polygon that is defined by a pair of coordinates in one row of the array argument. This function must immediately follow a CREATE.OBJECT or EXTEND.POLYGON function.

Use with macro sheets only.

Syntax

```
=EXTEND.POLYGON(array)
```

Array is an array of values, or a reference to a range of cells that contain values, that indicate the position of vertices in the polygon.

FILL.AUTO

The FILL.AUTO function copies a range of cells or automatically fills a selection.

Use with macro sheets only.

Syntax

```
=FILL.AUTO(destination_ref,copy_only)
```

Destination_ref is the range of cells into which you want to copy or fill the data.

Copy_only is a logical value that, if TRUE, copies the current selection in the destination_ref. If copy_only is FALSE or omitted, Excel automatically fills the cells in destination_ref based on the size and contents of the current selection.

FORMAT.AUTO

The FORMAT.AUTO function formats the selected range of cells using the built-in gallery of formats. This function is equivalent to choosing the AutoFormat command from the Format menu or of clicking the AutoFormat tool.

Use with macro sheets only.

Syntax

```
=FORMAT.AUTO(format_num,number,font,alignment,border,pattern,width)
=FORMAT.AUTO?(format_num,number,font,alignment,border,pattern,width)
```

Format_num is a number that corresponds to the formats in the Table Format list box in the AutoFormat dialog box. If format_num is omitted, the number defaults to 1.

The rest of the arguments are logical values that correspond to the Formats To Apply check boxes in the AutoFormat dialog box. If the argument is TRUE or omitted, the check box is selected; if the argument is FALSE, the check box is cleared.

Number corresponds to the Number check box; font corresponds to the Font check box; alignment corresponds to the Alignment check box; border corresponds to the Border check box; pattern corresponds to the Pattern check box; width corresponds to the Column Width/Row Height check box.

FORMAT.SHAPE

The FORMAT.SHAPE function is used to move, insert, or delete a vertex in a selected polygon. The function is equivalent to clicking the Reshape tool on the Drawing toolbar.

Use with macro sheets only.

Syntax

```
=FORMAT.SHAPE(vertex_num,insert,reference,x_offset,y_offset)
```

Vertex_num is a number that corresponds to the vertex you want to modify.

Insert is a logical value that specifies whether to move, insert, or delete a vertex in the selected polygon. If the value is TRUE, Excel inserts a vertex before the vertex_num. The vertex_num identified in FORMAT.SHAPE becomes vertex_num+1, and all vertex_nums are increased accordingly. If the value is FALSE, Excel deletes the vertex identified by vertex_num if the remaining arguments are omitted, or Excel moves the vertex to the location specified by the remaining arguments.

Reference refers to the range of cells that contain the vertex you are inserting or moving, and serves as the basis of the x and y offsets.

X_offset is the horizontal distance from the upper-left corner of the reference to the vertex, and is measured in points.

Y_offset is the vertical distance from the upper-left corner of the reference to the vertex, and is measured in points.

FORMULA

The FORMULA function is used to enter a formula in the active cell or in a reference.

Syntax 1

Use with worksheets and macro sheets.

```
=FORMULA(formula_text,reference)
```

Formula_text is a number, a reference, text (which must be enclosed in quotation marks), a formula in the form of text, or a reference to a cell that contains any of the above.

Reference specifies where formula_text is to be entered in the worksheet or macro, and can be a reference to a cell in the active worksheet or an external reference. If reference is omitted, the active cell is selected.

Syntax 2

Use with charts.

```
=FORMULA(formula_text)
```

Formula_text is the text label or series formula you wish to enter in the chart, as shown in the following table.

If	Then
Formula_text can be treated as a text label and the current selection is a text label.	The selected text label is replaced with formula_text.
Formula_text can be treated as a text label and there is no current selection, or the current selection is not a text label.	Formula_text creates a new text label.
Formula_text can be treated as a series formula and the current selection is a series formula.	The selected series formula is replaced with formula_text.
Formula_text can be treated as a series formula and the current selection is not a series formula.	Formula_text creates a new series formula.

FORMULA.ARRAY

The FORMULA.ARRAY function enters an array formula in the referenced range or current selection. This function is equivalent to pressing Ctrl+Shift+Enter.

Use with macro sheets only.

Syntax

```
=FORMULA.ARRAY(formula_text,reference)
```

Formula_text is a number, a reference, text (which must be enclosed in quotation marks), a formula in the form of text, or a reference to a cell that contains any of the above.

Reference specifies where formula_text is to be entered in the worksheet or macro sheet, and can be a reference to a cell in the active worksheet or an external reference. If reference is omitted, the active cell is selected.

FORMULA.FILL

The FORMULA.FILL function will enter a formula in the current selection or in a referenced range.

Use with macro sheets only.

Syntax

    =FORMULA.FILL(formula_text,reference)

Formula_text is a number, a reference, text (which must be enclosed in quotation marks), a formula in the form of text, or a reference to a cell that contains any of the above.

Reference specifies where formula_text is to be entered in the worksheet or macro, and can be a reference to a cell in the active worksheet or an external reference. If reference is omitted, the active cell is selected.

HIDE.OBJECT

The HIDE.OBJECT function is used to hide or display a specified object.

Use with macro sheets only.

Syntax

    =HIDE.OBJECT(object_id_text,hide)

Object_id_text is the number or name and number of the object (in text form enclosed in quotation marks) that appears in the reference area when the object is selected. The name of the object is the text returned by CREATE.OBJECT, so you can also use a reference to the cell that contains CREATE.OBJECT. If object_id_text is omitted, HIDE.OBJECT operates on all selected objects. If no object is selected, or if the selected object does not exist, HIDE.OBJECT returns an error value.

Hide is a logical value that, if TRUE or omitted, hides the object. If hide is FALSE, the object is displayed.

HLINE

The HLINE function scrolls horizontally through the active window by a specified number of columns.

Use with macro sheets only.

Syntax

    =HLINE(num_columns)

Num_columns is a number between –256 and 256 that specifies the number of columns through which you want to scroll. If num_columns is a positive number, HLINE scrolls to the right. If num_columns is a negative number, HLINE scrolls to the left.

HPAGE

The HPAGE function is used to change the displayed area of a worksheet or macro sheet. The function scrolls horizontally through the active window one pane at a time.

Use with macro sheets only.

Syntax

    =HPAGE(num_windows)

Num_windows specifies the number of windows to scroll through the active document. If num_windows is a positive number, HPAGE scrolls to the right. If num_windows is a negative number, HPAGE scrolls to the left.

HSCROLL

The HSCROLL function scrolls horizontally through the active document either by specifying a column number (starting with column A as number 1) or by percentage.

Use with macro sheets only.

Syntax

```
=HSCROLL(position, col_logical)
```

Position specifies the column to which you want to scroll. Position can be either the column number or a percentage that represents the horizontal position of the column in the active document. If position is 0, HSCROLL will scroll through the document to the furthest column on the left; if position is 1, HSCROLL will scroll through the document to the furthest column on the right.

Col_logical is a logical value that, if TRUE, scrolls through to the document to the designated column position. If FALSE, col_logical scrolls through the document to the horizontal position represented by a percentage.

PROMOTE

The PROMOTE function changes an outline by promoting rows or columns. This function is equivalent to clicking the promote button while in an outline.

Use with macro sheets only.

Syntax

```
=PROMOTE(rowcol)
=PROMOTE?(rowcol)
```

Row_col is a 1 or 2. If the value is 1 or omitted, rows are promoted. If the value is 2, columns are promoted. If the selection consists of an entire row or rows, then rows are promoted even if the value of row_col is 2. If the selection consists of an entire column or columns, then columns are promoted even if the value of row_col is 1.

REPORT.DEFINE

The REPORT.DEFINE function creates or replaces a report definition in the active document. This function is equivalent to choosing the Print Report command from the File menu and then choosing the Add option. This function is used in conjunction with the Reports add-in macro.

Use with macro sheets only.

Syntax

```
=REPORT.DEFINE(report_name,views_scenario_array,pages_logical)
```

Report_name specifies the name of the report.

Views_scenario_array is an array that contains one or more rows of the scenario and view pairs that define the report. If you do not want to change a position in the current view or scenario, use the #N/A error value in the argument.

Pages_logical is a logical value that, if TRUE or omitted, specifies continuous page numbers for multiple selections. If FALSE, pages_logical will reset page numbers to 1 for each new section.

REPORT.DELETE

The REPORT.DELETE function removes a report definition from the active document. This function is equivalent to choosing the Print Report command from the File menu, selecting a report in the Print Report dialog box, and choosing the Delete button. The REPORT.DELETE function will not work if the active document is protected. This function is used in conjunction with the Reports add-in macro.

Use with macro sheets only.

Syntax

```
=REPORT.DELETE(report_name)
```

Report_name is the name of the report to be deleted.

REPORT.PRINT

The REPORT.PRINT function prints a report. This function is equivalent to choosing the Print Report button from the Print Reports dialog box. The REPORT.PRINT function will not work if the active document is protected. This function works in conjunction with the Reports add-in macro supplied by Excel.

Use with macro sheets only.

Syntax

```
=REPORT.PRINT(report_name,copies_num,show_print_dllg_logical)
=REPORT.PRINT?(report_name,copies_num)
```

Report_name is the name of the report in the active document you want to print.

Copies_num is the number of copies you want to print. If copies_num is omitted, one copy will be printed.

Show_print_dllg_logical is a logical value that, if TRUE, will display a dialog box that asks how many copies you want to print. If FALSE or omitted, the dialog box will not be displayed and the report will print using the existing print settings.

SELECT

The SELECT function is used to select a cell or cells or to change the active cell. The SELECT function has three forms of syntax.

Syntax 1

```
=SELECT(selection,active_cell)
```

Syntax 1 is used to select cells on a worksheet or macro sheet

Selection is the cell or range of cells in the active document you want to select. Selection can be the cell addresses or a named reference to a range in the active document, and must be in text form. If selection is omitted, the current selection is used.

Active_cell is the cell contained in the argument selection that you wish to make the active cell.

Syntax 2

```
=SELECT(object_id_text,replace)
```

Syntax 2 is used to select worksheet and macro sheet objects.

Object_id_text is the number or name and number of the object (in text form enclosed in quotation marks) that appears in the reference area when the object is selected. The name of the object is the text returned by CREATE.OBJECT, so you can also use a reference to the cell that contains CREATE.OBJECT. If object_id_text contains the names or numbers of more than one object, the last object named in the list will be the active object.

Replace is a logical value that, if TRUE or omitted, instructs Excel to include only the objects specified by the object_id_text argument. If replace is FALSE, Excel includes the objects specified by the object_id_text argument and any other objects that were previously selected.

Syntax 3

```
=SELECT(item_text,single_point)
```

Syntax 3 is used to select chart items.

Item_text is text enclosed in parentheses that specifies which chart object to select, as shown in the following table.

Item_text	Selects
Chart	Entire chart
Plot	Plot area
Legend	Legend
Axis 1	Main chart value axis
Axis 2	Main chart category axis
Axis 3	Overlay chart value axis of 3-D series axis
Axis 4	Overlay chart category axis
Title	Chart title
Text Axis 1	Label for the main chart value axis
Text Axis 2	Label for the main chart category axis
Text Axis 3	Label for the main chart series axis
Text n	nth floating text item
Arrow n	nth arrow
Gridline 1	Major gridlines of value axis
Gridline 2	Minor gridlines of value axis
Gridline 3	Major gridlines of category axis
Gridline 4	Minor gridlines of category axis
Gridline 5	Major gridlines of series axis
Gridline 6	Minor gridlines of series axis
Dropline 1	Main chart droplines
Dropline 2	Overlay chart droplines
Hiloline 1	Main chart hi-lo lines
Hiloline 2	Overlay chart hi-lo lines
Up Bar 1	Main chart up bar
Up Bar 2	Overlay chart up bar

Item_text	Selects
Down Bar 1	Main chart down bar
Down Bar 2	Overlay chart down bar
Series line 1	Main chart series line
Series line 2	Overlay chart series line
Sn	Entire series (where n is a number)
SnPm	Data associated with point m in series n if single_point is TRUE
Text SnPm	Text attached to point m of series n
Text Sn	Series title text of series n of an area chart
Floor	Base of a 3-D chart
Walls	Back of a 3-D chart
Corners	Corners of a 3-D chart

Single_point is a logical value that, if TRUE, instructs Excel to select a single point. If FALSE or omitted, Excel selects a single point if there is only one series in the chart. If the chart contains more than one series, Excel selects the entire series.

SELECT.END

The SELECT.END function is used to select the cell at the end of the range in the direction specified in the function. This function is equivalent to pressing Ctrl+Arrow.

Use with macro sheets only.

Syntax

`=SELECT.END(direction_num)`

Direction_num is a number that specifies the direction in which to move, as shown in the following table.

Direction_num	Direction
1	Left (equivalent to Ctrl+Left arrow)
2	Right (equivalent to Ctrl+Right arrow)
3	Up (equivalent to Ctrl+Up arrow)
4	Down (equivalent to Ctrl+Down arrow)

SHOW.DETAIL

The SHOW.DETAIL function is used to expand or collapse the detail of a summary row under the specified Expand or Collapse button in an outline.

Use with macro sheets only.

Syntax

```
=SHOW.DETAIL(rowcol,rowcol_num,expand)
```

Rowcol is a number specifying whether to perform the operation on rows or columns. If the rowcol argument is 1, rows are operated on. If the rowcol argument is 2, columns are operated on.

Rowcol_num is a number that specifies the row or column to expand or collapse. If rowcol_num is not a summary row or column, the argument returns an error message and the macro will be interrupted.

Expand is a logical value that, if TRUE, expands the details under the designated row or column. If FALSE, the argument instructs Excel to collapse the detail under the row or column. If expand is omitted, Excel will use the default or previous setting.

SHOW.LEVELS

The SHOW.LEVELS function is used to display the specified number of row and column levels of an outline.

Use with macro sheets only.

Syntax

```
=SHOW.LEVELS(row_level,col_level)
```

Row_level specifies the number of row levels to display in an outline. If row_level specifies more levels in an outline than actually exist, Excel will display all of the levels in the outline. If row_level is omitted, rows are ignored in the outline.

Col_level specifies the number of column levels to display in an outline. If col_level specifies more levels in an outline than actually exist, Excel will display all of the levels in the outline. If col_level is omitted, columns are ignored in the outline.

SLIDE.COPY.ROW

The SLIDE.COPY.ROW function is used to copy selected slides, each of which is defined in a single row, to the clipboard. This function is equivalent to choosing the Copy Row button on a slide show. The SLIDE.COPY.ROW function is used in conjunction with the Slide Show add-in macro.

Use with macro sheets only.

Syntax

    =SLIDE.COPY.ROW()

SLIDE.CUT.ROW

The SLIDE.CUT.ROW function is used to cut selected slides, each of which is defined in a single row, and paste them to the clipboard. This function is equivalent to choosing the Cut Row button on a slide show. The SLIDE.CUT.ROW function is used in conjunction with the Slide Show add-in macro.

Use with macro sheets only.

Syntax

    =SLIDE.CUT.ROW()

SLIDE.DEFAULTS

The SLIDE.DEFAULTS function sets the default values for the speed, transition effect, sound, and advance rate on the active slide show. This function is equivalent to choosing the Set Defaults button on a slide show.

Use with macro sheets only.

Syntax

    =SLIDE.DEFAULTS(effect_num,speed_num,advance_rate_num,soundfile_text)
    =SLIDE.DEFAULTS?(effect_num,speed_num,advance_rate_num,soundfile_text)

Effect_num is a number that corresponds to the effects in the Effect list in the Edit Slide dialog box (starting with 1), and that specifies the transition effect you want to use when you display the slide. If effect_num is omitted, Excel will use the default setting. If effect_num is 1, the value of the argument is none.

Speed_num is a number from 1 to 10 that specifies the speed of the transition effect. If speed_num is omitted, the default setting is used. If effect_num is 1, speed_num is ignored. If speed_num is greater than 10, the value 10 will be used.

Advance_rate_num is a number that specifies how long (in seconds) the slide is displayed before you move on to the next slide. If advance_rate_num is omitted, the default setting is used. If advance_rate_num is 0, you must either click with the mouse or press a key to move on to the next slide.

Soundfile_text is the name of a file (enclosed in text surrounded by quotation marks) that specifies the sound that will be played when the slide is displayed. If soundfile_text is omitted, Excel will play the default sound for the slide. If soundfile_text is empty (" "), no sound will be played.

SLIDE.DELETE.ROWS

The SLIDE.DELETE.ROWS function is used to delete selected slides, each of which is defined on a single row. This function is equivalent to choosing the Delete Row button on a slide show.

Use with macro sheets only.

Syntax

```
=SLIDE.DELETE.ROW()
```

SLIDE.EDIT

The SLIDE.EDIT function is used to change the default values for the selected slides. This function is equivalent to choosing the Edit button in a slide show.

Use with macro sheets only.

Syntax

```
=SLIDE.EDIT(effect_num,speed_num,advance_rate_num,soundfile_text)
=SLIDE.EDIT?(effect_num,speed_num,advance_rate_num,soundfile_text)
```

Effect_num is a number that corresponds to the effects in the Effect list in the Edit Slide dialog box (starting with 1), and that specifies the transition effect you want to use when you display the slide. If effect_num is omitted, Excel will use the default setting. If effect_num is 1, the value of the argument is none.

Speed_num is a number from 1 to 10 that specifies the speed of the transition effect. If speed_num is omitted, the default setting is used. If effect_num is 1, speed_num is ignored. If speed_num is greater than 10, the value 10 will be used.

Advance_rate_num is a number that specifies how long (in seconds) the slide is displayed before you move on to the next slide. If advance_rate_num is omitted, the default setting is used. If advance_rate_num is 0, you must either click with the mouse or press a key to move on to the next slide.

Soundfile_text is the name of a file (enclosed in text surrounded by quotation marks) that specifies the sound that will be played when the slide is displayed. If soundfile_text is omitted, Excel will play the default sound for the slide. If soundfile_text is empty (" "), no sound will be played.

SLIDE.PASTE

The SLIDE.PASTE function is used to paste the contents of the clipboard as the next available slide of the active slide show and specify the default values. This function is equivalent to choosing the Paste button in a slide show.

Use with macro sheets only.

Syntax

```
=SLIDE.PASTE(effect_num,speed_num,advance_rate_num,soundfile_text)
=SLIDE.PASTE?(effect_num,speed_num,advance_rate_num,soundfile_text)
```

Effect_num is a number that corresponds to the effects in the Effect list in the Edit Slide dialog box (starting with 1), and that specifies the transition effect you want to use when you display the slide. If effect_num is omitted, Excel will use the default setting. If effect_num is 1, the value of the argument is none.

Speed_num is a number from 1 to 10 that specifies the speed of the transition effect. If speed_num is omitted, the default setting is used. If effect_num is 1, speed_num is ignored. If speed_num is greater than 10, the value 10 will be used.

Advance_rate_num is a number that specifies how long (in seconds) the slide is displayed before you move on to the next slide. If advance_rate_num is omitted, the default setting is used. If advance_rate_num is 0, you must either click with the mouse or press a key to move on to the next slide.

Soundfile_text is the name of a file (enclosed in text surrounded by quotation marks) that specifies the sound that will be played when the slide is displayed. If soundfile_text is omitted, Excel will play the default sound for the slide. If soundfile_text is empty (" "), no sound will be played.

SLIDE.PASTE.ROW

The SLIDE.PASTE.ROW function is used to paste, cut, or copy slides into the current selection. This function is equivalent to choosing the Paste Row button in a slide show.

Use with macro sheets only.

Syntax

```
=SLIDE.PASTE.ROW()
```

SLIDE.SHOW

The SLIDE.SHOW function is used to start a slide show. This function is equivalent to choosing the Start Show button in a slide show.

Use with macro sheets only.

Syntax

```
=SLIDE.SHOW(initialslide_num,repeat_logical,dialogtitle_text,
allownav_logical,allowcontrol_logical)
=SLIDE.SHOW?(initialslide_num,repeat_logical,dialogtitle_text,
allownav_logical,allowcontrol_logical)
```

Initialslide_num is a number that specifies the slide number to display first. If the argument is omitted, Excel will display the first slide in the slide show.

Repeat_logical is a logical value that, if TRUE, will instruct Excel to repeat the slide show after the last slide is displayed. If the argument is FALSE or omitted, Excel will end the slide show after the last slide is displayed.

Dialogtitle_text is text that is enclosed in quotation marks that specifies the title of the dialog boxes displayed during a slide show. If this argument is omitted, the text which is displayed will be *Slide Show*.

Allownav_logical is a logical value that, if TRUE or omitted, will permit you to use the arrow keys or the mouse to move between slides. If the value of the argument is FALSE, all movement is controlled by the slide show settings.

Allowcontrol_logical is a logical value that, if TRUE or omitted, allows you to press Esc to interrupt the slide show and display the Slide Show Options dialog box. If the argument is FALSE, you can press Esc to stop the slide show, but the dialog box will not be displayed.

SOUND.NOTE

The SOUND.NOTE function records sound into a cell note, erases sound from a cell note, or imports sounds from another file into a cell note. In order to use this function, you must be using Windows 3.0 with Multimedia Extensions 1.0 or later, or Windows 3.1.

Use with macro sheets only.

Syntax 1

Use for recording or erasing sound.

```
=SOUND.NOTE(cell_ref,erase_snd)
```

Syntax 2

Use for importing sound from another file.

```
=SOUND.NOTE(cell_ref,file_text)
```

Cell_ref is the reference to the cell that contains a note into which you want to record or import a sound, or from which you want to erase a sound.

Erase_snd is a logical value that, if TRUE, erases the sound from the note. If the argument is FALSE or omitted, Excel will display the Record dialog box so that you can record sound into the note.

File_text is the name of a file that contains sounds.

SOUND.PLAY

The SOUND.PLAY function plays the sound from a cell note or a file. This function is equivalent to choosing the Note command from the Formula menu and choosing Play, or choosing the Note command from the Formula menu and then choosing the Import button, opening a file, selecting a sound, and then choosing the Play button. This function can only be used if you are running Windows 3.0 with Multimedia Extensions 1.0 or later, or Windows 3.1.

Use with macro sheets only.

Syntax

```
=SOUND.PLAY(cell_ref,file_text)
```

Cell_ref is the reference to the cell that contains a note into which you want to record or import a sound, or from that you want to erase a sound.

File_text is the name of a file that contains sounds.

TEXT.BOX

The TEXT.BOX function is used to replace the characters in a text box or button with the text you want to use.

Use with macro sheets only.

Syntax

```
=TEXT.BOX(add_text,object_id_text,start_num,num_chars)
```

Add_text is the text you want to add to the text box or button.

Object_id_text is the name of the text box or button in which you want to place text. If object_id_text is omitted, the action will be performed on the current selection.

Start_num is a number that specifies the position of the first character you want to replace (or, if you do not want to replace text, the position at which you want to add text). If start_num is omitted, it is assumed to be 1.

Num_chars is the number of characters you want to replace. If num_chars is 0, no characters are replaced and the value of add_text is inserted at the position specified in start_num. If num_chars is omitted, all of the characters will be replaced.

UNLOCKED.NEXT

The UNLOCKED.NEXT function is used to move to the next unlocked cell in a protected document. This function is equivalent to pressing Tab in a protected document.

Use with macro sheets only.

Syntax

```
=UNLOCKED.NEXT()
```

UNLOCKED.PREV

The UNLOCKED.PREV function is used to move to the previous unlocked cell in a protected document. This function is equivalent to pressing Shift+Tab in a protected document.

Use with macro sheets only.

Syntax

```
=UNLOCKED.PREV()
```

VIEW.DEFINE

The VIEW.DEFINE function is used to create or replace a view. This function is equivalent to choosing the Add button from the Views dialog box. This function is used in conjunction with the View Manager add-in macro.

Use with macro sheets only.

Syntax

```
=VIEW.DEFINE(view_name,print_settings_log,row)col_log)
```

View_name is the name of the view you want to define (view_name must be in text enclosed in quotation marks).

Print_settings_log is a logical value that, if TRUE or omitted, includes current print settings in the view. If the argument is FALSE, the current print settings are not included in the view.

Row_col_log is a logical value that, if TRUE or omitted, includes the current row and column settings in the view. If the argument is FALSE, the current row and column settings are not included in the view.

VIEW.DELETE

The VIEW.DELETE function is used to remove a view from the active document. This function is equivalent to selecting a view and then choosing the Delete button from the Views dialog box. This function is used in conjunction with the View Manager add-in macro.

Use with macro sheets only.

Syntax

```
=VIEW.DELETE(view_name)
```

View_name is the name of the view (in text enclosed in quotation marks) that you want to delete.

VLINE

The VLINE function scrolls vertically through the active window by a specified number of rows.

Use with macro sheets only.

Syntax

```
=VHLINE(num_rows)
```

Num_rows is a number that specifies the number of rows you want to scroll through. If num_rows is a positive number, VLINE scrolls down the number of rows specified by the argument. If num_rows is a negative number, VLINE scrolls up the number of rows specified.

VPAGE

The VPAGE function is used to change the displayed area of a worksheet or macro sheet. The function scrolls vertically through the active window one window at a time.

Use with macro sheets only.

Syntax

```
=VPAGE(num_windows)
```

Num_windows specifies the number of windows to scroll through the active document. If num_windows is a positive number, VPAGE scrolls down. If num_windows is a negative number, VPAGE scrolls up. A window is defined by the number of rows that are visible.

VSCROLL

The VSCROLL function scrolls vertically through the active document either by specifying a row number or by percentage.

Use with macro sheets only.

Syntax

```
=VSCROLL(position, row_logical)
```

Position specifies the row to which you want to scroll. Position can be either the row number or a percentage that represents the vertical position of the row in the active document. If position is 0, VSCROLL will scroll through the document to the top edge (the first row); if position is 1, VSCROLL will scroll through the document to the bottom edge (which is row 16,384).

Row_logical is a logical value that, if TRUE, scrolls through the document to the designated row position. If FALSE, row_logical scrolls through the document to the vertical position represented by a percentage.

WORKBOOK.ACTIVATE

The WORKBOOK.ACTIVATE function is used to activate a specified document in a workbook. This function is equivalent to double-clicking a document in a workbook contents window.

Use with macro sheets only.

Syntax

```
=WORKBOOK.ACTIVATE(sheet_name, new_window_logical)
```

Sheet_name is the name of the document you want to activate in the active workbook. If sheet_name is omitted, the workbook contents window is displayed.

New_window_logical is a logical value that, if TRUE, displays the document in a new window. If the argument is FALSE or omitted, the document is displayed in the same size and location as the workbook contents window.

WORKBOOK.ADD

The WORKBOOK.ADD function is used to add documents to a workbook. This function is equivalent to choosing the Add button on the workbook contents window.

Use with macro sheets only.

Syntax

```
=WORKBOOK.ADD(name_array, dest_book, position_num,)
=WORKBOOK.ADD?(name_array, dest_book, position_num,)
```

Name_array is the name of the document, or an array of names of more than one document, that you want to add to the workbook.

Dest_book is the name of the workbook to which you want to add the document or documents. If dest_book is omitted, it is assumed to be the active workbook.

Position_num is a number that specifies the position of the document(s) within the workbook.

WORKBOOK.COPY

The WORKBOOK.COPY function is used to copy one or more documents from their workbook to another workbook. This function is equivalent to pressing the Ctrl key while dragging a document from one workbook to another.

Use with macro sheets only.

Syntax

```
=WORKBOOK.COPY(name_array,dest_book,position_num)
```

Name_array is the name of the document, or an array of names of more than one document, that you want to copy from one workbook to another.

Dest_book is the name of the workbook to which you want to copy the document or documents. If dest_book is omitted, the document specified in name_array becomes a separate document that is not part of any workbook.

Position_num is a number that specifies the position to copy the document(s) within the workbook. If position_num is omitted, the document(s) will be placed at the end of the workbook.

WORKBOOK.MOVE

The WORKBOOK.MOVE function is used to move a document or documents from one workbook to another, or to move a document to another position in its current workbook. This function can also be used to remove a document from the workbook.

Use with macro sheets only.

Syntax

```
=WORKBOOK.MOVE(name_array,dest_book,position_num)
```

Name_array is the name of the document, or an array of names of more than one document, that you want to move.

Dest_book is the name of the workbook to which you want to move the document or documents. If dest_book is omitted, the document is removed from the workbook and becomes a separate document.

Position_num is a number that specifies the target position of the document(s) within the workbook specified by dest_book.

WORKBOOK.OPTIONS

The WORKBOOK.OPTIONS function is used to bind and unbind documents within a workbook and to change the name of a document in a workbook. This function is equivalent to choosing the Options button in a workbook contents window.

Use with macro sheets only.

Syntax

```
=WORKBOOK.OPTIONS(sheet_name,bound_logical,new_name)
```

Sheet_name is the name of the document upon which you want to perform the action.

Bound_logical is a logical value that, if TRUE, binds the document. If the value is FALSE, the document is unbound. If the argument is omitted, the setting is unchanged.

New_name is the document name to assign to the document identified by sheet_name. If new_name is omitted, the document name is not changed. If the document is unbound, then new_name must be a filename.

WORKBOOK.SELECT

The WORKBOOK.SELECT function is used to select a document in an active workbook.

Use with macro sheets only.

Syntax

```
=WORKBOOK.SELECT(name_array,active_name)
```

Name_array is an array of text names (enclosed in quotation marks) of the documents you want to select. If this argument is omitted, no documents are selected.

Active_name is the name of a single sheet in the workbook that should be given priority when the selection is made. If the active_name is not in the selection, you will receive an error value. If active_name is omitted, the first sheet in the name_array argument is given priority.

The Information Functions

The following information functions are used to return information about specified parts of the Excel environment.

ACTIVE.CELL

The ACTIVE.CELL function is used to return the reference of the active cell as a reference or a value. The function returns a reference if it is used in a function that requires a reference argument, otherwise, the function returns the value contained in the active cell.

Use with macro sheets only.

Syntax

```
=ACTIVE.CELL()
```

CALLER

The CALLER function is used to return information about the cell, range of cells, command on a menu, tool on a toolbar, or the object that called the macro. Caller is used when the operation of a subroutine or custom function is dependent upon the location, size, name, or other attribute of the information returned by the caller. If the subroutine or custom function is entered in a single cell, CALLER returns the reference to the cell. If the subroutine or custom function is part of an array formula that was entered into a range of cells, CALLER returns the reference to the range. If CALLER is used in a macro called by an Auto_Open, Auto_Activate, Auto_Close, or Auto_Deactive macro, CALLER returns the name of the calling macro. If CALLER is used in a macro called by a menu command, CALLER returns the command's position or number, the menu number, and the menu bar number. If CALLER is used in a macro called by an assigned-to-object macro, CALLER returns the object identifier. If CALLER is used in a macro that is called by a tool, CALLER returns the position number of the tool and the toolbar name.

Use with macro sheets only.

Syntax

```
=CALLER()
```

DIRECTORIES

The DIRECTORIES function is used to return an array of all of the subdirectories in the current directories or in a specified directory.

Use with macro sheets only.

Syntax

```
=DIRECTORIES(path_text)
```

Path_text is the directory from which you wish to return a list of subdirectories. If path_text is omitted, Excel returns a list of all subdirectories in the current directory.

DIRECTORY

The DIRECTORY function is used to identify the name and path of the current directory, or to change to another directory.

Use with macro sheets only.

Syntax

```
=DIRECTORY(path_text)
```

Path_text is the path of the directory to which you want to change. If path_text is omitted, the argument returns the name of the current directory.

DOCUMENTS

The DOCUMENTS function is used to return the names of specified types of documents that are currently open. The documents are listed in alphabetical order. The

DOCUMENTS function will list workbooks and unbound sheets, but it will not list bound sheets.

Use with macro sheets only.

Syntax

    =DOCUMENTS(type_num,match_text)

Type_num is a number that specifies the type of document to include in the list. If type_num is 1 or omitted, Excel returns the names of all open documents, except add-in documents. If type_num is 2, Excel returns the names of add-in documents only. If type_num is 3, Excel returns the names of all open documents.

Match_text specifies the documents whose names you want returned. If match_text is omitted, the function returns the names of all open documents.

FILE.EXISTS

The FILE.EXISTS function is used to check for the existence of a file or a directory. If the file or directory exists, the function returns a value of TRUE. If the file or directory does not exist, the function returns a value of FALSE.

Use with macro sheets only.

Syntax

    =FILE.EXISTS(path_text)

Path_text is the name of the file or directory whose existence you want to verify. If the file or directory is not in the current directory, you must use the full path.

FILES

The FILES function is used to return a list of the names of the files in a specified directory.

Use with macro sheets only.

Syntax

    =FILES(directory_text)

Directory_text specifies the directory in which you want to list filenames. Directory_text can contain DOS wildcards. If directory_text is omitted, the function returns the filenames in the current directory.

GET.BAR

The GET.BAR function is used to return the number of the active number bar, or to return the name or position number of a command on a menu or a menu on a menu bar.

Use with macro sheets only.

Syntax 1

Returns menu bar numbers.

```
=GET.BAR()
```

Syntax 2

Returns command or menu names or numbers.

```
=GET.BAR(bar_num,menu,command)
```

Bar_num is the number of a menu bar that contains the menu or command for which you want information. Bar_num can be the number of a built-in menu bar that is returned by using the ADD.BAR function. A list of the ID numbers for Excel's built-in menu bars follows.

Bar_num	Built-in menu bar
1	Worksheet and macro sheet
2	Chart
3	Null (menu displayed when no documents are open)
4	Info
5	Worksheet and macro sheet (short menus)
6	Chart (short menus)
7	Cell, toolbar, and workbook
8	Object
9	Chart

Menu is the menu that contains the command or whose name and position you want. Menu can be the name of the menu as text enclosed in quotation marks, or the number of the menu (starting with 1 at the left of the menu bar).

Command is the command whose name or number you want returned. If the argument is the name of the command as text, the command number is returned. If the argument is the number of the command, the command name is returned. Commands are numbered starting with 1 at the top of the menu. If the argument is 0, the name or position number of the menu will be returned. If you use text in the command argument, the text must exactly duplicate the text in the command.

GET.CELL

The GET.CELL function is used to return information about the location, formatting or contents of a cell.

Use with macro sheets only.

Syntax

`=GET.CELL(type_num, reference)`

Type_num is a number that specifies the type of information you want the function to return, as shown in the following table.

Type_num	Information returned
1	Absolute reference of the upper-left cell in the reference argument, as text in the current workspace reference style.
2	Row number of the top cell in the reference argument.
3	Column number of the leftmost cell in the reference argument.
4	Same as reference Type.
5	Contents of the argument reference.
6	Formula in reference, as text, in either A1 or R1C1 style, depending on the style in the workspace.
7	Number format of the cell.

Type_num	Information returned
8	Number specifying the cell's alignment:

1 = General
2 = Left
3 = Center
4 = Right
5 = Fill
6 = Justify
7 = Center across cells

| 9 | Number indicating the left border style of the cell: |

0 = No border
1 = Thin line
2 = Medium line
3 = Dashed line
4 = Dotted line
5 = Thick line
6 = Double line
7 = Hairline

| 10 | Number indicating the right border style of the cell: |

0 = No border
1 = Thin line
2 = Medium line
3 = Dashed line
4 = Dotted line
5 = Thick line
6 = Double line
7 = Hairline

| 11 | Number indicating the top border of the cell: |

0 = No border
1 = Thin line
2 = Medium line
3 = Dashed line
4 = Dotted line
5 = Thick line
6 = Double line

7 = Hairline

Type_num	Information returned
12	Number indicating the bottom border of the cell:

        0 = No border
        1 = Thin line
        2 = Medium line
        3 = Dashed line
        4 = Dotted line
        5 = Thick line
        6 = Double line
        7 = Hairline

Type_num	Information returned
13	Number indicating which pattern is used in the cell. The number corresponds to the patterns in the Patterns dialog box in the Patterns command located in the Format menu. If no pattern is selected, a value of 0 is returned.
14	Returns a value of TRUE if the cell is locked; if the cell is not locked, returns a value of FALSE.
15	Returns a value of TRUE if the cell is hidden; if the cell is not hidden, returns a value of FALSE.
16	A two-item array that contains the width of the active cell and a logical value that, if TRUE, indicates that the cell's width is set to change as the standard width changes. If the value is FALSE, the cell's width is a custom width.
17	Row height of cell, in points.
18	Name of font, in text.
19	Size of font, in points.
20	Returns a value of TRUE if cell is bold; otherwise returns a value of FALSE.
21	Returns a value of TRUE if cell is italic; otherwise returns a value of FALSE.
22	Returns a value of TRUE if cell is underlined; otherwise returns a value of FALSE.
23	Returns a value of TRUE is cell is struck through; otherwise returns a value of FALSE.
24	Font color as a number. If font color is automatic, returns a value of 0.

Type_num	Information returned
25	Returns TRUE if cell is outlined; otherwise returns a value of FALSE.
26	Returns a value of TRUE if cell is shadowed; otherwise returns a value of FALSE.
27	Returns a number indicating whether a manual page break occurs at the cell: 0 = No break 1 = Row 2 = Column 3 = Both row and column
28	Row level (outline).
29	Column level (outline).
30	Returns TRUE if the row that contains the active cell is a summary row; otherwise returns a value of FALSE.
31	Returns TRUE if the column that contains the active cell is a summary column; otherwise returns a value of FALSE.
32	Name of the document containing the cell.
33	Returns a value of TRUE if the cell is formatted to wrap; otherwise returns a value of FALSE.
34	Returns the left border color as a number. If the color is automatic, returns a value of 0.
35	Returns the right border color as a number. If the color is automatic, returns a value of 0.
36	Returns the top border color as a number. If the color is automatic, returns a value of 0.
37	Returns the bottom border color as a number. If the color is automatic, returns a value of 0.
38	Returns the shade foregound color as a number. If the color is automatic, returns a value of 0.
39	Returns the shade backgound color as a number. If the color is automatic, returns a value of 0.
40	Style of the cell, as text.
41	Returns the formula in the active cell without translating it.

Type_num	Information returned
42	Returns the horizontal distance, measured in points, from the left edge of the active window to the left edge of the cell. The value may be a negative number if the window is scrolled beyond the cell.
43	Returns the vertical distance, measured in points, from the top edge of the active window to the top edge of the cell. The value may be a negative number if the window is scrolled beyond the cell.
44	Returns the horizontal distance, measured in points, from the left edge of the active window to the right edge of the cell. The value may be a negative number if the window is scrolled beyond the cell.
45	Returns the vertical distance, measured in points, from the top edge of the active window to the buttom edge of the cell. The value may be a negative number if the window is scrolled beyond the cell.
46	Returns TRUE if the cell contains a text note; otherwise returns a value of FALSE.
47	Return TRUE if the cell contain a sound note; otherwise returns a value of FALSE.
48	Returns TRUE if the cell contains a formula; returns a value of FALSE if the cell contains a constant.
49	Returns TRUE if the cell is part of an array; otherwise returns a value of FALSE.
50	Returns a number which indicates the cell's vertical alignment: 1 = Top 2 = Center 3 = Buttom
51	Returns a number that indicates the cell's vertical orientation: 0 = Horizontal 1 = Vertical 2 = Upward 3 = Downward
52	Returns the cell prefix (or text alignment) character, or empty text (" ") if the cell does not contain one.
53	Returns the contents of the cell as it is currently displayed, as text, including any additional numbers or symbols resulting from the formatting of the cell.

Reference is the cell or range of cells about which you want information. If the argument is a range of cells, the cell in the upper-left corner of the first range is used. If reference is omitted, the active cell is used.

GET.CHART.ITEM

The GET.CHART.ITEM function is used to return the vertical or horizontal position of a point on a chart item.

Use with macro sheets only.

Syntax

`=GET.CHART.ITEM(x_y_index,point_index,Item_text)`

X_y_index is a number that specifies which coordinate you want returned. A value of 1 will return a horizontal coordinate. A value of 2 will return a vertical coordinate.

Point_index is a number that specifies the point on the chart item as listed in the tables below. If point_index is omitted, it is assumed to be 1. If the item is a point, the value of the argument must be 1. If the specified item is a line other than a data line, use the following values for the point_index argument.

Point_index	Chart item position
1	Lower or left
2	Upper or right

If the specified item is a rectangle or an area in a area chart, use the following values for the point_index argument.

Point_index	Chart item position
1	Upper left
2	Upper middle
3	Upper right
4	Right middle
5	Lower right
6	Lower middle
7	Lower left
8	Left middle

If the selected item is an arrow, use the following values for the point_index argument.

Point_index	Chart item position
1	Arrow shaft
2	Arrowhead

If the selected item is a pie slice, use the following values for the point_index argument.

Point_index	Chart item position
1	Outermost counterclockwise point
2	Outer center point
3	Outermost clockwise point
4	Midpoint of the most clockwise radius
5	Center point
6	Midpoint of the most counterclickwise radius

Item_text is a code that specifies which item of a chart to select, as shown in the following table.

Item_text	Selects
Chart	Entire chart
Plot	Plot area
Legend	Legend
Axis 1	Main chart value axis
Axis 2	Main chart category axis
Axis 3	Overlay chart value axis of 3-D series axis
Axis 4	Overlay chart category axis
Title	Chart title
Text Axis 1	Label for the main chart value axis
Text Axis 2	Label for the main chart category axis
Text Axis 3	Label for the main chart series axis
Text n	nth floating text item
Arrow n	nth arrow
Gridline 1	Major gridlines of value axis
Gridline 2	Minor gridlines of value axis
Gridline 3	Major gridlines of category axis

Item_text	Selects
Gridline 4	Minor gridlines of category axis
Gridline 5	Major gridlines of series axis
Gridline 6	Minor gridlines of series axis
Dropline 1	Main chart droplines
Dropline 2	Overlay chart droplines
Hiloline 1	Main chart hi-lo lines
Hiloline 2	Overlay chart hi-lo lines
Up Bar 1	Main chart up bar
Up Bar 2	Overlay chart up bar
Down Bar 1	Main chart down bar
Down Bar 2	Overlay chart down bar
Series line 1	Main chart series line
Series line 2	Overlay chart series line
Sn	Entire series (where n is a number)
SnPm	Data associated with point m in series n if single_point is TRUE
Text SnPm	Text attached to point m of series n
Text Sn	Series title text of series n of an area chart
Floor	Base of a 3-D chart
Walls	Back of a 3-D chart
Corners	Corners of a 3-D chart

GET.DEF

The GET.DEF function is used to return the defined name, as text, for a particular area, value or formula.

Use with macro sheets only.

Syntax

```
=GET.DEF(def_text,document_text,type_num)
```

Def_text is the reference, value, or formula that contains the defined name.

Document_text specifies the worksheet or macro sheet in which the argument def_text is located.

Type_num is a number that specifies that type of name to return. If the value is 1 or omitted, the argument returns normal names only. If the value is 2, the argument returns hidden names only. If the value is 3, the argument returns all names.

GET.DOCUMENT

The GET.DOCUMENT function is used to return information about a document.

Use with macro sheets only.

Syntax

`=GET.DOCUMENT(type_num, name_text)`

Type_num is a number that specifies the type of document information you want. The following table lists the possible values you can use for type_num and the result of those values.

Type_num	Returns
1	Name of the document name_text argument, as text. The document name does not include the drive, directory, or window number.
2	The path of the directory containing the name_text argument, as text. If the document name_text has not been saved, it returns an error value.
3	Number that indicates the type of document: 1 = Worksheet 2 = Chart 3 = Macro sheet 4 = Infor window (if active) 5 = Workbook
4	Returns TRUE if changes have been made to the document since it was last saved; otherwise returns a value of FALSE.
5	Returns TRUE if the document is read-only; otherwise returns a value of FALSE.
6	Returns TRUE if the document is protected; otherwise returns a value of FALSE.

Type_num	Returns
7	Returns TRUE if the cells in a document, the contents of a workbook, or the series in a chart are protected; otherwise returns a value of FALSE.
8	Returns TRUE if the document windows are protected; otherwise returns a value of FALSE.
9	Applies to charts only. Returns a number that indicates the type of the main chart:

    1 = Area
    2 = Bar
    3 = Column
    4 = Line
    5 = Pie
    6 = XY (Scatter)
    7 = 3-D area
    8 = 3-D column
    9 = 3-D line
  10 = 3-D pie
  11 = Radar
  12 = 3-D bar
  13 = 3-D surface

Type_num	Returns
10	Applies to charts only. Returns a number that indicates the type of the overlay chart:

    1 = Area
    2 = Bar
    3 = Column
    4 = Line
    5 = Pie
    6 = XY (Scatter)
    7 = 3-D area
    8 = 3-D column
    9 = 3-D line
  10 = 3-D pie
  11 = Radar
  12 = 3-D bar
  13 = 3-D surface

Type_num	Returns
11	Applies to charts only. Returns the number of series in the main chart.
12	Applies to charts only. Returns the number of series in the overlay chart.
	Applies to worksheets, macro sheets, and charts, if applicable.
9	Applies to worksheets, macro sheets, and charts, if applicable. The number of the first used row. If the document is empty, returns a value of 0.
10	Applies to worksheets, macro sheets, and charts, if applicable. The number of the last used row. If the document is empty, returns a value of 0.
11	Applies to worksheets, macro sheets, and charts, if applicable. The number of the first used column. If the document is empty, returns a value of 0.
12	Applies to worksheets, macro sheets, and charts, if applicable. The number of the last used column. If the document is empty, return a value of 0.
13	Applies to worksheets, macro sheets, and charts, if applicable. The number of windows. If the document is a workbook, returns a value of 1.
14	Applies to worksheets, macro sheets, and charts, if applicable. A number that indicates the mode of calculation: 1 = Automatic 2 = Automatic except tables 3 = Manual
15	Applies to worksheets, macro sheets, and charts, if applicable. Returns TRUE if the iteration check box is selected in the Calculation dialog box; otherwise returns a value of FALSE.
16	Applies to worksheets, macro sheets, and charts, if applicable. Returns the maximum number of iterations.
17	Applies to worksheets, macro sheets, and charts, if applicable. The maximum change between iterations.
18	Applies to worksheets, macro sheets, and charts, if applicable. Returns TRUE if the Update Remote References check box is selected in the Calculation dialog box; otherwise returns a value of FALSE.

Type_num	Returns

Type_num	**Returns**
19	Applies to worksheets, macro sheets, and charts, if applicable. Returns TRUE if the Precision As Displayed check box is selected in the Calculation dialog box; otherwise returns a value of FALSE.
20	Applies to worksheets, macro sheets, and charts, if applicable. Returns TRUE if the 1904 Date System check box is selected in the Calculation dialog box; otherwise returns a value of FALSE.
21–29	Apply to previous versions of Excel.
30	A horizontal array of consolidation references for the document, in the form of text.
31	A number that indicates the function used in the current consolidation as shown in the following table. The default is SUM.

Function_num	**Function**
1	AVERAGE
2	COUNT
3	COUNTA
4	MAX
5	MIN
6	RODUCT
7	STDEV
8	STDEVP
9	SUM
10	VAR
11	VARP

32	Returns a three-item horizontal array indicating the status of the check boxes in the Data Consolidate dialog box. If TRUE, the check box is selected; if FALSE, the check box is not selected. The first item indicates the Top Row check box, the second item indicates the Left Column check box, and the third item indicates the Create Links to Source Data check box.
33	Returns TRUE if the Recalculate Before Saving check box is selected in the Calculation dialog box; otherwise returns a value of FALSE.

Type_num	Returns
34	Returns TRUE if the document is read-only recommended; otherwise returns a value of FALSE.
35	Returns TRUE if the document is write-reserved, otherwise returns a value of FALSE.
36	Returns the name of the user with current write permission for the document.
37	Returns a number that corresponds to the file type of the document as displayed in the Save As dialog box.
38	Returns TRUE if the Summary Rows Below Detail check box is the Outline dialog box is selected; otherwise returns a value of FALSE.
39	Returns TRUE if the Summary Columns To Right Of Detail check box in the Outline dialog box is selected; otherwise returns a value of FALSE.
40	Returns TRUE if the Create Backup File check box in the Save As dialog box is selected; otherwise returns a value of FALSE.
41	Returns a number from 1 to 3 that indicates whether objects are displayed. The number 1 displays all objects, 2 displays placeholders for pictures and charts, and 3 hides all objects.
42	Returns the horizontal array of all object in the document.
43	Returns TRUE if the Save External Link Values in the Calculation dialog box is selected; otherwise returns a value of FALSE.
44	Returns TRUE if the objects in a document or the documents in a workbook are protected; otherwise returns a value of FALSE.
45	Returns a number from 0 to 3 that indicates how the windows are synchronized. The number 0 indicates the windows are not synchronized, 1 indicates the windows are synchronized horizontally, 2 indicates the windows are synchronized vertically, and 3 indicates the windows are synchronized both horizontally and vertically.

Type_num	Returns
46	Returns a seven-item horizontal array of print settings that can be set by the LINE.PRINT function, as follows:

    ▼ Setup text
    ▼ Left margin
    ▼ Right margin
    ▼ Top margin
    ▼ Bottom margin
    ▼ Page length

A logical value that, if TRUE, indicates the output will be formatted. If the value if FALSE, the output will not be formatted.

Type_num	Returns
47	Returns TRUE if the Alternate Expression Evaluation check box in the Calculation dialog box is selected; otherwise returns a value of FALSE.
48	Returns the standard column width setting.
49	Returns the starting page number, or 1 if none is specified.
50	The total number of pages that would be printed based upon the current settings, excluding notes. If the document is a chart, the value returned is 1.
51	The total number of pages that would be printed out if only notes are printed.
52	A four-item horizontal array that indicates the margin settings (top, bottom, left, and right) in the current selection.
53	Return a number that indicates the orientation. The number 1 indicates portrait, 2 indicates landscape.
54	Returns the header, including formatting codes, as a text string.
55	Returns the footer, including formatting codes, as a text string.
56	Returns an array of two logical values that correspond to horizontal and vertical centering.
57	Returns TRUE if row or column headings are to be printed; otherwise returns a value of FALSE.

Type_num	Returns
58	Returns TRUE if gridlines are to be printed; otherwise returns a value of FALSE.
59	Returns TRUE if the cell colors are to be printed; otherwise returns a value of FALSE.
60	Returns a number from 1 to 3 that indicates how the chart will be sized when it is printed. A number 1 will print the size on the screen, 2 will scale the chart to fit the page, and 3 will use the full page.
61	Returns a number that indicates the pagination order. A number 1 indicates down, then over; 2 indicates over, then down.
62	Returns the percentage of enlargement or reduction of the document. If none is used, returns a value of 100 percent.
63	Returns a two-item array that indicates the number of pages to which the printout should be scaled to fit, with the first item equal to the width, and the second item equal to the height.
64	Returns an array of numbers that correspond to the rows that are immediately below a manual or automatic page break.
65	Returns an array of columns numbers that correspond to the columns immediately to the right of a manual or automatic page-break.
66	Returns TRUE if the Alternate Formual Entry check box in the Calculation dialog box is selected; otherwise returns a value of FALSE.
67	Returns TRUE if the workbook document is bound; otherwise returns a value of FALSE.
68	Returns the name of the workbook if the document is part of a workbook; otherwise returns a value of #N/A. If the workbook is part of multiple workbooks and is not bound, returns an array of the workbooks' names.

Name_text is the name of an open document. If the argument is omitted, it is assumed to be the active document.

GET.FORMULA

The GET.FORMULA function is used to return the contents of a cell (given as text) as they would appear in the formula bar of a worksheet.

Use with macro sheets only.

Syntax

`=GET.FORMULA(reference)`

Reference is a cell or range of cells, or an external reference to a cell or range of cells. If a range of cells is selected, the function returns the contents of the upper-left cell in the argument. Reference can also be the object identifier of a picture created by the camera tool, or a reference to a chart series.

GET.LINK.INFO

The GET.LINK.INFO function is used to return information about a specified link.

Use with macro sheets only.

Syntax

`=GET.LINK.INFO(link_text,type_num,type_of_link,reference)`

Link_text contains the path of the link.

Type_num is the number 1, which returns a value of 1 if the link is set to automatically update and a value of 2 if the link is not set to automatically update.

Type_of_link is a number from 1 to 6 that indicates the type of link about which you want information, as shown in the following table.

Type_of_link	Link document type
1	Not applicable
2	DDE link
3	Not applicable
4	Not applicable
5	Publisher
6	Subscriber

Reference is required if you have more than one publisher or subscriber of a single edition on the edition name on the active document, and must be in the R1C1 style.

GET.NAME

The GET.NAME function is used to return the definition of a name exactly as it appears in the Refers To box of the Define Name dialog box from the Formula menu.

Use with macro sheets only.

Syntax

```
=GET.NAME(name_text)
```

Name_text is a name defined on the macro sheet, or an external reference to a name defined on the active document. Name_text can be a hidden name.

GET.NOTE

The GET.NOTE function returns the characters from a note. Use this function to move the contents of a note to a cell or text box or to another cell note.

Use with macro sheets only.

Syntax

```
=GET.NOTE(cell_ref,start_char,num_chars)
```

Cell_ref is the cell to which the note is attached. If the argument is omitted, the note attached to the active cell is returned.

Start_char is the number of the first character in the note you wish to return. If the argument is omitted, it is assumed to be 1.

Num_chars is the number of characters in the note to return. It must be 255 characters or less. If the argument is omitted, it is assumed to be the entire length of the note attached to the cell identified in the argument cell_ref.

GET.OBJECT

The GET.OBJECT function returns information about a specified object.

Use with macro sheets only.

Syntax

`=GET.OBJECT(type_num,object_id_text,start_num,count_num)`

Type_num is a number that specifies the type of information you want returned, as shown in the following table.

Type_num	Returns
1	A number that specifies the type of the selected object:
	1 = Line
	2 = Rectangle
	3 = Oval
	4 = Arc
	5 = Embedded chart
	6 = Text box
	7 = Button
	8 = Picture
	9 = Closed polygon
	10 = Open polygon
2	Returns TRUE if the object if locked; otherwise returns a value of FALSE.
3	Z-order position (layering) of the object.
4	Returns a reference to the cell under the upper-left corner of the object as text in R1C1 style, or, for a line or arc, returns the start point.
5	Returns the X offset from the upper-left corner of the cell under the upper-left corner of the object.
6	Returns the Y offset from the upper-left corner of the cell under the upper-left corner of the object.
7	Returns the reference of the cell under the lower-right corner of the object as text, or, for a line or arc, returns the end point.
8	Returns the X offset from the upper-left corner of the cell under the lower-right corner of the object.
9	Returns the Y offset from the upper-left corner of the cell under the lower-right corner of the object.
10	Returns the name of the macro assigned to the object.

Type_num	Returns
11	Returns a number which indicates how the object moves and sizes. 1 = Object moves and sizes with cells 2 = Object moves with cells 3 = Object is fixed
12	Applies to text boxes and buttons. Returns text starting at start_num for count_num characters.
13	Applies to text boxes and buttons. Returns the font name of all text starting at the start_num argument for count_num argument characters.
14	Applies to text boxes and buttons. Returns the font size of all text starting with the start_num argument and ending with the character specified by the count_num argument.
15	Applies to text boxes and buttons. Returns TRUE if all text that starts with the start_num argument and ends with the character specified by the count_num argument is bold; otherwise returns a value of #N/A.
16	Applies to text boxes and buttons. Returns TRUE if all text that starts with the start_num argument and ends with the character specified by the count_num argument is italic; otherwise returns a value of #N/A.
17	Applies to text boxes and buttons. Returns TRUE if all text that starts with the start_num argument and ends with the character specified by the count_num argument is underlined; otherwise returns a value of #N/A.
18	Applies to text boxes and buttons. Returns TRUE if all text that starts with the start_num argument and ends with the character specified by the count_num argument is struck through; otherwise returns a value of #N/A.
19	Applies to text boxes and buttons. Returns TRUE if all text that starts with the start_num argument and ends with the character specified by the count_num argument is outlined. This argument is always FALSE in Excel for Windows.
20	Applies to text boxes and buttons. Returns TRUE if all text that starts with the start_num argument and ends with the character specified by the count_num argument is shadowed. This argument is always FALSE in Excel for Windows.

Type_num	Returns
21	Applies to text boxes and buttons. Returns a number that indicates the color of all text that starts with the start_num argument and ends with the count_num argument.
22	Applies to text boxes and buttons. Returns a number that indicates the horizontal alignment of text:

1 = Left
2 = Center
3 = Right
4 = Justified

23	Applies to text boxes and buttons. Returns a number that indicates the vertical alignment of text:

1 = Top
2 = Center
3 = Bottom
4 = Justified

24	Applies to text boxes and buttons. Returns a number that indicates the orientation of the text:

0 = Horizontal
1 = Vertical
2 = Upward
3 = Downward

25	Applies to text boxes and buttons. Returns TRUE if the text box or button is set to automatic sizing; otherwise the value of FALSE.
26	Applies to all objects. Returns TRUE if the object has been hidden by the HIDE.OBJECT function; otherwise returns a value of FALSE.
27	Applies to all objects. Returns a number that indicates the type of the border or line:

0 = Custom
1 = Automatic
2 = None

Type_num	Returns
28	Applies to all objects. Returns a number that indicates the style of the border or line:

0 = None
1 = Solid line
2 = Dashed line
3 = Dotted line
4 = Dashed dotted line
5 = Dashed double-dotted line
6 = 50 percent gray line
7 = 75 percent gray line
8 = 25 percent gray line

29	Applies to all objects. Returns a number that indicates the color of the border or line.
30	Applies to all objects. Returns a number that indicates the weight of the border or line:

1 = Hairline
2 = Thin
3 = Medium
4 = Thick

31	Applies to all objects. Returns a number that indicates the type of fill pattern. If the number is 0, the fill is custom; if the number is 1, the fill is automatic; and if the number is 2, there is no fill.
32	Applies to all objects. Returns a number that indicates the fill pattern.
33	Applies to all objects. Returns a number that indicates the foreground color of the fill pattern.
34	Applies to all objects. Returns a number that indicates the background color of the fill pattern.
35	Applies to all objects. Returns a number that indicates the width of the arrowhead, as follows:

1 = Narrow
2 = Medium
3 = Wide

Type_num	Returns
36	Applies to all objects. Returns a number that indicates the length of the arrowhead, as follows: 1 = Short 2 = Medium 3 = Long
37	Applies to all objects. Returns a number that indicates the style of the arrowhead, as follows: 1 = No head 2 = Open head 3 = Closed head
38	Applies to all objects. Returns TRUE if the border has round corners; otherwise returns a value of FALSE. If the object is a line, returns the #N/A error value.
39	Applies to all objects. Returns TRUE if the border has a shadow; otherwise returns a value of FALSE. If the object is a line, returns the #N/A error value.
40	Applies to all objects. Returns TRUE if the Lock Text check box in the Object Protection dialog box is selected; otherwise returns a value of FALSE.
41	Applies to all objects. Returns TRUE if the objects are to be printed; otherwise returns a value of FALSE.
42	Applies to all objects. Returns the horizontal distance from the left edge of the active window to the left edge of the object. If the window is scrolled beyond the object, this will be a negative number.
43	Applies to all objects. Returns the vertical distance from the top edge of the active to the top edge of the object. If the window is scrolled beyond the object, this will be a negative number.
44	Applies to all objects. Returns the horizontal distance from the left edge of the active window to the right edge of the object. If the window is scrolled beyond the object, this will be a negative number.
45	Applies to all objects. Returns the vertical distance from the top edge of the active window to the bottom edge of the object. If the window is scrolled beyond the object, this will be a negative number.
46	Applies to all objects. Returns the number of vertices in a polygon.

Type_num	Returns
47	Applies to all objects. Returns a count_num argument by 2 array of vertex coordinates starting at the start_num argument in a polygon's array of vertices.

Object_id_text is the name and number, or number, of the object about which you want information. Object_id_text is the information displayed in the reference when the object is selected. If object_id_text is omitted, it is assumed to be the current selected object. If object_id_text is omitted and no object is selected, the function returns an error value.

Start_num is the number of the first character in the text box or button, or the first vertex in a polygon, about which you want information.

Count_num is the number of characters in a text box or button, or the number of vertices in a polygon, that start with the start_num argument, about which you want information.

GET.TOOL

The GET.TOOL function returns information about a tool or tools on a toolbar.

Use with macro sheets only.

Syntax

`=GET.TOOL(type_num,bar_id,position)`

Type_num is a number that specifies the type of information you want returned, as shown in the following table.

Type_num	Returns
1	The tool's ID number.
2	The reference of the macro assigned to the tool.
3	Returns TRUE if the tool button is down; otherwise returns a value of FALSE.
4	Returns TRUE if the tool enabled; otherwise returns a value of FALSE.
5	Returns TRUE if the typeface on the tool is bitmapped; returns FALSE if the typeface on the tool is a default tool face.

Type_num	Returns
6	Returns the help_text reference associated with the custom tool.
7	Returns the balloon_text reference associated with the custom tool.

Bar_id specifies the name or number of the toolbar for which you want information.

Position specifies the position of the tool for which you are seeking information on the toolbar. Position starts with 1 at the left side of the toolbar (if horizontal) or at the top of the toolbar (if vertical).

GET.TOOLBAR

The GET.TOOLBAR function returns information about one or all of the toolbars.

Use with macro sheets only.

Syntax

`=GET.TOOLBAR(type_num, bar_id)`

Type_num is a number from 1 to 9 that specifies the type of information you want returned. If type_num is 8 or 9, GET.TOOLBAR returns an array of names or numbers of all visible toolbars or hidden toolbars; otherwise bar_id is required to identify the specific toolbar about which you seek information.

Type_num	Returns
1	A horizontal array of all tool IDs on the toolbar in position from left to right, or top to bottom.
2	A number that indicates the horizontal position of the toolbar in the docked or floating region.
3	A number that indicates the vertical of the toolbar in the docked or floating region.
4	A number that indicates the width of the toolbar.
5	A number that indicates the height of the toolbar.
6	A number that indicates the toolbar position. 1 = Top dock in the workspace 2 = Left dock in the workspace 3 = Right dock in the workspace 4 = Bottom dock in the workspace 5 = Floating

Type_num	Returns
7	Return TRUE if the toolbar is visible; otherwise returns a value of FALSE.
8	Returns an array of toolbar IDs (names or numbers) of all toolbars, visible and hidden.
9	Returns an array of toolbar IDs (names or numbers) for all visible toolbars.

Bar_id specifies the number or name of a specific toolbar for which you want information.

GET.WINDOW

The GET.WINDOW function returns information about a window.

Use with macro sheets only.

Syntax

```
=GET.WINDOW(type_num,window_text)
```

Type_num is a number that specifies the type of window information you are seeking, as shown in the following table.

Type_num	Returns
1	Returns the name of the document in the window.
2	Returns the number of the window.
3	Returns the X position from the left edge of the workspace to the left edge of the window.
4	Returns the Y position from the top edge of the workspace to the top edge of the window.
5	Returns the width.
6	Returns the height.
7	Returns TRUE if the window is hidden; otherwise returns a value of FALSE.
8	Returns TRUE if formulas are displayed; otherwise returns a value of FALSE.
9	Returns TRUE if gridlines are displayed; otherwise returns a value of FALSE.

Type_num	Returns

10   Returns TRUE if row and column headings are displayed; otherwise returns a value of FALSE.

11   Returns TRUE if zeros are displayed; otherwise returns a value of FALSE.

12   Returns a number indicating gridline and heading colors that corresponds to the colors in the Display Options dialog box.

13   Returns the leftmost column number of each pane.

14   Returns the top row number of each pane.

15   Returns the number of columns in each pane.

16   Returns the number of rows in each pane.

17   Returns a number that indicates the active pane:

1 = Upper, left, or upper-left
2 = Right or upper-right
3 = Lower or lower-right
4 = Lower-right

18   Returns TRUE if the window has a vertical split; otherwise returns a value of FALSE.

19   Returns TRUE if the window has a horizontal split; otherwise returns a value of FALSE.

20   Returns TRUE if the window is maximized; otherwise returns a value of FALSE.

21   Reserved.

22   Returns TRUE is the Outline Symbols check box is the Display Options dialog box is selected; otherwise returns a value of FALSE.

23   Returns a number that indicates the size of the document window, as follows:

1 = Restored
2 = Minimized (displayed as an icon)
3 = Maximized

24   Returns TRUE if the panes are frozen; otherwise returns a value of FALSE.

25   Returns the magnification of the active window (as a percentage). If none is specified, the default is 100 percent.

Windows_text is the name that appears in the title bar of the window about which you are seeking information. If the argument is omitted, it is assumed to be the active window.

GET.WORKBOOK

The GET.WORKBOOK function is used to return information about a workbook.

Use with macro sheets only.

Syntax

```
=GET.WORKBOOK(type_num, name_text)
```

Type_num is a number that specifies the type of workbook information you want, as shown in the following table.

Type_num	Returns
1	Returns the name of all document in the workbook.
2	Returns the name of the active document in the workbook.
3	Returns the name of the currently selected documents in the workbook.
4	Returns the number of documents in the workbook.

Name_text is the name of an open workbook. If the argument is omitted, it is assumed to be the active workbook.

GET.WORKSPACE

The GET.WORKSPACE function is used to return information about the workspace.

Use with macro sheets only.

Syntax

```
=GET.WORKSPACE(type_num)
```

Type_num is a number that specifies the type of workspace information you are seeking, as shown in the following table.

Type_num	Returns
1	Returns the name of the environment in which Excel is running.
2	Returns the version of Excel.
3	Return the number of decimals if fixed decimals is set; otherwise returns a value of 0.
4	Returns TRUE if in R1C1 style; otherwise, if in A1 style; returns FALSE.
5	Returns TRUE if scroll bars are displayed; otherwise returns FALSE.
6	Returns TRUE if the status bar is displayed; otherwise returns FALSE.
7	Returns TRUE if the formula bar is displayed; otherwise returns FALSE.
8	Returns TRUE if remote DDE requests are enabled; otherwise returns FALSE.
9	Returns the alternate menu key.
10	Returns a number that indicates special modes:

1 = Data Find
2 = Copy
3 = Cut
4 = Data Entry
5 = Unused
6 = Copy and Data Entry
7 = Cut and Data Entry

If no special mode is set, returns a value of 0.

Type_num	Returns
11	Returns the X position of the workspace window from the left edge of the screen to the left edge of the window.
12	Return the Y position of the workspace window from the top edge of the screen to the top edge of the window.
13	Returns useable workspace width.
14	Returns useable workspace height.
15	Returns a number that indicates either a maximized or minimized status.

1 = Neither
2 = Minimized
3 = Maximized

Type_num	Returns
16	Returns the amount of free memory.
17	Returns the total memory available to Excel.
18	Returns TRUE if a math processor is present; otherwise returns a value of FALSE.
19	Returns TRUE if a mouse is present; otherwise returns a value of FALSE.
20	Returns a horizontal array of documents in a group if a group is present.
21	Returns TRUE if the Excel version 3.0 toolbar is displayed; otherwise returns the value of FALSE.
22	Return the DDE application specific error code.
23	Returns the full path of the default startup directory.
24	Returns the full path of the alternate startup directory.
25	Returns TRUE if set for relative recording, FALSE if set for alternate recording.
26	Returns the name of the user.
27	Returns the name of the organization.
28	If alternate menus are switched to by the alternate menu or help key, returns a value of 1; if Lotus 1-2-3 help is switched to, returns a value of 2.
29	Returns TRUE if alternate navigations are enabled.
30	Returns a nine-item horizontal array of global print setting that can be set by the LINE.PRINT function:

▼ Setup text
▼ Left Margin
▼ Right margin
▼ Top margin
▼ Bottom margin
▼ Page length

Logical value indicating whether to wait after printing each page (TRUE) or use continuous form feed (FALSE).

Logical value indicating whether the printer has automatic line feeding (TRUE) or requires line-feed characters (FALSE).

The number of the printer port.

Type_num	Returns
31	Returns TRUE if a currently running macro is in step mode; otherwise returns a value of FALSE.
32	Returns the current location of Excel.
33	Returns a horizontal array of the names in the File New list.
34	Returns a horizontal array of template file in the File New list.
35	Returns TRUE if a macro is paused; otherwise returns a value of FALSE.
36	Returns TRUE if the Cell Drag and Drop check in the Options Workspace dialog box is selected; otherwise returns a value of FALSE.
37	Returns a 45-item array of the items related to country, versions, and settings, as follows. Numbers 1 and 2 are country codes, 3 to 5 are number separators, 6 to 11 are R1C1 style reference numbers, 12 to 16 are array characters, 17 to 26 are format code symbols, 27 to 32 are format codes, and 33 to 45 are logical value formats.

1   Number corresponding to the country version of Excel.
2   Number corresponding to the current country setting in the Windows Control Panel.
3   Decimal separator.
4   Zero (or 1000) separator.
5   List separator.
6   Row character.
7   Column character.
8   Lowercase row character.
9   Lowercase column character.
10 Character used instead of the left bracket.
11 Character used instead of the right bracket.
12 Character used instead of the left bracket.
13 Character used instead of the right bracket.
14 Column separator.
15 Row separator.
16 Alternate array item separator to use if the current array separator is the same as the decimal separator.
17 Date separator.
18 Time separator.

Type_num	Returns
19	Year symbol.
20	Month symbol.
21	Day symbol.
22	Hour symbol.
23	Minute symbol.
24	Second symbol.
25	Currency symbol.
26	"General" symbol.
27	Number of decimal digits to use in curency reports.
28	Number indicating the current format for negative currencies (where *currency* is a number and $ represents the current currency symbol): 0 = ($currency) or (currency$) 1 = -$currency or -currency$ 2 = $-currency or currency-$ 3 = $currency- or currency$-
29	Number of decimal digits to use in noncurrency numbers.
30	Number of characters to use in month names.
31	Number of characters to use in weekday names.
32	Number indicating date order: 0 = Month-Day-Year 1 = Day-Month-Year 2 = year-Month-Day
33	TRUE if using 24-hour time; otherwise FALSE.
34	TRUE if not displaying functions in English; otherwise FALSE.
35	TRUE if using the metric system; otherwise FALSE.
36	TRUE if a space is added before the currency symbol; otherwise FALSE.
37	TRUE if currency symbol precedes currency values; otherwise FALSE.
38	TRUE if using minus sign for negative numbers, FALSE if using parentheses.
39	TRUE if trailing zeros are displayed for zero currency values; otherwise FALSE.
40	TRUE if leading zeros are displayed for zero currency values; otherwise FALSE.

Type_num	Returns
	41 TRUE if leading zero is displayed in months; otherwise FALSE.
	42 TRUE if leading zero is displayed in days; otherwise FALSE.
	43 TRUE if using four-digit year, FALSE if displaying two-digit year.
	44 TRUE if date order is month-day-year when displaying dates in long form, FALSE if date order is day-month-year.
	45 TRUE if leading zero is shown in the time; otherwise FALSE.
38	Returns 0, 1, or 2, indicating the type of error-checking set by the ERROR function.
39	Returns a reference to the currently defined error-handling macro set by the ERROR function.
40	Returns TRUE if screen updating is turned on; otherwise returns a value of FALSE.
41	Returns a horizontal array of cell ranges that were previously selected with the Goto command from the Formula menu.
42	Returns TRUE if your computer is capable of playing sounds; otherwise returns a value of FALSE.
43	Returns TRUE if your computer is capable of recording sounds; otherwise returns a value of FALSE.
44	Returns a three-column array of all currently registered procedures in the dynamic link libraries. The first column contains the name of the DLLs that contain the procedures, the second columm contains the names of the procedures in the DLLs, and the third column contains text strings that contain the data type of the return values, and the number and data type of the arguments.
45	Returns TRUE if Windows for Pen Computing is running; otherwise returns a value of FALSE.
46	Returns TRUE if the More After Enter check box in the Options Workspace dialog box is selected; otherwise returns a value of FALSE.

LAST.ERROR

The LAST.ERROR function is used to return the reference of the cell where the last macro sheet error occurred.

Use with macro sheets only.

Syntax

```
=LAST.ERROR()
```

LINKS

The LINKS function is used to return the names of all worksheets referred to by external references in the document specified.

Use with macro sheets only.

Syntax

```
=LINKS(document_text,type_num)
```

Document_text is the name of the document, including its path. If the argument is omitted, the function operates on the active document.

Type_num is a number that specifies the type of linked documents to return, as shown in the following table.

Type_num	Returns
1 or omitted	Excel link
2	DDE link
3	Reserved
4	Not applicable
5	Publisher
6	Subscriber

NAMES

The NAMES function returns all specified names defined in the specified document. This is useful for locating named references, and so forth.

Use with macro sheets only.

Syntax

=NAMES(document_text,type_num,match_text)

Document_text specifies the document in which you want to locate the specified names. If this argument is omitted, it is assumed to be the active document.

Type_num is a number from 1 to 3 that specifies whether you want to include hidden names in the returned information. If the number is 1 or omitted, the function returns normal names only; if the number is 2, the function returns hidden names only; and if the number is 3, the function returns all names.

Match_text is text enclosed in quotation marks that specifies the names you want returned. This argument accepts DOS wildcards. If this argument is omitted, all names are returned.

REPORT.GET

The REPORT.GET function is used to return information about reports that have been defined in the active document. This function is used in conjunction with the Reports add-in macro that comes with Excel.

Use with macro sheets only.

Syntax

=REPORT.GET(type_num, report_name)

Type_num is a number from 1 to 3 that specifies the type of information you want returned, as shown below.

Type_num	Returns
1	An array of reports in the active document or, if none are specified, an error value.
2	An array of view and scenario pairs for the specified report in the active document. If the name is invalid or the document is protected, the argument returns an error value.
3	Returns TRUE if continuous page numbers are used, FALSE if page numbers start at 1 for each section.

Report_name specifies the name of the report in the active document for which you are seeking information. Report_name is required if type_num is a 2 or 3.

SELECTION

The SELECTION function is used to return information about the current selection. If a cell or range of cells is selected, you will usually get the value contained in the cells, not the reference. If an object is selected, Excel returns the object listed in the table in the syntax section of this function.

Use with macro sheets only.

Syntax

```
=SELECTION()
```

The following table lists the object identifiers that can be returned by the SELECTION function.

Items selected	Identifier returned
Imported graphic	Picture n
Linked graphic	Picture n
Chart picture	Picture n
Linked chart	Chart n
Worksheet range	Picture n
Linked worksheet range	Picture n
Text box	Text n
Button	Button n
Rectangle	Rectangle n
Oval	Oval n
Line	Line n
Arc	Arc n
Group	Group n
Freehand drawing	Drawing n

This function also returns the identifiers of the chart, as shown in the following table.

Item_text	Selects
Chart	Entire chart
Plot	Plot area

Item_text	Selects
Legend	Legend
Axis 1	Main chart value axis
Axis 2	Main chart category axis
Axis 3	Overlay chart value axis of 3-D series axis
Axis 4	Overlay chart category axis
Title	Chart title
Text Axis 1	Label for the main chart value axis
Text Axis 2	Label for the main chart category axis
Text Axis 3	Label for the main chart series axis
Text n	nth floating text item
Arrow n	nth arrow
Gridline 1	Major gridlines of value axis
Gridline 2	Minor gridlines of value axis
Gridline 3	Major gridlines of category axis
Gridline 4	Minor gridlines of category axis
Gridline 5	Major gridlines of series axis
Gridline 6	Minor gridlines of series axis
Dropline 1	Main chart droplines
Dropline 2	Overlay chart droplines
Hiloline 1	Main chart hi-lo lines
Hiloline 2	Overlay chart hi-lo lines
Up Bar 1	Main chart up bar
Up Bar 2	Overlay chart up bar
Down Bar 1	Main chart down bar
Down Bar 2	Overlay chart down bar
Series line 1	Main chart series line
Series line 2	Overlay chart series line
Sn	Entire series (where n is a number)
SnPm	Data associated with point m in series n if single_point is TRUE
Text SnPm	Text attached to point m of series n
Text Sn	Series title text of series n of an area chart

Item_text	Selects
Floor	Base of a 3-D chart
Walls	Back of a 3-D chart
Corners	Corners of a 3-D chart

SLIDE.GET

The SLIDE.GET function is used to return specified information about a slide show or about a particular slide in a slide show.

Use with macro sheets only.

Syntax

=SLIDE.GET(**type_num,** name_text, slide_num)

Type_num is the type of information you want to get about the slide show or slide. The following table lists the values you can use to return information about slide shows.

Type_num	Type of information returned
1	The number of slides in the slide show.
2	A two-item array that contains the numbers of the first and last slides in the current selection. Returns an error value if the selection is nonadjacent.
3	The version number of the Slide Show add-in macro used to create the slide show document.

The following table lists the values you can use to return information about single slides in a slide show.

Type_num	Type of information returned
4	The transition effect number.
5	The transition effect name.
6	The transition effect speed.
7	The number of seconds the slide is displayed before advancing to the next slide.
8	The name of the sound file which is associated with the slide. If no sound is specified, returns empty text (" ").

Name_text is the name of an open slide show about which you are seeking information. If this argument is omitted, it is assumed to be the active document.

Slide_num is the number of the slide about which you want information. If the argument is omitted, it is assumed to be the slide associated with the active cell on the document named in the name_text argument. If the value in the Type_num argument is 1, 2, or 3, the slide_num argument is ignored.

VIEW.GET

The VIEW.GET function is used to return an array of views from the active window. This function is equivalent to displaying a list of views in the Views dialog box, which appears when you choose the View command from the Window menu. This function is used in conjunction with the View Manager add-in macro.

Use with macro sheets only.

Syntax

`=VIEW.GET(type_num, view_name)`

Type_num is a number from 1 to 3 that specifies the type of information you want returned, as shown in the following table.

Type_num	Result
1	Returns an array of views in the active document. If none are defined, returns an error value.
2	Returns TRUE if print settings are included in the view; otherwise returns a value of FALSE. If the name is invalid or the document is protected, returns an error value.
3	Returns TRUE if row and column settings are included in the view; otherwise returns a value of FALSE. If the name is invalid or the document is protected, returns an error value.

View_name specifies the name of the view (in text enclosed in quotation marks) in the active document. If type_num is 2 or 3, view_name is required.

WINDOWS

The WINDOWS function is used to return the names of open windows in Excel, including hidden windows. The windows are listed in order, starting with the topmost window.

Use with macro sheets only.

Syntax

```
=WINDOWS(type_num,match_text)
```

Type_num is a number that specifies the type of documents returned by the function. If the number is 1 or omitted, the function returns all windows except those that belong to add-in documents. If the number is 2, the function returns add-in documents only. If the number is 3, the function returns all types of documents.

Match_text specifies the windows whose names you want to return. This argument accepts wildcards. If this argument is omitted, the function returns the names of all open windows.

Macro Control Functions

Macro Control Functions are commands used in macros in order to branch, loop, debug, and test macros.

ARGUMENT

The ARGUMENT function is used to describe the arguments in a custom function or subroutine. A custom function or subroutine must contain one argument function for each argument in the macro itself. You may use from one to thirteen arguments.

Use with macro sheets only.

Syntax

There are two forms of syntax for an argument function. Use the first if you want to store the argument as a name. Use the second syntax if you want to store the argument in a specific cell or cells.

Syntax 1

```
=ARGUMENT(name_text,data_type_num)
```

Name_text is the name of the argument or of the cells containing the argument.

Data_type_num is a number that determines what type of values are accepted for the argument. Data_type_num can also be a sum of the available numbers. For example, if data_type_num is 3, then the value can be a number or text. If data_type_num is omitted, it is assumed to be 7. The following table lists the numbers and their corresponding data types.

Data_type_num	Type of value
1	Number
2	Text
4	Logical
8	Reference
16	Error
64	Array

Syntax 2

```
=ARGUMENT(name_text,data_type_num,reference)
```

Reference is the cell or cells in which you want to store the argument's value.

BREAK

The BREAK function interrupts a For-Next, a For.Cell-Next, or a While-Next loop. If the Break function is placed within a loop, that loop is terminated and the macro looks for the Next statement at the end of the loop.

Use with macro sheets only.

Syntax

```
=BREAK()
```

ELSE

The ELSE function is used in conjunction with If, Else, If, and End.If to determine which functions are processed in a macro. Else is followed by a formula or group of formulas that will be processed if the results of all preceding Else.If statements and the preceding If statement are FALSE.

Use with macro sheets only.

Syntax

```
=ELSE()
```

ELSE.IF

The ELSE.IF function is used with If, Else, and End.If to determine which functions are processed in a macro. Else.If is followed by a formula or group of formulas that will be processed if the results of the preceding If or Else.If function returns FALSE and if logical_test is TRUE.

Use with macro sheets only.

Syntax

```
=ELSE.IF(logical_test)
```

Logical_test is a logical value that Else.If uses to determine where to branch. If logical_test is TRUE, Excel carries out the functions between the Else.If function and the next Else.If, Else, or End.If function. If logical_test is FALSE, Excel branches to the next Else, If, Else, or End.If function.

END.IF

The END.IF function ends functions associated with the preceding If function.

Use with macro sheets only.

Syntax

```
=END.IF()
```

FOR

The FOR function repeats the instructions between the For and Next functions a specified number of times. This is a For-Next loop.

Use with macro sheets only.

Syntax

```
=FOR(counter_text,start_num,end_num,step_num)
```

Counter_text is the name of the loop counter in the form of text.

Start_num is the value initially assigned to counter_text.

End_num is the last value assigned to counter_text.

Step_num is a value added to the loop counter after each iteration. The default is 1. The following table shows the steps in executing a For-Next loop.

Step	Action
1	Sets counter_text to the value start_num.
2	If counter_text is greater than end_num (or less than end_num if step_num is negative), the loop ends and the macro continues with the function after the Next function. If counter_text is less than or equal to end_num (or greater than or equal to end_num if step_num is negative), the macro continues in the loop.
3	Carries out functions up to the following Next function. The Next function must be below the For function and in the same column.
4	Adds step_num to the loop counter.
5	Returns to the For function and proceeds as described in step2.

FOR.CELL

The FOR.CELL function starts a For.cell-Next loop. The instructions between For.cell and Next are repeated over a range of cells, one cell at a time, and there is no loop counter.

Use with macro sheets only.

Syntax

```
=FOR.CELL(ref_name,area_ref,skip_blanks)
```

Ref_name is the name, in text, that Excel gives to the one cell in the range that is currently being operated on.

Area_ref is the range(s) of cells on which you want the For.Cell-Next loop to operate. Skip_blanks is a logical value that specifies whether blank cells are skipped. If the argument is TRUE, blank cells are skipped. If the argument is FALSE or omitted, blank cells are operated on.

GOTO

The GOTO function directs a macro execution to another cell or range. The macro will continue running at the upper-left cell of reference.

Use with macro sheets only.

Syntax

```
=GOTO(reference)
```

Reference is a cell reference or name that is defined as a cell reference. Reference can be an external reference if the macro sheet is open.

HALT

The HALT function stops all macros from running.

Use with macro sheets only.

Syntax

```
=HALT(cancel_close)
```

Cancel_close is a logical value that specifies whether a macro sheet, when encountering the HALT function in an Auto_close macro, is closed. If the argument is TRUE, the macro is halted, and the document is not closed. If the argument is FALSE or omitted, the macro is halted and the document is closed.

IF

The IF function conducts conditional tests on values and formulas, and branches based on the results of the tests. IF returns one value if the test is TRUE and another if the test is FALSE. There are two forms of syntax used with the IF function.

Use with macro sheets and worksheets.

Syntax 1

```
=IF(logical_test,value_if_true,value_if_false)
```

Logical_test is any value or expression that can be evaluated to TRUE or FALSE.

Value_if_true is the value that is returned if logical_test is TRUE.

Value_if_false is the value that is returned if logical_test is FALSE.

Up to seven IF functions can be nested as value_if_true and value_if_false arguments.

Syntax 2

Used with macro sheets only.

In Syntax 2, the IF function is used with Else, Else.if, and End.if to control which formulas in a macro are executed.

```
=IF(logical_test)
```

Logical_text is a logical value that IF uses to determine where to branch. If the argument is TRUE, Excel carries out the functions between the If function and the next Else, Else.If, or End.If function. If the argument is FALSE, Excel branches to the next Else.If, Else, or End.If function.

NEXT

The NEXT function ends a For-Next, For.Cell-Next, or While-Next loop and skips to the formula following the Next function.

Use with macro sheets only.

Syntax

```
=NEXT()
```

PAUSE

The PAUSE function pauses a macro, allowing user input.

Use with macro sheets only.

Syntax

```
=PAUSE(no_tool)
```

No_tool is a logical value that specifies whether to display the Resume toolbar when the macro is paused. If the argument is TRUE, the toolbar is not displayed. If the argument is FALSE or omitted, the toolbar is displayed.

RESTART

The RESTART function removes Return statements from the stack. You can use RESTART to determine which macro regains control when one macro calls another.

Use with macro sheets only.

Syntax

`=RESTART(level_num)`

Level_num is a number that specifies the number of previous Return statements you want to be ignored. If this argument is omitted, the next Return statement will halt macro execution.

RESULT

The RESULT function specifies the type of data returned by a macro or custom function. Use this function to make sure that your macros and custom functions return values of the correct data types.

Use with macro sheets only.

Syntax

`=RESULT(type_num)`

Type_num is a number that specifies the data type, as shown in the following table. Type_num can be a sum of the numbers. For example, if type_num is 3(1+2), the result can be a number or text. If you omit type_num, it is assumed to be 7.

Type_num	Type of returned data
1	Number
2	Text
4	Logical
8	Reference
16	Error
64	Array

RETURN

The RETURN function ends the currently running macro. In a subroutine macro that was called by another macro, control is returned to the calling macro. In a custom function, control is returned to the formula that called the function. In a command macro, control is returned to the user.

Use with macro sheets only.

Syntax

`=RETURN`(value)

Value specifies what value to return if the macro is a custom function or a subroutine. If the macro is a command macro, value should be omitted.

SET.NAME

The SET.NAME function defines a name on a macro sheet to refer to a value. Use this function to store values while the macro is calculating.

Use with macro sheets only.

Syntax

`=SET.NAME(name_text,`value)

Name_text is the name, in text, that refers to value.

Value is the value you want to store in name_text. If value is omitted, the name name_text is deleted.

SET.VALUE

The SET.VALUE function changes the value of a cell or cells on the macro sheet without changing any formulas entered in those cells. The value of cells in worksheets does not change. This function is useful for assigning and storing values during the calculation of a macro.

Use with macro sheets only.

Syntax

`=SET.VALUE`(reference,values)

Reference specifies the cell or cells on the macro sheet to which you want to assign a new value(s).

Values is the value(s) to which you want to assign the cell(s) in reference.

STEP

The STEP function stops the normal flow of a macro and calculates it one cell at a time. This is useful for debugging macros.

Use with macro sheets only.

Syntax

```
=STEP()
```

VOLATILE

The VOLATILE function specifies whether a custom function is volatile or nonvolatile. A volatile custom function is recalculated every time a calculation occurs on the worksheet. This function must precede every other formula in the function except Result and Argument.

Use with macro sheets only.

Syntax

```
=VOLATILE(logical)
```

Logical is a logical value that specifies whether the custom function is volatile or nonvolatile. If the argument is TRUE or omitted, the function is volatile. If the argument is FALSE, the function is nonvolatile.

WAIT

The WAIT function pauses the macro for a designated period of time. This function will suspend all Excel activity, except background (for example, printing) activities.

Use with macro sheets only.

Syntax

```
=WAIT(serial_number)
```

Serial_number is the date-time code used for date and time calculations. You can use text (for example, 5:00 PM) or a formula, such as NOW()+"00:00:10", instead of as a number. The text or formula is converted to a serial number.

WHILE

The WHILE function carries out the statements between the WHILE function and the next Next function until logical_test is FALSE.

Use with macro sheets only.

Syntax

```
=WHILE(logical_test)
```

Logical_test is a value or formula that evaluates to TRUE or FALSE. If Logical_text is TRUE, the execution continues. If Logical_test is FALSE, the macro skips to the statement after the next Next function.

The Customizing Functions

The customizing functions are used to customize Excel.

ADD.BAR

The ADD.BAR function creates a new menu bar and returns the bar ID number, which can then be used to identify the menu in other functions that allow you to display and add menus and commands to the menu bar. You must use SHOW.BAR to display a menu created by ADD.BAR.

Use with macro sheets only.

Syntax

```
=ADD.BAR(bar_num)
```

Bar_num is the number of a built-in menu bar to be restored after changes have been made. A list of ID numbers for built-in menu bars can be found in the following function, ADD.COMMAND.

ADD.COMMAND

The ADD.COMMAND function adds a command to a menu and returns the position number on the menu.

Use with menu sheets only.

Syntax

```
=ADD.COMMAND(bar_num,menu,command_ref,position)
```

Bar_num is a number that corresponds to the menu bar or type of shortcut menu to which you add a command. The following tables list the ID numbers of the built-in menu bars and the types of shortcut menus.

Bar_num	Built-in Menu Bar
1	Worksheet and macro sheet
2	Chart
3	Null (the menu displayed when no documents are open)
4	Info
5	Worksheet and macro sheet (short menus)
6	Chart (short menus)

Bar_num	Shortcut Menu
7	Cell, toolbar, and workbook
8	Object
9	Chart

Menu is the menu to which you want the new command added. It can be either a text name or a number. If bar_num is 1 through 6, menus are numbered starting with 1 from the left of the menu bar. If bar_num is 7 through 9, menu refers to a built-in shortcut menu. The combination of bar_num and menu determines which shortcut menu to modify, as shown in the following table.

Bar_num	Menu	Shortcut Menu
7	1	Toolbars
7	2	Toolbar tools
7	3	Workbook paging icons
7	4	Cells (worksheet)
7	5	Column selections
7	6	Row selections
7	7	Workbook items
7	8	Cells (macro sheet)
8	1	Drawn or imported objects
8	2	Buttons
8	3	Text boxes
9	1	Chart series
9	2	Chart text
9	3	Chart plot area and walls

Bar_num	Menu	Shortcut Menu
9	4	Entire charts
9	5	Chart axes
9	6	Chart gridlines
9	7	Chart floor and arrows
9	8	Chart legends

Command_ref is an array or a reference to an area on the macro sheet that describes the new command(s). It must be at least two columns wide, with the first column specifiying command names and the second specifying macro names.

Position specifies the placement of the new command. It can be either a number (starting with 1 at the top of the menu) or the text of an existing command above which you want to add a command.

ADD.MENU

The ADD.MENU function adds a menu to a menu bar and returns the position number in the menu bar of the new menu.

Use with macro sheets only.

Syntax

`=ADD.MENU(bar_num,menu_ref,position)`

See the ADD.COMMAND function for an explanation of syntax.

ADD.TOOL

The ADD.TOOL function adds tools to a toolbar.

Use with macro sheets only.

Syntax

`=ADD.TOOL(bar_id,position,tool_ref)`

Bar_id is a number from 1 to 9 that specifies either a built-in toolbar or the name, in text, of a custom toolbar. The following table lists each bar_id and its corresponding built-in toolbar.

Bar_id	Built-in Toolbar
1	Standard
2	Formatting
3	Utility
4	Chart
5	Drawing
6	Excel 3.0
7	Macro
8	Macro recording
9	Macro paused

Position specifies the position, starting with number 1, of the tool in the toolbar.

Tool_ref is a number that specifies a built-in tool, or is a reference to an area on the macro sheet that defines a custom tool or set of tools.

ALERT

The ALERT function displays a dialog box containing a message, and waits for the user to select a button.

Use with macro sheets only.

Syntax

`=ALERT`(message_text,type_num,help_ref)

Message_text is the message displayed in the dialog box.

Type_num is a number from 1 to 3 that specifies which type of dialog box to display. The default is 2. If type_num is 1, the dialog box displayed contains the OK and Cancel buttons. Alert returns TRUE if you choose OK and FALSE if you choose Cancel. If type_num is 2 or 3, the dialog box displayed contains the OK button (the difference between 2 and 3 is the icon displayed in the dialog box).

Help_ref displays a Help button in the dialog box.

APP.TITLE

The APP.TITLE function changes the title of the Excel application workspace to a title you specify.

Use with macro sheets only.

Syntax

```
=APP.TITLE(text)
```

Text is the title you want to assign to the Excel application workspace.

ASSIGN.TO.TOOL

The ASSIGN.TO.TOOL function assigns a macro to a tool. Inserting this function in a macro sheet is equivalent to choosing the Assign To Tool command from the Macro menu or the Tools shortcut menu.

Use with macro sheets only.

Syntax

```
=ASSIGN.TO.TOOL(bar_id,position,macro_ref)
```

Bar_id specifies the number or name of a toolbar to which you want to assign a macro. See the ADD.TOOL function for a table listing bar_id and corresponding built-in toolbars.

Position specifies the position, starting with 1, of the tool in the toolbar.

Macro_ref is the name of the macro you want to assign to the tool.

BEEP

The BEEP function sounds a tone or beep to get the user's attention.

Use with macro sheets only.

Syntax

```
=BEEP(tone_num)
```

Tone_num is a number from 1 to 4 that specifies the tone. The result depends on your computer (most computers produce the same sound or tone for all 4 numbers).

CANCEL.KEY

The CANCEL.KEY function disables macro interruption or specifies another macro to run when a macro is interrupted.

Use with macro sheets only.

Syntax

```
=CANCEL.KEY(enable,macro_ref)
```

Enable is a logical value that determines whether the macro can be disabled by pressing the ESC key. If Enable is FALSE, ESC does not interrupt a macro. If Enable is TRUE , ESC interrupts a macro. If Enable is TRUE and macro_ref is specified, macro_ref runs when ESC is pressed.

Macro_ref is a reference to a macro (cell reference or name) that runs when Enable is TRUE and ESC is pressed.

CHECK.COMMAND

The CHECK.COMMAND function adds or removes a check mark to or from a command name on a menu, thus choosing or not choosing the command.

Use with macro sheets only.

Syntax

```
=CHECK.COMMAND(Bar_num,menu,command,check)
```

Bar_num is the ID of the built-in or custom menu bar containing the command. See the ADD.COMMAND function for the Bar_num of built-in menus.

Menu is the menu containing the command, either as text or a number starting with 1 from the left of the screen.

Command is the command, as text, or a number starting with 1 (the first command on the menu) that you want to check.

Check is a logical value. If Check is TRUE, a check mark is added to the command. If Check is FALSE, the check mark is removed from the command.

COPY.TOOL

The COPY.TOOL function copies a tool face to the Clipboard. Inserting this function into a macro sheet is equivalent to choosing the Copy Tool Face command from the Edit menu. Use the Paste.Tool function to paste the tool from the Clipboard to a position on the toolbar.

Use with macro sheets only.

Syntax

```
=COPY.TOOL(bar_id,position)
```

Bar_id specifies the number or name of a toolbar from which you want to copy the tool face. Inserting this function into a macro sheet is equivalent to selecting a tool and choosing the Copy Tool Face command from the Edit menu. See ADD.TOOL for the Bar_id of built-in toolbars.

Position specifies the position of the tool, starting with 1, in the toolbar.

CUSTOM.REPEAT

The CUSTOM.REPEAT function allows custom commands to be repeated using the Repeat tool or the Repeat command on the Edit menu. It also allows custom commands to be recorded using the macro recorder.

Use with macro sheets only.

Syntax

```
=CUSTOM.REPEAT(macro_text,repeat_text,record_text)
```

Macro_text is the name of, or reference to, the macro you want to run when the Repeat command is chosen.

Repeat_text is the text you want to use as the command on the Edit menu.

Record_text is the formula you want to record to be run by the Repeat command. References must be in R1C1 format.

CUSTOM.UNDO

The CUSTOM.UNDO function creates a customized Undo tool and Undo or Redo command on the Edit menu for custom commands.

Use with macro sheets only.

Syntax

```
=CUSTOM.UNDO(macro_text,undo_text)
```

Macro_text is the name of, or an R1C1 reference to, the macro you want to run when the Undo command is selected.

Undo_text is the text you want to use as the Undo command.

DELETE.BAR

The DELETE.BAR function deletes a custom menu bar.

Use with macro sheets only.

Syntax

    =DELETE.BAR(bar_num)

Bar_num is the ID number of the custom menu bar you want to delete.

DELETE.COMMAND

The DELETE.COMMAND function removes commands from custom or built-in menus.

Use with macro sheets only.

Syntax

    =DELETE.COMMAND(bar_num,menu,command)

Bar_num is the menu bar from which you want to delete the command. See the Add.Command function for more information.

Menu is the menu from which you want to delete the command. See the Add.Command function for more information.

Command is the command, in text, or as a number starting with 1, that you want to delete.

DELETE.MENU

The DELETE.MENU function deletes a menu from a menu bar.

Use with macro sheets only.

Syntax

    =DELETE.MENU(bar_num,menu)

Bar_num is the menu bar from which you want to delete the menu. See the Add.Command function for the Bar_num ID numbers for built-in menu bars. You can also use an ID returned by the Add.Bar function.

Menu is the menu, as text or as a number starting with 1, that you want to delete.

DELETE.TOOL

The DELETE.TOOL function deletes a tool from a toolbar. Inserting this function into a macro sheet is equivalent to dragging a tool off the toolbar.

Use with macro sheets only.

Syntax

```
=DELETE.TOOL(bar_id,position)
```

Bar_id specifies the toolbar (name or number) from which you want to delete a tool. See the Add.Tool function for more information.

Position specifies the position of the tool, starting with 1, in the toolbar.

DELETE.TOOLBAR

The DELETE.TOOLBAR function deletes a custom toolbar. Inserting this function into a macro sheet is equivalent to choosing the Toolbars command from the Options menu and then choosing the Delete button from the Show Toolbars dialog box.

Use with macro sheets only.

Syntax

```
=DELETE.TOOLBAR(bar_name)
```

Bar_name specifies the name of the toolbar that you want to delete. For more information, see the Add.Tool function.

DIALOG.BOX

The DIALOG.BOX function displays the dialog box described in a dialog box definition table.

Use with macro sheets only.

Syntax

```
=DIALOG.BOX(dialog_ref)
```

Dialog_ref is a reference to a dialog box definition table. The dialog box definition table must be at least seven columns wide and two rows high. The following table shows the definitions of each column in a dialog box definition table.

Column type	Column number
Item number	1
Horizontal position	2
Vertical position	3
Item width	4
Item height	5
Text	6
Initial value or result	7

The first row of dialog_ref defines the position, size, and name of the dialog box. The position is specified in columns 2 and 3, the size in columns 4 and 5, and the name in column 6. To specify a default item, place the item's position number in column 7. Place the reference for the Help button in column 7.

The following table lists the numbers for the items you can display in a dialog box.

Dialog-box Item	Item Number
Default OK button	1
Cancel button	2
OK button	3
Default Cancel button	4
Static text	5
Text edit box	6
Integer edit box	7
Number edit box	8
Formula edit box	9
Reference edit box	10
Option button group	11
Option button	12
Check box	13
Group box	14
List box	15
Linked list box	16
Icons	17

Dialog-box Item	Item Number
Linked File list box	18
Linked Drive and Directory box	19
Directory text box	20
Drop-down list box	21
Drop-down combination edit/list box	22
Picture button	23
Help button	24

DISABLE.INPUT

The DISABLE.INPUT function blocks all input from the keyboard and mouse except in displayed dialog boxes.

Use with macro sheets only.

Syntax

`=DISABLE.INPUT(logical)`

Logical is a logical value that specifies whether input is blocked. If the argument is TRUE, input is disabled. If the argument is FALSE, input is reenabled.

ECHO

The ECHO function controls screen updating while a macro is running. This speeds up macros that have a lot of screen updating. Updating resumes when the macro ends.

Use with macro sheets only.

Syntax

`=ECHO(logical)`

Logical is a logical value that specifies whether screen updating is turned on or off. If the argument is TRUE, updating is selected. If the argument is FALSE, updating is cleared. If the argument is omitted, the current update condition is changed.

ENABLE.COMMAND

The ENABLE.COMMAND function enables or disables a custom command or menu. If a command is disabled, it appears dimmed on the menu. You cannot disable built-in commands.

Use with macro sheets only.

Syntax

`=ENABLE.COMMAND(bar_num,menu,command,enable)`

Bar_num is the menu bar on which the command is found. See the Add.Command function for more information about Bar_num.

Menu is the menu, in text or starting with number 1, on which the command is found.

Command is the command name, in text or starting with number 1, that you want to enable or disable.

Enable is a logical value that specifies whether the command is enabled or disabled. If the argument is TRUE, the command is enabled. If the argument is FALSE, the command is disabled.

ENABLE.TOOL

The ENABLE.TOOL function enables or disables a tool on a toolbar.

Use with macro sheets only.

Syntax

`=ENABLE.TOOL(bar_id,position,enable)`

Bar_id is the number or name of a toolbar where the tool is found. See the Add.Tool function for more information.

Position is the position of the tool, starting with number 1, on the toolbar.

Enable is a logical value that specifies whether the tool is enabled or disabled. If the argument is TRUE or omitted, the tool is is enabled. If the argument is FALSE, the tool is disabled.

ENTER.DATA

The ENTER.DATA function turns on Data Entry mode and allows the user to select and enter data in unlocked cells in the selected area.

Use with macro sheets only.

Syntax

`=ENTER.DATA(logical)`

Logical is a logical value that turns Data Entry mode on or off. If the argument is TRUE, Data Entry mode is turned on. If the argument is FALSE, Data Entry mode is turned off. To turn Data Entry on and prevent the ESC key from turning it off, enter 2 for Logical.

ERROR

The ERROR function determines what action is taken when an error is encountered. Error can ignore an error, return an Excel error message, or run the user's macro when an error is encountered.

Use with macro sheets only.

Syntax

`=ERROR(enable_logical,macro_ref)`

Enable_logical is a logical value or number that enables or disables error-checking. If the argument is FALSE or 0, error-checking is disabled. If an error is encountered while a macro is running, the error is ignored and the macro continues to run. If the argument is TRUE or 1, you can have Excel return a normal error message (the Excel Macro Error dialog box) by omitting the macro_ref argument, or you can run another macro by specifying it in the macro_ref argument.

Macro_ref specifies a macro to run if Enable_logical is TRUE or 1.

HELP

The HELP function displays the Excel Help Contents topic or a custom Help topic.

Use with macro sheets only.

Syntax

```
=HELP(help_ref)
```

Help_ref is a reference, in text, to a topic in a Help file, in the form

```
"filename!topic_number"
```

INPUT

The INPUT function displays a dialog box for user input and returns the information entered in the dialog box.

Use with macro sheets only.

Syntax

```
=INPUT(message_text,type_num,title_text,default,x_pos,y_pos,help_ref)
```

Message_text is the text, enclosed in quotation marks, to be displayed in the dialog box.

Type_num is a number that specifies the type of data to be entered. The following table lists each Type_num and its corresponding data type.

Type_num	Data type
0	Formula
1	Number
2	Text
4	Logical
8	Reference
16	Error
64	Array

You can also use the sum of data types for Type_num.

Title_text is text that specifies a title to be displayed in the title bar of the dialog box.

Default displays a value to be shown in the edit box when the dialog box is displayed. If default is omitted, the edit box is empty.

X_pos and Y_pos specify the horizontal and vertical position, in points, of the dialog box. A point is 1/72 of an inch.

Help_ref is a reference to custom online Help. See the Help function for more information.

MESSAGE

The MESSAGE function controls the display of messages in the message area of the status bar.

Use with macro sheets only.

Syntax

`=MESSAGE(logical,text)`

Logical is a logical value that specifies whether to display a message. If logical is TRUE, the information in the Text argument is displayed in the message area of the status bar. If logical is FALSE, the status bar is returned to normal.

Text is the text, enclosed by quotations marks, that you want to display in the status bar. To remove messages currently displayed, enter two double quotation marks (" ") to show empty text for this argument.

MOVE.TOOL

The MOVE.TOOL function moves or copies a tool from one toolbar to another.

Use with macro sheets only.

Syntax

`=MOVE.TOOL(from_bar_id,from_bar_position,to_bar_id,to_bar_position,`
`copy,width)`

From_bar_id specifies the number or name of a toolbar from which you want to move or copy the tool. See the Add.Tool function for more information.

From_bar_position specifies the current position, starting with 1, in the toolbar of the tool you want to move or copy.

To_bar_id specifies the number or name of a toolbar to which you want to move or paste the tool. See the Add.Tool function for more information.

To_bar_position specifies the position in the toolbar, starting with 1, to which you want to move or paste the tool.

Copy is a logical value that specifies whether to copy or move the tool. If the argument is TRUE, the tool is copied. If the argument is FALSE, the tool is moved.

Width is the width, in points, of a drop-down list. Width is ignored if the tool you are moving is not a drop-down list.

ON.DATA

The ON.DATA function runs a specified macro when another application sends data to a document via DDE. On.data remains in effect until you clear it or quit Excel. You can clear On.data by using the function and omitting the macro_text argument.

Use with macro sheets only.

Syntax

=ON.DATA(document_text,macro_text)

Document_text is the name of the document to which remote data is being sent or the name of the source of the remote data. The remove data source must be in the form

app|topic!item

Macro_text is the reference to (name or R1C1) a macro that you want to run when the document_text argument has been carried out.

ON.DOUBLECLICK

The ON.DOUBLECLICK function runs a macro when you double-click a cell or object on a specified worksheet, or macro sheet or when you double-click an item on a specified chart.

Use with macro sheets only.

Syntax

=ON.DOUBLECLICK(sheet_text,macro_text)

Sheet_text is text specifying the name of a document.

Macro_text is a reference, in text (name or R1C1), to a macro to be run when you double-click.

ON.ENTRY

The ON.ENTRY function runs a macro when you enter data into any cell on a specified document using the formula bar.

Use with macro sheets only.

Syntax

=ON.ENTRY(sheet_text,macro_text)

Sheet_text is the name, in text, of the document.

Macro_text is the reference, in text (name or R1C1), of the macro to be run when data is entered into the specified document.

ON.KEY

The ON.KEY function runs a macro when a particular key or key combination is pressed. On.key remains in effect until you clear (by using the function without the macro_text argument) or quit Excel.

Use with macro sheets only.

Syntax

=ON.KEY(key_text,macro_text)

Key_text specifies the key or key combination. You can use any single key, or any key combination using Alt, Ctrl, or Shift. Each key is represented by one or more characters such as a for the character a, or {ENTER} for the ENTER key. The following table lists the codes for characters that are not displayed when you press the key (such as ENTER).

Key	Code
Backspace	{BACKSPACE} or {BS}
Bread	{BREAK}
Caps Lock	{CAPSLOCK}
Clear	{CLEAR}
Delete or Del	{DELETE} or {DEL}
Down	{DOWN}

Key	Code
End	{END}
Enter (numeric keypad)	{ENTER}
Enter	~ (tilde)
Esc	{ESCAPE} or {ESC}
Help	{HELP}
Home	{HOME}
Ins	{INSERT}
Left	{LEFT}
Num Lock	{NUMLOCK}
Page Down	{PGDN}
Page Up	{PGUP}
Return	{RETURN}
Right	{RIGHT}
Scroll Lock	{SCROLLLOCK}
Tab	{TAB}
Up	{UP}
F1 through F15	{F1} through {F15}

To combine keys with Shift, Ctrl, or Alt, use the following table:

To combine with	Precede the key code by
Shift	+ (plus sign)
Ctrl	^ (caret)
Alt	% (percent sign)

Macro_text is a reference (R1C1), in text form and enclosed by quotation marks, to a macro to be run when key_text is pressed.

ON.RECALC

The ON.RECALC function runs a macro when a specified document is recalculated as long as the recalculation does not occur as a result of running another macro.

Use with macro sheets only.

Syntax

=ON.RECALC(sheet_text,macro_text)

Sheet_text is the name, in text, of the document.

Macro_text is the name of, or reference (R1C1) to, a macro to be run when the document specified by Sheet_text is recalculated.

ON.TIME

The ON.TIME function runs a macro at a specified time of day or after a specified period of time has elapsed.

Use with macro sheets only.

Syntax

=ON.TIME(time,macro_text,tolerance,insert_logical)

Time is the time and date (serial number) the macro is to be run.

Macro_text is the name of, or R1C1 reference to, the macro to be run.

Tolerance is the time and date (serial number) until which you want the macro to wait if it cannot run at the specified time and date (for example, if another macro is running). Insert_logical is a logical value that specifies whether you want Macro_text to run at Time. This is used to clear a previously set On.Time formula. If the argument is TRUE or omitted, the macro is run. If the argument is FALSE, and Macro_text is not set to run at Time, On.Time returns the #Value error value.

ON.WINDOW

The ON.WINDOW function runs a specified macro when you switch to a specified window.

Use with macro sheets only.

Syntax

=ON.WINDOW(window_text,macro_text)

Window_text is the name, in text, of the window.

Macro_text is the name of, or reference to, the macro to run when you switch to the window named in Window_text.

PASTE.TOOL

The PASTE.TOOL function pastes a tool face from the Clipboard to a specified position on a toolbar. Use the Copy.Tool function to copy the tool face to the Clipboard. Inserting this function into a macro sheet is equivalent to choosing the Paste Tool Face command from the Edit menu.

Use with macro sheets only.

Syntax

`=PASTE.TOOL(bar_id,position)`

Bar_id specifies the name or number of the toolbar into which you want to paste the tool face. See the Add.Tool function for more information.

Position specifies where you want to paste the tool face on the toolbar. Position starts with 1.

PRESS.TOOL

The PRESS.TOOL function formats a tool to appear either normal or depressed into the screen.

Use with macro sheets only.

Syntax

`=PRESS.TOOL(bar_id,position,down)`

Bar_id specifies the name or number of the toolbar that contains the tool whose appearance you want to change. For more information see the Add.Tool function.

Position specifies the position of the tool on the toolbar, starting with number 1.

Down is a logical value that specifies the appearance of the tool. If the argument is TRUE, the tool appears depressed into the screen. If the argument is FALSE or omitted, the tool appears normal.

RENAME.COMMAND

The RENAME.COMMAND function changes the name of a built-in or custom menu command or the name of the menu.

Use with macro sheets only.

Syntax

```
=RENAME.COMMAND(bar_num,menu,command,name_text)
```

Bar_num is either the number of one of the built-in menu bars or the number returned by a previously run Add.Bar function. See the Add.Command and Add.Bar functions for more information.

Menu is the name or number of the menu.

Command is the name or number of the command to be renamed. If Command is 0, the menu is renamed instead of the command.

Name_text is the new name for the command.

RESET.TOOL

The RESET.TOOL function resets a tool to its original tool face. Inserting this function into a macro sheet is equivalent to choosing the Reset Tool Face command from the Tool shortcut menu.

Use with macro sheets only.

Syntax

```
=RESET.TOOL(bar_id,position)
```

Bar_id is the name or number of the toolbar that contains the tool you want to reset. For further information see the Add.Tool function.

Position is the position of the tool within the toolbar, starting with number 1.

RESET.TOOLBAR

The RESET.TOOLBAR function resets built-in toolbars to the default Excel set.

Use with macro sheets only.

Syntax

```
=RESET.TOOLBAR(bar_id)
```

Bar_id specifies the name or number of the toolbar you want to reset. For further information see the Add.Tool function.

SAVE.TOOLBAR

The SAVE.TOOLBAR function saves toolbar definitions to a specified file.

Use with macro sheets only.

Syntax

`=SAVE.TOOLBAR(bar_id,filename)`

Bar_id is either the name or number of a toolbar or toolbars whose definition you want to save. Use an array to save several toolbar definitions at a time. For further information, see the Add.Tool function.

Filename specifies the name, in text, of the destination file.

SHOW.BAR

The SHOW.BAR function displays the specified menu bar.

Use with macro sheets only.

Syntax

`=SHOW.BAR(bar_num)`

Bar_num is the number of the built-in menu bar you want to display, a number returned by a previously executed Add.Bar function, or a reference to a cell containing a previously executed Add.Bar function. The following table lists windows and their corresponding bar numbers.

If active window contains	Bar displayed
Worksheet or macro sheet	1
Chart	2
No active window	3
Info window	4
Worksheet or macro sheet (short menus)	5
Chart (short menu)	6

SHOW.TOOLBAR

The SHOW.TOOLBAR function hides or displays a toolbar. Inserting this function into a macro sheet is equivalent to choosing the Show Toolbars or Hide Toolbars button in the Options Toolbars dialog box.

Use with macro sheets only.

Syntax

```
=SHOW.TOOLBAR(bar_id,visible,dock,x_pos,y_pos,width)
```

Bar_id is the name or number of a toolbar, or an array of names or numbers of toolbars, that you want to display or hide. For further information, see the Add.Tool function.

Visible is a logical value that specifies whether the toolbar is displayed or hidden. If the argument is TRUE, the toolbar is displayed. If the argument is FALSE, the toolbar is hidden.

Dock is a number from 1 to 5 that specifies the docking location of the toolbar. The following table lists the numbers and their corresponding docking positions.

Dock	Position of toolbar
1	Top of workspace
2	Left edge of workspace
3	Right edge of workspace
4	Bottom of workspace
5	Floating (not docked)

X_pos and Y_pos specify, in points, the horizontal and vertical position of the toolbar. A point is 1/72 of an inch.

Width specifies, in points, the width of the toolbar.

WINDOW.TITLE

The WINDOW.TITLE function changes the title of the active window. The new title appears at the top of the document window. Only the name of the window is changed, not the name of the document. Use the Save.As function to change the name of the document.

Use with macro sheets only.

Syntax

`=WINDOW.TITLE`(text)

Text is the title you want to assign the window. Empty text (" ") specifies no title.

The Text Functions

There is only one Text Function — SPELLING.CHECK.

SPELLING.CHECK

The SPELLING.CHECK function checks the spelling of a word and returns TRUE if the word is correctly spelled and FALSE if the word is incorrectly spelled. This function does not present a dialog box. If you want to display the Spelling dialog box, use the Spelling function.

Use with macro sheets only.

Syntax

`=SPELLING.CHECK(word_text,`custom_dic,ignore_uppercase)

Word_text is the word, in text or a reference, whose spelling you want to check.

Custom_dic is the filename of the custom dictionary you want to use.

Ignore_uppercase is a logical value that specifies case-sensitivity while checking the word. It corresponds to the Ignore Words In Uppercase check box in the Spelling dialog box. If the argument is TRUE, the check box is selected. If the argument is FALSE, the check box is cleared.

Chapter **4**

CREATING CUSTOM MACROS

What Is a Custom Macro?

Chapter 2 explains how to record simple macros using keystrokes and/or mouse movements. Custom macros allow you to add commands to your macros, which you cannot accomplish using keystrokes and/or mouse movements. By using Excel's macro functions and arguments, you can pause macros, display prompts in your macros for user input, branch or loop within a macro when a condition is met, search for text and/or numbers, and create and use variables. Macro functions and their arguments are discussed in detail in chapters 1 and 3.

Designing a Custom Macro

Before you begin creating a custom macro, it is a good idea to consider exactly what you want your macro to accomplish. Then you must list all of the steps the macro must perform. Write these steps down, using a diagram, a chart, or even an outline. For example, suppose you want to write a macro that will allow a user to save a worksheet and print it immediately, but you want the user to access custom dialog boxes, rather than the standard Excel dialog boxes, to accomplish this task. You could create the following outline to break down the steps necessary for your macro:

```
1. Save and Print

   A. Ask Save As or Save

      i. If Save, save worksheet with same name

      ii. If Save As, dialog box for new name

         a. If new name includes different path

            1. If path incorrect, error message
               informing user and asking for new
               path

            2. If path correct, save worksheet to
               user-supplied name

         b. If new name to same directory, save
            worksheet to new name

   B. Dialog box to determine print criteria

      i. Check for input errors

         a. If errors exist, error message asking
            user for acceptable criteria

      ii. Print worksheet using user-defined criteria.
```

The purpose of this outline is to break down and list every step the macro must perform. You must remember to take into account all of the possible choices a user will want to able to make when using the macro. For example, if you do not allow the user the option of saving the worksheet to the same name or to a different name, you limit the macro's uses. You must also take into account the possible errors a user can make when inputting choices in a macro. For example, if the user chooses to save the worksheet to a different name and a different directory, you must include an instruction telling the macro what to do if the user enters a directory that does not exist.

Using Control and Subroutine Macros

You could write the Save and Print macro following the steps outlined above. A better way is to use a control macro that contains all of the major steps the macro needs to accomplish, and use a subroutine macro to accomplish the specific tasks. Subroutine macros should be short. Shorter macros are easier to write, test, debug, modify, and reuse. For example, we could take the outline for the Save and Print macro above, and use it to determine the steps for a control macro and subroutine macros as follows:

```
1. Save — go to Save subroutine
   Save subroutine — choose Save or Save As

   A. If Save, save worksheet to same name
      If Save As, get user input for path, and name
      for worksheet

   B. Check for errors in user input

   C. Save worksheet to new name

2. Return to control macro

   A. Print — go to Print subroutine

      i. Get print criteria from user

     ii. Check for errors in user input

    iii. Print worksheet

3. Return to control macro

   A. Exit macro
```

Using the control macro and subroutine macros allows you to test each subroutine macro before combining them into one macro. It also allows you to use each subroutine macro individually or to reuse the subroutine macro in another macro. Finally, you can add as many subroutines as you want to the control macro. For example, you could add a subroutine that allows the user to format the worksheet, or one that allows the user to create reports using the data in the worksheet.

Writing the Save and Print Macro

The control macro and subroutine macros are each written and saved individually. They are actually three separate macros: the control macro contains the main steps involved in accomplishing the task; the Save subroutine accomplishes the first main step in the control macro; and the Print subroutine accomplishes the second main step in the control macro. Once you have determined the main steps to be accomplished, you should write the subroutine macros using macro functions and their arguments. Test them and, when they are functioning properly, save them. The control macro is the last macro you would create, since it runs the Save and Print macros. When the control macro is written, you must save it.

 Excel ignores blank cells in macros and continues to the next function. You must use =RETURN() or =HALT() to stop a macro.

NOTE

Naming a Command Macro

Once you have designed, written, tested, and saved the Save, Print, and Print and Save macros, you will want to define the name of the control macro so that it appears in the Macro/Run dialog box. To do this:

1. Be certain you have saved the macro.
2. Select the first cell of the macro.
3. Click on Formula in the menu bar to open the Formula menu.
4. Click on Define Name to display the Define Name dialog box, as shown in Figure 4.1.
5. In the Name text box, type a name for the macro. The name must start with a letter, and can only contain letters, numbers, periods (.), and underlines (_).
6. Select the Command option button if you want the name of the control macro to appear in the Macro/Run dialog box.

7. If you want to be able to invoke the macro using a shortcut key, select the Command option button, and then type a letter in the Key: Ctrl+ text box. Shortcut keys are case-sensitive, and both upper- and lowercase keys are valid. For example, you can assign the shortcut key *p* to one macro and the shortcut key *P* to another macro.

8. Click on OK.

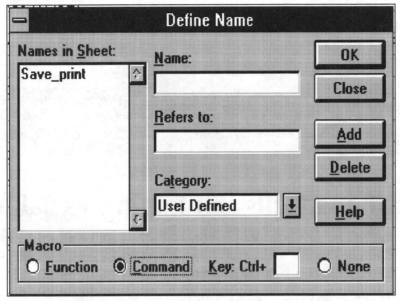

Figure 4.1 *The Define Name dialog box.*

Writing Macros Using the Paste Function

If you know the name of the function you want to use and the syntax of its arguments, you can type the function directly into a cell in the macro sheet.

If you do not know the exact name of the function you want to use, you can use the Paste Function command in the Formula menu to select a function. The function, including the argument(s), will appear in the formula bar. To use the Paste Function command:

1. Open the worksheet or macro sheet.

2. Select the cell in which you want to use the function.

3. Click on Formula in the menu bar to open the Formula menu.

4. Click on Paste Function.

5. The Paste Category list box shows lists the types of functions available to you in Excel. You can select any of these function types. Explanations of the function types used in macros can be found in Chapter 3.

6. The Paste Function list box shows you all of the functions available in the function category you selected. The default function category is All, and all of the worksheet functions available in Excel are listed in the Paste Function list box when that category is selected.

7. Select the function you want in the Paste Function list box.

8. Click on OK.

If you are entering a function and cannot remember the argument(s), you can type the equal sign (=), the function name, and the opening parenthesis, then press Ctrl+A. The argument(s) will be pasted into the function.

N O T E

Identifying Cells Containing Variables

When you are identifying cells or cell ranges in a macro function, use names instead of references (cell addresses) whenever possible. Using names guarantees that the function will always refer to the correct cells. To name a cell or range:

1. Select the cell or range you wish to name.

2. Click on Formula in the menu bar to open the Formula menu.

3. Click on Define Name to display the Define Name dialog box.

4. In the Name text box, type a name for the cell or range.

5. Click on OK.

Types of References in Macro Functions

References are the addresses of cells, ranges, or nonadjacent ranges. You can use either the A1 or R1C1 style of reference. The **A1** style reference refers to cell A1 in the worksheet. The **R1C1** style refers to Row 1, Cell 1 of the worksheet. Excel defaults to the A1 reference style. There are a variety of references you can use in a macro function. The reference you use will depend upon what you are referring to. The following table shows each type of reference available:

A1 style	R1C1 style	Description
$A$1	R1C1	Absolute reference to a cell in the macro sheet that contains the macro.
A1	R[1]C[1]	Relative reference to a cell in the macro sheet that contains the macro.
!$A$1	!R1C1	Absolute reference to a cell in the active sheet.
!A1	!R[1]C[1]	Relative reference to a cell in the active sheet. This reference refers to the cell on the macro sheet that contains the reference, not to the active cell on the active sheet.
DocName!$A$1	DocName!R1C1	Absolute reference to a cell in an external sheet.
DocName!A1	DocName!R[1]C[1]	Relative reference to a cell in an external sheet.

These references can be used as arguments in a function. When you use a reference as an argument in a function, the contents of the cells being referenced are used as the argument. If you want to select a cell whose address is relative to the active cell on the active sheet, you must use the R1C1 reference style, and the reference must be enclosed in quotation marks. For example, the function

```
=SELECT("R[1]C[1]")
```

selects the cell that is one row down and one column to the right of the active cell on the active sheet. You can achieve the same result using the OFFSET function:

```
=SELECT(OFFSET(ACTIVE.CELL(),1,1))
```

The function

```
=SELECT(OFFSET(ACTIVE. CELL(),5,2))
```

selects the cell that is five rows down and two columns to the right of the active cell.

References preceded by an exclamation point (!) must be given in the reference style that is currently used in your workspace. For example, if your workspace is currently set to A1 style, the function =SELECT(!$A$2) selects cell A2 on the active sheet. If your workspace is currently set to R1C1 style, the function =SELECT(!R2C1) selects the cell in Row 2, Column 1 of the active sheet—cell A2.

Converting Data Types

If you enter an argument containing an incorrect data type into a macro function, Excel will try to convert the data in the argument. For example, the function =LEN(text) requires a text data type to be used in the argument. If you enter the function =LEN("data"), all of the characters between the opening and closing quotation marks will be counted, and the function will return a value of 4. If you enter a number type argument instead of a data type argument in the function, Excel will convert the number to text. For example, the function =LEN(12345) contains the number type argument (12345) instead of a data type argument. Excel will convert the number to a text value of *12345*, and will count all of the characters between the opening and closing quotation marks. The value of the function =LEN(12345) will be returned as 5. Excel will try to convert numbers, text, and logical values to the correct data type. For a list of data types and how they are converted, see "Converting Data Types" in Chapter 1.

Editing a Macro

Macros are edited in exactly the same way as any worksheet in Excel. Open the document, type your changes in the cell that contains the data you want to change, and save the macro sheet.

Using Conditions in Macros

There are several programming elements that enable your custom macro to respond to varying conditions. **Looping** repeats an action until a certain condition is met. **Branching** allows your macros to perform different actions depending upon the user's choice or whether a certain condition is met. **User Input** allows you to ask for input from the user. Finally, you can start one macro from another.

Branching

When you use branching in a macro, the macro performs an action depending upon certain conditions. Your macro can decide whether or not to perform an action depending upon a certain condition, such as, "If today is Tuesday, print database; otherwise, do not print database." Your macro can also decide between multiple actions, such as, "If today is Tuesday, print database; if today is Wednesday, print worksheet; otherwise, do not print anything." You also use branching to determine which action to perform depending upon user input. For example, "If save, save document to same name; if save as, save document to new name; otherwise, do not save document." The following functions are used in branching: IF(logical_test), ELSE.IF(logical_test), ELSE(), END.IF(), and GOTO(reference). The IF function cannot be used alone; it must either be used with the GOTO function, or in a block of IF, ELSE, END.IF functions.

IF

The IF function is used to make a macro branch to another part of an existing macro. If the value returned by the IF function is TRUE and the GOTO function is used, the macro will branch to another macro or cell reference, or will follow the functions immediately following the IF function until it reaches the next ELSE.IF or ELSE function. All functions between the ELSE.IF or ELSE and the next ELSE.IF or ELSE will be carried out.

If the value returned by the IF function is FALSE, the macro skips to the next ELSE.IF or ELSE function in the macro, without performing any of the functions between the IF and ELSE.IF or ELSE functions.

Use with worksheets and macro sheets.

Syntax

```
=IF(logical_test,value_if_true,value_if_false)
```

Example of use with GOTO

```
=IF(Age!A1>=18,GOTO(Vote),GOTO(Non_vote))
```

Or,

```
=IF(Age!A1>=18,GOTO(Vote)
=ALERT("Cell A1 is too young to vote")
=RETURN()
```

The first example determines whether the value of the contents of cell A1 in the Age worksheet is greater than or equal to 18. If the value is greater than or equal to 18, then the logical test is TRUE, and the value_if_true argument is used; the macro jumps to the GOTO(Vote) macro. If the value is less than 18, then the logical test is FALSE, and the value_if_false argument is used; the macro jumps to the GOTO(Non_vote) macro.

In the second example, the IF function does not include an action if the logical test argument is FALSE. If the logical test argument is TRUE, the value_if_true statement is

used and the macro jumps to the GOTO(Vote) macro. Since no value_if_false statement is included in the IF function, if the logical test argument is FALSE, the macro
ignores the GOTO function, and continues to run the original macro.

Example of use with ELSE() and END.IF()

```
=INPUT("Do You Want to (S)ave or Save and (P)rint?",2)
=IF(Print="P")
=ALERT("Check to see if printer on",1)
=SAVE()
=PRINT()
=ELSE()
=SAVE()
=END.IF()
=RETURN()
```

Or,

```
=INPUT("Do You Want to (S)ave, Save and (P)rint, or Save and Print a
(R)eport?",2)
=IF(Print="P")
=ALERT("Check to see if printer on",1)
=SAVE()
=PRINT()
=ELSE.IF(Print="R")
=SAVE()
=Reports()
=ELSE()
=SAVE()
=END.IF()
=RETURN()
```

The first example asks the user to choose between saving the document (S) or saving and printing the document (P). The user's input is recorded to the defined name,
Print. (To define a name, select the cell that contains the INPUT function, click on
Formula, click on Define Name in the Formula menu, type *Print* in the Name text box,
and click on OK.) If Print (the defined name) is equal to *P* (the user's input), the macro
will save and print the document. Otherwise (ELSE), the macro will save the document. Finally, the IF, ELSE, END.IF block *must* end with the END.IF function.

User input is not case-sensitive. The macro will identify both *P* and *p* as Save and Print, and *S* and *s* as Save.

N O T E

In the second example, the user chooses between saving the document (S), saving and printing the document (P), or saving the document and printing a report (R). The user's input is recorded to the defined name, Print. If Print (the defined name) is equal to *P* (the user's input), the macro will save and print the document. Otherwise (ELSE.IF), if Print is equal to *R*, the macro will save the document and branch to the Reports macro. If Print is not equal to *P* or *R*, then it is equal to (ELSE), and the macro will save the document. Finally, the IF, ELSE.IF, ELSE, END.IF block *must* end with the END.IF function. You can have as many ELSE.IF functions as you wish between the IF and END.IF functions. You must, however, precede the END.IF function with an ELSE function. For example:

Two conditions	Three conditions	Four conditions
=IF	=IF	=IF
=ELSE	=ELSE.IF	=ELSE.IF
=END.IF	=ELSE	=ELSE.IF
	=END.IF	=ELSE
		=END.IF

We have not made any provision for typos in user inputs. If you type a *T* instead of an *R*, for instance, the macro will save the document, since the ELSE is *SAVE*. If you wanted to save the document and print a report, you would have to re-run the macro. We will cover this kind of error trapping later in the chapter.

N O T E

Looping

A **loop** is a series of macro commands that continuously repeat until a certain condition is met or until the user presses a key to end the loop. For example, the following macro will print *This is a loop* in the message bar until the Esc key is pressed:

```
=SET.NAME("done",TRUE)
=WHILE(done)
```

```
=MESSAGE(TRUE,"This is a loop")
=NEXT()
=MESSAGE(FALSE)
=RETURN()
```

The WHILE function sets the condition for the loop. If the condition is TRUE, the loop continues to run; if the condition is FALSE, the loop never starts. The SET.NAME function establishes the value of TRUE for "done." In the cell below the WHILE function, the MESSAGE function changes the message in the status bar to *This is a loop*. The macro performs each function that follows the WHILE function until it encounters the NEXT function, which starts the loop again. If the condition is still TRUE, the loop will run again; if the condition is FALSE, the loop will never start and the macro will jump to the function that follows NEXT. In the above example, the loop is endless because there is no condition that forces the macro to end the loop. The only way to exit the loop is to press the Esc key.

There are three loop functions: FOR-NEXT, FOR.CELL-NEXT, and WHILE-NEXT. Each of these functions performs a different kind of loop.

FOR-NEXT

The FOR-NEXT function is used when you want to repeat actions a specified number of times within a loop.

Use with macro sheets.

Syntax

```
=FOR(counter_text,start_num,end_num,step_num)
```

Actions to be performed

```
=NEXT()
```

Example of use

```
=FOR("Counter",1,10,1)
=MESSAGE(TRUE,"This is a Loop")
=NEXT()
=MESSAGE(FALSE)
=RETURN()
```

The first line sets the conditions for the loop. The first argument, Counter, is the name of the loop counter; the second argument, 1, is the initial value assigned to

Counter; the third argument, 10, is the highest value that can be assigned to Counter before the loop stops. The last argument, 1, is the value added to the loop counter each time the loop repeats. If you do not include this argument in the function, the value will default to 1. When you run this macro, the FOR function sets the initial value (1) to the loop counter (Counter). It checks to see if the value of Counter is greater than the highest value (10) that the Counter can reach before the loop stops. If the value of Counter is less than 10, the loop carries out the MESSAGE function and proceeds to the NEXT function. The value of the last argument in the FOR function (1) is added to the loop counter (Counter), and the macro loops back to the FOR function. On the second pass through the loop, the value of Counter is 2, since every time you pass through the loop, the value of Counter increments by 1. When the value of Counter is greater than 10, the loop will stop and the macro will jump to the action following NEXT. To stop the macro while it is looping, press Esc.

FOR.CELL-NEXT

The FOR.CELL-NEXT function is used when you want to perform actions for all of the cells in a specified reference area or selected range.

Use with macro sheets.

Syntax

```
=FOR.CELL(ref_name,area_ref,skip_blanks)
```

Actions to be performed

```
=NEXT()
```

Example of use

```
=FOR.CELL("cell_ref","Change",TRUE)
=FORMULA(cell_ref-10,cell_ref)
=NEXT()
=RETURN()
```

Assume that you have a worksheet that lists your expenses for the month. You discover that somehow you have made a mistake, and the expenses entered in cells A1:B15 are $10 over the actual amounts. You can use the FOR.CELL function to quickly change the amount in each cell in the range A1:B15. The macro subtracts 10 from the contents of each of the nonblank cells in the referenced area. The first line starts the loop with the FOR.CELL function. The first argument (cell_ref) is the name that refers to the cell on which the action is currently being performed. Cell_ref refers to a new cell on each pass through the loop. The second argument, Change, is the name of the range or multiple ranges upon which you want to perform the actions in the loop. If you do not want to name a range, you can select a range or multiple ranges before you run the macro. When the macro encounters the FOR.CELL function, it will perform the actions in the loop on each cell in the currently selected range. The third argument tells Excel whether or not to perform the actions in the loop on blank cells in the selected or referenced area. If you choose TRUE, blank cells will be skipped; if you choose FALSE, the actions will be performed on all cells in the selected or referenced area. If you do not include this argument, Excel will default to a value of FALSE.

The second line of the loop contains the formula to subtract 10 from the contents of each cell in the referenced area. The first argument (Cell_ref-10) subtracts 10 from the contents of the current cell in the range. The current cell changes during each pass through the loop until Excel has performed the action on each cell in the referenced area. The second argument (Cell_ref) tells Excel where you want the result of the formula to appear in the worksheet, which is the current cell. Since the current cell changes with each pass through the loop, the result of the formula will appear in each cell in which the calculation takes place. If you have used a referenced area in the FOR.CELL function and do not include this argument, the result of the formula will appear in whatever cell is selected in the worksheet, and will change for each pass through the loop. If you have used a selected area in the FOR.CELL function and do not include this argument, the result of the formula will appear in the first cell in the selected range. If you want the result of the formula to appear in the cell in which the action is currently being performed, you must include the second argument in the FORMULA function.

The third line contains the NEXT function, which causes the macro to loop back to FOR.CELL. When the current cell goes beyond the last cell in the referenced or selected range, the loop stops and the macro jumps to the function following NEXT.

WHILE-NEXT

The WHILE-NEXT function is used when you want to perform an action or actions only if a specified condition is met.

Use with macro sheets.

Syntax

```
WHILE(logical_test)
```

Actions to be performed

```
=NEXT()
```

Example of use

```
=SET.NAME("Typos",TRUE)
=WHILE(Typos)
=INPUT("Do You Want to (S)ave, Save and (P)rint, or Save and Print a
(R)eport?",2)
=IF(Print="P")
=ALERT("Check to see if printer on",1)
=SAVE()
=PRINT()
=SET.NAME("Typos",FALSE)
=ELSE.IF(Print="R")
=SAVE()
=Reports()
=SET.NAME("Typos",FALSE)
=ELSE.IF(Print="S")
=SAVE()
=SET.NAME("Typos",FALSE)
=ELSE.IF(Print=FALSE)
=SET.NAME("Typos",FALSE)
=ELSE()
=ALERT("You Must Enter ""S""", ""P""", or ""R."" Please enter your
selection again",2)
=END.IF()
=NEXT()
=RETURN()
```

This is the same Save and Print macro we created in the IF section earlier in this chapter. This time, we have added a WHILE loop to send the user an error message and return the user to the original dialog box ((S)ave, Save and (P)rint, or Save and Print a (R)eport) if the user enters a letter other than *S, P,* or *R* and does not select the Cancel button. The WHILE function sets the condition for the loop. If the condition is TRUE, the loop continues to run; if the condition is FALSE, the loop never starts.

The SET.NAME function establishes the value of TRUE for *Typos*. As long as *Typos* retains the value TRUE, the loop will start. If the value of *Typos* changes to FALSE, the loop does not start on the next pass, and the macro will jump to the command that follows the NEXT function. The SET.NAME function is entered before the WHILE function to set (**initialize**) the original value of Typos. Since the original value of Typos is TRUE, the loop starts and the macro performs the function that follows the WHILE function. If the user enters *P* for the action to be performed, the value of the first IF condition becomes TRUE, and the actions following it are performed. A dialog box is displayed reminding the user to check to be sure the printer is on. Then the document is saved and printed. The next SET.NAME function changes the value of Typos to FALSE. Unless the macro encounters another SET.NAME function inside the loop that changes the value of Typos back to TRUE, the value FALSE will remain in effect. The macro then proceeds to the next IF statement, ELSE.IF(Print="R"). Since the user entered *P* and not *R*, the value of that statement is FALSE and none of the actions between the ELSE.IF and the following ELSE.IF statement are performed. The third IF statement, ELSE.IF(Print="S"), is also FALSE, and none of the actions will be performed. The fourth IF statement, ELSE.IF(Print=FALSE), allows the user to cancel the macro. When a user selects the Cancel button in a dialog box, Excel automatically returns a value of FALSE. Therefore, if the user selects the Cancel button, Print is equal to FALSE, the condition of the IF statement is TRUE, and all actions following the IF statement will be performed until the next IF statement is encountered. The action that follows this IF statement sets the SET.NAME function to FALSE.

Finally, we come to the last IF statement (ELSE). The first four IF statements perform an action (or actions) if the user enters *P, R,* or *S,* or selects the Cancel button in the dialog box. If the user enters any other letter for the action to be performed and does not select CANCEL, the value of the fourth IF condition becomes TRUE and the macro performs the actions that follow the IF statement. The next function (ALERT) displays a message on the screen telling the user to enter *S, P,* or *R.* Notice that this IF statement is the only one that does not change the value of Typos to FALSE. The macro then encounters the END.IF function and continues on to the NEXT function. When the macro reaches the NEXT function, it loops back to the WHILE function to start the next pass through the loop. If the user entered *P, R, S,* or selected the Cancel button, the value of *Typos* is FALSE, the loop will not start, and the macro will jump to the function following the NEXT function. If the user entered any other letter and did not select the Cancel button, the value of Typos is TRUE, and the macro will begin another pass through the loop.

You can enter all of the functions in a macro in a straight line, but it is easier to read and edit the macro if you indent the functions to be performed inside a loop or condition. For example, the following macro is much easier to read if you indent all of the functions between the WHILE and NEXT functions, and all of the functions between the IF, ELSE.IF, ELSE, and END.IF statements in the Save and Print macro to look like this:

```
=SET.NAME("Typos",TRUE)
=WHILE(Typos)
  = INPUT("Do You Want to (S)ave, Save and (P)rint, or Save and
Print            a (R)eport?",2)
  = IF(Print="P")
    = ALERT("Check to see if printer on",1)
    = SAVE()
    = PRINT()
    = SET.NAME("Typos",FALSE)
  = ELSE.IF(Print="R")
    = SAVE()
    = Reports()
    = SET.NAME("Typos",FALSE)
  = ELSE.IF(Print="S")
    = SAVE()
    = SET.NAME("Typos",FALSE)
  = ELSE.IF(Print=FALSE)
    = SET.NAME("Typos",FALSE)
  = ELSE()
    = ALERT("You Must Enter ""S""", ""P""", or ""R."" Please enter
your            selection again",2)
  = END.IF()
=NEXT()
=RETURN()
```

The WHILE and NEXT commands stand out, as do the IF, ELSE.IF, ELSE, and END.IF commands. If you write a macro and, upon running it, receive an error message saying that you are missing an ELSE command, it is much easier to locate the missing command if you have indented the commands between all of the IF, ELSE.IF, ELSE, and END.IF commands.

User Input

You can use the INPUT function to ask for input from the user. The macro can then take certain actions depending upon the input. For example, in the Save and Print macro, the macro performs different actions depending upon whether the user inputs P, R, or S, or selects the Cancel button.

Use with macro sheets.

Syntax

```
INPUT(message_text,type_num,title_text,default,x_pos,y_pos,help_ref)
```

Example of use

```
=INPUT("Do You Want to (S)ave, Save and (P)rint, or Save and Print a
(R)eport?",2)
```

This example, which is taken from the Save and Print macro, will display a dialog box on the screen asking the user to choose whether to (S)ave, Save and (P)rint, or Save and Print a (R)eport. If the user does not wish to do any of these, he or she has the option of canceling the entire procedure. The first argument, "Do You Want to (S)ave, Save and (P)rint, or Save and Print a (R)eport?" is the text that appears in the dialog box. The second argument in the INPUT function is the type_num argument. Use this argument if you want to require a specific data type for your arguments. If you omit the type_num argument, Excel will assign a default type_num of 7 to the argument, which will allow the user to enter numbers, text, or logical values into the function's argument. If you want to restrict the user to entering a text data type for the argument, you must specify a type_num argument of 2. For example, if you want to allow only text entries for the response to the message_text, you would enter the following in the INPUT function:

```
=INPUT("Do You Want to (S)ave, Save and (P)rint, or Save and Print a
(R)eport?",2)
```

The first argument (message_text) requests that the user enter a response, the second argument (type_num) specifies that only text entries will be accepted for the response. Each data type you can specify in an argument is shown in the following table, along with its value.

Data type	Value
Number	1
Text	2
Logical	4
Reference	8
Error	16
Array	64

An argument can be a formula, a reference to a single cell, or a constant value, as long as it produces a result that is allowed by the data type. For example, if you specify a data type of 1 for the message_text argument, the user will only be able to enter a number in response to the request for input. If you specify a data type of 64 for the message_text argument, the user can enter a formula, a cell reference, a range, or a constant value.

If you want to specify more than one data type for an argument, you can add together the values of the data types. For example, if you want to allow the user to enter either text or a logical value, you would add the value of the text data type (2) to the value of the logical data type (4), and enter the data type for the argument as 6.

The INPUT function returns the data the user enters. If the user selects the Cancel button, the function returns a value of FALSE. In order for this data to be used in a macro, it must be stored using a name that the macro can identify. To store the input data with a name, select the cell that contains the INPUT function, click on Formula in the menu bar, click on Define Name, type the name you want in the Name text box, and select OK. For example, if you define the name of the cell as *Print*, when the user enters *P*, the value P is returned and Print is equal to P. If the user enters *S*, the value S is returned and Print is equal to S. If the user selects the Cancel button, the value FALSE is returned, and Print is equal to FALSE.

If you enter an argument for title_text, the argument you enter will be displayed in the title bar of the dialog box. For example:

```
=INPUT("Do You Want to (S)ave, Save and (P)rint, or Save and Print a
(R)eport?",2,"Save and Print")
```

will display the text *Save and Print* in the title bar of the dialog box. If you omit this argument, the text *Input* is displayed in the title bar.

If you want to specify a default value in the edit box of the dialog box, use the default argument. For example, the function:

```
=INPUT("Do You Want to (S)ave, Save and (P)rint, or Save and Print a
(R)eport?",2,"Save and Print","S")
```

will display the letter *S* in the edit box when the dialog box is displayed. If you omit this argument, the dialog box will be empty.

Use the x_pos and y_pos arguments to specify the horizontal and vertical positions, respectively, of the dialog box on the screen. If you omit one of these arguments, the dialog box will use the position you specify, and will be centered for the omitted argument. If you omit both arguments, the dialog box will be centered on the screen.

The last argument, help_ref, allows the user to access a custom help topic. A detailed explanation of custom help topics can be found in Chapter 5.

Starting One Macro from within Another Macro

You can start one macro while you are in another macro by typing an equal sign (=) followed by the name of the macro. For example, the command:

```
=Reports()
```

used in the Save and Print macro, will start a macro named Reports. When the Reports macro is done, the user will be returned to the Save and Print macro.

If the macro you want to invoke is on a different macro sheet than the original macro, you must use an external reference. For example, the command:

```
=MACRO1.XLM!Reports
```

will run the macro Reports, which is located on the macro sheet named MACRO1.XLM. The sheet to which the macro refers (MACRO1.XLM) must be active, or the macro (Reports) will not run.

Using Add-in Macros

When you save your macros as add-in macros, you do not have to use an external reference to access them from another macro sheet. For example, if you save the macro Reports as an add-in macro and then want to run Reports from another macro sheet, you do not have to include an external reference to run the macro—you only have to open the add-in macro sheet and enter =Reports. When you open an add-in macro sheet, the sheet is hidden and cannot be displayed by using the Unhide command on the Window menu. Macros in add-in macro sheets do not appear in, and cannot be run from, the Macro/Run dialog box.

Saving a Macro Sheet as an Add-in Macro Sheet

To save a macro sheet as an add-in macro sheet:

1. Switch to the macro sheet if it is not the active document.
2. Click on File to open the File menu.
3. Click on Save As to display the Save As dialog box.
4. Type a name for the macro sheet.
5. Under Save File as Type, select Add-In.
6. Select OK.

WARNING The Close All command in the File menu does not close add-in macro sheets. When you exit Excel, you will not be asked if you want to save changes to an add-in macro sheet. If you have made any changes to the sheet, you must remember to save the sheet before you exit, or your changes will be lost.

Opening an Add-in Macro Sheet as a Regular Macro Sheet

When you want to read or edit an add-in macro sheet, you must open it as a regular macro sheet. To do this:

1. Click on File in the menu bar to open the File menu.
2. Click on Open to display the Open dialog box.
3. Select the name of the add-in macro sheet.
4. Press Shift and click on OK.

You can automatically open an add-in macro sheet every time you start Excel, by either adding it to the working set of add-in macros or by placing it in the startup directory or folder.

Speeding Up a Macro

If your macro seems to run very slowly, there are a number of steps you can take to speed it up.

▼ Check the functions inside any loops in your macro. Since most of the work in a macro is done within a loop, do not include any functions that are not absolutely necessary.

▼ Turn off screen updates in sections of the macro where users do not need to see what is happening on the screen. To turn off screen updates, enter the function =ECHO(FALSE) in the macro. Turn screen updates back on only when users need to see what is on the screen. To turn screen updates on, enter the function =ECHO(ON) in the macro. You can also hide the macro sheet to reduce the number of screen updates.

▼ If your macro runs a large worksheet with many numbers that are frequently recalculated, use manual calculation instead of automatic calculation. Use the CALCULATE.NOW and CALCULATE.DOCUMENT functions to calculate the worksheet only when necessary.

▼ Use the MESSAGE function to tell the user what is happening. This will not help your macros to operate more quickly, but it will reduce the anxiety level of the user.

Slowing Down a Macro

If you include information that the user needs to read in a macro, you might want to slow down the macro for a certain period of time to give the user an opportunity to read the message. You can use the WAIT function to make a macro wait a specified amount of time or to resume at a specific time. If you want the user to control the amount of time the message is displayed on the screen, use the ALERT function. The user must respond by clicking on OK or CANCEL to remove the dialog box from the screen.

Testing a Macro

When you have written a macro, you will need to switch to a document window to test the macro. Testing a macro goes beyond just running it. You must check the results of the macro to be certain that it is doing exactly what it is supposed to do. For example, if you write a macro that subtracts 10 from every number greater than 100 on a worksheet, you must run the macro, then check the changed worksheet against the original to be sure that every number greater than 100 on the worksheet has been reduced by exactly 10, and that none of the numbers that are less than 100 have been changed. You should also run the macro again to be certain that it works equally well with the changed worksheet.

If you write a macro that contains a dialog box requesting user input, you must test the macro for every possible type of input. Just because your message says *Enter Sales Tax* does not mean that the user is going to enter *.0825* or *8¼%* for the sales tax for the State of New York. You must anticipate and test as many variations of input from the user as you can think of. For example, what happens if the user enters *eight and one-quarter*, or just *8¼*, without the percent sign?

If your macro is not working properly, you must locate the function in the macro that is causing the problem. There are several ways you can accomplish this.

Stepping through a Macro Using the Run Command

When it encounters a function that is incorrect, your macro will stop and a dialog box will be displayed informing you of the error and the location of the function. You can then exit the macro and fix the function. If you have a function in your macro that does not give you the proper results, but whose syntax is correct, the macro will run but will not produce the result intended. You must then determine which functions are not operating correctly. When you step through a macro, you can check its individual steps to make sure the formulas are being calculated in the correct order. You cannot edit a macro while you are stepping through it. To step through a macro:

1. Click on Macro in the menu bar to open the Macro menu.

2. Click on Run to open the Run Macro dialog box, as shown in Figure 4.2.

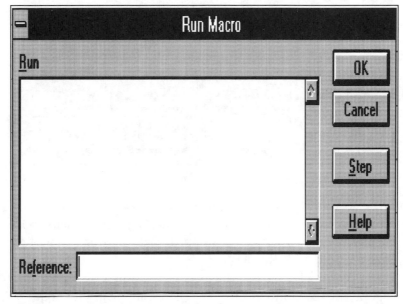

Figure 4.2 *The Run Macro dialog box.*

3. Select the macro you want to run, and click on Step to display the Single Step dialog box, as shown in Figure 4.3.

4. Select Step Into to step through the macro. When you select Step Into, Excel allows you to step through each function in the main macro and each function in all subroutine macros. The Single Step dialog box will display the first cell in the macro and will tell you the formula (or function) the macro is executing. When you click on Step Into again, Excel will show you the result of the formula. If the formula does not produce a result—for example, if you set a variable such as =SET.NAME("Typos",TRUE)—Excel will continue to the next cell in the macro and will show you the formula to be calculated next.

Every time you click on Step Into, you will either get the result of the formula displayed in the Single Step dialog box, or go to the next cell in the macro. You can continue to Step Into each formula in the macro and all subrou-

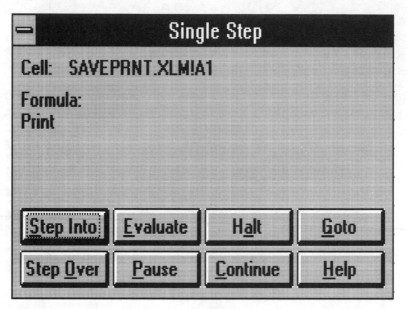

Figure 4.3   *The Single Step dialog box.*

tine macros until you locate the formula that is giving you inaccurate results. You can then press the Goto button in the Single Step dialog box to stop the macro and go to the cell where it stopped. Make the changes in the formula and begin the testing procedure again.

5. If you have already tested all of your subroutines and do not wish to step through all of the formulas in them, choose the Step Over button. When you choose Step Over, Excel steps through each formula in the main macro and runs the subroutine macros in their entirety. Once you have located the problem, press the Goto button to stop the macro and go to the cell where it stopped.

6. To stop a macro, press the Halt button. To resume running a stopped macro, press the Continue button.

7. If you have a very complex formula and you suspect that it is not calculating the result in the proper order (for example, a parenthetical expression is not set up correctly), choose the Evaluate button. It calculates the formula one operator at a time, giving you the result of each operator. Continue pressing the Evaluate button to view the result of each succeeding operator until you locate the problem. Once you have located the problem, press the Goto button to stop the macro and to go to the cell where the macro was stopped. You can then correct the problem and test the macro again.

8. If you choose the Pause button, you will pause the macro and remove the Single Step dialog box from the screen. You can then perform other tasks in

Excel or in other programs. When you pause a macro, the Macro Resume tool appears on the screen. To resume running the macro at the point where it was paused, click on the Resume Macro tool.

Stepping through a Macro Using Step Macro

The Step Macro tool allows you to start the macro at the active cell.

1. To display the Macro toolbar, click on Options to display the Options menu, then choose the Toolbars command.

2. Select the cell where you want to start the macro.

3. Click the Step Macro tool on the Macro toolbar to display the Single Step dialog box, as shown in Figure 4.3. Follow steps 4 through 8 in the preceding section, as though you were stepping through the macro using the Run command.

Automatically Stepping through a Command Macro

You can use the =STEP function in your macro to automatically step through a macro. When you run the macro, it will operate normally until it encounters the =STEP function. At that point it will automatically begin to step through the remaining functions in the macro. This is useful if you know that the beginning of your macro is functioning properly and you want to step through only the formulas or functions that you believe are causing the problem. To step through a macro automatically:

1. Insert an empty cell at the point in the macro where you want the stepping to start. Be certain that the cell is part of the range you named as a macro.

2. Type =STEP() in the cell where you want the macro to start stepping.

3. Run the macro. When the macro encounters the =STEP function, the Single Step dialog box will be displayed. Again, follow steps 4 through 8, as though you were stepping through the macro using the Run command.

Remember to remove the =STEP function from the macro when you have made all corrections and the macro is running properly.

WARNING

Manually Interrupting a Macro that is Running

You can manually interrupt a macro while it is running:

1. Press Esc to display a dialog box.
2. To step through the macro, choose the Step button.
3. To stop the macro, choose the Halt button.
4. To resume running the macro, choose the Resume button.
5. To go to the cell where the macro stopped, choose the Goto button.

 Interrupting a macro while it is running works only if you have not set up a condition to exit the macro if certain keys are pressed. For example, the Save and Print macro shown earlier in this chapter changes the N O T E condition Typos to FALSE if the Esc key is pressed, and automatically exits the macro without executing any of the macro choices.

Displaying the Returned Values of Formulas on the Macro Sheet

You can tell Excel to return values instead of formulas. When you display values, you can quickly determine which formulas return FALSE values or error values.

1. Click on Options in the menu bar to display the Options menu.
2. Click on Display to open the Display Options dialog box.
3. Clear the Formulas check box.
4. Click on OK.

Chapter 5

DESIGNING A PROGRAM

Defining Your Needs

The first step in creating any program is to define your needs. What exactly do you want the program to accomplish? If you are creating a program that will be used to automate procedures that the user has done manually until this time, it is a good idea to talk to the user. Ask the user what he or she likes and doesn't like about the current method of doing things. Ask to see hard copy of any forms and reports. Remember, the reason for custom programming is not only to increase efficiency, but to make life easier for the user. For example, if you are creating an accounting program, talk to the bookkeeper. Find out what forms he or she is using now. Ask for a wish list of things that the user would like to be able to accomplish electronically. Then, sit down and start planning. Rather than try to plan the entire program at once, plan one section at a time. For example, instead of trying to design the entire accounting program all at once, break it into manageable sections. The accounting program will consist of accounts payable, accounts receivable, general ledger and trial balance, and reports. Since the general ledger and the reports will depend upon the information entered into accounts receivable and accounts payable, logically you should start with one of these sections. Let's start with accounts receivable. What do you need to include in this section? Be sure to have a pencil and paper handy to jot down all of your ideas—otherwise you are likely to leave something out.

When you enter a receivable, you must include, at a minimum, the name of the company or person from whom it was received; the amount; whether it was paid by check, credit card, or in cash; the check or credit card number; the date received; and the account number to credit for the payment. Once you have decided what to include in this section, talk to the user again. See if there is anything else he or she wants included. Check your list against the existing system. Remember, your job is to enable to user to increase efficiency and produce information more easily. If you do not include everything the user needs to accomplish this, your program will not be efficient. After you decide what the program will do and how, it is time to design the menus, menu commands, dialog boxes, tools, and toolbars that the user will need. Finally, you must design the macros that will comprise the program.

Using the Structured Macro Template

When you write a program, keep it organized and easy to read and understand. If you need to go back and change or add something in six months, you do not want to have to figure out what you did previously. The structured macro template included with Excel that will help you to do this. The structured macro template also includes utilities that you can use to make programming your macros easier. For example, it allows you to modify and use the auto_open and auto_close macros and include them in your own macros; to automatically indent macro commands, making them easier to read and understand; and to test macro functions with the included utilities.

Indenting Macro Commands Using the Structured Macro Template

When you indent commands inside a macro, you make the macro easier to read and understand. For example, the following macro has all of its commands at the left margin.

```
=SET.NAME("Typos",TRUE)
=WHILE(Typos)
=INPUT("Do You Want to (S)ave, Save and (P)rint, or Save and
Print a (R)eport?",2)
=IF(Print="P")
```

```
=ALERT("Check to see if printer on",1)
=SAVE()
=PRINT()
=SET.NAME("Typos",FALSE)
=ELSE.IF(Print="R")
=SAVE()
=Reports()
=SET.NAME("Typos",FALSE)
=ELSE.IF(Print="S")
=SAVE()
=SET.NAME("Typos",FALSE)
=ELSE.IF(Print=FALSE)
=SET.NAME("Typos",FALSE)
=ELSE()
=ALERT("You Must Enter ""S"", ""P"", or ""R."" Please enter
your selection again",2)
=END.IF()
=NEXT()
=RETURN()
```

If you indent the macro commands as shown below, you can see how much easier it is to read the macro.

```
=SET.NAME("Typos",TRUE)
=WHILE(Typos)
  =INPUT("Do You Want to (S)ave, Save and (P)rint, or Save
  and Print a (R)eport?",2)
  =IF(Print="P")
    =ALERT("Check to see if printer on",1)
    =SAVE()
    =PRINT()
    =SET.NAME("Typos",FALSE)
  =ELSE.IF(Print="R")
    =SAVE()
    =Reports()
    =SET.NAME("Typos",FALSE)
  =ELSE.IF(Print="S")
    =SAVE()
    =SET.NAME("Typos",FALSE)
  =ELSE.IF(Print=FALSE)
```

```
    =SET.NAME("Typos",FALSE)
  =ELSE()
    =ALERT("You Must Enter ""S"", ""P"", or ""R."" Please
    enter your selection again",2)
  =END.IF()
=NEXT()
=RETURN()
```

When you indent the commands that follow the IF and ELSE.IF statements, you can easily find them and the commands they affect. The IF statements are indented under the WHILE statement. If the macro were several pages long and included loops within loops, imagine the difficulty of reading and understanding where each loop begins and ends.

Indenting Selected Macro Commands

To indent selected macro commands using the structured macro template:

1. Open the STRUCTM.XLT macro sheet template.
2. Open the macro sheet in which you wish to indent commands.
3. Select the cells which contain the commands you wish to indent.
4. Press Ctrl+N.

Removing Indents from Selected Macro Commands

To remove indents from selected macro commands using the structured macro template:

1. Open the STRUCTM.XLT macro sheet template.
2. Open the macro sheet that contains the macro indents you want to change.
3. Select the macro commands from which you want to remove indents.
4. Press Ctrl+M.

The structured macro template also contains the command window macro, which allows you to calculate a macro function simply by clicking the cell in the macro that contains the function. This is a valuable and time-saving tool for debugging your macros.

Using the Command Window Macro

To use the Command Window macro on the structured macro template:

1. Open the STRUCTM.XLT macro sheet template.
2. Open the macro sheet that contains the function you want to test.
3. Press Ctrl+Shift+C.
4. Either type the macro function in a cell or click on the cell that contains an existing macro function.
5. Choose the Run button.
6. Choose the OK button. The Command Window macro will calculate the function and display the result.
7. Choose the Close button.

Programming in Modules

Modules are sections of a program that, when linked together, comprise the entire program. There are several reasons for creating a program using modules. First, it is easier to find and correct bugs in a program when the program is done in smaller segments. Second, certain sections of the program may be reused (such as print macros), and if they are created as separate modules you do not have to retype them. Third, the program is more efficient and easier to maintain.

When you write a module for a program, you should first test the module and then, if it runs as expected, link the module to the main program and test it again. Otherwise, you cannot be sure that both the module and main program are still operating correctly.

Creating a Basic Accounting Program

Once you have defined and outlined your needs, you are ready to go on to the next step, the actual programming. Since all accounting programs must begin with a chart of accounts, setting it up will be the first step. The next step is to set up the data files and establish the links.

Setting Up the Chart of Accounts

The chart of accounts is the lynchpin of the program. It must list all of the income and expense accounts of your company. In order to produce reports that can track all of the company's financial information, the chart of accounts must also include assets, liabilities, and equity. Let's set up a sample chart of accounts on a worksheet for a small law firm. The account numbers will be typed into Column A and the account descriptions will be typed into Column B. We will save the worksheet as CHRTACCT.XLS, and it will look like the following:

1000	Checking account
1050	Savings account
1060	Payroll account
1070	Trust account cash
1080	Petty cash
1099	Cash transfers
1100	Accounts receivable—billed
1190	Accounts receivable—unbilled
1200	Allowance for bad debts
1350	Prepaid expenses
1370	Prepaid insurance
1390	Prepaid taxes
1400	Loans and exchanges
1500	Land
1510	Buildings
1511	Accum depreciation—building
1520	Building improvements
1521	Accum depreciation—building improvements
1550	Leasehold improvements
1551	Accum depreciation—lease improvements
1570	Equipment
1571	Accum depreciation—equipment
1580	Furniture and fixtures
1581	Accum depreciation—furniture and fixtures
1650	Vehicles
1651	Accum depreciation—vehicles
1680	Other fixed assets
1681	Accum depreciation—other fixed assets
1700	Partners' loan receivable
1800	Utility deposits

1810	Other assets
1900	Organization costs
2000	Accounts payable
2010	Credit card—Visa
2020	Credit card—Mastercard
2030	Credit card—American Express
2090	Notes payable—short term
2100	Employee health insurance payable
2150	Clients' funds in trust
2190	Sales taxes payable
2200	Federal withholding tax payable
2210	FICA withholding tax payable
2220	State withholding taxes payable
2250	Local withholding taxes payable
2280	Accrued FUTO
2290	Accrued SUTA
2300	Long term notes—current portion
2500	Accrued corporation taxes
2610	Accrued interest
2690	Accrued other expenses
2800	Long term notes—net of current
2900	Notes payable—partner
3020	Common Stick
3030	Additional paid in capital
3040	Retained Earnings
3099	Initial Cash Balance Offset
3110	Partner's Capital #1
3120	Partner's Capital #2
3160	Partner's Drawing #1
3170	Partner's Drawing #2
3210	Capital
3220	Drawing
4000	Fees—billed
4100	Fees—unbilled
4290	(Less) fees absorbed
4300	Other income
5000	Client postage
5050	Client photocopy
5100	Client telephone

5230	Client travel
5550	Other client-related expenses
5650	(Less) expenses recovered
6000	Associates' salaries
6030	Office salaries
6100	Auto expense
6120	Bank service charges
6140	Contributions
6160	Depreciation expense
6180	Due and subscriptions
6200	Equipment rental
6220	Utilities
6230	Insurance—employee group
6240	Insurance—general
6250	Insurance—partner's life
6260	Interest expense
6270	Legal and accounting
6280	Miscellaneous expense
6300	Office expense
6310	Outside services
6340	Postage expense
6360	Rent expense
6380	Repairs and maintenance
6440	Supplies expense
6480	Taxes—real estate
6490	Taxes—payroll
6500	Taxes—other
6520	Telephone
6540	Travel and entertainment
7010	Fines and penalties
7030	Interest income
7100	Finance charge income
7150	Other income
7210	Federal income tax
7220	State income tax
9999	Temporary distribution

Set up a chart of accounts that suits your company's needs. If the company for which you are writing the program already has a chart of accounts, simply copy the existing chart of accounts into a worksheet. Once you have set up the chart of accounts, you are ready to set up the initial data files. This is a good time to create one or two dialog boxes, which will be needed in the macros we will be writing for the data files.

Setting Up the Initial Data Files

A basic accounting program must be able to record receipts (monies received) and disbursements (monies paid). Therefore, the next step is to set up worksheets for disbursements and receipts, as shown in figures 5.1 (DISBURSE.XLS) and 5.2 (RECEIPTS.XLS). The account numbers and account names in these worksheets are linked to the account numbers and account names in the chart of accounts (CHRTACCT.XLS). All of these worksheets are included in the floppy disk that accompanies this book. Linking these items allows changes to the chart of accounts to be automatically reflected in the disbursements and receipts worksheets. Remember, you can use the Format command in the menu bar to format your worksheets so that they are easy to use and the user will be comfortable with them.

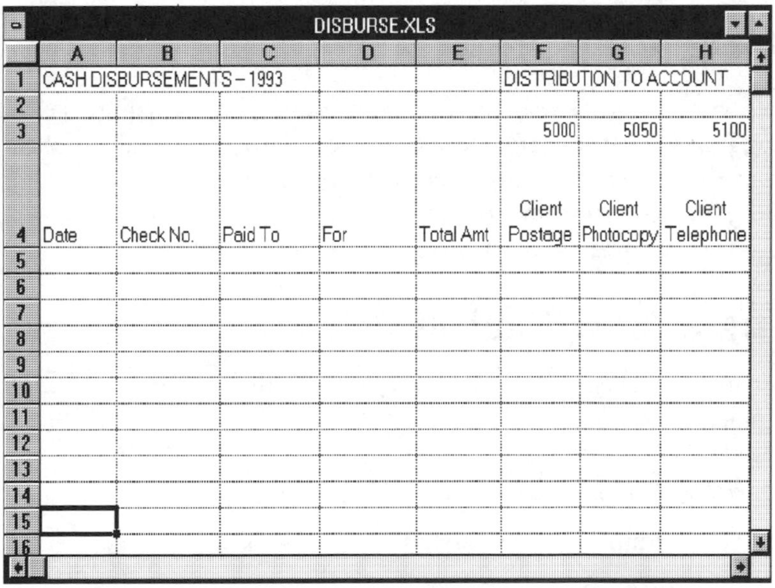

Figure 5.1 *DISBURSE.XLS worksheet.*

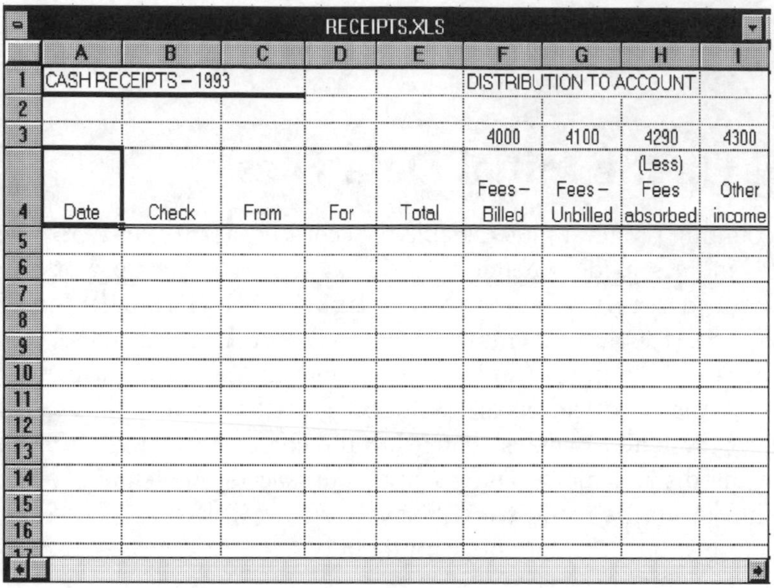

Figure 5.2   *Receipts.XLS worksheet.*

Creating Dialog Boxes

Excel allows you to create your own custom dialog boxes using the Dialog Editor. These dialog boxes look and operate like the standard Excel dialog boxes. We will be using custom dialog boxes to create custom data entry forms and to display custom error messages to the user. A custom dialog box can contain 64 items —32 items that can take or return arguments, 8 list boxes, and 1,024 text characters.

Creating a New Dialog Box

When you run the Dialog Editor, it creates a blank dialog box in which you can add, move, and delete items.

Starting the Dialog Editor

To start the Dialog Editor:

1. Select Run from the Control menu.
2. Select the Dialog Editor option button. A blank dialog box appears, as shown in Figure 5.3.
3. Click on OK.

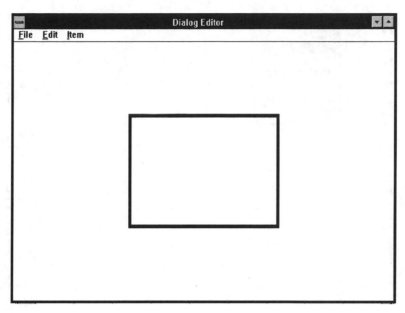

Figure 5.3   *Dialog Editor.*

Adding an item to the dialog box

To add an item to the dialog box, click on Item in the menu bar to see a list of items you can add, as shown in Figure 5.4. All of the items except group boxes and fixed text have more than one possible kind. When you select an item from the Item menu, a dialog box appears listing the choices you have in that item. For a complete list of the items that can be used in a dialog box, see the section entitled "Items Used in a Custom Dialog Box" later in this chapter.

If you select a Group box and then press Enter, an option button will be added to the Group box.

N O T E

Selecting an item in the dialog box

Once you have added an item to the dialog box, you can change the text in the item to reflect the text you want to appear in the dialog box. For example, if you select Text in the Item menu, the word *Text* will appear in the dialog box enclosed in a box. You can then type *Date,* for instance, and *Text* will be replaced by *Date.* If you move your mouse and click, the text is no longer enclosed in a box and you cannot edit it. If you

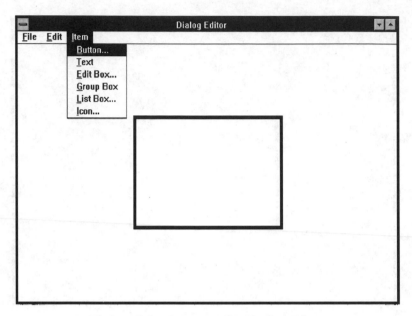

Figure 5.4   *Item menu in Dialog Editor.*

click on the text it will again be enclosed in a box. You can either edit the text or, if you press Enter, the existing text will be copied to the area directly below the existing text.

To select an item in a dialog box, click on the item you want to select. To deselect an item in a dialog box, click on the item you want to deselect.

Selecting multiple items in a dialog box

To select more than one item in a dialog box:

1. Click on the first item you wish to select.
2. Press Shift and click on the next item you wish to select.
3. Repeat Step 2 until you have selected all of the items you want.

Deleting an item from a dialog box

To delete an item from a dialog box:

1. Select the item you want to delete.
2. Click on Edit in the menu bar and select Clear.

Deleting multiple items from a dialog box

To delete more than item from a dialog box:

1. Click the first item you want to delete.
2. Press Shift and click the next item you wish to delete.
3. Repeat Step 2 until you have selected all of the items you want to delete.
4. Click on Edit in the menu bar and choose Clear.

Moving an item in a dialog box

To move an item in a dialog box:

1. Click on the item you want to move.
2. Drag the item to the location you want.

To cancel the move, press Esc before pressing Enter or releasing the mouse button.

If the item does not move, you may have to select the item and then choose Info from the Edit menu. In the Info dialog box, clear the Auto check boxes for the x and y positions.

Resizing an item in a dialog box

To resize an item in a dialog box:

1. Click on the item you want to resize.
2. Drag the border of the item until it is the size you want.

To cancel moving or resizing an item, press Esc before pressing Enter or releasing the mouse button.

If the item does not resize, you may have to select the item and then choose Info from the Edit menu. In the Info dialog box, clear the Auto check boxes for height and width.

Clearing automatic formatting of items in a dialog box

When you add items to a dialog box, the Dialog Editor automatically assigns a location and size to the item. Some of the dimensions of items in a dialog box (for example, the height of a Cancel button) cannot be changed until you clear the Auto check box.

1. Double-click the item you want.
2. Clear the Auto check box for the dimension you want to change.
3. Type the location or size you want.
4. Click on OK.

Creating a group of items in a dialog box

In a dialog box, a group is used for a set of related items that you want to place together in a group box. You can move, resize, or delete an entire group box. To create a group of items in a dialog box:

1. First create the group box by clicking in Item in the menu bar and selecting Group Box.

2. Click on Item in the menu bar and choose the items you wish to add. If you want to add option buttons, you can simply select the group and press Enter for each option button you want to create. Remember to type the text you want for the option button immediately after you create it. Otherwise, you must select the option button and edit the text.

Moving an existing item to a group in a dialog box

You can drag an existing item into a dialog box only if it was created after the Group box was created. To move an existing item to a group:

1. Select the item.

2. Click on Edit in the menu bar and choose Cut.

3. Select the group box.

4. Click on Edit in the menu bar and choose Paste.

5. Drag the item into the Group box.

Moving, resizing, or deleting a group of items in a dialog box

To move, resize, or delete a group of items in a dialog box:

1. Select the Group box.

2. Click on Edit in the menu bar and choose Select Group.

3. Move, resize, or delete the group as you would a single item.

 You can move, resize, edit, or delete a single item within a group box the way in which you move, resize, edit, or delete an item that is not in a Group box.

NOTE

Copying a Dialog Box Definition to a Macro Sheet

Once you have created a dialog box, you must copy the dialog box definition to a macro sheet. When your dialog box is set up the way you want it:

1. Click on Edit in the menu bar and choose Select Dialog.
2. Click on Edit in the menu bar again and select Copy.
3. Open the macro sheet to which you want to add the dialog box definition.
4. Select the cell in the upper-left corner of the range where you want the dialog box definition to be pasted.

Remember, when you paste data into a macro sheet, any existing data on the range to which you are pasting will be overwritten. Be careful to select a range that has enough empty space.

WARNING

5. Click on Edit in the menu bar and choose Paste.
6. Click on Define Name in the Formula menu to define the name of the dialog box definition.
7. Type a name in the Name box, and click on OK.

Quitting the Dialog Editor

After you have copied the dialog box definition to a macro sheet, you can quit the Dialog Editor. Simply click on File in the Dialog Editor menu bar, and select Exit.

If you have created a dialog box and have not copied it to the Clipboard, you will receive a message asking whether you want to copy the dialog box to the clipboard. If you say no, any changes made to the dialog box will be lost.

The Dialog Box Definition

When you paste the information contained in a dialog box into a macro sheet, the information is pasted into the macro sheet in a table containing the numeric and text values that define the dialog box. The dialog box definition contains seven values (each placed in a separate column) for each item in the dialog box, as shown in the following table:

Column	Value
1	Item number
2	X position of the item's upper-left corner
3	Y position of the item's upper-left corner
4	Width of the item
5	Height of the item
6	Text associated with the item
7	Initial value or result for the item

Each item in the dialog box will contain these seven values placed in seven column across one row.

Displaying a Dialog Box

To display your dialog box, you must create a macro that uses the dialog box definition you created and copied to the macro sheet. In the macro, you use the following DIALOG.BOX function syntax:

```
=DIALOG.BOX(dialog_ref)
```

where dialog_ref is the named range that contains the dialog box definition. This function is used in the Main Macro described later in this chapter.

Editing an Existing Dialog Box

To change an existing dialog box, you must copy the dialog box definition from the macro sheet to the Clipboard, then paste it into the Dialog Editor:

1. Open the macro sheet that contains the dialog box definition you want to change.
2. Select all of the cells in the range that contain the dialog box definition. Remember, all dialog box definitions are seven columns wide, and must be at least two rows long.
3. Click on Edit in the menu bar and choose Copy.
4. Open the Dialog Editor (select Run from the Control menu and then select Dialog Editor).

5. Make your changes to the dialog box.

6. Click on Edit in the menu bar and choose Select Dialog.

7. Click on Edit in the menu bar and choose Copy.

8. Switch to the macro sheet in which you want to paste the revised dialog box definition.

9. Select the cell in the upper-left corner of the range where you want to place the dialog box definition.

10. Click on Edit in the menu bar and choose Paste.

Moving a dialog box

To move a dialog box:

1. Click the border of the dialog box to select the box.

2. Drag the dialog box to the location you want.

If the dialog box does not move, click on Edit in the menu bar, choose Info, and clear the Auto check boxes for the x and y positions. Then either type in the location you want in the x and y boxes or follow the steps listed above.

Resizing a Dialog Box

To resize a dialog box:

1. Click the border of the dialog box to select the box.

2. Drag a corner or side of the box until it is the size you want.

If the dialog box does not move, click on Edit in the menu bar, choose Info, and clear the Auto check boxes for height and width. Then either type in the height and width you want or follow the steps listed above.

Specifying Values in a Dialog Box Definition

If you want the dialog box to contain a value determined by you when it is displayed, use the SET.VALUE function as follows:

```
=SET.VALUE(reference,values)
```

Reference refers to the cell address of the initial/result column of the item, and values refers to the value you want displayed for that item when the dialog box is displayed. For example, if you create a dialog box that contained an edit box called Tax, and you want the value in that edit box to be .0825 whenever the dialog box is displayed, you would enter following function into your macro sheet:

```
=SET.VALUE(G8,.0825)
```

G8 is the cell address of the initial/result column of the item called Tax, and .0825 is the value you want displayed.

If you want to use the values that a user enters into the dialog box, you can create formulas that refer to the initial/results columns.

Items Used in a Custom Dialog Box

There are twenty-four types of items that can be used in a custom dialog box.

- ▼ **OK button (default).** This item closes the dialog box, enters the data from the dialog into the initial/result column, and returns control to the macro. The name of the button in the dialog box can be edited—it does not have to be OK. This button is already selected when the dialog box appears.

- ▼ **Cancel button (not default).** This item closes the dialog box and returns control to the macro. Any data entered or options selected are ignored. The name of the button can be edited—it does not have to be Cancel.

- ▼ **OK button (not default).** This item closes the dialog box, enters the data from the dialog box into the initial/result column, and returns control to the macro. The name of the button can be edited—it does not have to be OK.

- ▼ **Cancel button (default).** This item closes the dialog box and returns control to the macro. Any data entered or options selected are ignored. The name of the button can be edited—it does not have to be Cancel. This button is already selected when the dialog box appears.

- ▼ **Text.** This item contains fixed text that you use to label items in the dialog box.

- ▼ **Text edit box.** This item is a box in which you can enter text. You can make this box more than one line high by entering the height box in the height column. The text column for this item is left blank. The initial/result column contains the contents entered into the edit box.

- ▼ **Integer edit box.** This item is just like the text edit box, except that you can only enter integers ranging from −32765 to 32,765. The text column for this item is left blank. The initial/result column contains the contents entered into the edit box.

▼ **Number edit box.** This item is like a text edit box, except that you can only enter numbers. The number edit box accepts formatted dates. The initial/result column contains the contents entered in the edit box.

▼ **Formula edit box.** This item is like a text edit box, except you can only enter formulas. References in the initial/result column are always R1C1 style references in the form of text. When these references are displayed in the dialog box, they reflect the current style of the Excel workspace (the default is the A1 style). If you enter a constant, an equal sign is added before it. If you enter text, it is enclosed in quotation marks.

▼ **Reference edit box.** This item is like a text edit box, except that you can only enter references. References in the initial/result column are always R1C1 style references in the form of text. When these references are displayed in the dialog box, they reflect the current style of the Excel workspace (the default if the A1 style).

▼ **Option button group.** This item must appear in the row directly above a group of option buttons. The item does not produce a visible object in the dialog box. Its purpose is to logically group option buttons, and it is required for a button group. This item is automatically created when you create option buttons in a group.

The text column for this item can contain a label for the group. The initial/result column contains the number of the selected option button for the following group. The button in the row directly below the option button group item is button number 1, the next option button is button number 2, and so on. If the initial/result column is blank, button 1 is assumed. If the initial/result column is #N/A, no buttons are selected. The initial/result column also returns the number of the button that you selected.

▼ **Option button.** If this item is part of the group of option buttons, only one button can be selected. The text column contains the name of the button.

▼ **Check box.** In this item, the text column contains the name of the check box. The initial/result column contains the logical value TRUE if the box is checked, and the logical value FALSE if the box is not checked. If the box is dimmed, the initial/result column contains the value #N/A.

▼ **Group box.** This item visually groups items with a dialog box. The text column contains a label for the group.

▼ **List box.** The list box contains a list of items. The text column contains a reference to the items contain in the list. This reference can be an R1C1 style reference given as text, the name of a reference, or the name of an array. You can also specify the list by using any function that returns an array (do not include the equal sign for the function). If the reference is to blank cells or is invalid, no items will be displayed in the list box. The initial/result column contains the number of the item selected in the list box. If the initial/result column is blank, number 1 is assumed. If the initial/result column contains #N/A, no items have been selected.

If the initial/result column contains a valid name, the list box turns into a multiple-selection list box, which allows you to select more than one item from the list (for example, you can choose more than one item in the Apply Name dialog box in the Apply Name command in the Formula menu). The name in the initial/result column must refer to a single number or a one-dimensional array of numbers corresponding to the positions in the list of the initially select-ed values. Once you select items from the list and close the dialog box, the numbers in the named array change to match the selected items. The numbers appear in ascending order in the array. If a name that matches the text in the initial/result column does not exist when the dialog box is opened, Excel will create a name.

▼ **Linked list box.** This item is like a list box, except that it must be preceded by a text edit box. When an item is selected in the linked list box, the text of that item is displayed in the edit box. The text column contains a reference to the items contained in the list. This reference can be an R1C1 style reference given as text, the name of a reference, or the name of an array. You can also specify the list by using any function that returns an array (do not include the equal sign for the function). If the reference is to blank cells or is invalid, no items will be displayed in the list box.

The initial/result column contains the number of the selected item in the list box. The first item in the list box is number 1, the second item is number 2, and so on. If the initial/result column is blank, number 1 is assumed. If the initial/result column contains #N/A, no items have been selected.

▼ **Icon.** This item displays an icon. The text column contains 1 when the user must make a choice, 2 for presenting information to the user, and 3 when an error has occurred.

▼ **Linked file list box.** This item lists files in a directory. It must precede a linked Drive and Directory list box and must follow a Text edit box. The edit box is used to filter filenames that appear in the linked file list box. The text column in this item is ignored.

▼ **Linked Drive and Directories list box.** This item lists available drives and directories. It must immediately follow a linked file list box. If a text item (type 5) immediately follows this item, the text item will display the name of the current drive and directory, and will be updated if the drive or directory changes. The text and initial/result columns in this item are ignored.

▼ **Directory text.** This item displays the name of the current directory. The name will not change once the dialog box is displayed, even if you change directories. If you want the name of the directory to change every time you change directories, you must use the linked drive and directory list box (item 19) followed by a text item (item 5). The text and initial/result columns in this item are ignored.

▼ **Drop-down list box.** This item contains a list of items. The text column contains a reference to the items contained in the list. This reference can be an R1C1 style reference given as text, the name of a reference, or the name of an array. You can also specify the list by using any function that returns an array (do not include the equal sign for the function). If the reference is to blank cells or is invalid, no items will be displayed in the list. The height column contains the length of the list when it is displayed in the dialog box. The initial/result column contains the number of the selected list item. The first item in the list is item number 1, the second is item number 2, and so on. If the initial/result column is blank, 1 is assumed. If no items are selected, the initial/result column contains #N/A.

▼ **Drop-down combination edit/list box.** This item is like a drop-down list box, except that it must be preceded by a text edit box (item 6). You can edit the item in the edit box before the list is displayed. The height column contains the length of the list when it is displayed in the dialog box. The text column contains a reference to the items contained in the list. This reference can be an R1C1 style reference given as text, the name of a reference, or the name of an array. You can also specify the list by using any function that returns an array (do not include the equal sign for the function). If the reference is to blank cells or is invalid, no items will be displayed in the list. The initial/result column contains the number of the selected list item. The first item in the list is item number 1, the second item is item number 2, and so on. If the initial/result column is #N/A, the initial value is taken from the preceding text edit box. If the initial/result column is blank, number 1 is assumed. If you type text in the box that is not contained in the list, the text is returned to the initial/result column of the preceding text edit box (item 6).

▼ **Picture button.** This item closes the dialog box, enters the data from the dialog box into the initial/result column, and returns control to the macro. The button can be any graphic object created on the macro sheet using Excel drawing tools. The text chart column contains the object identifier, for example, *Chart 2*. If you want to find the object identifier for an object, select the object, and the object identifier will appear in the formula bar.

If you simply want to display a graphic object that is not a button in a dialog box, type *223* in column 1. The graphic object will appear in the dialog box, but it is not a button and you cannot press it.

▼ **Help button.** This item displays the custom help topic for the dialog box. The custom help topic reference is entered in the first cell in the dialog box definition table. Although the default name for the button is Help, you can rename it by typing a new name in the text column.

Creating a Custom Data Entry Form

Creating a custom data entry form is very much like creating a custom dialog box. The custom data entry form allows you to design your own data entry form for your worksheets, instead of using the default data form, which can be accessed by clicking on the Form command in the Data menu. The custom data form contains only two of the items that are available in the Item men when you create a dialog box. The two items you can use are Text and Edit Boxes, as shown in the dialog box shown in Figure 5.5.

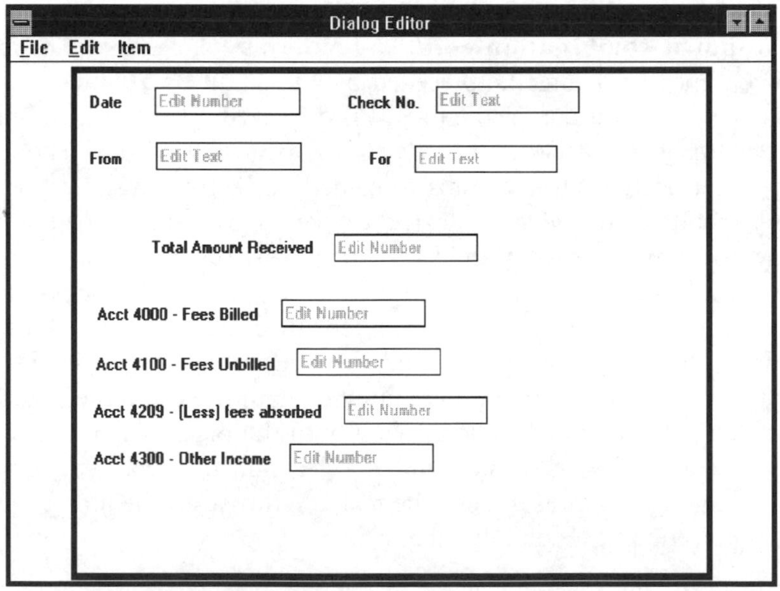

Figure 5.5 *Custom data form with text and edit boxes.*

This dialog box is going to be a custom data entry form for accounts receivable in our basic accounting program. You will notice that none of the command buttons (such as OK and Cancel) have been included in the dialog box. This is because a custom data form only replaces the section of the default data form that is to the left of the scroll bar; all of the command buttons remain the same. To create the custom data entry form:

1. Open the worksheet for which you want to create a custom data entry form.

2. Define your database range using the Set Database command on the Data menu.

3. Select Run from the Control Menu.

4. Select the Dialog Editor option button.

5. Click on OK to display an empty dialog box.

6. Click on Item in the menu bar to select the items you want to add to the dialog box. Remember that you can only use the Text Boxes and Edit Boxes commands from the Item menu in a custom data entry form. Recreate the dialog box shown in Figure 5.5.

7. Once you have created a dialog box that has the text and edit boxes arranged in the way you want them to appear on the data entry form, select the first edit box.

8. Choose Info from the Edit menu and type the name of the database field in which you want to store the information entered in the edit box.

9. Click on OK.

10. Repeat steps 8 and 9 for each edit box in the dialog box.

11. Click on Edit in the menu bar and choose Select Dialog.

12. Click on Edit in the menu bar and choose Copy.

13. Switch to the worksheet that contains the database for which you want to use the custom data entry form.

14. Select the cell that you want to be the upper-left corner of the pasted information. Remember, the data you paste will be seven columns wide and a minimum of two rows long; be certain to choose an area on the worksheet that will not interfere with your database.

15. Click on Edit in the menu and choose Paste. The dialog box description has been pasted and remains selected.

16. Click on Formula in the menu and choose Define Name.
17. In the Name box, type Data_Form. Check to be certain that the cell range identified in the Refers To box is correct.
18. Choose OK.
19. Save the worksheet.

You have now created a custom data entry form. If you select the Form command from the Data menu, your custom data form will be displayed, as shown in Figure 5.6.

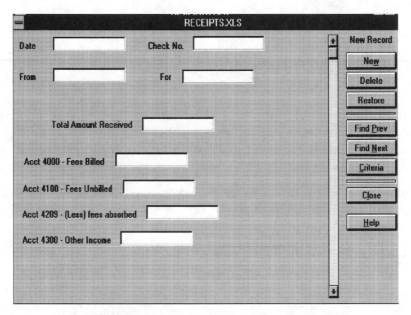

Figure 5.6 *Custom data form when displayed.*

When you enter data into this form, the data will be stored in the database on the worksheet. The custom data entry form is located in the RECEIPTS.XLS worksheet on the disk included with this book.

Creating a Main Entry Screen and Macros

Now that we have created a chart of accounts and linked it to the income and expense worksheets, and have created a custom data entry form for our income worksheet, we need to put it all together into a cohesive whole. We are going to create a custom dialog box that will allow the user to access the chart of accounts and the income and expense worksheets, and to print any of these documents by choosing an option button in the custom dialog box.

The Main Entry Screen

First, create a custom dialog box that looks like the one shown in Figure 5.7. To do this:

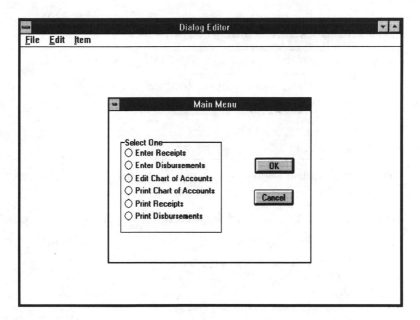

Figure 5.7   *Custom dialog box which will be the main entry screen.*

1. Open the macro sheet for which you want to create a custom dialog box.

2. Select Run from the Control Menu.

3. Select the Dialog Editor option button.

4. Click on OK to display an empty dialog box.

5. Click on Item in the menu bar to select the items you wish to add to the dialog box. We are using a Group Box with Option Buttons, plus the OK and Cancel option buttons.

7. Once you have created a dialog box that has the appearance you want, click on Edit in the menu bar and choose Select Dialog.

8. Click on Edit in the menu bar and choose Copy.

9. Switch to the macro sheet into which you want to paste the definition of the dialog box.

10. Select the cell which you want to be the upper-left corner of the pasted information. Remember, the data you paste will be seven columns wide and a minimum of two rows long; be certain to choose an area on the worksheet that will not interfere with any other macros.

11. Click on Edit in the menu and choose Paste. The dialog box description has been pasted and remains selected.

12. Click on Formula in the menu and choose Define Name.

13. In the Name box, type *Main*. Check to be certain that the cell range identified in the Refers To box is correct.

14. Choose OK.

15. Save the macro sheet.

If you have recreated the dialog box shown in Figure 5.7, the definition on your macro sheet will look like this:

Item	X	Y	Width	Height	Text	Init/Result
			452	204	Main Menu	
1	325	63	88		OK	
2	324	105	88		Cancel	
14	26	36	225	127	Select One	
11						
12					Enter Receipts	
12					Enter Disbursements	
12					Edit Chart of Accounts	
12					Print Chart of Accounts	
12					Print Receipts	
12					Print Disbursements	

The first column contains the item numbers for the dialog box. The second and third columns reflect the x and y positions of the item's upper-left corner. The fourth and fifth columns reflect the width and height of the item. The sixth column contains the text that is used for the item, and the seventh column contains the initial value or result for the item. You will notice that the seventh column is now blank. This is because we did not set any initial values for any of our items. When an option block is selected, the result of that selection will appear in the init/result column in the row that contains item 11, the Option Button Group. The result will appear as a number, starting with 1 for the first option button and continuing consecutively. Notice that in the Text column in the first row, the words *Main Menu* appear, although they did not appear when you created the dialog box. You can put any text you wish to use in the title bar of the dialog box in the Text column in the first row of any dialog box by simply typing the text after you have pasted the dialog box into your macro sheet. This not only provides you with a title for your dialog box, but also with a title bar that allows you to move the dialog box.

The Control Macro

The next step is to create a control macro that will, upon specified conditions, branch to subroutine macros. This will allow you to enter, edit, or print the chart of accounts and worksheets, as shown.

```
Main Macro
=SET.NAME("Box",TRUE)
=WHILE(Box)
=DIALOG.BOX(main)
=IF(N5=1)
=Receipts()
=ELSE.IF(N5=2)
=Disburse()
=ELSE.IF(N5=3)
=Chart()
=ELSE.IF(N5=4)
=Printchart()
=ELSE.IF(N5=5)
=PrintReceipts()
=ELSE.IF(N5=6)
=PrintDisburse()
=ELSE.IF(N5="")
=SET.NAME("Box",FALSE)
=END.IF()
=NEXT()
=RETURN()
```

The first two lines of the control macro set the condition for the macro loop. The value of Box is set to TRUE, and the macro will continue to loop until the value of Box changes to FALSE. The third line uses the DIALOG.BOX function to display the dialog box that we just created and named *Main*. The rest of the control macro sets the condition upon which the macro will branch to a subroutine. IF(N5=1) specifies that if the result in the init/result column (which is column N) is 1 (indicating that the first option button has been selected) the macro will branch to a subroutine macro called Receipts. If this condition is not TRUE, the commands following the IF statement will be ignored, and the control macro will proceed to the next IF statement. If there is no number in the init/result column, the macro changes the value of Box to FALSE, and exits the loop and the macro. For a complete explanation of branching and looping, see Chapter 4.

The Subroutine Macros

Once the control macro is created, you must create the subroutine macros that will allow the user to perform the operations indicated by the option buttons. The first sub-routine is RECEIPTS, and looks like this:

```
Receipts
=OPEN("F:\EXCEL4\RECEIPTS.XLS",1)
=DATA.FORM()
=FILE.CLOSE(TRUE)
=SELECT($N$5)
=CLEAR(1)
=RETURN()
```

The first function in this macro opens the RECEIPTS.XLS worksheet and informs Excel to update all links. The second function instructs Excel to use the custom data entry form that we created earlier in this chapter. These functions will open the work-sheet and display the custom data form on the screen. When you have finished editing and you close the data form, the worksheet will remain open. Therefore, the third function (FILE.CLOSE(TRUE)) automatically closes and saves the worksheet when the data form is closed. The next two functions clear the number in the init/result column in the dialog box definition. When you selected the first option button, the result (1) appeared in the init/result column. After you have cleared this number and selected another option button, the resulting number of the newly selected option box will be reflected in the init/result column. If you select Cancel, the number in the init/result remains blank, the value of Box in the control macro changes to FALSE, and the macro ends. Finally, the macro ends with the RETURN function. Remember, all macros must end with either a RETURN or a HALT function, or you will receive an error message when you run the macro.

The second subroutine, DISBURSE, uses some functions that were not used in the RECEIPTS macro, and looks like this:

```
Disburse
=OPEN("DISBURSE.XLS",3)
=SELECT("R1C1")
=MESSAGE(TRUE,"Click on Tool When Finished")
=PAUSE(FALSE)
=MESSAGE(FALSE)
=FILE.CLOSE(TRUE)
=SELECT($N$5)
=CLEAR(1)
=RETURN()
```

The first function opens the DISBURSE.XLS worksheet and the second function selects the first cell in the worksheet. The PAUSE function pauses the execution of the macro to enable the user to edit the worksheet. When the PAUSE function is used with an argument of FALSE, the Resume tool appears on the screen. The MESSAGE function is used to display a message in the status bar that informs the user to click on the tool when he or she is finished and wants to leave the worksheet. When the user clicks on the Resume tool, the second MESSAGE function resets the status bar to reflect normal Excel messages and the FILE.CLOSE(TRUE) function closes and saves the worksheet. Finally, the number that is the result of choosing option button 2 is cleared and the user is returned to the control macro.

The third subroutine, CHART, is almost an exact duplicate of the DISBURSE subroutine macro, as shown.

```
Chart
=OPEN("F:\EXCEL4\CHRTACCT.XLS")
=SELECT("R1C1")
=MESSAGE(TRUE,"Click on Tool When Finished")
=PAUSE(FALSE)
=MESSAGE(FALSE)
=FILE.CLOSE(TRUE)
=SELECT($N$5)
=CLEAR(1)
=RETURN()
```

The only difference between this subroutine and the DISBURSE subroutine is that a different worksheet is opened by the macro. Though it is not always necessary to include the entire path of the document, it is not a bad idea to get into the habit.

The next three subroutines allow the user to print the chart of accounts and the income and expense worksheets. The first of the print subroutines uses the

PAGE.SETUP and PRINT functions to instruct Excel as to how you want the chart of accounts printed, as shown below.

```
Printchart
=OPEN("F:\EXCEL4\CHRTACCT.XLS")
=PAGE.SETUP("&F","Page
&P",0.75,0.75,1,1,FALSE,FALSE,FALSE,FALSE,1,1,100,1,1,FALSE)
=PRINT(1,,,1,FALSE,FALSE,1,FALSE,1,-2)
=FILE.CLOSE(TRUE)
=SELECT($N$5)
=CLEAR(1)
=RETURN()
```

The first function opens the CHRTACCT.XLS worksheet. The second and third functions set the options you want for the printout and send the document to the printer. These functions and their arguments are explained in detail in Chapter 3. You can also use the Macro Record function in the Macro menu to record the steps needed to set the options for the functions. When you have stopped recording, you can add the rest of the functions to the macro. The fourth function saves and closes the worksheet. Finally, the value in the init/result column is cleared and the user is returned to the control macro.

The second print subroutine is a little different. This subroutine displays the Print dialog box (which is accessed on the File menu):

```
PrintReceipts
=OPEN("F:\EXCEL4\RECEIPTS.XLS",1)
=PRINT?()
=FILE.CLOSE(TRUE)
=SELECT($N$5)
=CLEAR(1)
=RETURN()
```

The function PRINT?() displays the Print dialog box on the screen. If you have not used any of the possible arguments for the function, the last settings that were used for printing will be displayed. If you have included any arguments in the function, the Print dialog box will be displayed with the settings you selected in the arguments.

The third print subroutine also uses the PAGE.SETUP and PRINT functions. As you can see below, the arguments used for these functions is different from the arguments used in the PRINTCHART subroutine.

```
PrintDisburse
=OPEN("F:\EXCEL4\DISBURSE.XLS",1)
=PAGE.SETUP("&F","Page
&P",0.75,0.75,1,1,FALSE,TRUE,FALSE,FALSE,2,5,100,1,1,FALSE)
=PRINT(1,,,1,FALSE,FALSE,1,FALSE,1,-2)
=FILE.CLOSE(TRUE)
=SELECT($N$5)
=CLEAR(1)
=RETURN()
```

The arguments used in the PAGE.SETUP and PRINT functions in the PRINTCHART subroutine eliminate gridlines and print the chart of accounts as a list using portrait orientation. The arguments used in the PAGE.SETUP and PRINT functions in the PRINTDISBURSE subroutine print the worksheet with gridlines in a landscape orientation.

These custom dialog boxes and macros automate and simplify the user's task. They can all be found in the macro sheet entitled ACCTING.XLM on the disk that accompanies this book. You do not have to stop here. Using the techniques demonstrated in this book, you can continue to add subroutines to the control macro to expand the beginnings of this accounting system. You could use the CROSSTAB.CREATE function (or use the Record Macro command on the Macro menu) to create reports that will organize and analyze the data that has been input into the income and expense worksheets. For example, you could create an income and expense report, a Trial Balance, and a General Ledger. All of these subroutines can be added to the custom dialog box using the Dialog Editor. In fact, if you are really ambitious, you can create an accounting system that will allow the user to project earnings and to answer "what-if" questions. You can automatically open the macro sheet and activate the macro when the user executes Excel (see Chapter 8).

The main thing to remember when you are programming is to have patience and flexibility. If your macro does not work, step through the macro and evaluate the result of each function to locate the problem. If one function does not give you the result you want, try another function. Create your macros in modules and test each one thoroughly before you combine the module with another macro. When you have combined one module with another, test them again. Always enter sample data to test your macros. When you have created all of the modules and they have all been combined, test again. Try your best to make the program malfunction. Remember, if users are able to trap themselves in the program, they are not going to want to use it. Finally, remember to keep the programming as simple as possible and still achieve the results you want.

DATABASES, DATABASE FUNCTIONS, AND MACROS

What Is a Database?

A database in Excel allows you to organize, retrieve, and analyze all or some of the data in your worksheets. It allows you to take an entire worksheet or ranges of a worksheet, and reorder the data alphabetically and/or numerically by rows or columns. You can use the data in an existing worksheet, or you can create a worksheet for the express purpose of using its data as a database. You can search a database to find specific data, extract portions of the database, perform statistical calculations on all or part of the data in a database, and print the database.

The Parts of a Database

Before you can use a database in Excel, you must select the data you wish to use and inform Excel that this data will be used as a database. Once you have identified the area of your worksheet that will be used as a database, Excel identifies columns, rows, and data as parts of the database that make up the whole. These parts are used for organizing and retrieving data from your database. Figure 6.1 shows the parts of a database.

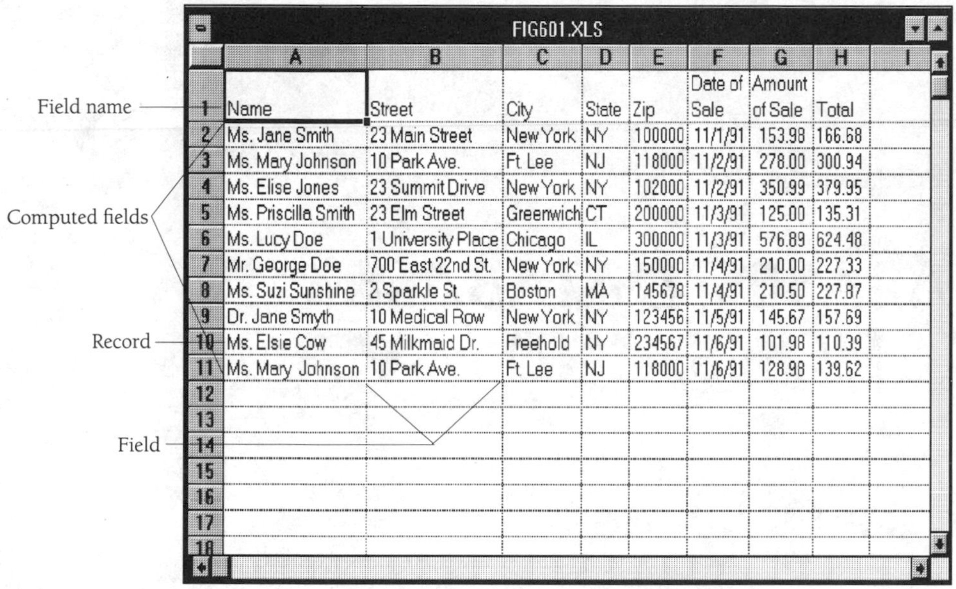

	A	B	C	D	E	F	G	H
1	Name	Street	City	State	Zip	Date of Sale	Amount of Sale	Total
2	Ms. Jane Smith	23 Main Street	New York	NY	100000	11/1/91	153.98	166.68
3	Ms. Mary Johnson	10 Park Ave.	Ft Lee	NJ	118000	11/2/91	278.00	300.94
4	Ms. Elise Jones	23 Summit Drive	New York	NY	102000	11/2/91	350.99	379.95
5	Ms. Priscilla Smith	23 Elm Street	Greenwich	CT	200000	11/3/91	125.00	135.31
6	Ms. Lucy Doe	1 University Place	Chicago	IL	300000	11/3/91	576.89	624.48
7	Mr. George Doe	700 East 22nd St.	New York	NY	150000	11/4/91	210.00	227.33
8	Ms. Suzi Sunshine	2 Sparkle St.	Boston	MA	145678	11/4/91	210.50	227.87
9	Dr. Jane Smyth	10 Medical Row	New York	NY	123456	11/5/91	145.67	157.69
10	Ms. Elsie Cow	45 Milkmaid Dr.	Freehold	NY	234567	11/6/91	101.98	110.39
11	Ms. Mary Johnson	10 Park Ave.	Ft Lee	NJ	118000	11/6/91	128.98	139.62

Figure 6.1 *The parts of a database.*

Database Range

A **database range** contains the area of the worksheet that is defined as a database. The first row of a database contains the **field names**.

Record

A **record** contains all of the data in a row of the database. The fields that appear in each record are identical. For example, all of the records shown in Figure 6.1 contain the data for the Names, Street, City, State, Zip, Date of Sale, Amount of Sale, and Total fields.

Field

Every column in a database is identified as a separate **field**. Every cell within the column is also identified as a field. You can enter numbers, text, dates, or formulas in your fields, and can leave a field blank if there is no data for it. Figure 6.1 contains seven fields: Names, Street, City, State, Zip, Date of Sale, Amount of Sale, and Total.

Computed Field

A field that contains formulas or functions is a **computed field**. In Figure 6.1 for example, the Total field contains a formula to compute the amount of the sale plus the tax.

Field Name

A field name identifies the data that is stored in each field. Each column in the database must have a field name, which appears in the first row of the database. Field names can contain up to 255 characters. Field names must be text constants; do not use formulas, blank cells, logical values, or error values as field names. If a field name contains numbers, the numbers must be formatted as text. If you do not follow these rules, the database will not perform its operations properly. In Figure 6.1 Names, Street, City, State, Zip, Date of Sale, Amount of Sale, and Total are all field names.

Creating a Database

The first step in creating a database is planning. Your original goal may be to send a mailing to everyone on the list, but in the future you might want to extract of portion of the list for limited mailings. You might want to sort the list by city, state, zip code, date, or amount spent. All of these considerations should be taken into account when planning your database. You must use a separate field for each item you might want to use for a sort. For example, if you think that someday you will want to sort by last names, you should create separate fields for first and last names. Let's create the sample database shown in Figure 6.1.

1. Enter the field names in the first row of the area that will become a database.
2. Enter the records in each row of the database directly below the field names. Each record in our database contains eight fields. These fields can contain numbers, text, or formulas. The data is entered exactly as you would enter it in a

worksheet. In the first Total field, enter a formula to compute 8.25 percent of the Amount of Sale and add this figure to the Amount of Sale (=G2*.0825+G2). Leave the rest of the fields in this column blank for now.

3. Select all of the fields you want to include in the database range. This selection must include the field names, and should have an extra blank row below the last record in the database.

4. Click on Data in the menu bar to open the Data menu, as shown in Figure 6.2.

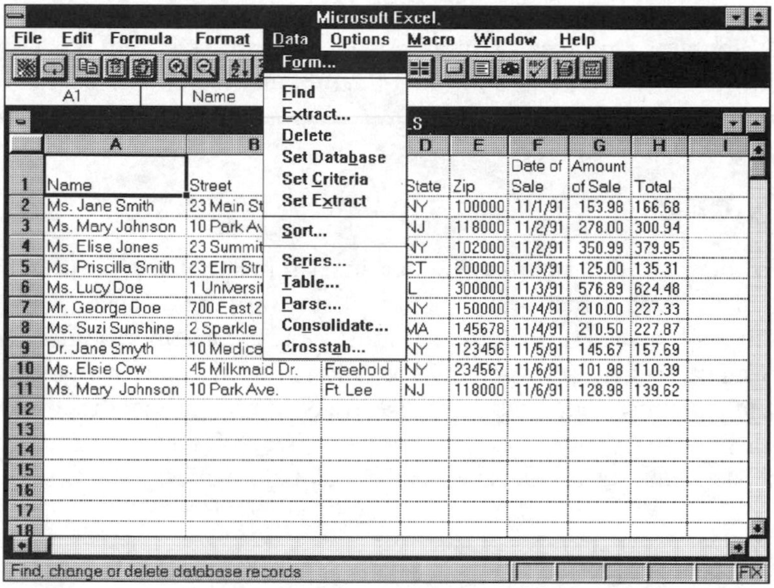

Figure 6.2 *The Data menu.*

5. Click on Set Database to define the database range. Excel automatically names the database range "Database."

Editing and Formatting a Database

You can edit or format a database using any of the editing and formatting features available for worksheets—you can change the data in fields, copy or cut data, change formatting styles, and so forth. For example, to copy the formula in Cell H2 to the rest of the cells in Column H:

1. Select Cell H2.

2. Click on Edit in the menu bar to open the Edit menu.

3. Click on Copy.

4. Select the range to which you wish to copy the formula. In this case it is Cell H3: H10.

5. Click on Paste. The formula for the total is now copied into each field in the column.

Adding Records to a Database

When you add records to a database, you must be careful to insert them within the defined range. This means that you must either add records between rows of existing data, or include a blank record at the end of the database. Otherwise, you must redefine the range each time you add records or the information will not be included in your database. To add a record to a database:

1. Select a row heading within the defined range of the database—preferably a blank record at the end.

2. Click on Edit to open the Edit menu.

3. Click on Insert.

You have added a blank record to the database within the defined database range. When you enter data into the fields in this record, all of the information you entered will be included in all of the operation of the database.

Adding Fields to a Database

When you add fields to a database, you must either add the column inside the defined range, or redefine the database range. This is one reason that planning is important. To add a field within the defined range of a database:

1. Click on the column heading where you want to add a field.

2. Click on Edit in the menu bar to open the Edit menu.

3. Click on Insert.

Deleting Records from a Database

To delete a record from a database:

1. Click on the row heading of the record you want to delete.

2. Click on Edit in the menu bar to open the Edit menu.

3. Click on Delete.

The record has been deleted from the database.

Deleting Fields from a Database

When you delete a field from a database, you must delete the entire column, including the field name.

1. Click on the column heading of the field you want to delete.

2. Click on Edit in the menu bar to open the Edit menu.

3. Click on Delete.

Be careful when deleting fields that contain values used in formulas. All of the rules concerning worksheet formulas and functions apply to databases.

Data Forms

A **data form** is a dialog box that Excel creates by using the field names in your database. It allows you to view one record at a time; to change, add, or delete records from your database; or to find specific records in your database based on criteria you supply. You can use the data form supplied by Excel, or you can create a custom data form (creating custom data forms is covered later in this chapter). To see the data form Excel created for your current database:

1. Click on Data in the menu bar to open the Data menu.

2. Click on Form. The Data Form dialog box Excel created for this defined database range is displayed, as shown in Figure 6.3.

    ▼ **Control Box.** The control box allows you to move or close the Data Form dialog box.

    ▼ **Title Bar.** The title bar shows you the name of the worksheet that contains the currently defined database.

    ▼ **Field Names.** The field names are the field names in your database.

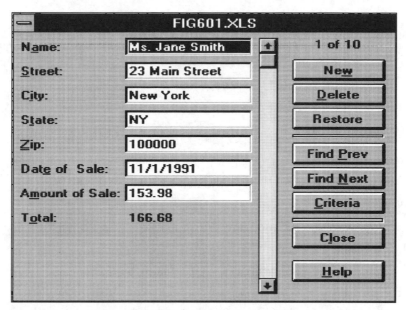

Figure 6.3   *The Data Form dialog box for Figure 6.1.*

▼ **Fields.** The Fields column in the dialog box contains the data for each field within a record in your database. The data form defaults to the first record in your database when you open it.

▼ **Fields with Text Boxes.** Fields with text boxes contain data that can be edited using the data form.

▼ **Fields without Text Boxes.** Fields without text boxes indicate fields that you cannot edit while using the data form. These include fields that are the result of a formula and fields that are locked while the worksheet is protected.

▼ **Scroll Bar.** The scroll bar allows you to scroll through the records quickly, and shows your approximate position in the database.

▼ **Record Number Indicator.** The record number indicator tells you which record is currently displayed and how many records there are in the entire database. Blank records at the end of the database are not counted. The record number indicator changes its message to *New Record* when you scroll to the first blank record after the last nonblank record in the database.

▼ **Command Buttons.** The command buttons in the data form are explained later in this chapter.

If your database contains more fields than the data form can display, you will not be able to view the remaining fields. Also, you will not be able to edit the information in those fields or add data to them when you add **N O T E** a new record.

Editing Records Using a Data Form

You can use a data form to edit the data in certain fields in any of the records in your database. You cannot edit computed fields or fields that are protected.

To edit a record:

1. Open the worksheet that contains the database you want to edit.
2. Click on Data in the menu bar to open the Data menu.
3. Click on Form to display the Data Form dialog box.
4. Scroll to each record that contains a field you wish to edit and make your changes.
5. Click on Close.

When you make changes to a record, they are permanently saved as soon as you move to a new record. If you have not yet moved to a new record you can undo the changes by clicking on the Restore command **WARNING** button. If you have moved to a new record, the changes have been saved and you will have to re-edit the record to restore its original contents.

Adding Records Using a Data Form

The New command button in the data form allows you to add a new record to the database. To do this:

1. Open the worksheet that contains the database you want to use.
2. Click on Data in the menu bar to open the Data menu.
3. Click on Form to display the Data Form dialog box.
4. Click on New. Excel scrolls to the first blank record at the end of the database. You can also scroll past the last record in the database. If no blank record exists, Excel will add one. The record number changes its message to *New Record*.
5. Enter the data in the first field of the record. To move to the next field, either click the field with the mouse or press Tab.

6. Continue until you have finished entering all of the data, then press Enter. The record has been added to the database and a new blank record is displayed.

7. Repeat steps 2 and 3 to add as many records as you wish.

8. Click on Close when you have finished adding records.

If there is no room to add a new record at the bottom of the database because the row below the defined range contains data, Excel will display a message. You must either move or delete the data below the defined range if you want to add more records to your database. You **N O T E** cannot enter data into a computed field. Excel automatically copies the formula to the new record.

Defining Criteria in a Data Form

You can define **criteria** to find records in a database. Criteria are the instructions you give to Excel that determine which records it will find. For example, you could tell Excel to find all of the records in the current database with an amount of sale greater than $200. You could tell Excel to find all of the records in the State field whose contents are equal to NY. You could tell Excel to find all of the records in the database where the contents of the Amount of Sale field is greater than or equal to 200 *and* the contents of the State field are equal to NY, as shown in Figure 6.4.

```
┌──────────────────────────────────────────────────────┐
│ ▬              FIG601.XLS                             │
├──────────────────────────────────────────────────────┤
│  Name:          [              ]        Criteria      │
│                                                       │
│  Street:        [              ]       ┌──────────┐   │
│                                        │   New    │   │
│  City:          [              ]       └──────────┘   │
│                                        ┌──────────┐   │
│  State:         [=NY          ]        │  Clear   │   │
│                                        └──────────┘   │
│  Zip:           [              ]       ┌──────────┐   │
│                                        │ Restore  │   │
│  Date of Sale:  [              ]       └──────────┘   │
│                                        ┌──────────┐   │
│  Amount of Sale:[>200         ]        │Find Prev │   │
│                                        └──────────┘   │
│  Total:         [              ]       ┌──────────┐   │
│                                        │Find Next │   │
│                                        └──────────┘   │
│                                        ┌──────────┐   │
│                                        │   Form   │   │
│                                        └──────────┘   │
│                                        ┌──────────┐   │
│                                        │  Close   │   │
│                                        └──────────┘   │
│                                        ┌──────────┐   │
│                                        │   Help   │   │
│                                        └──────────┘   │
└──────────────────────────────────────────────────────┘
```

Figure 6.4 *Defining criteria for finding records.*

When you search for records in a data form you can specify only one criterion for each field. If you want to search for more than one criterion in a field—such as all of the records that contain NY and all of the records that contain MA in the State field—you must specify a criteria range in your worksheet and use the Set Criteria command. You must also use the Set Criteria command to search for records that meet criteria based on a formula. The Set Criteria command is discussed later in this chapter.

When you are using a data form to find records, you are using comparison criteria. Comparison criteria are used to find records whose field contents either match or fall within limits you specify. For example, you can search for all of the records that contain NY or all of the records that contain MA.

Criteria names must be the names of fields in which you are searching. For example, in Figure 6.4, the criteria name is State and the criteria is "ny."

Text used as a criteria is not case-sensitive. For example, in Figure 6.4 the criterion for state is "ny." This criterion will find all of the records that contain NY, ny, Ny, or nY in the State field.

There are two types of criteria: a series of characters you want to match or a quantity you want to compare.

Using matching character string criteria

To search for a series of characters, simply enter the text, numbers, or logical values you want to match into a specified field. Excel will find all of the records whose contents begin with or exactly match the text, numbers, or logical values you entered.

The question mark (?) and asterisk (*) DOS wildcards can be used to search for matching character strings. For example, you could type *sm?th to locate all records in the current database that end with sm?th, where the question mark represents a single letter. The asterisk tells Excel to find any characters in the Name field in any record that precede the letters *sm?th*. The question mark tells Excel to find the letters *sm* and *th*, and any single character between them. You would locate the records for Ms. Jane Smith and Dr. Jane Smyth. When you search for matching character strings, Excel assumes there is an asterisk at the end of the text you enter as a criterion. For example, if your criterion name is State and you type in *new*, Excel will locate all of the records whose State fields begin with the word *new*, such as New York and New Jersey.

If the text you wish to find contains an asterisk (*) or question mark (?), precede the text with a tilde (~). This indicates to Excel that you are searching for a character and not using a DOS wildcard.

Using comparison criteria

You can search for criteria whose data falls within specified limits by typing a comparison operator in front of the value. For example, you could search for all records whose Amount of Sales fields are greater than or equal to 200 by typing in *>=200*. The following table shows the six comparison operators that are available to you:

Operator	Meaning
=	Equal to
>	Greater than
<	Less than
>=	Greater than or equal to
<=	Less than or equal to
<>	Not equal to

If you use an equal sign (=) with nothing after it, you will locate only blank fields. If you use a "not equal to" operator (<>) with nothing after it, you will locate only fields that are not blank.

> If you have many records you want to search, do not use a data form. Use criteria defined on your worksheet with the Set Criteria command. The criteria you use in a data form does not replace the criteria you defined on your worksheet with the Set Criteria command. The Set N O T E Criteria command is covered later in this chapter.

Finding Records Using a Data Form

To find records that match the criteria you specify:

1. Open the worksheet that contains the database you want to search.
2. Click on Data in the menu bar to open the Data menu.
3. Click on Form to display the Data Form dialog box.
4. Click on Criteria. The Data Form dialog box changes to accept criteria. The record number indicator changes its message to *Criteria*. The fields are blank.

The New button is dimmed, the Delete button changes to the Clear button, and the Criteria button changes to the Form button.

5. Type the criteria you want for each field in the blank text box next to the field name. If you want to select all of the records for that field, leave the text box blank.

6. To search forward in the database and display the first record that matches the criteria, click on Find Next. To search backward and display the previous record that matches the criteria, click on Find Prev. If there are no matching records in the direction in which you are searching, Excel will beep and the last matching record remains selected. If there are no matching records at all, the last selected record is displayed. Note that when you click on Find Next or Find Prev and a matching record is found, you are returned to the regular data form. To return to the criteria form, click on Criteria.

7. To return to the regular data form without searching for any records, click on Form. When you have returned to the regular data form, you can use Find Next and Find Prev to search for matching records. The criteria you have selected are still in effect and you will not be able to use the Find Next and Find Prev buttons to move between any records other than those that match the criteria. You can move throughout the database and display records that do not match the criteria by using the scroll bar. To return to the criteria form, click on Criteria.

8. The Clear button clears all existing criteria. The Restore button restores the last existing criteria.

9. Click on Close to clear the existing criteria exit both the criteria form and the regular data form.

When you select criteria and click on Form, the criteria you selected are still in effect. If you want to clear the criteria and return to the regular data form, click on Clear. If you want to clear the criteria and exit both the criteria form and the regular data form, click on Close.

Deleting Records Using a Data Form

To delete a record from a database:

1. Open the worksheet that contains the database.

2. Click on Data in the menu bar to open the Data menu.

3. Click on Form to display the Data Form dialog box.

4. Display the record you want to delete. You may either use the scroll bar or specify criteria to locate the record or records you want to delete.

5. Click on Delete. You will see a message asking you to confirm the deletion.

6. Click on OK. The current record is deleted along with all of its data. All of the records following this one in the database will be moved up to fill the empty space left by the deleted record.

> You cannot undo a delete command in a data form. Before you confirm a deletion, be certain you want to delete all of the information contained in the record.
>
> WARNING

Using Find Next and Find Prev

The Find Next button searches forward through your database and finds and displays each successive record that matches your criteria until you reach the end of the database. If your criteria range is blank, Find Next displays the next record in the database.

The Find Prev button searches backward through your database and finds and displays each successive record that matches your criteria until you reach the beginning of the database. If your criteria range is blank, Find Prev displays the previous record in the database.

Moving Around the Data Form

The following table shows the mouse actions and keyboard selections you can use to move around a data form.

To	With mouse	With keyboard
Select a field	Click on the field	Press Alt+key for underlined letter in the field name
Choose a command button	Click on the button	Press Alt+key for underlined letter in button
Move to the same field in the same field	Click the down arrow in scroll bar	Press Down Arrow

To	With mouse	With keyboard
Move to the same field in the previous record	Click the up arrow in scroll bar	Press Up Arrow
Move to the next field that you can edit in the record	—	Press Tab
Move to the previous field that you can edit in the record	—	Press Shift+Tab
Move to the first field in the next record	—	Press Enter
Move to the first field in the previous record	—	Press Shift+Enter
Move to the same field ten records forward	Click below the scroll box the in scroll bar	Press PgDn
Move to the same field ten records back	Click above the scroll box in the scroll bar	Press PgUp
Move to the new record	Drag the scroll box to the bottom of the scroll bar	Press Ctrl+PgDn
Move to the first record	Drag the scroll box to the top of the scroll bar	Press Ctrl+PgUp1.5
Move to a field	Click on the location to which you want to move	Press Home; End; Left Arrow; or Right Arrow
Delete the previous character	—	Press Backspace
Delete the selected text or the next character	—	Press Delete
Select within a field	Drag mouse through selection	Press Shift+Home; Shift+End; Shift+Left Arrow; or Shift+Right Arrow

Creating a Custom Data Form

You may, for a variety of reasons wish to create a custom data form. For instance, default data forms list the fields in your database in the order in which they were created; a custom data form will allow you to determine the order in which the fields in your database appear, which will make it easier for end users to use your programs.

You can also add explanatory text, use a name other than the database field name to precede the field, and add characters in the data form to simplify entry. But you can change only the part of the data form to the left of the scroll bar. The scroll bar and command buttons *must* remain the same.

Let's assume that we want to change the default data form. We want the State and Zip fields to be on one line, and the Total field to indicate that both the Amount of Sale and the tax are included in the Total. We also want to separate names and addresses from the rest of the data, and to identify the amount of tax being calculated. In short, we want to create the custom data form shown in Figure 6.5.

	A	B	C	D	E	F	G	H	I
5	Ms. Elsie Cow	45 Milkmaid Dr.	Freehold	NY	234567	11/6/91	101.98	110.39	
6	Ms. Jane Smith	23 Main Street	New York	NY	100000	11/1/91	153.98	166.68	
7	Ms. Lucy Doe	1 University Place	Chicago	IL	300000	11/3/91	576.89	624.48	
8	Ms. Mary Johnson	10 Park Ave.	Ft Lee	NJ	118000	11/2/91	278.00	300.94	
9	Ms. Mary Johnson	10 Park Ave.	Ft Lee	NJ	118000	11/6/91	128.98	139.62	
10	Ms. Priscilla Smith	23 Elm Street	Greenwich	CT	200000	11/3/91	125.00	135.31	
11	Ms. Suzi Sunshine	2 Sparkle St	Boston	MA	145678	11/4/91	210.50	227.87	

Figure 6.5 Database sorted by name.

When we create this data form we are replacing two of the elements in the default data form: the **static text**, which includes the text that is used to identify the fields (the field names on the default data form) and any other text you want to include in the custom data form, and the **edit boxes**, in which you can add or edit data in fields. Each edit box corresponds to a field in the database, and should be of the same type as the data type of the field. Edit boxes for fields that contain referenced or computed data will display the contents of the field, but will be contained in a box since you cannot edit these fields.

To create this custom data form you must use the Dialog Editor (explained in detail in Chapter 5).

1. Open the Control menu.
2. Click on Run.
3. Select the Dialog Editor option button.
4. Click on Item in the menu bar to open the Item menu.
5. Click on Text.
6. A box contains the word *Text* appears in the dialog box. Type in the text you want to appear before the field (in the default data form, this would be the name of the field). To recreate the custom data form shown in Figure 6.5, type in the word *Name* and either press Enter or click on another area of the dialog box. If you want to be able to access the Name field using the Alt key plus a letter, precede the letter you want to use with an ampersand (&). For example, instead of typing *Name* in the text box, you would type *Na&me*. The word will appear in the custom dialog box as *Name*, and the Alt+M combination will automatically bring you to the Name edit box.
7. Click on Item in the menu bar.
8. Click on Edit Box to display the Edit Box menu.
9. Click on Text. The Name field in the database is a text field, and the Edit Box type must correspond to the type of data in that field.
10. Move and size the text and edit box entries in the dialog box to the location and size you see in Figure 6.5.
11. You have created the static text and edit box for the first field in the database, the Name field.
12. Repeat steps 4 through 10 for each field in the database. Remember that the fields Zip, Date of Sale, and Amount of Sale are number fields. You must select a Number Edit Box to correspond to the data type of the field in your database. The Total field is a computed field, and you must select a Formula Edit Box for it.
13. To create the single and double underscores and to add the tax information to your custom form, click on Item in the menu bar and click on Text. All of these entries are Text entries. Type the entries just as you would type any text. Move and size all of the existing entries in the dialog box to reflect the locations and sizes shown in Figure 6.5 (or rearrange them to suit yourself).
14. Select the first edit box in the dialog box (the Name edit box).
15. Click on Edit in the menu bar to display the Edit menu.
16. Click on Info.
17. Select the Init/Result text box and type in the field name *Name*.
18. Click on OK.

19. Select the next edit box in the dialog box, click on Info in the menu bar and click on Info. Type the name of the field that corresponds to the edit box and click on OK. Continue for each edit box in the dialog box.

20. Click on Edit in the menu bar to display the Edit menu.

21. Click on Select All Items.

22. Click on Copy to copy all of the information in the dialog box to the clipboard.

23. Open or switch or Excel and open the worksheet that contains the database for which you created the custom data form.

24. Select the first cell of the range into which you wish to paste the dialog box information. This cell will become the upper-left corner of the range.

Remember, when you add records to a database, they will overwrite any data that already exists in the cells where the data is added. Be careful about the placement of your data form information or it could be over-written by records added to the database. **N O T E**

25. Click on Edit in the worksheet menu bar to display the Edit menu.

26. Click on Paste. The dialog box information is pasted into seven columns in the worksheet, as shown in Figure 6.6. It contains the following information about the dialog box (starting at column one):

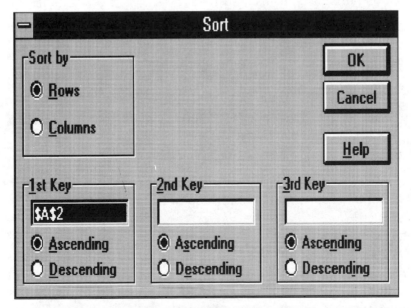

Figure 6.6   *The Sort dialog box.*

- ▼ **Item Field.** The Item Field identifies the item type. Static text is identified by the number 5, text edit boxes are identified by 6, integer edit boxes by 7, number edit boxes by 8, formula edit boxes by 9, and reference edit boxes by 10.

- ▼ **X Field.** The X Field indicates the horizontal position of the item in the dialog box.

- ▼ **Y Field.** The Y Field indicates the vertical position of the item in the dialog box.

- ▼ **Width Field.** The Width Field column tells you width of each item in the dialog box and of the dialog box itself.

- ▼ **Height Field.** The Height Field column is empty since Excel automatically adjusts the height of the field to reflect the font you are using.

- ▼ **Text Field.** The Text Field column contains the static text you entered in the dialog box. Notice that if you preceded any letters with an ampersand (&), they will appear in the Text Field column.

- ▼ **Init/Result Field.** The Init/Result Field column contains the names of the fields in your database that are linked to the edit boxes.

27. If the pasted range does not include a blank row, reselect the range to include a blank row at the top of the range and all of the data in the pasted range.

28. Click on Formula in the menu bar.

29. Click on Define Name.

30. Type *Data_form* in the Name text box. Double check to be certain that the range in the Refers To text box is correct. Then click OK.

You *must* type *Data_form* in the Name text box. You cannot redefine the range of the existing Data_form definition.

N O T E

To use your new custom data form, click on Data in the menu bar and then click on Form. Your new custom data form will appear on the screen.

Sorting a Database

Once you have created your database, you can use it to sort your data. You can sort rows or columns in any database range, alphabetically or numerically and in ascending or descending order.

Using One Sort Key to Sort a Database

When you sort a database in Excel you must select at least one sort key. The sort key specifies which column to sort by when you are sorting by rows, or which row to sort by when sorting by columns. You can specify as many as three sort keys at a time. When you sort by more than one key, the first sort key is the primary key. The data will be sorted by that specification first. If you have one or more of the same data entries in cells, those cells will then be sorted according to the second and third sort keys you specified. If you do not identify more than one sort key, rows or columns with duplicate data entries in the first sort key are left in the order in which they are found. For example, if you sort the database in Figure 6.1 by name and do not select any other sort key, the database will look like the one shown in Figure 6.7.

	A	B	C	D	E	F	G	H	I
	Name	Street	City	State	Zip	Date of Sale	Amount of Sale	Total	
1	Name	Street	City	State	Zip	Sale	of Sale	Total	
2	Dr. Jane Smyth	10 Medical Row	New York	NY	123456	11/5/91	145.67	157.69	
3	Mr. George Doe	700 East 22nd St.	New York	NY	150000	11/4/91	210.00	227.33	
4	Ms. Elise Jones	23 Summit Drive	New York	NY	102000	11/2/91	350.99	379.95	
5	Ms. Elsie Cow	45 Milkmaid Dr.	Freehold	NY	234567	11/6/91	101.98	110.39	
6	Ms. Jane Smith	23 Main Street	New York	NY	100000	11/1/91	153.98	166.68	
7	Ms. Lucy Doe	1 University Place	Chicago	IL	300000	11/3/91	576.89	624.48	
8	Ms. Mary Johnson	10 Park Ave.	Ft. Lee	NJ	118000	11/6/91	128.98	139.62	
9	Ms. Mary Johnson	10 Park Ave.	Ft. Lee	NJ	118000	11/2/91	278.00	300.94	
10	Ms. Priscilla Smith	23 Elm Street	Greenwich	CT	200000	11/3/91	125.00	135.31	
11	Ms. Suzi Sunshine	2 Sparkle St.	Boston	MA	145678	11/4/91	210.50	227.87	
12									
13									
14									
15									
16									
17									

Figure 6.7 *Database sorted by name and amount of sale.*

To sort a database using one sort key:

1. Open the worksheet that contains the database you want to sort.

2. Select the range inside the defined database range you want to sort. You do not have to select the entire database range. Everything inside the range you select will be sorted. Any fields not included in the sort range will not be affected by the sort. You will want to select a range that includes all data that belongs together. For example, if you selected only D2:D11 from Figure 6.1, all of the

data in the State field would be sorted, but none of the data in any other field would be affected. This would invalidate the rest of the data, since all of the rest of the information in the row would not have been moved. Therefore, row 2 would contain the following information: cell A2, *Ms. Jane Smith*; cell B2, *23 Main Street*; cell C2, *New York*; cell D2, *CT*; cell E2, *100000*; cell F2, *11/1/91*; cell G2, *153.98*; and cell H2, *166.68*. If you had selected all of the cells together, all of the data in row 5 would have been reordered along with the data in the State field. In this instance, select A2:H11 as your range.

Do not include field names as part of a range to be sorted. The field names for a database must always be in the top row of the database. Save your worksheet before you sort.

NOTE

3. Click on Data in the menu bar to open the Data menu.

4. Click on Sort to display the Sort dialog box, as shown in Figure 6.8.

	A	B	C	D	E	F	G	H	I
						Date of	Amount		
1	Name	Street	City	State	Zip	Sale	of Sale	Total	
2	Ms. Lucy Doe	1 University Place	Chicago	IL	300000	11/3/91	576.89	624.48	
3	Dr. Jane Smyth	10 Medical Row	New York	NY	123456	11/5/91	145.67	157.69	
4	Ms. Mary Johnson	10 Park Ave.	Ft. Lee	NJ	118000	11/6/91	128.98	139.62	
5	Ms. Mary Johnson	10 Park Ave.	Ft. Lee	NJ	118000	11/2/91	278.00	300.94	
6	Ms. Suzi Sunshine	2 Sparkle St.	Boston	MA	145678	11/4/91	210.50	227.87	
7	Ms. Priscilla Smith	23 Elm Street	Greenwich	CT	200000	11/3/91	125.00	135.31	
8	Ms. Jane Smith	23 Main Street	New York	NY	100000	11/1/91	153.98	166.68	
9	Ms. Elise Jones	23 Summit Drive	New York	NY	102000	11/2/91	350.99	379.95	
10	Ms. Elsie Cow	45 Milkmaid Dr.	Freehold	NY	234567	11/6/91	101.98	110.39	
11	Mr. George Doe	700 East 22nd St.	New York	NY	150000	11/4/91	210.00	227.33	

FIG608.XLS

Figure 6.8 *Database sorted by street.*

5. To keep the rows in your database intact, select the Rows option. To keep the columns intact, select the Columns option.

6. You are going to sort by name. In the 1st Key text box, enter the address of any cell in the column that contains the field name.

7. Select Ascending.
8. Click on OK.

You can undo a sort immediately after it has finished by using the Undo key.

You will notice that all of the names in the database are in alphabetical order and that the two entries for Ms. Mary Johnson have been left in their original order.

Using More than One Sort Key to Sort a Database

If you sort the database first by name and then by amount of sale, the database will look like the one shown in Figure 6.9.

	A	B	C	D	E	F	G	H	I
						FIG609.XLS			
1	State	Sales			State	Sales			
2	NY	24			NY	>50			
3	MA	50							
4	OH	75							
5	NY	56							
6	NY	75							
7	NY	150							
8	NJ	98							
9	CT	34							
10									
11									
12									
13									
14									
15									
16									
17									
18									

Figure 6.9 *A criteria range.*

To sort by more than one key:

1. Open the worksheet that contains the database you want to sort.
2. Select the range inside the defined database range you want to sort. You do not have to select the entire database range. Everything inside the range you select

will be sorted. Any fields not included in the sort range will not be affected by the sort. Select A2:H11 as your range.

3. Click on Data in the menu bar to open the Data menu.

4. Click on Sort to display the Sort dialog box.

5. To keep the rows in your database intact, select the Rows option. To keep the columns intact, select the Columns option.

6. You are going to sort first by name and then by amount of sale. In the 1st Key text box, enter the address of any cell in the column that contains the field. In the 2nd Key text box, enter the address of any cell in the column that contains the field name.

7. Select Ascending for each sort key.

8. Click on OK.

Now, not only are all of the names in the database in alphabetical order, the entries for Ms. Mary Johnson have been reorganized so that the amount of sale entries are in numerical order.

Ascending Sort Order

For each sort key you identify you must indicate whether you want to sort the column or row in ascending or descending order. In ascending order, Excel sorts from top to bottom for rows and from left to right for columns, following a specific sort order, as follows:

▼ **Numbers.** Sorts from the largest negative number to the largest positive number.

▼ **Text.** Text sorts in Excel are not case-sensitive. Numbers that are entered as text values are sorted as text. Numbers that are entered as numeric values are sorted before text values. Figure 6.10 shows how the database looks when it is sorted by street. Since all of the numbers in the State field are entered as text values, the field is sorted by alphabetically and not numerically. The following list shows the order in which text is sorted: 0 1 2 3 4 5 6 7 8 9 Space ! " # $ % & " ( ) * + , - . / : ; < = > ? @ [\ } ^ _ ` { | } ~ A B C D E F G H I J K L M N O P Q R S T U V W X Y Z

▼ **Logical Values.** False values come before true values in the sort.

▼ **Error Values.** Error values are equal.

▼ **Blanks.** Blanks are always sorted last.

	A	B	C	D	E	F	G	H	I
1	State	Sales			State	Sales	Sales		
2	NY	24			NY	>50	<100		
3	MA	50							
4	OH	75							
5	NY	56							
6	NY	75							
7	NY	150							
8	NJ	98							
9	CT	34							
10									
11									
12									
13									
14									
15									
16									
17									
18									

FIG610.XLS

Figure 6.10 *A criteria range using an AND relation.*

Descending Sort Order

If you specify descending order, Excel reverses the order of everything except blanks. Blanks are always sorted last. The sort order is as follows:

- ▼ **Error Values.** Error values are equal.
- ▼ **Logical Values.** True values come before False values in the sort.
- ▼ **Text.** Text sorts in Excel are not case-sensitive. Numbers that are entered as text values are sorted as text. Numbers that are entered as numeric values are sorted before text values. The following list shows the order in which text is sorted in descending order: Z Y X W V U T S R Q P O N M L K J I H G F E D C B A ~ } | { ` _ ^] \ [@ ? > = < ; : / . - , + *) (" & % $ # " ! Space 9 8 7 6 5 4 3 2 1 0
- ▼ **Numbers.** Sorts from the largest positive number to the largest negative number.
- ▼ **Blanks.** Blanks are always sorted last.

Be sure that you have entered all numbers either as text values or numeric values. If you haven't and you are doing an ascending sort, Excel will sort the numbers entered as numeric values before it sorts the numbers entered as text values. If you are doing a descending sort, Excel will sort the numbers you have entered as text values before sorting the numbers you have entered as numeric values.

WARNING

Using Names in Sort Key Text Boxes

If you have defined names for your ranges, you can type a defined name instead of a cell address in the 1st, 2nd, and 3rd Key text boxes. The cell in the upper-left corner of the named range will be the address in the Key text box. For example, if you selected cells D2:D11 and defined the name of the range as City, you could type City in the 1st, 2nd, or 3rd Key text box. Cell D2 would be used as the sort key.

Using a Criteria Range

You have already learned how to find records in a data form by setting criteria. This method limits you to locating records that contain only one criterion for each field. You cannot search for multiple criteria. For example, you cannot search for records in which the amount of sale is greater than $100 and less than $200. You cannot search for records that meet criteria based on a formula. You cannot search for and extract the records that match your specified criteria. To do all of this you must use a criteria range in your worksheet and use the Set Criteria command.

You can search for two types of criteria when you use a criteria range: **comparison criteria** and **computed criteria**. Comparison criteria allow you to find records in which the contents of the specified fields either match or fall within the criteria limits. For example, you could search for all records in which the contents of the Amount of Sale field are between $100 and $150. You used this type of criteria to search for records in a data form. The other type of criteria is computed criteria. Computed criteria are used to find records that meet specified criteria based on a formula. For example, if your database contains a field for the amount of sale and a field for the tax rate for each state, and you want all of the records in which the amount of sale plus the tax rate is equal to or greater than $200, you would use computed criteria and enter this formula: =Amount of Sale*Tax Rate+Amount of Sale>=200.00. Excel will find all the records where the amount of sale plus the tax rate is greater than $200.

Defining a Criteria Range for Comparison Criteria

Setting up a criteria range is basically the same as setting up a database. To set up a criteria range:

1. Select a row in the worksheet where you want to enter the field names that contain the criteria for which you wish to search. These names are called the **criteria names**.

2. Enter the criteria you want to search for in the rows beneath the field names. The syntax and rules discussed earlier in this chapter to define criteria may also be used to define criteria in data forms. In addition, you can search for several criteria at the same time. For example, if your database contains fields for states and fields for sales, you could create a criteria range that will search for all sales greater than $50 in the state of New York, as shown in Figure 6.10. You can select records that match any combination of AND or OR relationships. For example, you can search for all of the records whose state is NY AND whose sales are greater than 50, or you can search for all of the records whose state is NY OR whose sales are greater than 50. Excel recognizes an AND or OR condition by the position of the criteria in your criteria range. To select criteria using the AND relationship, you must enter the criteria in the same row, as shown in Figure 6.10. If the AND relationship applies to the same field name—for example, all records in the state of NY AND all records with sales greater than 50 AND sales less than 100—you must enter the field name twice, as shown in Figure 6.11. If you want to find all of the records in the database that contain the state of NY OR the state of NJ, you must enter the criteria in different rows under the same field name, as shown in Figure 6.12.

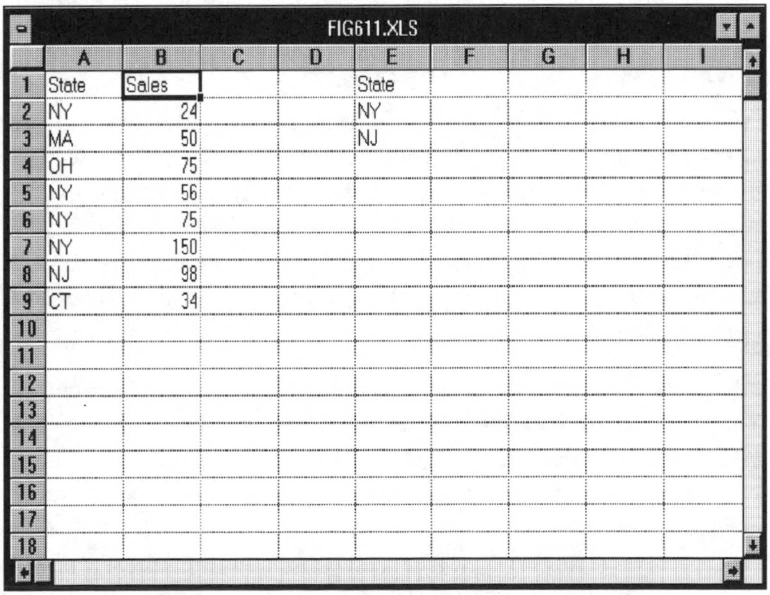

Figure 6.11   *A criteria range using an OR relation.*

3. Select the range that contains the criteria names and the criteria.
4. Click on Data in the menu bar to open the Data menu.
5. Click on Set Criteria.

| D2 | | =OR(State="NY",State="NJ") | | | | | | |

FIG612.XLS

	A	B	C	D	E	F	G	H	I
1	State	Sales		Selected					
2	NY	24		TRUE					
3	MA	50							
4	OH	75							
5	NY	56							
6	NY	75							
7	NY	150							
8	NJ	98							
9	CT	34							
10									
11									
12									
13									
14									
15									
16									
17									
18									

Figure 6.12   *A formula to search for multiple criteria.*

Defining a Criteria Range for Computed Criteria

When you set up a criteria range for computed criteria, you enter formulas instead of constant values as your criteria. The criteria formula must refer to values contained in one or more fields in your database. All criteria formulas compare the resulting value of the formula to another value, and must produce either a TRUE or FALSE value. For example, if cell A1 contains the value $25 and cell B1 contains the value $30 the criteria formula A1+B1>50.00 will produce the logical value TRUE since the sum of $25 plus $30 is greater than $50. To set up criteria:

1. Select a row in the worksheet where you want to enter names to indicate the criteria for which you wish to search. These names are called the **criteria names**. Unlike entering criteria names for comparison criteria, you *cannot* enter field names for your criteria names when you are searching records for computed criteria. When Excel encounters field names used as criteria names in the first row of a criteria range, it automatically assumes you are searching for comparison criteria. For example, if you want to find all of the records in a database where the amount of sale plus the tax is greater than $200 you would enter the formula =sales*tax+sales>200.00, and your criteria name could be Totals.

2. Enter the criteria you want to search for in the rows beneath the criteria names. A computed criteria formula can use either field names or the relative reference of the first record in the database. If you use an absolute reference, Excel will evaluate only the record referred to by the absolute reference, and will not search the rest of the database for records that match your computed criteria. For example, if you have the field names Sales and Tax, and the database records containing the values for these fields begins in cells A7 and B7, to find all of the records whose sales plus tax is greater than $200 you could enter the formula

   ```
   =Sales*Tax+Sales>200
   ```

   or the formula

   ```
   =A7*B7+A7>200.00
   ```

to search the entire database for all records that match this computed criteria. To search for multiple criteria using computed criteria, you can use the AND and OR functions in your formulas. For example, to search for all of the records for the states of New York OR New Jersey, you would enter the formula =OR(State="NY",State="NJ"), as shown in the formula bar in Figure 6.13.

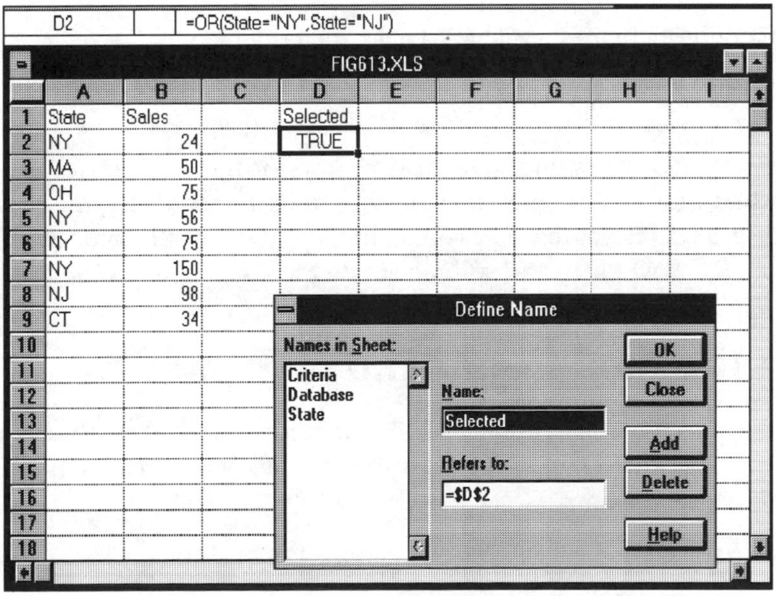

Figure 6.13 *The Field State defined.*

NOTE If you enter field names as your criteria, you must first define them, using the Define Names command in the Formula menu. The range you define must contain all of the fields you wish to search. If a field is not included in the defined range, Excel will ignore the field when it searches for the field name criteria. Figure 6.14 shows the field name State defined.

3. Select the range that contains the criteria names and criteria.

4. Click on Data in the menu bar to open the Data menu.

5. Click on Set Criteria.

Finding Records that Match a Criteria Range

When you have set your criteria and defined your range, you can search through the database for all of the records that match the criteria. If the active cell is outside the database when you begin your search, Excel selects the first record in the database that matches the criteria; if the active cell in located inside the database, Excel selects the first record that matches the criteria below the active cell.

1. Click on Data in the menu bar to open the Data menu.

2. Click on Find.

3. Excel has selected the first record in the database that matches the specified criteria.

4. Use your Up Arrow and Down Arrow keys or the scroll boxes to scroll backward and forward through the database to each record that matches the specified criteria. If you have reached the last matching record and continue to scroll, Excel will beep and will remain on the last selected record.

Exiting the Find Command

Once you have used the Find command to search for records that match specified criteria, you must exit the command in order to access all of the records in your database. To exit the Find command:

1. Click on Data in the menu bar to open the Data menu.

2. Click on Exit Find.

You can now access all of the records in your database.

Extracting Records that Match Specified Criteria

When you set your criteria and define your criteria range, you can elect to extract the records that match the specified criteria and copy them to another section of your worksheet. To do this, you must set an **extract range**. You can copy any or all of the fields in your database. To set and copy your data to an extract range:

1. Define both the database and criteria ranges.

2. Enter the exact names of the fields you want to extract in a row on the worksheet. These names must exactly match the field names in your database. Only the fields whose names are included in the extract range will be copied into the extract range.

3. Select either a range that contains the field names or a range that contains the field names and the cells into which the extracted data will be copied. If you select a range that contains both field names and cells, only as much data as will fit into the selected cells will be copied. Any data that does not fit in the selected range will not be copied, and Excel will display a message informing you that the extract range is full. If this happens you must either make the extract range larger or select a range that contains only the field names (Excel will copy all matching records when only the field names are selected as the extract range).

4. Click on Data in the menu bar to open the Data menu.

5. Click on Set Extract.

6. Click on Data in the menu bar to open the Data menu.

7. Click on Extract. If you do not want to extract duplicate records, select the Unique Records Only check box.

The records that match the specified criteria have been copied to the rows below the field names you entered.

> When you copy data to an extract range, all of the data in the cells included in the extract range are replaced by the data that has been copied. If you selected only field names as your extract range, all of the data in the cells below the field names to the bottom of the worksheet is cleared, whether data is copied into them or not. Be very careful about the placement of your extract range. You cannot Undo an Extract command. **WARNING**

Deleting Records that Match Specified Criteria

You can simultaneously delete all of the records in your database that match the specified criteria.

1. Define your database and criteria ranges.

2. Click on Data in the menu bar to open the Data menu.

3. Click on Delete. Excel displays a message informing you that matching records will be permanently deleted from the database.

4. Click on OK.

All of the records that match the specified criteria will be deleted.

 WARNING Save your database before using the Delete command. Once you have deleted records, you cannot Undo it. If you save your worksheet and then discover that you made a mistake defining the criteria range and deleting your data, you can exit the worksheet without saving and retain your original data.

Using Database Functions

Excel provides you with twelve functions created specifically for use in a database. Database functions contain three different arguments: database, field, and criteria. The syntax for database functions is as follows:

```
=FUNCTION(Database,Field,Criteria)
```

The **database argument** is the range of cells that make up the database. If you have used the Set Database command in the Data menu to define your database, you can use the defined name Database instead of a range address. For example, the database we created in Figure 6.1 extends from cell A1 to H11. We used the Set Database command to define the database with the defined name Database. This means we can enter either the range address A1:H11 or the defined name Database for the first argument in a database function.

The **field argument** identifies the field that the function will use to calculate the result. The field argument will allow you to enter only a text data type. You must enter the name of the field enclosed in parenthesis (" ").

The last argument, **criteria**, is the range of cells that contain the criteria you want to use in the function. If you have used the Set Criteria command in the Data menu to define your criteria, you can use the defined name Criteria instead of a range address. For example, if you want to know how many total sales are over $150 and you entered into cells J1 and J2 the criteria:

```
Total
>150
```

you can enter either the range address J1:J2 or the defined name Criteria for the last argument.

> You can also use the worksheet functions in a database, but you cannot use the database functions in a worksheet.

N O T E

The following functions be used in a database.

DAVERAGE

The DAVERAGE function averages all of the numbers in a database field that match the selected criteria. Using this command is the same as extracting all of the records in the database that match the specified criteria and then averaging all of the numbers in one field of the database. If you want to average all of the numbers in the database (not just the numbers which match the specified criteria), use the AVERAGE function.

Use with databases only.

Syntax

=DAVERAGE(Database,Field,Criteria)

Examples of use

=DAVERAGE(Database,"Total",Criteria)

=DAVERAGE(A1:H11,"Total",J1:J2)

Both examples will give you the average of all of the numbers in the database (A1:H11 or the defined name Database) in the Total field for the specified criteria (J1:J2 or the defined name Criteria). Since the criterion specifies all numbers in the Total column over $150, the DAVERAGE function will return the average of all numbers in the Total field over $150 for a result of 297.85.

DCOUNT

The DCOUNT function counts all of the cells containing numbers in a database field that match the selected criteria. Using this command is the same as extracting all of the records in the database that match the specified criteria and then counting all of the cells that contain numbers in one field of the database. If you want to count all of the cells that contain numbers in a specified field in the database (not just the cells which match the specified criteria), use the COUNT function.

Use with databases only.

Syntax

    =DCOUNT(Database,Field,Criteria)

Examples of use

    =DCOUNT(Database,"Total",Criteria)
    =DCOUNT(Database,,Criteria)

The first example will count the number of cells that contain numbers over 150 in the Total field for the specified database. The second example (which omits the optional Field argument) will count the number of records in the database that match the specified criteria.

DCOUNTA

The DCOUNTA function counts all of the cells in a database field that are not blank and that match the selected criteria. Using this command is the same as extracting all of the records in the database that match the specified criteria and then counting all of the cells that are not blank in one field of the database. If you want to count all of the cells that are not blank in a specified field in the database (not just the cells that match the specified criteria), use the COUNTA function.

Use with databases only.

Syntax

    =DCOUNTA(Database,Field,Criteria)

Examples of use

```
=DCOUNTA(Database, "Total",Criteri
=DCOUNTA(A1:H11, "Total",J1:J2)
```

Both examples will count the nonblank cells that match the specified criteria in the Totals field of the defined database. In this case the criteria specifies all states in the State column that are equal to NY; the DCOUNTA function will return the number of nonblank cells in the Total field of each record where the State=NY for a result of 5.

DGET

The DGET function extracts from the database the value of a single field that matches the specified criteria. If none of the values matches the specified criteria, the DGET function returns an error value of #VALUE. If more than one record matches the specified criteria, the DGET function returns an error value of #NUM.

Use with databases only.

Syntax

```
=DGET(Database,Field,Criteria)
```

Examples of use

```
=DGET(Database, "Total",Criteria)
=DGET(A1:H11, "Total",J1:J2)
```

Both examples will count the nonblank cells that match the specified criteria in the Totals field of the defined database. In this case the criteria specifies a value of over $600 in the Total column, and the DGET function will return the value of 624.48.

DMAX

The DMAX function returns from the database the largest number in a single field that matches the specified criteria.

Use with databases only.

Syntax

```
=DMAX(Database,Field,Criteria)
```

Examples of use

```
=DMAX(Database,"Total",Criteria)
=DMAX(A1:H11,"Total",J1:J2)
```

Both examples will return the largest value in the Total field that match the specified criteria in the defined database. In this case the criterion specifies a value of over $200 in the Total column, and the DMAX function will return the value of 624.48.

DMIN

The DMIN function returns from the database the smallest number in a single field that matches the specified criteria.

Use with databases only.

Syntax

```
=DMIN(Database,Field,Criteria)
```

Examples of use

```
=DMIN(Database,"Total",Criteria)
=DMIN(A1:H11,"Total",J1:J2)
```

Both examples will return the smallest value in the Total field that match the specified criteria in the defined database. In this case the criteria specifies a value of over $200 in the Total column, and the DMAX function will return the value of 227.33.

DPRODUCT

The DPRODUCT function multiplies the values in the field column that match the specified criteria.

Use with databases only.

Syntax

```
=DPRODUCT(Database,Field,Criteria)
```

Examples of use

```
=DPRODUCT(Database,"Total",Criteria)
=DPRODUCT(A1:H11,"Total",J1:J2)
```

Both examples will multiply the values in the Total field that match the specified criteria in the defined database. In this case the criterion specifies a value of over $350 in the Total column, and the DPRODUCT function will return the value of 237,270.40.

DSTDEV

The DSTDEV function estimates the standard deviation of a population based on a sample, using the values in the Total column in the database that matches the specified criteria.

Use with databases only.

Syntax

    =DSTDEV(Database,Field,Criteria)

Examples of use

    =DSTDEV(Database,"Total",Criteria)
    =DSTDEV(A1:H11,"Total",J1:J2)

Both examples will estimate the standard deviation of a population based on a sample, using the values in the Total field that match the specified criteria in the defined database. In this case the criteria specifies a value of over $350 in the Total column, and the DSTDEV function will return the value of 172.9136.

DSTDEVP

The DSTDEVP function estimates the standard deviation of an entire population using the values in the Total column in the database that matches the specified criteria.

Use with databases only.

Syntax

    =DSTDEVP(Database,Field,Criteria)

Examples of use

    =DSTDEVP(Database,"Total",Criteria)
    =DSTDEVP(A1:H11,"Total",J1:J2)

Both examples will estimate the standard deviation of an entire population using the values in the Total field that match the specified criteria in the defined database. In this case the criteria specifies a value of over \$350 in the Total column, and the DSTDEVP function will return the value of 122.2684.

DSUM

The DSUM function adds the numbers in the field column that match the specified criteria.

Use with databases only.

Syntax

```
=DSUM(Database,Field,Criteria)
```

Examples of use

```
=DSUM(Database, "Total",Criteria)
=DSUM(A1:H11, "Total",J1:J2)
```

Both examples will add the numbers in the Total column that match the specified criteria in the defined database. In this case the criteria specifies a value of over \$350 in the Total column, and the DSUM function will return the value of 1004.43.

DVAR

The DSTDEV function estimates the variance of a population based on a sample, using the values in the field column in the database that match the specified criteria.

Use with databases only.

Syntax

```
=DVAR(Database,Field,Criteria)
```

Examples of use

```
=DVAR(Database, "Total",Criteria)
=DVAR(A1:H11, "Total",J1:J2)
```

Both examples will estimate the variance of a population based on a sample, using the values in the Total field that match the specified criteria in the defined database. In this case the criteria specifies a value of over \$350 in the Total column, and the DVAR function will return the value of 29,889.11.

DVARP

The DVARP function estimates the variance of an entire population using the values in the field column in the database that match the specified criteria.

Use with databases only.

Syntax

```
=DVARP(Database,Field,Criteria)
```

Examples of use

```
=DVARP(Database,"Total",Criteria)
=DVARP(A1:H11,"Total",J1:J2)
```

Both examples will estimate the variance of an entire population using the values in the Total field that match the specified criteria in the defined database. In this case the criteria specifies a value of over $350 in the Total column, and the DVARP function will return the value of 14,949.56.

Using Database Macro Functions

In addition to the twelve database functions listed above, Excel also provides you with twelve database macro functions, which are the equivalent of executing Chart menu commands or tools. Macro functions can be created using the macro recorder.

CROSSTAB.CREATE

The CROSSTAB.CREATE function creates a cross-tabulation table from specified data in a database. It is equivalent to choosing the Crosstab command from the Data menu, which activates the Crosstab Wizard. It is strongly recommended that you use the macro recorder rather than the CROSSTAB.CREATE function to create a cross-tabulation table.

Use with macro sheets only.

Syntax

```
=CROSSTAB.CREATE(row_array,columns_array,values_array, create_out-
line,Create_names,multiple_values,auto_drilldown, new_sheet)
```

Or,

`=CROSSTAB.CREATE?()`

Rows_array is a two-dimensional array that specifies a set of fields that appear in each row of the cross-tabulation table. Rows_array consists of the following elements:

▼ **Field_name.** Specifies a field name either as text or as a reference to a cell you wish to include in the cross-tabulation table.

▼ **Grouping_index.** Specifies how to group numeric and date values in the cross-tabulation table. For numeric fields, the grouping_index is the size of the group. For text fields, or to specify no grouping at all, use the number 0. The grouping_index for date values is as follows:

Index	Description of group
0	No grouping or text field
1	Group by days
2	Group by weeks
3	Group by months
4	Group by 30-day periods
5	Group by quarters
6	Group by years

▼ **From.** Specifies the value for the starting field. If the field is numeric, From is a number; if the field is a character field, From is a text string; if the field is a data field, From is a serial number or date enclosed in quotation marks (" "). If you enter FALSE for the From value, you specify that you wish to start at the minimum possible value for the field.

▼ **To.** Specifies the value for the ending field. If the field is numeric, To is a number; if the field is a character field, To is a text string; if the field is a data field, To is a serial number or date enclosed in quotation marks (" "). If you enter FALSE for the To value, you specify that you wish to end at the maximum possible value for the field.

▼ **Subtotals.** Represents a string of seven characters. Each character in the string corresponds to a type of subtotal. If you want a type of subtotal, set the character in the string to Y. If you want to skip a type of subtotal, set the character in the string to N. Following is a list of the types of subtotals and their corresponding position within the character string.

Position	Type of subtotal
1	Sum
2	Count
3	Average
4	Minimum
5	Maximum
6	Standard deviation
7	Variance

Columns_array is a two-dimensional array that specifies a set of fields that appear in each column of the cross-tabulation table. Columns_array consists of the same elements as Rows_array.

Values_array is a two-dimensional array the identifies each field that appears as a value field in the cross-tabulation table. Following is a list of the elements which comprise the Values_array.

- ▼ **Field_label**. Specifies a label for the summary field.

- ▼ **Summary_expression.** The summary expression is a text string that identifies the expression (including an aggregation operator) to compute.

- ▼ **Display_items**. This is a five-character text string that specifies whether or not to display certain values. To specify a display value, type *Y* for the corresponding character. To omit a display value, type *N* for the corresponding character. The Display_items values and their corresponding positions in the character string are as follows:

Position	Type of display
1	Values
2	Row percent
3	Column percent
4	Total percent
5	Index

- ▼ **Use_all_values.** A logical value that indicates what values to use when calculating subtotals and percentages. If the logical value is TRUE, the CROSSTAB.CREATE function uses any table values that it needs,—even values that appear outside the From and To range. These values will not, however, appear in the cross-tabulation table. If the logical value is FALSE, the CROSSTAB.CREATE function will use only values that appear in the cross-tabulation table.

▼ **Create_outline.** A logical value. If the logical value is TRUE, the argument creates an outline for the cross-tabulation table; if the logical value is FALSE, the argument does not create an outline.

▼ **Create_names.** A logical value. If the logical value is TRUE, the argument creates names for the values from the cross-tabulation table; if the logical value is FALSE, the argument does not create names for the values. Names can be used instead of cell addresses for rows and columns.

▼ **Multiple_values.** A numerical value that indicates how to handle multiple summaries. Following is a list of multiple_values and their descriptions:

Values	Description
1	Inner columns
2	Outer columns
3	Inner rows
4	Outer rows

▼ **Auto_drilldown.** A logical value. If TRUE, the argument places drilldown formulas in the result cells; if FALSE, the argument does not place drilldown formulas in the result cells.

▼ **New_sheet.** A logical value. If TRUE, the argument creates the cross-tabulation table on a new sheet; if FALSE, the argument creates the cross-tabulation table on the existing sheet.

The CROSSTAB.CREATE?() function will access the Crosstab Wizard.

CROSSTAB.DRILLDOWN

The CROSSTAB.DRILLDOWN function performs a database query that retrieves records summarized in the cell. This function is equivalent to double-clicking on a cell that contains a summary value in a cross-tabulation table.

Use with macro sheets only.

Syntax

```
=CROSSTAB.DRILLDOWN()
```

Example of use

`=CROSSTAB.DRILLDOWN()`

The function will return a logical value of TRUE if successful, or an error value of #N/A is the active cell is not in a cross-tabulation table or if the active cell does not contain a summary value.

CROSSTAB.RECALC

The CROSSTAB.RECALC function recalculations a cross-tabulation table. This function is equivalent to the Recalculate Existing Crosstab command in the Data menu.

Use with macro sheets only.

Syntax

`=CROSSTAB.RECALC(rebuild)`

Examples of use

`=CROSSTAB.RECALC(TRUE)`
`=CROSSTAB.RECALC(FALSE)`
`=CROSSTAB.RECALC`

If the logical value rebuild is true, the CROSSTAB.RECALC function recreates the cross-tabulation table from row, column, and value definition. If the logical value is FALSE or omitted, the CROSSTAB.RECALC function recalculates the cross-tabulation with its current layout and elements.

DATA.DELETE

The DATA.DELETE function deletes data that matches the specified criteria in the defined database. This function is equivalent to using the Delete command on the Data menu.

Use with macro sheets only.

Syntax

`=DATA.DELETE()`
`=DATA.DELETE?()`

Examples of use

```
=DATA.DELETE()
=DATA.DELETE?()
```

The first example deletes all records that match the specified criteria in the defined database, without first issuing a warning message. The second example displays a message warning you that matching records will be deleted, and gives you a choice of approving or canceling the action. If you approve, all records that match the specified criteria will be deleted. If you cancel, the action will be canceled, and the records will not be deleted.

DATA.FIND

The DATA.FIND function selects records that match the specified criteria in the defined database. This function is equivalent to using the Find and Exit Find commands on the Data menu.

Use with macro sheets only.

Syntax

```
=DATA.FIND(logical)
```

Examples of use

```
=DATA.FIND(TRUE)
=DATA.FIND(FALSE)
```

If the DATA.FIND function returns a logical value of TRUE, this function will find and select all records that match the selected criteria. If the DATA.FIND function returns a logical value of FALSE, this function will execute the Exit Find command.

DATA.FIND.NEXT

The DATA.FIND.NEXT function finds the next record that matches the specified criteria in the defined database. This function is equivalent to using the Down Arrow key after the Find command in the Data menu has been selected. If the DATA.FIND.NEXT function cannot find any more matching records, it will return a value of FALSE. You will hear a beep and your insertion point will remain in the last matching record.

Use with macro sheets only.

Syntax

```
=DATA.FIND.NEXT()
```

Examples of use

```
=DATA.FIND.NEXT()
```

If you have selected all records that match the specified criteria in the defined database, this function will find the next matching record in the database.

DATA.FIND.PREV

The DATA.FIND.PREV function finds the previous record that matches the specified criteria in the defined database. This function is equivalent to using the Up Arrow key after the Find command in the Data menu has been selected. If the DATA.FIND.PREV function cannot find any more matching records, it will return a value of FALSE. You will hear a beep and your insertion point will remain in the last matching record.

Use with macro sheets only.

Syntax

```
=DATA.FIND.PREV()
```

Example of use

```
=DATA.FIND.PREV()
```

If you have selected all records that match the specified criteria in the defined database, this function will find the previous matching record in the database.

DATA.FORM

The DATA.FORM function displays the data form for the defined database. If you have created a custom data form for the database, it will be displayed; otherwise, the default data form will be displayed. This function is equivalent to using the Form command in the Data menu. If no database has been defined, the DATA.FORM function will return an error value of #VALUE.

Use with macro sheets only.

Syntax

```
=DATA.FORM()
```

Example of use

=DATA.FORM()

This function will display either the default data form for the defined database or, if you have created one, the custom data form.

EXTRACT

The EXTRACT function finds records that match the specified criteria, and copies them into a separate extract range. This function is equivalent of using the Extract command in the Data menu.

Use with macro sheets only.

Syntax

=EXTRACT(unique)
=EXTRACT?(unique)

Examples of use

=EXTRACT(TRUE)
=EXTRACT(FALSE)
=EXTRACT()
=EXTRACT?(TRUE)
=EXTRACT?(FALSE)
=EXTRACT?()

If unique is TRUE, this function will exclude duplicate records from the extract list. If unique is FALSE or omitted, this function extracts all records that match the specified criteria including duplicate records. If EXTRACT is followed by a question mark (?), the Extract dialog box will be displayed on the screen.

SET.CRITERIA

The SET.CRITERIA function defines the name Criteria for the selected criteria range on the database. This function is equivalent to using the Set Criteria command in the Data menu.

Use with macro sheets only.

Syntax

```
=SET.CRITERIA()
```

Examples of use

```
=SET.CRITERIA(Criteria)
=SET.CRITERIA("Criteria")
```

This function defines the criteria range on a database with the defined name Criteria. When creating a macro, SET.CRITERIA should precede any database function or database macro function.

SET.DATABASE

The SET.DATABASE function defines the name Database for the selected range on the database. This function is equivalent to using the Set Database command in the Data menu.

Use with macro sheets only.

Syntax

```
=SET.DATABASE()
```

Examples of use

```
=SET.DATABASE(Database)
=SET.DATABASE("Database")
```

This function defines the database range on a database with the defined name Database.

SET.EXTRACT

The SET.EXTRACT function defines the name Extract for the selected extract range on the database. This function is equivalent to using the Set Extract command in the Data menu.

Use with macro sheets only.

Syntax

```
=SET.EXTRACT()
```

Examples of use

```
=SET.EXTRACT(Extract)
=SET.EXTRACT("Extract")
```

This function defines the extract range on a database with the defined name Extract.

CHARTS, GRAPHICS, AND SLIDES

A chart is a pictorial representation of worksheet data. For most people, it is easier to read a chart or graph than to read numbers in a worksheet. In addition, charts can represent the data in a worksheet in several ways. Charts are linked to worksheet data. When you upgrade the data in a worksheet, the chart is automatically upgraded.

A chart can be created as a graphic object included in the worksheet and saved with the worksheet. This is called an **embedded chart**. You can also create a **chart document**, which is a chart that is created as a separate document in its own window. A chart document is also linked to a worksheet. You can change your mind and save an embedded chart as a chart document, or save a chart document as an embedded chart.

Understanding the Parts of a Chart

Charts, like worksheets, are comprised of various parts. Before you create a chart, you should be familiar with the parts of a chart:

▼ **Chart window.** The chart window is exactly the same as the document window in worksheets, except that it contains a chart instead of a worksheet, and the menu bar changes to reflect the different type of document.

▼ **Chart.** The chart comprises the entire area inside the chart window, including labels, axes, and data markers.

▼ **Chart toolbar.** The Chart toolbar allows you to change chart types, format charts, and select the ChartWizard.

▼ **Plot area.** The plot area is the area in the chart window that Excel uses to plot your chart, including the axes and all data markers. The plot area does not include chart titles, unattached text, legends, and so forth.

▼ **Data marker.** A data marker is a bar, line, dot, or other symbol that represents one value in the chart. All of the data markers together comprise a chart data series.

▼ **Chart data series.** A group of related values, such as the figures in a row or column, that are being charted. For example, if you created a bar chart to show expenses for each day of the week, each bar would be a data marker, and all of the data markers together would be a chart data series. A chart can contain one or more data series. When you have more than one data series in a chart, the data markers for each series will contain the same color, pattern, or symbol.

▼ **Axis.** The axis is the line on which data in a chart is plotted. A chart contains two axes: the x-axis, on which categories of data are plotted, and the y-axis, on which data values are plotted. The x-axis contains the names of all of the categories of data that are being charted, and the y-axis lists all of the values along which the data is being charted. Bar charts reverse the axes: the categories are plotted along the y-axis, and the values are plotted along the x-axis.

▼ **Category names.** Category names appear along the x-axis, and are the labels taken from the worksheet data used in the chart.

▼ **Chart data series name.** The data chart series name corresponds to the labels included in your worksheet data, which is plotted along the y-axis. If your worksheet data does not contain any labels (for example, if you selected a row or column of numbers only), the data chart series name defaults to the number of the series chosen—for example, Series 1, Series 2, and so on. You can replace the data chart series name with any name you choose.

▼ **Tick mark.** The tick mark is the small line that intersects the axes and marks off each category on the x-axis and each data value on the y-axis.

▼ **Tick mark label.** The tick mark label is the text attached to the tick mark.

▼ **Gridlines.** Gridlines in charts are the same as gridlines in worksheets. Gridlines in charts are optional.

▼ **Chart text.** Chart text is the text in a chart that describes the data in the chart. Attached text is linked to a specific object in a chart (such as the chart title, the descriptions you add to the axes, or descriptions of series or data points) and cannot be moved unless the chart object is moved. Unattached text is text that is independent of chart objects and can be moved anywhere in the chart window.

▼ **Legend.** The legend is an optional box that identifies the color or pattern of the data markers in a data series, and shows the name of each data series.

Creating an Embedded Chart

The easiest way to create a chart in Excel is to use the ChartWizard tool on your toolbar, as shown in Figure 7.1. Using the ChartWizard tool, we are going to create a basic chart that contains the income for some of the accounts for the month of January, as shown in Figure 7.2.

1. Open the INCOME.XLS worksheet.

2. Select the nonadjacent ranges A7:A18 and C7:F18. We want the chart to contain the names of all the items in the worksheet for which we received income, as well as the income for each account. We do not want the chart to contain any blank columns. Therefore, we need to select the nonadjacent ranges that contain all of this information.

3. Click on the ChartWizard in the toolbar.

4. Move to the section of the worksheet where you want to position the chart, and drag your pointer to create a rectangle of the size and shape you want.

5. The ChartWizard—Step 1 of 5 dialog box is displayed, as shown in Figure 7.3. Excel arbitrarily assigns the order in which your selected data will be plotted, and displays your selection in this order in the Range text box. Excel takes the category names for the x-axis from the first column or row if your selection contains one range. If you have multiple ranges containing columns that all start with the same row number, Excel will take the category names from the first column.

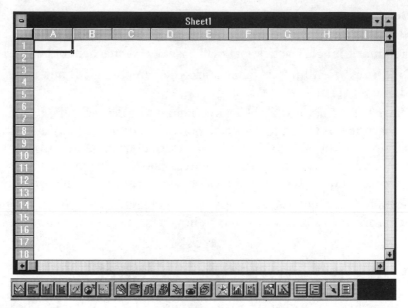

Figure 7.1   *The ChartWizard tool is the fifth button from the right.*

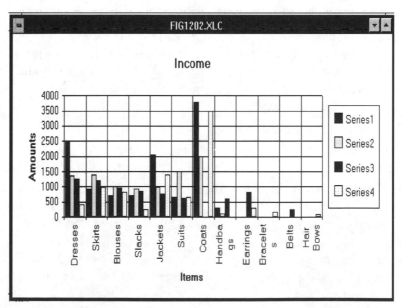

Figure 7.2   *Chart showing January income for each account.*

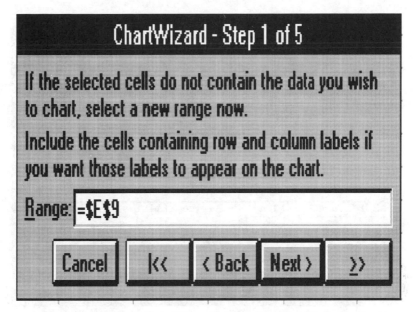

Figure 7.3   *The ChartWizard tool—Step 1 of 5 dialog box.*

6. Click on Next. The ChartWizard—Step 2 of 5 dialog box is displayed, as shown in Figure 7.4. You can choose one of fourteen chart types.

7. Select Column and click on Next. The ChartWizard—Step 3 of 5 dialog box is displayed, showing ten styles of column charts. Select style 1.

8. Click on Next. The ChartWizard—Step 4 of 5 dialog box is displayed, as shown in Figure 7.5. You will see how your chart will appear, and you will be given three formatting choices. The Data Series In choice determines whether your data will be plotted in columns or rows. If you choose Rows, each selected row of data will appear as a data series in the chart; if you choose Columns, each selected column of data will appear as a data series in the chart. Since we want each column to be used as a data series, we will choose Columns.

The second choice, Use First Column For, lets you choose whether the contents of the first row or column will appear as labels or a data series along the x-axis. Since we want to use labels, select the Category [X] Axis Labels option.

The final choice, Use First Row For, lets you choose whether you want the values in the first row or column to appear as labels or values along the y-axis. If you choose Series (Y) Axis Labels, the y-axis will have labels; if you choose First Data Point, the y-axis will contain values. We want the y-axis to have values, and so we will choose First Data Point. The sample chart in the dialog box will change to reflect your choices.

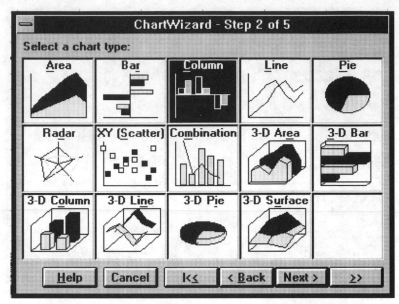

Figure 7.4 *The ChartWizard—Step 2 of 5 dialog box.*

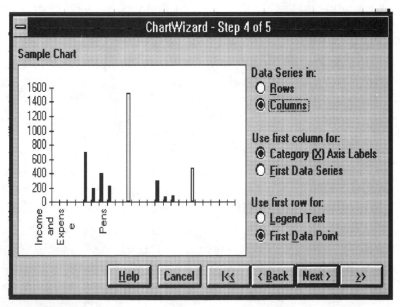

Figure 7.5 *The ChartWizard—Step 4 of 5 dialog box.*

9. Click on Next. The ChartWizard—Step 5 of 5 dialog box is displayed, as shown in Figure 7.6. Choose Yes to add a legend to the chart. To complete your chart, type the title *Income* into the Chart Title text box, type *Items* in the Category [X]: text box, and type *Amounts* in the Value [Y] text box to complete your chart. Notice how the sample chart in the dialog box changes to reflect each change.

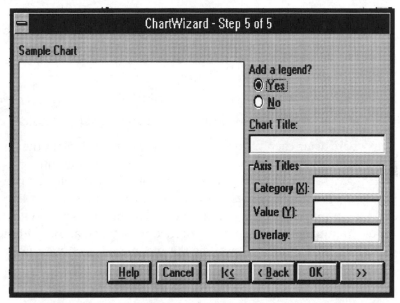

Figure 7.6   *The ChartWizard—Step 5 of 5 dialog box.*

10. Click on OK. Your embedded chart has been created. If necessary, size your chart to accommodate the data it contains by dragging the handles located in the center of the top, bottom, left, and right borders.

Before continuing we should save our chart. To save the chart as part of the worksheet (embedded into the worksheet), simply save your worksheet. When you save a chart as an embedded document, the worksheet and the chart are all located in the same document. When you open the worksheet, the chart is there as part of the document. When you make changes in the worksheet data included in the chart, the chart will reflect these changes. To format or edit an embedded chart, you must double-click on the chart to open it. When you open an embedded chart, the menu bar choices change. To close the chart, click on File and then on Close.

Saving a Chart Document

You can also save your chart as a separate document. When you create a chart document, you must open the chart as a separate document. This will allow any changes made in the worksheet data contained in the chart to take effect in the chart. If your worksheet is particularly large, saving the chart as a separate document is usually a better choice, since this makes it easier to locate the chart, and you can format and edit it without taking up RAM with a large document. To save a chart as a separate document:

1. Double-click on the chart to open it.
2. Click on File in the menu bar to open the File menu.
3. Click on Save As to display the Save As dialog box.
4. Name the chart. Excel automatically gives charts an XLC entension.

Save your chart using each of the above methods. If you look at the chart you will see that the legend contains four series, each of which represents one of the four accounts. Each series is preceded by a box that contains the color or pattern for the columns corresponding to that series in the chart. Each income item is listed along the x-axis, and dollar amounts in thousands are plotted along the y-axis. When you look at the chart, you can quickly see the amounts of income for each account in proportion to the other accounts for that item, as well as the income for each item in proportion to the income for all of the other items.

Creating an Embedded 3-D Chart

We have just created a very simple, basic chart, using two ranges. Now let's take it one step further. Let's create a 3-D chart using three nonadjacent ranges to show the income and expense for some of the items for the month of January.

1. Open the INC&EXP.XLS worksheet.
2. Select the nonadjacent ranges A25:A46, R6:617, and R25:R46. For our category names we want to use range A25:A46, which contains the names of all the income and expense items in the worksheet. For our data series, we want to use ranges R6:R17 and R25:R46, which contain the totals for each item.
3. Click on the ChartWizard in the toolbar. The shape of your mouse pointer will change. Move to the section of the worksheet where you want to position the chart and drag your pointer to create a rectangle of the size and shape you want.
4. The ChartWizard—Step 1 of 5 dialog box is displayed. Excel arbitrarily assigns the order in which your selected data will be plotted, and displays your selection in this order in the Range text box. Excel takes the category names for the

x-axis from the first column or row if your selection contains one range. If your selection contains nonadjacent ranges, Excel takes the category names for the x-axis from the first column or row of the first range shown in the Range text box. We want our category names in the x-axis of our chart to reflect the labels in range A25:A46. To accomplish this, we will have to edit the contents of the Range text box by typing:

```
=$A$25:$A$46,$R$6:$R$17,$R$25:$R$46
```

This indicates to Excel that the labels in the range A25:A46 will be the category labels for the x-axis.

5. Click on Next to display the ChartWizard—Step 2 of 5 dialog box. You can choose one of fourteen chart types.

6. Select 3-D Column and click on Next. The ChartWizard—Step 3 of 5 dialog box is displayed, showing ten styles of column charts. Select style 1.

7. Click on Next to display the ChartWizard—Step 4 of 5 dialog box. You will see how your chart will appear, and will be given three formatting choices. The Data Series In choice determines whether your data will be plotted in columns or rows. If you choose Rows, each selected row of data will appear as a data series in the chart; if you choose Columns, each selected column of data will appear as a data series in the chart. Since we want each column to be used as a data series, we will choose Columns.

   The second choice, Use First Column For, lets you choose whether the contents of the first row or column will appear along the x-axis as labels or as a data series. Since we want to use labels, select the Category [X] Axis Labels option.

   The final choice, Use First Row For, lets you choose whether you want the values in the first row or column to appear as labels or values along the y-axis. If you choose Series (Y) Axis Labels, the y-axis will contain labels; if you choose First Data Point, the y-axis will contain values. We want the y-axis to contain values, so we will choose First Data Point. The sample chart in the dialog box will change to reflect your choices.

8. Click on Next to display the ChartWizard—Step 5 of 5 dialog box. Choose Yes to add a legend to the chart. To complete your chart, type in the title *Income and Expense* in the Chart Title text box, type *Items* in the Category [X] text box, and type *Amounts* in the Value [Y] text box. Notice that the sample chart in the dialog box changes to reflect each change.

9. Click on OK. Your embedded chart has been created. If necessary, size your chart to accommodate the data it contains by dragging the handles located in the center of the top, bottom, left, and right borders.

Before we continue, save your chart as either an embedded chart or a separate chart document.

If you look at the chart you will see that the legend contains two series, one representing income and the other representing expenses. Each of the series is preceded by a box that contains the color or pattern for the columns corresponding to that series in the chart. Series 1 charts expenses for the month of January, and Series 2 charts income. Each income and expense item is listed along the x-axis, and dollar amounts in thousands are plotted along the y-axis. When you look at the chart, you can quickly see the amounts of income and/or expense for each item in proportion to one another and in proportion to the greatest amount of income and/or expense for the month.

Changing Types of Charts

Using the Chart Toolbar

When you are using an embedded chart, you may choose one of two ways to edit the chart: using the Chart menu, and using the Chart toolbar. To use the Chart toolbar:

1. Use GoTo or scroll through the worksheet until you have the chart on the screen.
2. Click on Options in the menu bar to open the Options menu.
3. Click on Toolbars to display the Toolbars dialog box.
4. Select Chart in the Show Toolbars list box.
5. Click on Show.

The Chart toolbar is now shown at the bottom of the Excel application window. Each of the first seventeen buttons on the Chart toolbar represents a type of chart. Clicking on any of these buttons will change your chart to a different type. Click on a few to see the changes in your chart.

Using the Chart Menu

If you have saved your chart as a separate chart document or if you have opened your embedded chart, you can change your chart type by using the chart menu.

1. If you have saved your chart as a separate document, open it now. If you have saved an embedded chart, open the worksheet, use GoTo or scroll through the worksheet to position the chart on the screen, and double-click on the chart to

open it. The menu bar choices in the application window have changed to reflect a different kind of document.

2. Click on Gallery in the menu bar to open the Gallery menu.

3. The Gallery menu lists fourteen types of charts. Selecting any of these will take you to a dialog box that contains the various styles available for that type of chart. For example, if you select Area in the Gallery menu, the Chart Gallery dialog box, containing all available styles for area charts, will be displayed.

4. Select one of the styles and click on OK to change your chart type, or click on Cancel to exit the Chart Gallery without changing your chart type.

To view and select a style for a different type of chart, click on Next or Previous in the Chart Gallery dialog box.

N O T E

Setting a Default Type for New Charts

At some point, you will probably decide that you prefer one type of chart for your data. If this is not the column chart, you will want to change the default.

1. Open a chart document or an embedded chart to display the chart menu.

2. Click on Gallery in the menu bar to open the Gallery menu.

3. If the chart displayed is not the type you want as your default, change it.

4. Select Set Preferred from the Gallery menu. The style of the currently displayed chart is now your default chart type.

To change any other chart to the default type, simply click on Preferred in the Gallery menu.

N O T E

Selecting Chart Items

Now that you have created two charts, you will want to format and edit them. Before you can format or edit an item in a chart, you must open the chart and select the item or text you want to edit. The following sections show the mouse and keyboard movements you can use to select items in a chart.

Selecting Chart Items Using a Mouse

To	Do this
Select an item	Click the chart item you want to select.
Select a chart data series	Click any tick mark in the chart data series.
Select a single data marker	Hold down the Ctrl key and click the data marker.
Select gridlines	Click on a gridline.
Select an axis	Click the axis or the area containing the axis tick mark labels.
Select the entire plot area of a chart	Click on any area in the plot area that is not occupied by any other item, including gridlines.
Select the entire chart	Click anywhere outside the plot area that is not occupied by any other item.

Selecting Chart Items Using the Keyboard

When you select chart items using the keyboard, you can move from item to item or among the following categories of items:

- ▼ Charts
- ▼ Plot areas
- ▼ 3-D floors
- ▼ 3-D walls
- ▼ 3-D corners
- ▼ Legends
- ▼ Axes
- ▼ Text
- ▼ Arrows
- ▼ Gridlines
- ▼ First chart data series
- ▼ Second and subsequent chart data series
- ▼ Drop lines
- ▼ Hi-Lo lines
- ▼ Up/Down bars
- ▼ Series lines

You can use the Up and Down arrow keys to move among categories of items in the chart, and the Left and Right arrow keys to select individual items within categories.

Press	To
Up arrow	Go to the first item in the next category
Down arrow	Go to the last item in the previous category
Right arrow	Go to the next item in the same category
Left arrow	Go to the previous item in the same category

Selecting Items Using Chart Menu Commands

You can use the chart menu commands to select either the entire chart or the plot area of a chart.

1. Click on Chart in the menu bar to open the Chart menu.
2. Click on either Select Chart or Select Plot Area.

You have selected either the entire chart or the plot area of the chart.

When you select a chart item or text, it is marked with black or white selection squares. When a selected item or text is marked with black selection squares, it can be moved or sized using the mouse. Selected items or text marked with white selection squares cannot be moved or sized.

N O T E

Canceling a Selection

To cancel a selection for a chart item or text, click an area inside the chart window that is not occupied by any other chart item.

To cancel a selection for the entire chart, either click outside the chart window or press Esc.

Adding, Deleting, or Editing a Data Series

Using the ChartWizard

The easiest way to add or delete a chart data series in an existing chart is to use the ChartWizard tool. You can also use the ChartWizard tool to change whether you plot the chart series by columns or rows.

1. Open the source document and select the chart you want to change.
2. Click on the ChartWizard tool to display the ChartWizard—Step 1 of 2 dialog box.
3. Either reselect the data in the worksheet you want to include in the chart or enter the range or nonadjacent ranges in the Range text box.
4. Click on Next. The ChartWizard—Step 2 of 2 dialog box is displayed.
5. Pick the options you want for the Data Series In, Use First Column For, and Use First Row For options in the dialog box.

Using the Edit Command

If you only want to add or delete data series in a chart, or change whether you are going to plot the chart by rows or columns, the ChartWizard is the easiest method to use. If, however, you want to do any of the above and also change the name of a data series in your chart, you must use the Edit command. Let's change the names of the data series in the chart we created using the INCJAN.XLS worksheet.

1. Open the chart you want to change (if the chart is embedded, double-click on it, if the chart is a separate document, open it).

2. Click on Chart in the menu bar to open the Chart menu.

3. Click on Edit Series to display the Edit Series dialog box, shown in Figure 7.7.

4. Select New Series if you want to add a new data series to the chart. Type in the range for the new data series using an external absolute reference. For example, if you wanted to add the totals from column G in the INCOME.XLS worksheet to the chart, the reference would look like this:

    =INCOME.XLS!$G$7:$G$18

5. If you want to give the data series a name of your own choosing, type the name into the Name text box.

6. We do not want to add a data series, but we do want to change the names of our data series. Click on Series 1 in the Edit Series dialog box. Select the Name text box and type *Acct 100*. Click on Define so that the dialog box remains open. Rename Series 2 *Acct 101*, Series 3 *Acct 102*, and Series 4 *Acct 103*.

7. To delete a data series from your chart, select the data series in the Edit Series dialog box and click on Delete.

8. If you want to change the order in which your data is plotted in the chart, select the data series and change the number in the Plot Order text box.

9. Click on OK.

When you want to edit more than one chart data series, click on Define after making the change to leave the Edit Series dialog box open; when you want to edit only one chart data series, click on OK after making the change to close the Edit Series dialog box.

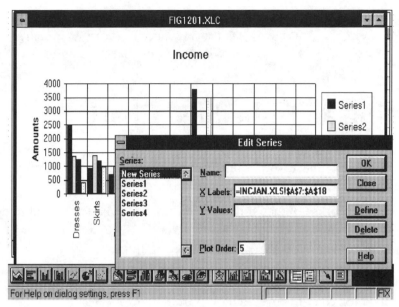

Figure 7.8   *The Edit Series dialog box.*

Changing Data Values in a Chart

When you change the values of the data in your source worksheet, the data automatically changes in the chart. You can also change the data in some chart types and have the change reflected in the worksheet. The chart types that allow you to do this are: column charts, bar charts, and 2-D line charts, including xy (scatter) charts. You can drag the data markers to increase or decrease the values they show, allowing you to quickly view a "what-if" scenario on your chart.

To change data values:

1. Open the source worksheet.
2. Open the chart (if the chart is embedded, double-click on the chart to open it).
3. Hold down the Ctrl key and click on the data marker you want to change.
4. Drag the black selection square to change the value of the data marker. As you drag, the changing values will be reflected in the reference area and a line along the y-axis will also appear, reflecting the change.

You cannot go beyond the values already established by the y-axis. For example, you cannot change the data marker in your chart to reflect a value of 4,000 if the values in the y-axis do not go beyond 3,500.

Deleting an Embedded Chart

Deleting an embedded chart is not the same as deleting a document in Excel. If you delete the entire document, your worksheet will also be deleted. If you want to delete only the chart and leave the worksheet and all objects in it intact:

1. Open the worksheet that contains the embedded chart you want to delete.
2. Click once on the embedded chart.
3. Click on Edit in the menu bar to open the Edit menu.
4. Click on Clear.

The embedded chart has been removed from the worksheet.

If you change your mind you can click on Undo Clear in the Edit menu immediately after you clear the chart.

Deleting a Chart Document

You can delete a chart document the same way you delete any other document in Excel.

1. Be sure the chart document you want to delete is not open.
2. Click on File in the menu bar to open the File menu.
3. Click on Delete to display the Delete Document dialog box.
4. Select the chart you want to delete and click on OK.

You cannot undo a Delete command. Be certain you want to delete the chart before choosing OK.

Clearing a Chart of Data or Formats

You can clear a chart of data, formats, or both. If you have formatted your chart and decide that you want to replace its data, you can quickly clear all of the data and leave the formatting intact. If you decide that you do not like the formatting you have applied, you can clear all formatting and leave the data intact. Or you can clear everything from your chart and start from scratch, creating a new chart from a source worksheet using the Copy and Paste Special commands. To clear a chart:

1. Open the chart.
2. Select the entire chart.
3. Click on Edit in the menu bar to open the Edit menu.
4. Click on Clear to display the Clear dialog box, as shown in Figure 7.8.

   ▼ To clear everything and leave a blank chart, select the All option.
   ▼ To clear the formatting and leave the data, select the Formats option.
   ▼ To clear the data and leave the formatting intact, select the Formulas option.

5. Click on OK.

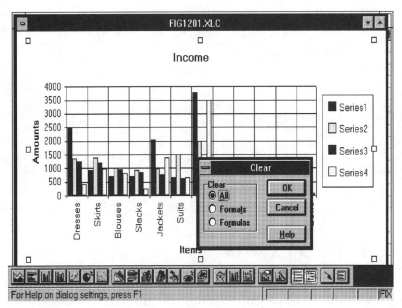

Figure 7.8 *The Clear dialog box.*

Copying Data to a Chart

To copy data from a source worksheet to a chart:

1. Open the source worksheet and the chart. It is easier to work with both document windows on the screen simultaneously. Click on Window in the menu bar to open the Window menu. Hide all documents except the ones you want to view. From the Windows menu, click on Arrange and choose Tiled.

2. Make the worksheet the active document.

3. Select the data you want to include in your chart.

4. Click on Edit in the menu bar to open the Edit menu.

5. Click on Copy.

6. Switch to the chart window.

7. Click on Edit in the menu bar to open the Edit menu.

8. Click on Paste Special to display the Paste Special dialog box.

9. Select the options you want in the Paste Special dialog box. Replace Existing Categories is applicable only when you are pasting data into an existing chart for which you have selected Categories [X Labels] in First Column/Row. If you select Replace Existing Categories, the categories in the chart will be replaced with the categories you are pasting.

10. Select OK.

Formatting Charts

Using charts adds punch to your spreadsheet data. Charts allow for an easy-to-read visual representation of data usually contained in rows and columns. You can enhance your charts with formatting features. You can add text to describe your data or to make a special point, add and delete gridlines, and even put arrows into your charts.

Adding Text to Charts

When you created the chart from the INCOME.XLS worksheet in this chapter, you added some text—a chart title and descriptions of the data along the x and y axes. Later, you renamed the data series to reflect the accounts represented by the data markers. This change was reflected in the chart legend, making it easy to identify exactly which account each data marker represented. Now you are going to use text to further enhance your chart.

Charts contain two types of text: attached and unattached. **Attached text** is attached to a chart object. For example, tick mark labels are attached to tick marks and describe the data along the corresponding axes. This text can be moved only if the chart object is moved. **Unattached text** can be inserted anywhere in a chart window, and can be moved around at will. When you select attached text, it is surrounded by white selection squares. When you select unattached text, it is surrounded by black selection squares.

Adding or editing a chart title or axis title

You can add or change a chart title or an axis title whenever you like. This is useful if your information has changed, or if you just want your text to be more descriptive. We are going to change the chart title and the axis titles in our income chart.

1. Open the chart that you created from the INCOME.XLS worksheet.
2. Click on Chart in the menu bar to open the Chart menu.
3. Click on Attach Text to display the Attach Text dialog box.
4. Click on Chart Title.
5. Click on OK. The title area in the chart is surrounded by white selection sqares containing the word *Title,* which also appears in the formula bar. You can edit this text just as you would any text in a worksheet cell. Type *Income for the Month of January* in the formula bar. Insert a line break by pressing Alt+Enter where you want the break to appear. Press Alt+Enter after the words *Income for the*.
6. Press Enter. Your title has now been changed to look like this:

    Income for the
    Month of January

7. Select Value [Y] Axis.
8. Click on OK. The description area for the y-axis is surrounded by white selection squares that contain a Y. Type *Dollar Amounts* in the formula bar.
9. Press Enter.
10. Select Category [X] Axis.
11. Click on OK. The description area for the x-axis is surrounded by white selection squares that contain an X. Type the words *Items Listed for Income* in the formula bar.
12. Press Enter.

If your chart already contains chart titles or axis titles, and you can edit them simply by selecting the item and clicking on the existing text in the formula bar.

SHORT CUT

Adding a Label to a Data Marker

You can add labels to data markers in your charts to emphasize information. Labels added to data markers are attached text attached to the data marker. Let's add a label to the data marker in our income chart to pinpoint the item that brought in the most income in January. First, open the chart you created from the INCOME.XLS worksheet.

There are two ways to add this label. The first is to:

1. Click on Chart in the menu bar to open the Chart Menu.

2. Click on Attach Text to display the Attach Text dialog box.

3. Select Series and Data Point. Enter the number of the series and the data point to which you want to add a label. To add a label to the data marker that reflects the highest income for the month, enter 1 in Series Number and 7 in Point Number.

4. Click on OK.

5. Type in the words "Highest Income" in the formula bar.

6. Press Enter.

The second way to add this label is to:

1. Select the data marker to which you want to add a label by clicking on it while holding down the Ctrl key. In this case, select the data marker that reflects the highest income for the month. The data marker is surrounded by white and black selection squares.

2. Click on Chart in the menu bar to open the Chart menu.

3. Click on Attach Text. The Attach Text dialog box is displayed. The Series and Data Point option has been selected automatically and the Series and Data numbers that correspond to the data marker you selected appear in the Series and Point Numbers text boxes.

To unselect (remove the selection squares from) a chart item, click on any area in the chart that is not occupied by a chart area.

N O T E

Adding Unattached Text

You can add unattached text anywhere in the chart window. Unattached text is surrounded by black selection squares and can be moved and resized at will. We are going to add unattached text to our income chart to identify the type of chart we created.

1. If it is not still open, open the chart that contains the data from the INCOME.XLS worksheet.
2. While no other text is selected (the formula bar is blank), type: *This is a Column Chart*. If you want to add more than one line of unattached text, press Alt+Enter after the word where you want the text to break.
3. Press Enter.
4. Excel has placed the text in the chart window and surrounded it with black selection squares.
5. Drag the text to the upper-left corner of the chart window. To see how it will look when it is printed, click on File and then on Print Preview in the File menu.

Editing Unattached Text

To edit unattached text in a chart, click on the text you want to edit. Then click on the formula bar to either edit some of the text or retype the text in its entirety. Press Enter.

Deleting Text from Charts

To delete either attached or unattached text from a chart:

1. Open the chart.
2. Click on the text to select it. It will be surrounded by white or black selection squares.
3. Click on Edit in the menu bar to open the Edit menu.
4. Click on Clear.

The text has been deleted from the chart.

Changing the Fonts Used by Chart Text

You can change the font type and size of the text in your charts. (Remember, if your printer is not capable of printing the fonts you select, the fonts will show on screen, but will not print.) You can format all of the text in a chart using one font, or apply different fonts to each text selection.

First, open the chart that contains the text you want to change.

▼ To change the font for all of the text in the chart, click on Chart in the menu bar to open the Chart menu and choose Select Chart.

▼ To change the font for a single piece of attached or unattached text, click on the text to select it.

▼ To change to font of the tick mark labels in an axis, click the axis to select it.

▼ To change the font of the text in a legend, click the legend to select it.

After selecting the item you wish to edit:

1. Click on Format in the menu bar to open the Format menu.
2. Click on Font to display the Font dialog box. Select the font you wish to use.
3. If you want to add or change the border or pattern of the area you have selected, click on Patterns. Select the border and pattern you want from the options and drop down boxes in the Pattern dialog box.
4. If you want to change the alignment or orientation of the text you have selected, click on Text. Select the options you want in the Text dialog box. The Text button is not available if you selected the entire chart or the legend.
5. Click on OK.

Changing the Border and Patterns in Selected Text Areas

You can add, delete, and change border and patterns styles in selected areas of attached and unattached text to add even more interest and/or emphasis to your charts.

1. Open the chart you want to format.
2. Select the text you want to format.
3. Click on Format in the menu bar to open the Format menu.
4. Click on Patterns to display the Patterns dialog box. Select the border style and pattern you want for the selected text.
5. If you want to delete a border or pattern, select None in the Border or Pattern option boxes. This is the default for charts.
6. Click on OK.

Changing Text Alignment and Orientation in Selected Text

You can change the alignment and orientation of selected text in your charts. The selected text will align between the area outlined by the selection squares. To change text alignment or orientation:

1. Open the chart you want to format.
2. Select the text you want to format.
3. Click on Format in the menu bar to open the Format menu.
4. Click on Text to display the Text dialog box.
5. Select the options you want.
6. To return attached text to the default alignment and orientation, select the Automatic Text option.
7. Click on OK.

Spell-Checking a Chart

You can check the spelling of all attached and unattached text in your chart.

1. Open the chart.
2. Click on Chart in the menu bar to open the Chart menu.
3. Click on Spelling. If Excel finds any misspelled words or words it cannot identify, you will be prompted.
4. You will be prompted when spelling check is completed. Choose OK.

Adding, Deleting, and Formatting a Chart Legend

The chart legend identifies each data series in your chart and shows you the color or pattern used for each data marker in the series. The text used in the legend is taken from the worksheet cells that contain the data series. If your data series does not contain any text that can be used as a data series label, Excel automatically names each data series in consecutive order—Series 1, Series 2, and so on. You can change the name of the series in the legend by either changing the text in the worksheet cells that contain the data series labels or by using the Edit command in the menu bar. Changing the name of a series in a legend by using the Edit command is covered earlier in this chapter in the section titled "Adding, Deleting, or Editing a Data Series." When you create a legend, it is automatically positioned at the right edge of the chart. When you create a chart, you can add a legend to it. If you do not select this option, you can still add a legend to your chart later. If you do select this option and then change your mind, you can delete the legend from the chart. You can also add, delete, or change borders and patterns for the legend, change the text size and type, and move the legend to another location on the chart.

Adding a legend

To add a legend to your chart:

1. Open the chart (if the chart is embedded, double-click on it).
2. Click on Chart in the menu bar to open the Chart menu.
3. Click on Add Legend.

The legend will be inserted at the right border of the chart, and the chart will be resized to accommodate the legend.

Deleting a legend

To delete a legend:

1. Open the chart (if the chart is embedded, double-click on it).
2. Click on Chart in the menu bar to open the Chart menu.
3. Click on Delete Legend.

The legend will be deleted from your chart.

Formatting or moving a legend

You can move a legend to any location on your chart by dragging the mouse or by using the Legend command on the Format menu. If you use the mouse to position the legend on sections of the chart that cannot be moved (such as data markers), the legend will overlap that section of the chart. If you move the legend to the edge of the chart window, Excel will adjust the size of the chart to accommodate the change. Excel will also automatically change the vertical or horizontal arrangement of the data series in the legend to accommodate the space available. For example, if you move the legend to the top of the chart, Excel will arrange the data series in the legend horizontally, instead of vertically.

Moving a legend using the mouse

To move a legend using the mouse:

1. Open the chart that contains the legend you want to move. (If the chart is embedded, double-click on it.)
2. Select the legend by clicking on it.
3. Drag the legend to its new position in the chart.

Moving and/or formatting a legend using the Legend command

To move and/or format a legend using the Legend command:

1. Open the chart that contains the legend you want to move or format. (If the chart is embedded, double-click on it.)
2. Select the legend by clicking on it.
3. Click on Format in the menu bar to open the Format menu.
4. Click on Legend to display the Legend dialog box.
5. Select the option that will position the legend at the location you want.
6. Click on Patterns in the Legend dialog box to display the Patterns dialog box.
7. Select the border and pattern styles you want to use for the legend.
8. Click on Font in either the Legend dialog box or the Patterns dialog box to display the Font dialog box. Select the options you want.
9. Click on OK. The dialog box will be closed and all of your changes will take effect.

Adding, Deleting, and Formatting Axes

You may choose either, both, or none of the axes on your chart. You can delete one or both (the axes automatically show when you create a chart). You can also format each axis independently of the other. You can change the appearance of the axes, tick marks, and tick mark labels. For example, you can change the size and font of the text in the tick mark labels. When you create a chart, Excel automatically decides how many categories are displayed in the x-axis and how many values are displayed in the y-axis. You can change either of these defaults. For example, in the chart created from the INCOME.XLS worksheet, the values along the y-axis (the **major units**) increment by 500. You can change this so that the major units increment by 250. You can also change the increment values of the **minor units** along the axis. The minor units are the tick marks that mark values within the major units. You can decide whether the x and y axis will intersect at the top or bottom of the chart. You can reverse the order of the values in the chart, placing the lowest value at the top of the y-axis and the highest value at the bottom. You can decide what the beginning and ending values will be in the y-axis. You can also change the orientation of the tick mark labels and the format of the axis itself.

Adding or deleting an axis

You can determine whether to display one, both, or neither of the axes in your chart.

1. Open the chart you want to change. (If the chart is embedded, double-click on it.)
2. Click on Chart in the menu bar to open the Chart menu.
3. Click on Axes to display the Axes dialog box.
4. Select the check boxes for the axis or axes you want to show on the chart. Clear the check boxes for the axis or axes you do not want displayed.
5. Click on OK.

Formatting an axis

When you format an axis, your formatting choices will change depending upon whether you are formatting an x-axis or a y-axis. When you format a y-axis you can control the beginning and ending values of the axis, the increments between the major units and the increments between the minor units, whether the axis starts with the highest or lowest value, and where the x and y axes will intersect. You can also change the format of the axis line, the position of the tick marks and tick mark labels, and the font and orientation of the tick mark labels.

To format a y-axis

1. Open the chart you want to change.
2. Select the axis by clicking on the axis line or a tick mark label attached to the axis line.
3. Click on Format in the menu bar to open the Format menu.
4. Click on Scale to display the Axis Scale dialog box, as shown in Figure 7.9.

    Notice that the text in the upper-left corner of the dialog box identifies this as the Value [Y] Axis Scale.

5. Make the changes you want in the dialog box. You have the following choices:

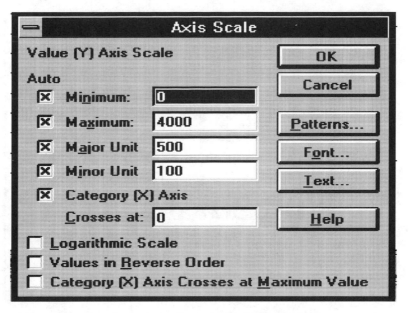

Figure 7.9 *The Axis Scale dialog box.*

▼ **Minimum.** This selection lets you decide the lowest value you want to appear on the axis. If the Auto check box is selected, the Minimum text box displays the lowest value found in all of the data series in the chart. To change the automatic value, type a new value into the text box.

▼ **Maximum.** This selection lets you decide the highest value you want to appear on the axis. If the Auto check box is selected, the Maximum text box displays the highest values found in all of the data series in the chart. To change the automatic value, type a new value in the text box.

▼ **Major Unit.** This selection lets you decide how much the values on the axis will increment between major tick marks. If the Auto check box is selected, Excel automatically calculates the increment. To change the increment, type a new value into the Major Unit text box.

▼ **Minor Unit.** Minor units are the tick marks that incicate the values between major units on the axis. Figure 7.10 shows the minor units along the y-axis indicating each 100-value increment between the major units. To change this value, type a new number into the Minor Unit text box.

If you want the minor units to be displayed along the y-axis, you must change the default options in the Patterns dialog box. To access the Patterns dialog box, click on Patterns in the Axis Scale dialog box.

SHORT CUT

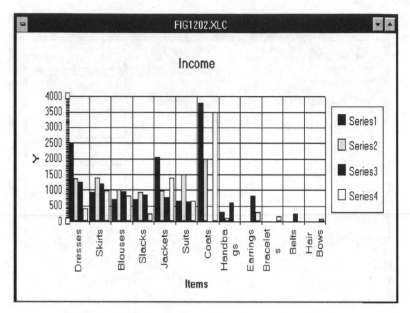

Figure 7.10   *Chart with minor units added.*

▼ **Category (X) Axis Crosses At.** This choice lets you decide where you want the x and y axes to intersect. If the Auto check box is selected, Excel automatically intersects the x and y axes at the lowest value along the y axis. To change the location where the x and y axes intersect, type a new value in the Category (X) Axis Crosses At text box.

▼ **Logarithmic Scale.** This selection recalculates the Minimum, Maximum, Major Unit, and Minor Unit values as powers of 10. The values are based on the range of values in the data series in the chart. You cannot use a zero or a negative value to recalculate values on a logarithmic scale, and the Major and Minor Units must both contain a value of at least 10. If you have a value in the Minimum or Maximum text boxes that is not a power of 10, Excel will round the value up or down to the next power of 10.

▼ **Values in Reverse Order.** This selection reverses the values along the y-axis. Instead of displaying the lowest value at the bottom of the axis line, the lowest value is displayed at the top and the highest value is displayed at the bottom.

▼ **Category (X) Axis Crosses At Maximum Value.** When this selection is enabled, the x and y axes intersect at the point where the highest value is located along the y-axis. This selection overrides the Category (X) Axis Crosses At option.

6. To change the formatting of the axis line, tick marks, and tick mark labels, click on Patterns in the Axis Scale dialog box. Select the options you want from the Patterns dialog box.

7. To change font, color, size, and background of the tick mark labels, click on Fonts in the Axis Scale dialog box. Make the selections you in the Font dialog box.

8. To change to orientation of the text along the axis, click on Text in the Axis Scale dialog box to display the Text dialog box, and make your selection.

9. Click on OK to close the dialog box and have your changes take effect.

To format an x-axis:

1. Open the chart you want to change.

2. Select the axis by clicking on the axis line or a tick mark label attached to the axis line.

3. Click on Format in the menu bar to open the Format menu.

4. Click on Scale to display the Axis Scale dialog box. Notice that the text in the upper-left corner of the dialog box identifies this as the Value [X] Axis Scale.

5. Make the changes you want in the dialog box. You have the following choices:

   ▼ **Value (Y) Axis Crosses At Category Number.** This selection lets you specify the number of the category at which the x and y axes will intersect. Categories start with the number 1 and increment by one for each category. A category does not have to be labelled and does not necessarily have to have tick mark. Each category does, however, contain the data markers for each data series. To change the value at which the x and y axes intersect, type a new value in the Value (Y) Axis Crosses At Category Number text box.

   ▼ **Number of Categories Between Tick Labels.** This selection lets you specify which categories will have tick mark labels. For example, if you type 1 in the Number of Categories Between Tick Labels text box, Excel will assign a tick mark label for every category; if you type 2 in this text box, Excel will assign a tick mark label for every other category along the axis. Typing 3 in the text box would assign a tick mark label for every third category along the axis, and so on.

   ▼ **Number of Categories Between Tick Marks.** This selection lets you choose the number of categories along the axis that will be included between each set of tick marks. If you type 1 in the Number of Categories Between Tick Marks text box, each tick mark will have one category assigned to it; if you type 2 in the text box, two categories will be included between each set of tick marks; and so forth.

▼ **Category (Y) Axis Crosses At.** When this selection is checked, the x and y axes will intersect at the edge of the category indicated in the Value (Y) Axis Crosses At text box. When this selection is cleared, the y axis intersects in the center of the first category.

▼ **Values in Reverse Order.** This selection reverses the values along the x-axis. The first value is shown last and the last value is shown first.

▼ **Category (Y) Axis Crosses At Maximum Value.** When this selection is enabled, the x and y axes intersect at the last category along the x axis. This selection overrides the Category (Y) Axis Crosses At value.

6. To change the formatting of the axis lines, tick marks, and tick mark labels, click on Patterns in the Axis Scale dialog box to display the Patterns dialog box. Select the options you want.

7. To change font, color, size, and background of the tick mark labels, click on Fonts in the Axis Scale dialog box. Make the selections you want within the Font dialog box.

8. To change to orientation of the text along the axis, click on Text in the Axis Scale dialog box. Select the orientation you want from the Text dialog box.

9. Click on OK.

Formatting Data Markers

You can change the pattern, color, spacing, and border styles of the data markers in your charts. You can change all or some of the data markers within a data series. To change the formatting of the data markers in your chart:

1. Open the chart you want to change. (If the chart is embedded, double-click on it.)

2. To format all of the data markers in a data series, click on one of the data markers. To format one of the data markers in a data series, hold down the Ctrl key and click on the data marker you want to format.

3. Click on Format in the menu bar to open the Format menu.

4. Click on Patterns to display the Patterns dialog box.

5. Use the drop-down boxes under Border and Area to select the formatting you want to use for the data markers.

6. If you select the Apply To All check box, the options you have chosen will be applied to every data marker in every data series in the chart.

7. If you select the Invert If Negative check box, the foreground and background colors of the data markers that represent negative values will be reversed.

8. Click on OK.

Adding, Deleting, and Formatting Gridlines

You can add and delete major and minor gridlines to make it easier locate and identify the values and categories on your charts, even if the chart style you originally selected does not include gridlines. Major gridlines intersect with the major units along the axes, and minor gridlines intersect with the minor units along the axes. You can change the color, style, and thickness of the gridlines in your charts.

Adding or deleting major gridlines using the Chart toolbar

To add or delete major gridlines using the Chart toolbar:

1. Open the chart you want to change. (If it is embedded, double-click on it.)

2. Click the Horizontal Gridlines tool in the Chart toolbar. If the chart does not have gridlines, Excel will add them. If the chart has gridlines, Excel will delete them.

Adding or deleting major and minor gridlines using the Gridlines command

To add or delete major and minor gridlines using the Gridlines command:

1. Open the chart you want to change. (If it is embedded, double-click on it.)

2. Click on Chart in the menu bar to open the Chart menu.

3. Click on Gridlines to display the Gridlines dialog box.

4. Select the check boxes to add gridlines to your chart. Clear the check boxes to delete any gridlines you do not want in your chart.

5. Click on OK.

Formatting gridlines

To format gridlines:

1. To format a major gridline, double-click on one of the major gridlines. To format a minor gridline, double-click on one of the minor gridlines.

2. The Patterns dialog box is displayed.

3. Select the options you want to use for the gridlines.

4. Click on OK.

Adding, Deleting, and Formatting a Chart Arrow

You can add arrows to your charts to point to information you want to emphasize, or to identify data. Once you have added an arrow to your chart, you can change the style, color, and line weight of the arrow shaft, as well as the style, width, and length of the arrowhead. You can move and resize the arrow by dragging the handles at either end.

Adding one arrow to a chart using the Chart toolbar

You can add one arrow to your chart using the Arrow tool on the Chart toolbar. To add an arrow:

1. Open the chart you want to change. (If the chart is embedded, double-click on the chart to open it.)

2. Click on the Arrow tool (identified by its Arrow icon) on the Chart toolbar.

3. Drag the handles at either end of the arrow to move and size it.

Adding one or several arrows to a chart using the Add Arrow command

You can add more than one arrow to your chart using the Add Arrow command. To add one or several arrows to a chart:

1. Open the chart you want to change. (If the chart is embedded, double-click on it.)

2. Click on Chart in the menu bar to open the Chart menu.

3. Click on Add Arrow to insert an arrow into your chart.

4. Drag the handles at either end of the arrow to move or size it.

 If the Delete Arrow command is displayed instead of the Add Arrow command, it means that you have selected an existing arrow. To add another arrow, select any item in the chart that is not an arrow and **N O T E** repeat steps 2, 3, and 4 above.

Deleting a chart arrow

You can select and delete any arrow in a chart. To delete an arrow:

1. Open the chart you want to change. (If the chart is embedded, double-click on it.)
2. Select the arrow you want to delete.
3. Click on Chart in the menu bar to open the Chart menu.
4. Click on Delete Arrow.

The arrow will be deleted from the chart.

Formatting an arrow

To change the format of the arrow:

1. Double-click on the arrow to display the Patterns dialog box.
2. Under Line, select the options you want for the arrowshaft.
3. Under Arrow Head, select the options you want for the arrowhead.
4. Click on OK.

Drawing Graphic Objects

You can use the tools in the drawing toolbar to create lines, ovals, rectangles, arcs, and polygons. You can also create freehand drawings and filled shapes. The shapes you create with the drawing tools are know as **graphic objects**. If you have never tried drawing with a mouse before, you might find it a bit cumbersome. Keep at it—you'll get the knack eventually. If you have worked with other drawing programs, you will find it very easy to create graphic objects in Excel.

You can create transparent or filled shapes by selecting the Oval tool or the Filled Oval tool. For example, if you select the Oval tool, you will create a transparent oval. If you select the Filled Oval tool, you will create a filled oval. Later in the chapter, you will learn how to fill shapes with different colors and patterns.

Drawing Lines and Shapes

Let's start off by drawing simple shapes. You must have the drawing toolbar displayed.

1. Click on the Line tool. The mouse pointer changes shape.
2. Place the pointer where you want to begin drawing a line.

3. Drag with the mouse until the line is the position and angle you want.

4. Release the mouse button. The line has been drawn.

Practice creating other shapes using the Unfilled Oval, Rectangle, and Arc tools in the drawing toolbar. To restrict lines to horizontal, vertical, or 45-degree angles, hold down the Shift key while you draw. To change the Oval tool to a Circle tool, or the Rectangle tool to a Square tool, hold down the Shift key while you draw.

You can align graphic objects with gridlines in a worksheet by holding down the Alt key while you draw.

When you select a tool by double-clicking on it, the tool stays selected until you click on it again, select another tool, or click on another part of the worksheet. This makes it easy to draw the same shape over and over. To draw multiple lines, rectangles, or other graphic objects:

1. Double-click on the tool you want to use to create the shape.

2. Draw the first graphic object.

3. Release the mouse button. The tool is still selected and you can move to another location on the worksheet.

4. Draw additional shapes with the same tool.

5. When you are finished, deselect the tool.

Creating a Drawing Using the Freehand Tool

You can draw your own freehand shapes and drawings using the Freehand tool. To draw in a continuous line, click on the tool and start drawing. When you release the mouse button, the tool will be deselected.

To keep the tool selected so that you can continue drawing even after releasing the mouse button, double-click on the freehand tool. The tool will stay selected until you click on it again, select another tool, or double-click on another location in the worksheet.

To create a freehand drawing:

1. Click on the freehand tool.

2. Place the pointer where you want to start the drawing and click.

2. Drag to create the drawing you want.

3. When you are finished, release the mouse button.

Creating a Drawing Using the Freehand Polygon Tool

A polygon is simply a flat plane enclosed by many angles. You can create a polygon using the Freehand tool or the Freehand Polygon tool. To draw a polygon with straight lines or a combination of straight lines and freehand lines, use the Freehand Polygon tool. If your drawing is comprised of all freehand lines, use the Freehand tool, as described in the previous section.

Drawing straight lines using the Freehand Polygon tool

To draw straight lines using the Freehand Polygon tool:

1. Click on the Freehand Polygon tool.
2. Place the mouse pointer where you want to begin drawing and click.
3. Without pressing the mouse button, move the mouse in the direction you want to draw the line. As you move the mouse, the line will be drawn. Move the mouse to where you want the next line to begin.
4. Click to form a vortex of the polygon, and begin the next line.
5. Move the mouse in the direction you want to draw the next line.
6. Repeat steps 4 and 5 until the polygon is complete.
7. Double-click to end the drawing or, if the last line closes the polygon, click at the location where you began the drawing.

Drawing a combination of straight lines and freehand lines

To draw a combination of straight lines and freehand lines using the Freehand Polygon tool:

1. Click on the Freehand Polygon tool.
2. Place the mouse pointer where you want to begin drawing.
3. To draw freehand, drag the mouse as you draw.
4. To draw straight lines, click where you want to begin and, without pressing down on the mouse button, move the mouse to draw the line. Click and draw the next line.
5. To switch from a straight line to a freehand line, drag the mouse. To switch from a freehand line to a straight line, release the mouse button and move the mouse. Click to end the line.

6. Double-click to end the drawing or, if the last line closes the polygon, click where you began the drawing.

Selecting Graphic Objects

To move or size a drawn or imported graphic object, you must first select it. When you select a graphic object, handles appear on the object's border. The handles are attached to a frame. For a rectangle or line, the frame is the actual border of the graphic. For an arc, polygon, or oval, the frame is an invisible rectangle surrounding the object.

You can select an object by clicking on it or by using the Selection tool. You can select an object only when the mouse pointer is in the shape of an arrow.

Selecting a Graphic Object Using the Mouse Pointer

To select a graphic object using the mouse pointer:

1. Place the mouse pointer on the border of the graphic object.
2. Click on the object. The object is selected if handles appear. If you do not see handles, the object is not selected. Try again, making sure the pointer is in the shape of an arrow before you click.

Selecting Multiple Graphic Objects Using the Mouse Pointer

To select multiple graphic objects using the mouse pointer:

1. Place the mouse pointer on the border of the first graphic object you want to select.
2. Click on the object. The object is selected if handles appear. If you do not see handles, the object is not selected. Try again, making sure the pointer is in the shape of an arrow before you click.
3. Holding down the Ctrl key, repeat steps 1 and 2 for each object you want to select.

Selecting Multiple Graphic Objects in One Area Using the Selection Tool

Use the Selection tool to select multiple graphic objects in one area.

1. Click on the Selection tool.

2. Place the mouse pointer on one corner of the area containing the objects you want to select.

3. Drag the mouse to create a large rectangle enclosing all of the objects you want to select. An object must be entirely enclosed in the rectangle to be selected.

4. Release the mouse button. All of the objects in the selection rectangle are selected.

5. To deselect the selection tool, click on it again.

Selecting Graphic Objects in Multiple Areas Using the Selection Tool

You can also use the selection tool to select graphic objects in multiple areas.

1. Click on the Selection tool.

2. Place the mouse pointer on one corner of the first area containing the objects you want to select.

3. Drag the mouse to create a large rectangle enclosing all of the objects you want to select in the first area. An object must be entirely enclosed in the rectangle to be selected.

4. Release the mouse button. All of the objects in the selection rectangle are selected.

5. To select objects in additional areas, hold down the Ctrl key and repeat steps 2 through 4.

6. To deselect the Selection tool, click on it again.

Selecting All Graphic Objects in a Worksheet

You can select all graphic objects in a worksheet at once:

1. Click on Formula in the menu bar to open the Formula menu.

2. Click on Select Special to display the Select Special dialog box.

3. Select Objects in the Select box.

4. Click on OK. All of the graphic objects have been selected.

 When you select a graphic object, its number and type appear in the formula bar.

N O T E

Removing a Graphic Object from a Selection

If you have selected only one graphic object, you can deselect it by selecting another object or by clicking on another location in the worksheet.

If you have selected more than one graphic object, you can remove one or more objects from the selection.

To remove an object from the selection, hold down the Ctrl key and click on the graphic object you want to deselect.

To remove a group of objects from a selection, click on the Selection tool, and, while holding down the Ctrl key, enclose the objects you want to deselect from the selection rectangle.

Object Groups

If you are working with many graphic objects, you can create an object group. Objects that are grouped together can be moved, sized, edited, and formatted as a group. If you want to work with an individual object that is part of a group, you must first ungroup the objects.

Creating an Object Group

To group graphic objects:

1. Select the objects you want to group together.

2. Click on the Group tool, or choose the Group command from the Format menu.

Ungrouping Graphic Objects

To ungroup graphic objects:

1. Select the grouped objects you want to ungroup.
2. Click the Ungroup tool; or choose the Ungroup command in the Format menu.

Editing Graphic Objects

Graphic objects can be cell-oriented or page-oriented. If an object is attached to its underlying cell or cells, it will be moved or sized when the cell is moved or sized. Graphics that are not attached to cells are page-oriented and will remain in place even if the underlying cell is moved or sized. Objects can be attached so that they move with their underlying cells, but do not change size if the size of the cells changes.

When an object is moved and sized with its underlying cells, it maintains the position and size of the upper-left corner and lower-right corner of the underlying cells. When an object is moved but not sized with its underlying cells, it is positioned with the upper-left corner of the underlying cells.

All objects that are not imported from other applications are initially formatted to move and size with their underlying cells.

Attaching and Unattaching Objects from Cells

To attach or unattach objects from their cells:

1. Select the object you want to attach or unattach.
2. Click on Format in the menu bar to open the Format menu.
3. Click on Object Properties to display the Object Properties dialog box.
4. Select the option you want.
5. Click on OK.

An attached object moves only when the cell it is attached to moves. Using the Cut or Copy commands to move the contents of a cell will not affect the object, since these commands affect only the cell contents, not the cell structure.

N O T E

Sizing a Graphic Object

You size a graphic object by dragging its handles. If more than one object is selected, all of the selected objects will be sized proportionately. If you size one object in an object group, all of the objects in the group will be sized.

Graphic handles appear in the corners and on the sides of the frame of a graphic object. To size an object vertically or horizontally, drag the handles that appear on the sides of the object. To drag an object in both dimensions at once, drag a corner handle.

To size a graphic object:

1. Select the object you want to size.
2. Position the mouse pointer (it should be in the shape of a double-headed arrow) over a handle.
3. Drag the handle to size the object. To proportionally size an object, hold down the Shift key while you drag a corner handle.

Moving a Graphic Object

To move a graphic object, drag the object to a new location or use the Cut and Paste command. Using Cut and Paste gives you more control over where you place the object.

To move a graphic object by dragging:

1. Select the object you want to move.
2. Position the mouse pointer on the border of the object.
3. Drag the object to its new location. To move the object horizontally or vertically, hold down the Shift key while you drag.

To move a graphic object using Cut and Paste:

1. Select the object you want to move.
2. Click on Edit in the menu bar to open the Edit menu.
3. Click on Cut to move the object to the Windows Clipboard.
4. Select the cell to which you want to move the object.
5. Click on Edit in the menu bar to open the Edit menu.
6. Click on Paste to paste the object from the Clipboard to its new location.

Copying a Graphic Object

You can copy a graphic object by dragging it or by using the Copy and Paste commands.

To copy an object by dragging:

1. Select the object you want to copy.

2. Place the mouse pointer on the border of the graphic object.

3. While holding down the Ctrl key, drag the object to its new location. To drag vertically or horizontally, hold down the Ctrl and Shift keys while you drag.

When copying or moving an object, you can align the object to a cell gridline by holding down the Alt key while dragging the object.

N O T E

To copy a graphic object using the Copy and Paste command:

1. Select the object you want to copy.

2. Click on Edit in the menu bar to open the Edit menu.

3. Click on Copy. The object is copied to the Windows Clipboard.

4. Select the cell to which you want to copy the object.

5. Click on Edit in the menu bar to open the Edit menu.

6. Click on Paste. The object is pasted from the Clipboard to its new location.

Sometimes when you create, move, or size graphic objects they will overlap. If an object is completely covered, select the object overlapping it and click the Send to Back tool. The overlapped object will be brought to the forefront. If an object is partially covered, select the object you want to bring to the forefront and click the Bring to Front tool.

N O T E

Deleting a Graphic Object

To delete a graphic object:

1. Select the object you want to delete.

2. Click on Edit in the menu bar to open the Edit menu.

3. To move the object into the Clipboard, click on Cut. The object can then be pasted to another location in the document. If you want to clear the object completely, click on Clear.

You can undo the deletion immediately after deleting. To undo the deletion:

1. Click on Edit in the menu bar to open the Edit menu.
2. Click on Undo.

Formatting and Editing Graphic Objects

Editing most graphic objects is very simple—you can change the size or placement of the object by sizing or moving it. However, graphics created using the Freehand tool or Freehand Polygon tool are a little more complex to edit, since it is often necessary to reshape only sections of the drawing. This is done using the Reshape tool. When you select the Reshape tool, selection handles appear at close intervals along the freehand line and at the beginning and end of each straight line. You can reshape the drawing using any of these handles.

Editing Polygons and Freehand Drawings

To edit a polygon or freehand drawing:

1. Select the drawing you want to edit.
2. Click on the Reshape tool. Selection handles appear at close intervals along the drawing.
3. Drag a handle to reshape the drawing.
   - ▼ To delete a vertex in a polygon, hold down the Shift key and click the vertex handle.
   - ▼ To add a vertex to a polygon, hold down the Shift key, position the mouse on a line of the polygon, and drag the pointer to the location where you want the new vertex.
4. Repeat steps 2 and 3 until you have finished reshaping the drawing.
5. Click on the Reshape tool to deselect it.

Formatting Graphic Objects

You can format an object's borders and fill the object with a color and/or a pattern. You can format both transparent and filled objects.

To format an object:

1. Place the mouse pointer on the object you want to format and double-click, to display the Patterns dialog box.

2. In the Border options box, select the border options you want to apply to the object.

3. In the Fill options box, select the fill options you want to apply to the object. The Sample box in the lower-right corner of the dialog box will display the object with the selected options.

4. Click on OK. The selected graphic object has been formatted with your choices.

You can also change the color of an object using the Color tool.

1. Select the object whose color you want to change.

2. Click on the Color tool. Continue clicking on the tool until the object turns the color you want.

3. To return to previous colors in the Color tool, hold down the Shift key while you click on the Color tool.

Printing Graphic Objects

You can determine which graphic objects, if any, will print when the worksheet is printed. If you print a graphic object that has been formatted with colors or patterns, the colors and patterns will print only if your printer is capable of supporting them.

To print a worksheet that contains objects:

1. Select the objects you want to print.

2. Click on Format in the menu bar to open the Format menu.

3. Click on Object Properties to display the Object Properties dialog box.

4. Select Print Object.

5. Click on OK. The selected objects will print.

To print a worksheet without graphic objects:

1. Select the objects you do not want to print.

2. Click on Format in the menu bar to open the Format menu.

3. Click on Object Properties to display the Object Properties dialog box.

4. Clear the Print Object check box.

5. Click on OK. The selected objects will not print.

Creating Pictures

You can create pictures from charts, cells, or graphic objects and then copy the pictures to different locations in a worksheet or to a different worksheet.

When you copy a chart as a picture, the chart is not linked to its original source data on the worksheet. You can copy an embedded chart or a chart document as a picture.

When you copy a picture of a linked cell, you can link the picture so that it automatically updates when you update the data. Both the data and the cell format will be updated.

If you want a picture to appear as it would print, the formatting and colors will be changed to reflect the formatting and colors supported by the printer that was selected when the picture was created. You can select this option when you create the picture.

After a picture is pasted into a worksheet, it can be moved or sized using the same techniques for moving and sizing any graphic object.

You can import graphics from other applications and export graphics from Excel to other applications. Excel will accept graphics from and export graphics to any application that can support the Clipboard picture and bitmap formats. Consult your Windows manual for more information about acceptable formats. Once the graphic is in the Clipboard, it can be pasted into Excel or another application using the Paste command.

To create a picture by copying a chart, cell, or object:

1. Select the chart, cell(s), or object(s) you want to copy.

2. Hold down the Shift key and click on Edit in the menu bar to open the Edit menu.

3. Click on Copy Picture to display the Copy Picture dialog box, shown in Figure 7.11.

4. Select from the following options:

   ▼ To copy the graphic as it appears on screen, choose As Shown On Screen in the Appearance box.

   ▼ To copy the graphic as it would be printed, choose As Shown When Printed in the Appearance box.

▼ To create the picture as a bitmapped image, choose Bitmap in the Format box. A bitmapped image is comprised of pixels and may not scale proportionately when you size it.

▼ To create the picture as a picture image, choose Picture in the Format box. A picture image is a line drawing that will scale proportionately when the picture is sized.

5. Choose OK. The picture has been copied to the Clipboard. Once you have created a picture, you can copy it to a different worksheet, or to another location in the same worksheet.

6. Click on the location where you want to paste the picture.

7. Click on Edit in the menu bar to open the Edit menu.

8. Click on Paste. The picture is pasted to the new location.

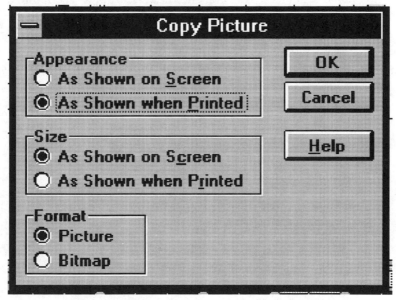

Figure 7.11 *The Copy Picture dialog box.*

To copy and paste a linked cell to a picture:

1. Select the cell(s) you want to copy.

2. Click on Edit in the menu bar to open the Edit menu.

3. Click on Copy.

4. Select the location where you want to paste the cell(s).

5. Hold down the Shift key and click on Edit in the menu bar to open the Edit menu.

6. Choose Paste Picture Link.

To paste a picture into another application, switch to the application and follow that application's instructions for copying graphics from the Clipboard.

Creating Slide Shows

Slide shows are an exciting new feature of Excel 4.0 that allow you to really jazz up your presentations. You can select data or graphics, incorporate them into a slide show, and then show the slides on a computer screen. This is a great accompaniment to any presentation, and is much more efficient and cost-effective than having your graphs, worksheets, and so forth turned into transparencies or other display devices. You can even use sounds in your slides if you are using Windows 3.1 or Windows 3.0 with Multimedia Extensions 1.0 or later.

Slides are pasted from the Clipboard into a slide show template. To open the template:

1. Click on File in the menu bar to open the File menu.

2. Click on New to display the New dialog box.

3. Select Slides and click on OK. A slide show template is opened, as shown in Figure 7.12.

The mouse pointer changes shape when you move it to any of the command buttons in the slide show template.

Creating a Slide from a Range of Cells

You can create a slide from a cell or a range of cells in a worksheet. If you do not want the gridlines to show in the slide, turn them off in the Options Display command before you copy the cell or range. Before you start, open the slide show template. To create a slide from a range of cells:

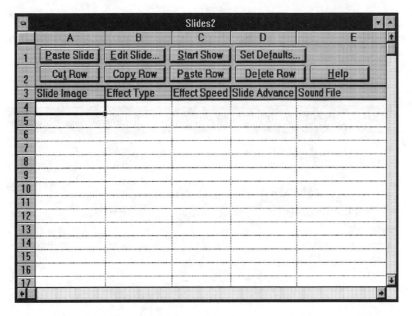

Figure 7.12 *A slide show template.*

1. Select the cell or range you want to use in the slide.

2. Click on the Copy tool in the standard toolbar, or on the Copy command in the Edit menu.

3. Switch to the slide show template.

4. Choose the Paste Slide button. The slide is pasted into the template and the Edit Slide dialog box is displayed, as shown in Figure 7.13.

5. Select from the following options:

   ▼ **Effect.** You can choose the effect you want during the transition from one slide to the next. Clicking on the Test button will show you the results of each choice.

   ▼ **Speed.** This choice allows you to control the speed of the transition effect. Use the scroll arrows or move the scroll box to speed up or slow down the transition effect.

   ▼ **Advance.** This choice allows you to choose between manual and timed advancement between slides. If you choose Manual, you can advance the slide by clicking the left mouse button or pressing the Spacebar. If you choose Timed, the slides will automatically advance at the timed intervals (in seconds) that you enter in the Timed text box.

▼ **Sound.** If your system is capable of using the sound feature, you can use the sound option to import and record sounds to be used during the transition between slides.

6. Choose OK.

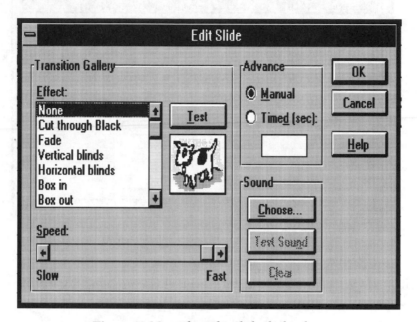

Figure 7.13   *The Edit Slide dialog box.*

The image is pasted into the template and the options to be used with the image in the slide show are selected. A picture of the range of cells selected is pasted into Column A of the template as a slide. Columns B, C, D, and E contain information about how the slide is to be used in the slide show.

Creating a Slide Show from an Embedded Chart or a Graphic

You can use embedded charts, chart documents, or graphics in a slide show. You can copy an embedded chart or graphic into the Clipboard by selecting the range of cells under the chart or graphic and then using the Copy tool or the Copy command to copy the data to the Clipboard. However, an easier and more effective way is to copy the chart or graphic as a picture using the Copy Picture command. To create a slide from a chart or graphic:

1. Select the range of cells under the embedded chart or graphic and click on the Copy tool, or select Copy from the Edit menu. Or, select the chart or graphic and, while holding down the Shift key, select the Copy Picture command from the Edit menu.

3. Switch to the slide show template.

4. Choose the Paste Slide button. The slide is pasted into the template and the Edit Slide dialog box is displayed.

5. Select the options you want in the Edit Slide dialog box.

6. Choose OK.

Do not use the Cut command to copy the data into the Clipboard. The graphic you use must remain in its original position in the worksheet in order to be used as a slide.

Changing a Slide Show's Defaults

To change a slide show's defaults, click on the Set Defaults button in the template. The Set Defaults dialog box is displayed, which provides you with the same choices as the Edit Slide Dialog box. The choices you make will affect any new slides you create.

Editing, Moving, Copying, or Deleting Slides

You can edit the attributes of any slide in a slide show and move, copy, or delete slides.

Editing a slide

When you edit a slide, you can change the transition effects in the Edit Slide dialog box. To edit a slide:

1. On the slide show template, select any cell in the row that contains the slide you want to edit.

2. Click on the Edit Slide button to display the Edit Slide dialog box.

3. Choose the options you want in the slide.

4. Click on OK. The new options have been applied to the slide.

Moving a slide

You can rearrange the order of slides by moving them. To move a slide:

1. On the slide show template, select any cell in the row that contains the slide you want to move.
2. Click on the Cut Row button.
3. Select the row above which you want to insert the slide.
4. Choose the Paste Row button to paste the slide above the currently selected row.

Copying a slide

You can repeat a slide by copying it to another location in the slide show. To copy a slide:

1. On the slide show template, select any cell in the row that contains the slide you want to copy.
2. Click on the Copy Row button.
3. Select the row above which you want to copy the slide.
4. Click on the Paste Row button. The slide is pasted above the currently selected row.

Deleting a slide

To delete a slide:

1. On the slide show template, select any cell in the row that contains the slide you want to delete.
2. Click on the Delete Row button to delete the slide.

Running a Slide Show

You can choose to run a slide show only once or have it repeat in a continuous loop until you stop it. You can also choose with which slide to start the show. To run a slide show:

1. In the slide show template, click on the Start Show button. The Start Show dialog box is displayed, as shown in Figure 7.14.
    ▼ If you want the show to run in a continuous loop until you stop it, select the Repeat Show Until Esc is Pressed box.

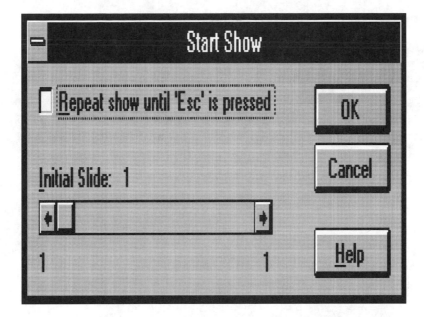

Figure 7.14   *The Start Show dialog box.*

▼ If you want to begin with a slide other than the first one, use the Initial Slide bar to select the slide with which you want to begin the show.

2. Select OK. The show will begin running. If you have selected a manual transition in the Edit Slide dialog box, click the left mouse button or press the Spacebar to advance to the next slide.

To interrupt the slide show at any time, press the Esc key. The Slide Show Options dialog box is displayed. Select the options you want.

Saving a Slide Show

To save a slide show:

1. Switch to the slide show template.

2. Click on File in the menu bar to open the File menu.

3. Click on Save to display the Save As dialog box.

4. Give the slide show a name. Excel will automatically save the slide show as a worksheet, giving it an .XLS extension.

5. Click on OK.

Opening an Existing Slide Show

To open an existing slide show:

1. Click on File in the menu bar to open the File menu.
2. Select the slide show you want to open from the file list.
3. Click on OK to open the slide show.

Chapter 8

REFINING THE PROGRAM

Once you have designed and written a custom program, you can refine it by running the macros automatically and by using the macro functions to create custom menu bars, commands, and toolbars. Taking advantage of these functions allows you to auto-mate the program completely, making life easier for the end user.

Creating Macros that Run Automatically

You can define a macro that runs automatically every time you open or close a docu-ment, when you switch document windows, or when a specific event occurs. You can also define a macro that prevents a document from being closed unless it has been saved, recalculated, or printed.

Defining a Macro that Runs Automatically

You can define a macro to run automatically whenever a specific document is opened or closed, or when you switch document windows.

1. Open the document for which you want to define a macro to run automatically.
2. Click on Formula in the menu bar to open the Formula menu.
3. Choose Define Name to display the Define Name dialog box, as shown in Figure 8.1.
4. In the Name text box, enter a name as follows:

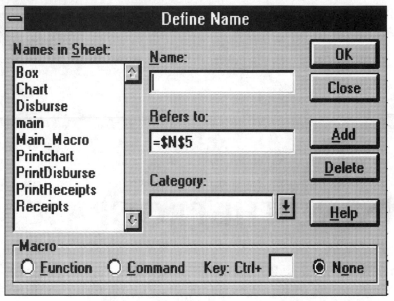

Figure 8.1 *The Define Name dialog box.*

▼ Type a name that starts with AUTO_OPEN to run the macro when the document is opened.

▼ Type a name that starts with AUTO_CLOSE to run the macro when the document is closed. You can include the formula =HALT(TRUE) within the auto-close macro to stop the macro and prevent the document from being closed. This formula is usually used with the IF function to prevent the document from being closed unless the user has performed a certain action, such as saving or printing the document.

▼ Type a name that starts with AUTO_ACTIVATE to run the macro when the document window is activated (when you switch to the document window that contains the document).

▼ Type a name that starts with AUTO_DEACTIVATE to run the macro when the document window is deactivated (when you switch from one document window to another).

5. In the Refers To text box, enter the name or reference of the macro you want to run. If you enter an external reference, Excel will automatically open the macro sheet before running the macro.

6. Select OK.

When you enter a name that begins with AUTO_ACTIVATE or AUTO_DEACTIVATE, the macro will run only when you switch to or from a document window.

Using Event-Triggered Macros

You can trigger a macro to run when an event occurs other than opening or closing a document or switching a document window. Certain functions will automatically run a macro when a specific event occurs. The macro sheet that contains these functions must be opened before the macros can run automatically. The following table lists the functions that run a macro automatically when a specific event or keystroke occurs. For a more detailed explanation of these functions, refer to Chapter 3.

Function	Action
CANCEL.KEY	Runs a specified macro when you cancel an operation or macro.
ERROR	Runs a specified macro when an error is encountered in a macro that is currently running.
ON.DATA	Runs a specified macro when another application sends data to Excel using Dynamic Data Exchange.
ON.DOUBLECLICK	Runs a specified macro when you double-click a cell or an object.
ON.ENTRY	Runs a specified macro when data is entered.
ON.KEY	Runs a specified macro when a certain key is pressed. This functions allows you to assign a Help key or a Save key.
ON.RECALC	Runs a specified macro when a certain document is recalculated.
ON.TIME	Runs a specified macro at a specified time. For this function to work, both Excel and the macro sheet must be open at the time specified.

Function	Action
ON.WINDOW	Runs a specified macro when the user switches to a specified window.

Creating a Custom Menu Bar

You can create or delete custom menu bars in Excel. Each menu bar must contain one or more menus (creating custom menus is explained in the "Creating a Custom Menu" section later in this chapter).

Restoring a Built-in Menu Bar

To restore a built-in menu bar in Excel, you must use the =ADD.BAR macro function, which uses the following syntax:

```
=ADD.BAR(bar_num)
```

When you want to restore a built-in menu bar, bar_num is the number of the built-in menu bar that you want to restore. The ID numbers of all the built-in menu bars in Excel for Windows can be found in the section entitled "Setting Up a Menu Table" later in this chapter.

Adding a Custom Menu Bar

To add a new menu bar in Excel, use the =ADD.BAR macro function with the following syntax:

```
=ADD.BAR()
```

The =ADD.BAR function creates a new, empty menu bar and returns the menu bar number, but it does not display the menu bar or add any menus to it. Excel allows you to define up to fifteen custom menu bars at one time. If you try to carry out an =ADD.BAR function when you already have fifteen custom menu bars defined, Excel will return the #VALUE error value.

Displaying a Custom Menu Bar

Once you add a custom menu bar, you must use the =SHOW.BAR macro function to display it. The =SHOW.BAR function uses the following syntax:

```
=SHOW.BAR(bar_num)
```

When you want to display a custom menu bar or add menus or commands to it, you identify the menu bar by using its ID number. Another way to identify the menu bar is by using the cell address that contains the =ADD.BAR() function on your macro sheet. For example, if cell A1 contains the =ADD.BAR() function, you can use the following function to display the new menu bar:

```
=SHOW.BAR(A1)
```

When you display a custom menu bar, you disable the automatic menu bar switching for different document types in Excel. For example, if you display a custom menu bar and then switch to a chart, the built-in chart menu will not be displayed. To enable automatic menu bar switching after you have displayed a custom menu bar, display a built-in menu bar using the =SHOW.BAR(bar_num) function where bar_num is one of the built-in menu bar ID numbers.

The =SHOW.BAR() function can also be used in combination with other functions to switch between menu bars. For example, you could use the =ON.KEY macro function to run the Account macro, which contains the =SHOW.BAR function, and display a custom menu bar whenever you press the F1 key:

```
=ON.KEY("{F1}","ACCOUNT")
```

Deleting a Custom Menu Bar

To delete a custom menu bar, use the macro function:

```
=DELETE.BAR(bar_num)
```

where bar_num is the ID number of the menu bar you have added. You can also name the cell on the macro sheet containing the =ADD.BAR function that creates the menu bar you want to delete, then use the named reference instead of the ID number of the menu bar. For example, if cell A1 on the macro sheet contains the function =ADD.BAR(), and you name the cell AccountBar, the following function will delete the menu bar:

```
=DELETE.BAR(AccountBar)
```

Creating a Custom Menu

You can use macros to create custom menus and to add, delete, rename, or disable built-in or custom menus on built-in or custom menu bars in Excel. For example, you can add a new menu to the Accounting worksheet menu bar. When you click on

Accounting in the menu bar, the Accounting menu is displayed and you can then click on the command you want to execute.

Setting Up a Menu Table

To add a menu to an existing menu bar, you must first create a **menu table**. This is an area on your macro sheet that contains the information Excel needs to set up the menu. The menu table is four columns wide and contains menu and command names, command macro names, status messages, and Help topics, as shown in Figure 8.2.

The first cell in column 1 contains the menu name (Accounting) that will appear in the menu bar, followed by the commands that will appear in the Accounting menu (Reports, Accounts Receivable, Accounts Payable, and General Ledger). Cells B2 through B5 contain the command macros that will be executed when the user selects one of the commands from the menu. The third column produces a status bar message for the selected command. For example, if the user selects the command in cell A2 (Reports), the Reports macro listed in cell B2 will run, and the status bar message will say *Choose a Report*. The last column contains the custom Help topic for each command in the menu.

If you want to include a separator line in the menu between one command and another, you must insert a cell that contains a single hyphen (-) between the two commands, as shown in Figure 8.3.

If you want to be able to use a specified key to choose a command or select a menu, precede the letter for that key by an ampersand (&). For example, to use the letter *a* to select the Account menu, type:

```
&Account
```

into cell A1 of the menu table shown in Figure 8.2.

If you want an ampersand to appear in the menu name or command, you must type two ampersands. For example, to have the Account menu name appear as *Account&Reports,* type:

```
Account&&Reports
```

into cell A1 of the menu table.

Before you can add a menu to an existing menu bar in Excel, you must know the number of the menu bar to which you want to add a menu. Only one menu bar at a time can be displayed in Excel. Excel has four menu bars:

1. The Worksheet menu bar has an ID number of 1 or 5, and looks like this:

```
File Edit Formula Format Data Options Macro Window Help
```

Figure 8.2   *Macro sheet with menu table for columns wide.*

Figure 8.3   *The menu table with a separator line.*

2. The Chart menu bar has an ID number of 2 or 6, and looks like this:

```
File Edit Gallery Chart Format Macro Window Help
```

3. The Null menu bar has an ID number of 3, and looks like this:

```
File Help
```

4. The Info Window menu bar has an ID number of 4, and looks like this:

```
File Info Macro Window Help
```

Adding a Menu

If you want to add a menu to a menu bar, you must use the following macro function:

```
=ADD.MENU(bar_num,menu_ref,position)
```

Bar_num is replaced by the ID number of the menu bar to which you want to add a menu. Menu_ref is replaced by the range of cells on the macro sheet that contain the menu table. Position is optional. If no position is specified, the menu is added immediately to the right of the rightmost menu on the menu bar. If you want to place the new menu anywhere else on the menu bar, you must specify the position of the new menu. Menus on a menu bar are numbered from left to right, starting with number 1, and are added to the left of the menu position specified. For example, the function:

```
=ADD.MENU(1,A1:D5,2)
```

adds the menu described in Figure 8.2 (cells A1:D5) to the Worksheet menu bar (bar_num = 1) between the File and Edit menus on the menu bar (position = 2).

Renaming a Menu

To rename a menu, use the RENAME.COMMAND function, which contains the following arguments:

```
=RENAME.COMMAND(bar_num,menu,command,name_text)
```

where bar_num is the ID number of the menu bar you wish to rename, menu is the name of the menu you want to change, command is replaced with a zero (0) when you want to rename a menu, and name_text is the new name you want the menu to have. For example,

```
=RENAME.COMMAND(1,"Accounting",0,"Accounts")
```

will rename the Accounting menu in the Worksheet menu bar to Accounts.

Disabling a Menu on a Menu Bar

When you disable a menu, the menu name is dimmed and you cannot select the menu. You cannot disable built-in menus. To disable a menu, use the ENABLE.COMMAND:

```
=ENABLE.COMMAND(bar_num,menu,command,enable)
```

Bar_num is the number of the menu bar that contains the menu, menu is the name of the menu on the menu bar, command must be replaced by a zero (0), and enable is a logical value. If enable is TRUE, the menu is enabled; if enable is FALSE, the menu is disabled. Therefore, the function

```
=ENABLE.COMMAND(1,"Accounting",0,FALSE)
```

disables the Accounting menu on the Worksheet menu bar.

Deleting a Menu from a Menu Bar

To delete a menu from a menu bar, use the =DELETE.MENU function:

```
=DELETE.MENU(bar_num,menu)
```

Bar_num is the menu bar from which you want to delete a menu, and menu is the name of the menu you want to delete. For example:

```
=DELETE.MENU(1,"Accounting")
```

will delete the Accounting menu from the Worksheet menu bar. When you delete a menu from a menu bar, all of the menus to the right of the deleted menu shift one position to the left.

Creating a Custom Command

You can create custom menu commands to add, delete, rename, or disable built-in or custom commands on built-in or custom menus in Excel. Custom commands added to a menu run macros that you have created, making life easier for the user.

Setting Up a Command Table

To add a command to an existing menu, you must first create a **command table**. This is an area on your macro sheet that contains the information Excel needs for the command. The command table is four columns wide and contains the command names, command macro names, status messages, and Help topics, as shown in Figure 8.2. The first cell in column 1 contains the menu name (Accounting) that will appear in the menu bar, followed by the commands that will appear in the Accounting menu (Reports, Accounts Receivable, Accounts Payable, and General Ledger). Cells B2 through B5 contain the command macros that will be executed when the user selects one of the commands in the menu. For example, if the user selects the command in cell A2 (Reports), the Reports macro listed in cell B2 will run. The third column produces a status bar message for the selected command. For example, if the user selects Reports, the status bar message will say *Choose a Report*. The last column contains the custom Help topic for each command in the menu.

If you want to include a separator line in the menu between one command and another, you must insert a cell that contains a single hyphen (-) between the two commands, as shown in Figure 8.3.

If you want to be able to use a specified key to choose a command or select a menu, precede the letter for that key by an ampersand (&). For example, in the screen shown in Figure 8.2, to use the letter *r* to select the Reports command in the Accounting menu, type:

```
&Report
```

into cell A2.

If you want an ampersand to appear in the menu name or command, you must type two ampersands. For example, to have the Reports command appear as *Reports&Statements,* type:

```
Reports&&Statements
```

into cell A2.

Before you can add a command to an existing menu, you must know the number of the menu bar and the name of the menu to which you want to add a command.

Adding a Command to a Menu

If you want to add a command to a menu, use the macro function:

```
=ADD.COMMAND(bar_num,menu,command_ref,position)
```

Bar_num is replaced by the ID number of the menu bar to which you want to add a command. Menu indicates the menu to which you want to add a new command; it can be either the name or the number of the menu to which you want to add a command. Menus are numbered from left to right in the menu bar, and from 1 to 6. Bar_nums 7, 8, and 9 refer to built-in shortcut menus in Excel. The combination of bar_num and menu determines which shortcut menu the command will be added to, as shown in the following table:

Bar_num	Menu	Shortcut menu modified
7	1	Toolbars
7	2	Toolbar tools
7	3	Workbook paging icons
7	4	Cells (worksheet)
7	5	Column selections
7	6	Row selections
7	7	Workbook items
7	8	Cells (macro sheet)
8	1	Drawn or imported objects
8	2	Buttons
8	3	Text boxes
9	1	Chart series
9	2	Chart text
9	3	Chart plot area and walls
9	4	Entire charts
9	5	Chart axes
9	6	Chart gridlines
9	7	Chart floor and arrows
9	8	Chart legends

Any commands added to the Toolbar Tools shortcut menu will be dimmed.

N O T E

Menu_ref is replaced by the range of cells on the macro sheet that contain the command table. Position is optional. If no position is specified, the command is added to the bottom of the menu. If you want to place the new command anywhere else on the menu, you must specify its position. Commands on a menu are numbered from top to bottom, starting with number 1. Position can also be the name of an existing command as text. The new command will be added to the menu directly above the name of the existing command. For example, the function

```
=ADD.COMMAND(1,"Options",A1:D1,"Color Palette")
```

adds the command contained in cells A1:D1 of the macro sheet to the Options menu in the Worksheet menu bar directly above the Color Palette command.

Renaming a Command

To rename a command, use the RENAME.COMMAND function, which contains the following arguments:

```
=RENAME.COMMAND(bar_num,menu,command,name_text)
```

Bar_num is the ID number of the menu bar you wish to rename, menu is the name of the menu that contains the command you want to change, command is replaced with either the name of the command as text or the number of the command in the menu (commands on a menu are numbered from top to bottom starting with 1), and name_text is the new name you want the command to have. For example,

```
=RENAME.COMMAND(1,"Options",Reports,"Accounts")
```

will rename the Reports command menu in the Options menu of the worksheet menu bar to *Accounts*.

Disabling a Command on a Menu

When you disable a command, it is dimmed on the menu to indicate that you cannot select it. To disable a command, use the ENABLE.COMMAND function:

```
=ENABLE.COMMAND(bar_num,menu,command,enable)
```

Bar_num is the number of the menu bar that contains the menu, menu is the name of the menu on the menu bar that contains the command you want to disable, command is the name of the command that you want to disable, and enable is a logical value. If enable is TRUE, the menu is enabled; if enable is FALSE, the menu is disabled. Therefore, the function

```
=ENABLE.COMMAND(1,"Options","Accounting",FALSE)
```

disables the Accounting command on the Options menu on the Worksheet menu bar.

Deleting a Command from a Menu

When you want to delete a command from a menu, use the =DELETE.COMMAND function:

```
=DELETE.COMMAND(bar_num,menu,command)
```

Bar_num is the menu bar that contains the menu, menu is the name of the menu that contains the command you want to delete, and command is the command you want to delete from the menu. For example:

```
=DELETE.COMMAND(1,"Options","Accounting")
```

will delete the Accounting command from the Options menu in the worksheet menu bar. When you delete a command from a menu, all of the commands that follow the deleted command will shift up one position.

Adding or Deleting Checkmarks from a Command

A checkmark next to a command indicates that the command is in effect. Checkmarks are usually used with menu commands that indicate a setting. To add or remove a checkmark from a command, use the macro function:

```
=CHECK.COMMAND(bar_num,menu,command.check)
```

Bar_num is the number of the menu bar that contains the command, menu is the menu that contains the command (menus can be either the name of the menu or its number), and command.check is a logical value that corresponds to the checkmark. If command.check is TRUE, Excel adds a checkmark to the command; if command.check if FALSE, Excel removes the checkmark. For example, the following function adds a checkmark to the Accounting command in the Options menu of the Worksheet menu bar:

```
=CHECK.COMMAND(1,"Options","Accounting",TRUE)
```

Creating a Custom Toolbar

In addition to the built-in toolbars that come with Excel, you can create custom toolbars. When you create a new toolbar, you start with a blank bar and add tools to it.

Let's create a Formula toolbar containing tools we can use to build formulas:

1. From the Options menu or the toolbar shortcut menu, choose Toolbar to display the Toolbars dialog box.

2. In the Toolbar Name textbox, type *Formula*.

3. Choose the Add or Customize command button. Excel displays a new blank toolbar in its own toolbar window, and displays the Customize dialog box so that you can add tools to the new toolbar.

4. In the Categories box, select Formula to display the tools used in building formulas.

5. Drag each of the formula tools to the new Formula toolbar. Excel will resize the toolbar as you add new tools.

6. Click on the Close command button to close the dialog box. You have created a new toolbar called Formula.

You can now display or hide the Formula toolbar, move it in or out of a toolbar dock, and edit it.

 You can also drag tools from another displayed toolbar to the new toolbar as you create it by holding down the Ctrl key and dragging the tool to the new toolbar. If you change your mind while creating the toolbar, N O T E you can remove a tool by dragging it off the toolbar and placing it anywhere there is no toolbar.

Deleting a Custom Toolbar

You can delete custom toolbars, but not built-in toolbars. To delete a custom toolbar:

1. From the Options menu or the toolbar shortcut menu, choose Toolbars.

2. In the Show Toolbars box, highlight the toolbar you want to delete.

3. Click on the Delete command button. The toolbar is deleted.

4. Click on the Close command button to close the dialog box.

Customizing Tools

You can use the built-in tools that come with Excel to create custom tools. You can then use these custom tools to execute macros. You can also copy a tool face to another tool.

Copying a Tool Face to Another Tool

You can use this feature to copy a built-in tool face to another tool in a displayed toolbar. Only the picture on the tool changes; the action remains the same. To copy a tool face to another tool:

1. From the Toolbar shortcut menu, choose Customize or Toolbars; or choose Toolbars from the Options menu.

2. While the Customize or Toolbars dialog box is open, point to the tool you want to copy and click the right mouse button. The Tool shortcut menu is displayed. (Either the Toolbars or Customize dialog box must be open to use the Tool shortcut menu.)

3. Choose Copy Tool Face in the Tool shortcut menu.

4. If the tool you want to copy is not displayed in a toolbar, click the tool you want to copy in the Customize dialog box and choose Copy Tool Face in the Edit menu.

5. Click on the toolbar tool to which you want to copy the face. You can only copy a face to a tool in a displayed toolbar.

6. From the Edit menu or the Tool shortcut menu, choose Paste Tool Face.

You can restore a tool to its original face by clicking on the tool you want to reset and choosing Reset Tool Face from the tool shortcut menu.

N O T E

Creating a Custom Tool and Assigning a Macro to It

You can assign an existing macro to a custom tool.

1. In the Toolbar shortcut menu, choose Customize; or in the Toolbars dialog box click on the Customize command button. The Customize dialog box is displayed.

2. In the Categories box, select Custom to display the Custom tools. None of the custom tools in the dialog box have a macro or an action assigned to them.

3. Drag the tool you want from the Tools box to the position on the toolbar where you want to add the tool. The Assign To Tool dialog box is displayed.

4. In the Assign Macro box, select the name of the command macro 1you want to assign to the tool, or type a macro name or cell reference in the Reference text box.

5. Click on OK. The macro has been assigned to the custom tool.

Creating a Custom Tool and Recording a New Macro for It

1. In the Toolbar shortcut menu, choose Customize; or in the Toolbars dialog box click on the Customize command button. The Customize dialog box is displayed.

2. In the Categories box, select Custom to display the Custom dialog box. None of the tools in the Custom dialog box has a macro or an action assigned to it.

3. Drag the tool you want from the Tools box to the position on the toolbar where you want to add the tool. The Assign To Tool dialog box is displayed.

4. In the Assign To Tool dialog box, click on the Record command button to display the Record Macro dialog box. See Chapter 2 for a detailed explanation of how to use the Record Macro dialog box.

5. When you are finished, choose Stop Recorder from the Macro menu.

Displaying a Custom Toolbar

Once you have created your custom toolbar and custom tools, you can use the SHOW.TOOLBAR macro function to automatically display the toolbar. The SHOW.TOOLBAR function uses the following syntax:

```
=SHOW.TOOLBAR(bar_id,visible,dock,x_pos,y_pos,width)
```

Bar_id is the name or number of the custom toolbar. Visible is a logical value that, if TRUE, specifies that the toolbar is visible; if FALSE, it specifies that the toolbar is hidden. Dock specifies the docking location of the toolbar as described in the following table:

Dock	Position of toolbar
1	Top of workspace
2	Left edge of workspace
3	Right edge of workspace
4	Bottom of workspace
5	Floating

X_pos specifies the horizontal position of the toolbar. Y_pos specifies the vertical position of the toolbar. Finally, width specifies the width of the toolbar measured in points (a point is 1/72 of an inch). For example, the following macro function displays the Accounting toolbar as a floating toolbar:

```
=SHOW.TOOLBAR("Accounting",TRUE,5)
```

Creating a Custom Help Topic

You can create custom Help information that can then be used for custom dialog boxes, commands, and menus, and for messages to be displayed in the course of running a macro. You can enter Help topics in one or several Help files. A Help topic starts with an asterisk, followed by a topic number and a short optional comment describing the Help topic (this description is not shown when the user executes Help). This is followed by the actual Help information. Topics do not have to be in consecutive order in the Help file. For example, to create a Help topic to inform users how to fill in a custom report form, type:

```
*15 Using the report form
Fill in all of the blanks and then choose OK.
```

Save the Help file as a plain-text format. You can also create Help files and Help topics using your word processor. Save the file in plain-text format. Once you have created and saved your Help file, you must convert the file from a plain-text format to the Windows Help file format. To do this, you will need to obtain a copy of the custom Window Help conversion program from Microsoft Corp.

Using a Help topic in a command is explained in the section earlier in this chapter entitled "Setting Up a Command Table." Using a Help topic in a dialog box is discussed in Chapter 5.

Saving and Converting Help Files

Save the Help file as a plain-text format. You can also create Help files and Help topics using your word processor. Save the file in plain-text format. Once you have created and saved your Help file, you must convert the file from a plain-text format to the Windows Help file format. To do this, you will need to obtain a copy of the custom Window Help conversion program from Microsoft.

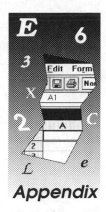

MACROS USED IN THIS BOOK

Examples of Use with ELSE() and END.IF()

```
=INPUT("Do You Want to (S)ave or Save and (P)rint?",2)
  =IF(Print="P")
    =ALERT("Check to see if printer on",1)
    =SAVE()
    =PRINT()
  =ELSE()
    =SAVE()
  =END.IF()
=RETURN()
```

```
=INPUT("Do You Want to (S)ave, Save and (P)rint, or Save and Print a
(R)eport?",2)
  =IF(Print="P")
    =ALERT("Check to see if printer on",1)
    =SAVE()
    =PRINT()
  =ELSE.IF(Print="R")
    =SAVE()
    =Reports()
  =ELSE()
    =SAVE()
  =END.IF()
=RETURN()
```

Examples of Looping.

```
=SET.NAME("done",TRUE)
  =WHILE(done)
    =MESSAGE(TRUE,"This is a Loop")
  =NEXT()
    =MESSAGE(FALSE)
=RETURN()

=FOR("Counter",1,10,1)
  =MESSAGE(TRUE,"This is a Loop")
=NEXT()
  =MESSAGE(FALSE)
=RETURN()

=FOR.CELL("cell_ref","Change",TRUE)
  =FORMULA(cell_ref-10,cell_ref)
=NEXT()
=RETURN()

=SET.NAME("Typos",TRUE)
  =WHILE(Typos)
    =INPUT("Do You Want to (S)ave, Save and (P)rint, or Save and
    Print a (R)eport?",2)
      =IF(Print="P")
        =ALERT("Check to see if printer on",1)
        =SAVE()
        =PRINT()
        =SET.NAME("Typos",FALSE)
      =ELSE.IF(Print="R")
        =SAVE()
```

```
        =Reports()
        =SET.NAME("Typos",FALSE)
    =ELSE.IF(Print="S")
        =SAVE()
        =SET.NAME("Typos",FALSE)
    =ELSE.IF(Print=FALSE)
        =SET.NAME("Typos",FALSE)
    =ELSE()
        =ALERT("You Must Enter ""S"", ""P"", or ""R.""
    Please enter your selection again",2)
    =END.IF()
  =NEXT()
=RETURN()
```

Macros Used to Create a Basic Accounting Program

Main Macro

```
=SET.NAME("Box",TRUE)
  =WHILE(Box)
    =DIALOG.BOX(main)
      =IF(N5=1)
        =Receipts()
      =ELSE.IF(N5=2)
        =Disburse()
      =ELSE.IF(N5=3)
        =Chart()
      =ELSE.IF(N5=4)
        =Printchart()
      =ELSE.IF(N5=5)
        =PrintReceipts()
      =ELSE.IF(N5=6)
        =PrintDisburse()
      =ELSE.IF(N5="")
        =SET.NAME("Box",FALSE)
      =END.IF()
    =NEXT()
=RETURN()
```

Receipts

```
=OPEN("F:\EXCEL4\RECEIPTS.XLS",1)
=DATA.FORM()
=FILE.CLOSE(TRUE)
=SELECT($N$5)
=CLEAR(1)
=RETdURN()
```

Disburse

```
=OPEN("DISBURSE.XLS",3)
=SELECT("R1C1")
=MESSAGE(TRUE,"Click on Tool When Finished")
=PAUSE(FALSE)
=MESSAGE(FALSE)
=FILE.CLOSE(TRUE)
=SELECT($N$5)
=CLEAR(1)
=RETURN()
```

Chart

```
=OPEN("F:\EXCEL4\CHRTACCT.XLS")
=SELECT("R1C1")
=MESSAGE(TRUE,"Click on Tool When Finished")
=PAUSE(FALSE)
=MESSAGE(FALSE)
=FILE.CLOSE(TRUE)
=SELECT($N$5)
=CLEAR(1)
=RETURN()
```

PrintChart

```
=OPEN("F:\EXCEL4\CHRTACCT.XLS")
=PAGE.SETUP("&F","Page
&P",0.75,0.75,1,1,FALSE,FALSE,FALSE,FALSE,1,1,100,1,1,FALSE)
=PRINT(1,,,1,FALSE,FALSE,1,FALSE,1,-2)
=FILE.CLOSE(TRUE)
=SELECT($N$5)
=CLEAR(1)
=RETURN()
```

PrintReceipts

```
=OPEN("F:\EXCEL4\RECEIPTS.XLS",1)
=PRINT?()
=FILE.CLOSE(TRUE)
=SELECT($N$5)
=CLEAR(1)
=RETURN()
```

PrintDisburse

```
=OPEN("F:\EXCEL4\DISBURSE.XLS",1)
=PAGE.SETUP("&F","Page
&P",0.75,0.75,1,1,FALSE,TRUE,FALSE,FALSE,2,5,100,1,1,FALSE)
=PRINT(1,,,1,FALSE,FALSE,1,FALSE,1,-2)
=FILE.CLOSE(TRUE)
=SELECT($N$5)
=CLEAR(1)
=RETURN()
```

The Definition of the Custom Dialog Box

```
        452 204     Main Menu
1  325  63 88            OK
2  324  105 88           Cancel
14 26 36 225 127    Select One
11
12          Enter Receipts
12          Enter Disbursements
12          Edit Chart of Accounts
12          Print Chart of Accounts
12          Print Receipts
12          Print Disbursements
```

Index

Special Characters Index

\# (number sign), as error value indicator, 7

$ (dollar sign), in A1-style of cell referencing, 269

% (percent sign), as percentage operator, 10

^ (caret), as exponentiation operator, 10

& (ampersand), as text join operator, 10

* (asterisk)
  as multiplication operator, 10
  as wildcard in searches, 330-331

+ (plus sign)
  as addition operator, 10
  as key combination indicator, vi

: (colons), for separating values in ranges, 3

< > (angle brackets), as comparison operators, 10

= (equal sign)
  as comparison operator, 331
  prefix for functions, 2, 49

> < (greater than/less than symbols), as comparison operators, 331

? (question mark)
  as dialog box indicator, 50
  as wildcard in searches, 330-331

, (commas)
  in arguments, 9-10
  in functions, 3

! (exclamation point), in cell references, 269

~... (ellipses), as used with arguments, 3

~ (periods), for separating values in ranges, 3

- (minus sign)
  as negation operator, 10
  as subtraction operator, 10

( ) (parentheses)
  for enclosing database func-

tion field names, 350
  for enclosing function arguments, 2

{ } (brackets), in array formulas, 13, 15

" " (quotation marks), for text in arguments, 6

/ (slash), as division operator, 10

~ (tilde), for searches for wildcard characters, 331

Alphabetical Index

A

A1.R1C1 function, 156

A1-style references to cells, 268-269

accounting program. *See* programs

ACCTING.XLM macro sheet, 319

action-equivalent functions, 2

ACTIVATE function, 156-157

ACTIVATE.NEXT function, 157-158

ACTIVATE.PREVIOUS function, 158

ACTIVE.CELL function, 188

Add Arrow command, 398

ADD.ARROW function, 50

ADD.BAR function, 239, 422

ADD.COMMAND function, 239-241, 428-430

add-in macros
  opening as macro sheet, 283
  saving macro sheets as, 282

ADD.MENU function, 241, 426

ADD.OVERLAY function, 51

ADD.TOOL function, 241-242

ALERT function, 242, 284

alignment
  of cell contents, 94-95
  of chart text, 389
  returning information about, 192-197

ALIGNMENT function, 94-95

ampersand (&), as text join operator, 10

angle brackets (< >), as comparison operators, 10

applications
  function for pasting from, 78
  function for saving documents for, 90-91

APPLY.NAMES function, 128-129

APPLY.STYLE function, 117-118

APP.MAXIMIZE function, 55

APP.MOVE function, 55-56

APP.RESTORE function, 57

APP.SIZE function, 57-58

APP.TITLE function, 242-243

arcs
  function for creating, 161-163
  function for returning information about, 208-214, 226-228

area charts
  function for converting to, 122-123
  function for embedding, 161-163
  function for selecting, 158-160

ARGUMENT function, 19-22, 230-231

argument names, 7

arguments
  automatic paste feature, 268
  commas in, 9-10
  data types in, 8-9
  function for describing in custom functions, 230-231
  how to use in functions, 6-10
  maximum allowable, 3
  purpose in functions, 1-2
  types of, 6-7

ARRANGE.ALL function, 152-153

array constants, 15-17

array ranges, 11-14
  converting to constants, 14-15

arrays
  as arguments, 7
  in formulas and functions, 11-17

445

DAVERAGE database function, 351-352
DBF file format, function for saving documents in, 90
DCOUNTA database function, 352-353
DCOUNT database function, 352
DDE, function for running macros upon receipt of data from, 254
debugging. *See* errors; error trapping
defaults
    appearing upon omission of function arguments, 50
    for cell reference style, 268
    for new charts, 377
    for slide shows, 415
Define Name dialog box, 267, 420
DEFINE.NAME function, 129-130
DELETE.ARROW function, 52
DELETE.BAR function, 246, 423
DELETE.COMMAND function, 246, 431
DELETE.DIRECTORY function, 164
DELETE.FORMAT function, 103, 164-165
DELETE.MENU function, 246, 427
DELETE.OVERLAY function, 52-53
DELETE.TOOLBAR function, 247
DELETE.TOOL function, 247
deleting
    array ranges, 14
    buttons, 46
    cells, 72
    chart arrows, 399
    chart axes, 392
    chart data or formats, 383
    chart data series, 379-381
    chart legends, 390
    charts, 382
    chart text, 387
    custom menu bars, 246
    custom toolbars, 432
    database fields, 326
    database records, 325-326, 332-333
    dialog box items, 300-301
    directories, 164
    files, 80
    graphic objects, 407-408
    gridlines, 397
    matches for criteria ranges, 350

menus, 246
number formats, 103, 164-165
page breaks, 145-146, 147
report definitions, 172
rows on slide shows, 178
slides, 416
toolbars, 247
tools, 48, 247
views, 183-184
DEMOTE function, 165
DGET database function, 353
dialog boxes
    copying to macro sheets, 303
    creating in custom programs, 298-310
    function for displaying, 247-249, 252-253
DIALOG.BOX function, 247-249
Dialog Editor, 298-303
DIF file format, function for saving documents in, 90
directories
    functions for,
        creating, 160
        deleting, 164
        returning array of, 189
        returning path of current, 189
    for sample chart of accounts, vi
DIRECTORIES function, 189
DIRECTORY function, 189
directory text, in customized dialog boxes, 309
DISABLE.INPUT function, 249
DISBURSE.XLS worksheet, 317
disks, included with this book, vi
DISPLAY function, 145-146
displays
    of dialog boxes, 304
    functions for,
        help topics, 251-252
        returning information on, 216-218
        selecting style for row and column headings, 156
    of menu bars, 260
    of toolbars, 261, 434-435
    of values in place of formulas, 288
    See also views
#DIV/0! error message, 28
DMAX database function, 353-354
DMIN database function, 354

docking toolbars
    function for, 149-150
    function for returning information on, 214-215
documents
    charts as, 367
    functions for,
        calculating, 142-143
        closing, 79, 89
        creating, 83
        previewing before printing, 89
        printing, 87-88
        protecting, 147
        returning current, 189-190
        returning information on, 200-206
        saving, 89-92
        zooming, 155-156
    See also workbooks; worksheets
DOCUMENTS function, 189-190
dollar sign ($), in A1-style of cell referencing, 269
DPRODUCT database function, 354-355
drawing, graphic objects, 399-402
drop-down combination edit/list boxes, in customized dialog boxes, 309
drop-down list boxes, in customized dialog boxes, 309
DSTDEV database function, 355
DSTDEVP database function, 355-356
DSUM database function, 356
DUPLICATE function, 165
DVAR database function, 356
DVARP database function, 356

E

ECHO function, 249
edit boxes, 335
EDIT.COLOR function, 144-145
Edit command, for editing chart data series, 380-381
EDIT.DELETE function, 72
editing
    chart data series, 379-381
    custom macros, 270
    databases, 324-325
    dialog boxes, 298-310
    graphic objects, 405-408
    polygons, 408
    records with data forms, 328

formatting, 84-87

headings, functions for setting display, 145-146

height (of charts), functions for altering, 92-94

height (of rows), functions for altering, 113-114

help
  customizing, 435
  functions for displaying, 251-252

help buttons, in customized dialog boxes, 310

HELP function, 251-252

HIDE function, 153

HIDE.OBJECT function, 169-170

HLINE function, 170

HPAGE function, 170

HSCROLL function, 170-171

I

icons
  in customized dialog boxes, 308
  functions for arranging, 152-153

IF function, 234-235
  with ELSE( ) and END.IF( ), 272-273
  used with GOTO, 271-272

IF values, as function arguments, 7

INC&EXP.XLS worksheet, 374

INCOME.XLS worksheet, 369

indenting, in structured macro templates, 290-292

information functions, 188-230

Info window, functions for displaying, 150

INPUT function, 252-253

INSERT function, 74

INSERT.OBJECT function, 74-75

integer edit boxes, in customized dialog boxes, 306

interrupting macros. See pausing

intersections of axes, 394

iterations, functions for returning information about, 200-206

J

justification. See alignment

K

keyboard

functions for,
  blocking input from, 249
  running macros, 254-256
  for selecting chart items, 378
  See also key combinations

key combinations
  caution on re-using in macros, 32-33
  indicated by plus sign (+), vi

keystroke macros, 31

L

labels
  on chart data markers, 386
  on chart tick marks, 369

landscape orientation, functions for, 85

LAST.ERROR function, 224

Legend command, 391

LEGEND function, 50-51

legends
  functions for,
    adding to charts, 50-51
    formatting, 100-101
    returning identifiers of, 226-228
    returning point position, 197-199
  on charts, 369, 389-391

line charts
  functions for,
    converting to, 125
    embedding, 161-163
    selecting, 158-160

lines
  drawing, 399-402
  functions for,
    creating, 161-163
    returning information about, 208-214, 226-228
  See also borders

linked drive and directories list boxes, in customized dialog boxes, 309

linked file list boxes, in customized dialog boxes, 308

linked list boxes, in customized dialog boxes, 308

links
  between charts and worksheets, 367
  functions for,
    changing, 80
    displaying, 81

opening, 81-82

pasting, 75

pasting components with, 76

returning information about, 207-208

returning worksheet names with, 224

updating, 82
  between pictures and worksheet cells, 410

LINKS function, 81, 224

list boxes, in customized dialog boxes, 307-308

LIST.NAMES function, 135-136

locking, functions for, 97, 105

logarithmic scale, selecting for chart axes, 394

logical data type. See logical values

logical values, as arguments, 7

looping, 270, 273-274
  with FOR.CELL-NEXT function, 275-276
  with FOR-NEXT function, 274-275
  functions for interrupting, 231
  functions for performing, 232-233, 235, 238-239
  performance considerations, 283
  sample custom macro for, 438-439
  with WHILE-NEXT function, 276-279

M

macro control functions, 230-239

macro functions, 31
  advantages, 1
  for assigning macros,
    to objects or tools, 140
    to tools, 243
  for disabling interruption, 243-244
  for halting macros, 234
  for naming values, 237
  for pausing macros, 235
  for pausing macros for specified periods, 238
  for performing macros step by step, 237-238
  for restarting macros, 235-236
  for resuming paused macros, 141

returning information
about, 208-214
pie charts
functions for,
converting to, 125-126
embedding, 161-163
selecting, 158-160
placeholders, 9-10
plot area, 368
plus sign (+)
as addition operator, 10
as key combination indicator,
vi
polygons
drawing, 401
editing, 408
functions for,
creating, 161-163
extending, 165-166
reshaping, 167
returning information
about, 208-214
portrait orientation, functions for,
85
pound sign (#), as error value
indicator, 7
precedence of calculations, altering with parentheses, 10-11
precedence of sorts, in database
sorts, 342-343
PRECISION function, 144
PREFERRED function, 127
PRESS.TOOL function, 258
PRINT function, 87-88
printing
functions for,
returning information
about, 200-206
selecting area to print, 148
graphic objects, 409-410
reports, 172-173
PRINT.PREVIEW function, 89
print quality, functions for, specifying, 88
product, obtaining with database
searches, 354-355
programs
chart of accounts, 293-297
custom data entry forms,
310-312
data files, 297-298
defining needs and designing,
289-290, 293
dialog boxes, 298-310
main entry screen and

macros, 312-319
sample macros for basic
accounting, 439-441
using structured macro templates, 290-293
See also custom macro samples
projections of trends, using array
constants, 16-17
PROMOTE function, 171
PROTECT.DOCUMENT func-
tion, 147
protection, function for returning
information about, 200-206

Q

question mark (?)
dialog box indicator, 50
as wildcard in searches, 330-
331
QUIT function, 89
quotation marks (" "), for text in
arguments, 6

R

R1C1-style references to cells,
268-269
radar charts
functions for,
converting to, 126
embedding, 161-163
selecting, 158-160
ranges of cells
advantage of using names in
macros, 268
creating slides from, 412-413
functions for,
adding borders, 96-97
copying, 166
copying to Clipboard, 70-
71
formatting, 166-167
going to, 132-133, 233-234
inserting blank, 74
naming, 129
returning information on,
188-189, 226-228
selecting last cell in, 175
functions for selecting by criteria match, 138-139
read-only status, function for
returning information about,
200-206
recalculation

functions for,
immediate recalculation of
worksheets, 52
running macros upon, 256-
257
and macro performance considerations, 283
RECEIPTS.XLS worksheet, 312
Recorder
pausing, 40
starting with Set Recorder
command, 34
stopping with Stop Recorder
command, 34
Record Macro dialog box, 32-33
records, 322
adding and editing with data
forms, 328-329
adding to databases, 325
deleting from databases, 325-
326, 332-333
finding in databases, 331-
332, 333
functions for,
extracting, 64
selecting, 65-66
sorting, 68-69
rectangles
functions for,
creating, 161-163
returning information
about, 208-214, 226-228
reference arguments, 7
in custom functions, 21-22
reference edit boxes, in customized dialog boxes, 307
references, 268
#REF error message, 29
REMOVE.PAGE.BREAK function,
147
RENAME.COMMAND function,
258-259, 426, 430
REPORT.DEFINE function, 171-
172
REPORT.DELETE function, 172
REPORT.GET function, 225
REPORT.PRINT function, 172-173
reports
functions for,
defining in documents,
171-172
deleting definitions, 172
printing, 172-173
returning information
about, 225

454